JOHN H. ARMS

The Railroad
What It Is, What It Does

5th Edition

Edited by
William C. Vantuono

Contributors:
Roger W. Baugher
Kendrick Bisset
Roy H. Blanchard
Rick Ford
Stephen T. Gerbracht
Thomas R. Gerbracht
Thomas White
Frank N. Wilner
Dr. Allan M. Zarembski

Simmons-Boardman Books, Inc., 1809 Capitol Avenue, Omaha, NE 68102
402-346-4300 • 800-228-9670 • www.transalert.com

The information presented in this book is in no way intended to supersede or negate any rules or regulations of government bodies, the AAR, or individual carriers. Further, it is not intended to conflict with any currently effective manufacturer's operating, application, or maintenance instructions and/or specifications. The publisher is not responsible for any technical errors that might appear.

Printings

First Edition, First Printing, May 1978
Second Printing, January 1979
Second Edition, First Printing, March 1982
Second Edition, Second Printing, February 1984
Second Edition, Third Printing, January 1987
Second Edition, Fourth Printing, August 1988
Third Edition, First Printing, August 1990
Third Edition, Second Printing, March 1993
Third Edition, Third Printing, May 1994
Third Edition, Fourth Printing, December 1995

Third Edition, Fifth Printing, November 1996
Third Edition, Sixth Printing, July 1997
Fourth Edition, First Printing, May 1998
Fourth Edition, Second Printing, December 1998
Fourth Edition, Third Printing, December 2000
Fourth Edition, Fourth Printing, April 2003
Fourth Edition, Fifth Printing, August 2005
Fourth Edition, Sixth Printing, November 2006
Fourth Edition, Seventh Printing, July 2007
Fifth Edition, First Printing, June 2008

Library of Congress Control Number: 2008930800

ISBN-13: 978-0-911382-58-7

Printed in the USA.

Tribute to John H. Armstrong

This fifth edition of *The Railroad: What It Is, What It Does* is dedicated to John Armstrong, this book's original author in 1978. Having gone through four editions in the past thirty years, Armstrong's book has become an invaluable training and resource tool for thousands of professional railroaders.

Armstrong (1920-2004) was born and raised in Canandaigua, New York. He graduated from Purdue University with a degree in mechanical engineering and worked at the Naval Ordnance Laboratory (later known as the Naval Surface Weapons Laboratory) at the Naval Gun Factory in Washington, D.C., contributing to the design of weapons systems for nuclear submarines.

After his retirement in 1979, he became a contributing editor to *Railway Age* for ten years, crafting beautifully written, highly detailed articles on complex mechanical and engineering subjects. He wrote scores of articles for various other publications and published thirteen books, mostly in the field of model railroading, for which he was widely known as a master layout designer and track planner. His track plan books introduced generations of model railroaders to the principles of realistic layout design.

Armstrong's lifelong project was the "Canandaigua Southern," an O-scale (1/48-scale) model of an imaginary railroad in Upstate New York and western Pennsylvania. He began the railroad in his teens and continued working on it until shortly before his death. The railroad filled his 24-by-36-foot basement and attracted thousands of visitors over the years. It was called "arguably the most well documented layout in O Scale."

Armstrong was active for many years with various railroad-related organizations, including the National Model Railroad Association, Capital Area O Scalers, and the Lexington Group. He was named to the O Scale Hall of Fame in 1998, was the 1968 and 1997 recipient of the NMRA's Distinguished Service Award, and was named an NMRA Pioneer of Model Railroading in 2001.

Acknowledgments

Throughout the previous four editions of this book many people have provided valuable technical assistance. Although much of the text has been revised in an effort to keep this book current we wish to recognize and thank the following people for the assistance they have offered: J. A. Pinkepank, Burlington Northern Railroad Company; and W. J. Nail, Union Pacific Railroad.

We are similarly grateful to the following for their help in providing illustrations used throughout this text:

AAR (Association of American Railroads)
Amtrak
APTA (American Public Transportation Association)
BNSF Railway
Cambridge Systematics, Inc.
Canadian National Railway
Canadian Pacific Railroad
CSX Transportation
Eno Foundation for Transportation
FRA (Federal Railroad Administration)
FreightCar America
GE Transportation
The Greenbrier Companies
KASGRO Rail Corporation
Kratville, Bill, Photographer, Omaha, NE
National Railway Equipment Company
New York Air Brake
ORX
Plasser American Corporation
Railway Age Magazine
Rescar Incorporated
Specialized Rail Transport
Starfire Engineering
Trinity DIFCO Incorporated
TTCI (Transportation Technology Center, Inc.)
TTX Company
Union Pacific Railroad
Union Switch & Signal
U.S. DOT (United States Department of Transportation)
Wabtec Corporation
Wilson, Don, Photographer, Port of Seattle

Contents at a Glance

Contents

1

Railroad Technology—The Tools of the Trade 1

2

A Hypothetical Railroad 7

3

The Track: Alignment and Structure 21

4

The Locomotive **51**

Contents

7

Signals and Communication 135

Contents

8

Railroad Operation—Moving From Here to There 163

9

Car Types, Commodities, and Carloadings **177**

10

Car Ownership and Distribution **195**

11

Terminal Operations **203**

Contents

16

Special Freight and Package Services 245

17

Rail Passenger Services 251

18

The Railroad Organization 263

Contents

Illustrations

Illustrations

8

Railroad Operation—Moving From Here to There

9

Car Types, Commodities, and Carloadings

11

Terminal Operations

12

Classification and Blocking

14 Unit-Train Operations

15 Intermodal Traffic

16 Special Freight and Package Services

17 Rail Passenger Services

18 The Railroad Organization

22 Operations

24 The Engineering and Mechanical Departments

Tables

Preface to the Fifth Edition

The Railroad: What It Is, What It Does is intended to present a basic yet comprehensive overview of the railroad industry in North America as it currently exists and functions. Its primary perspective is a description of railroad operations and their supporting technology, with an interpretation of the specialized terminology involved.

In the 30 years since publication of John Armstrong's first edition, and increasingly in the 10 years since the fourth edition, organizational and legislative matters—largely shaped by a wave of consolidations that resulted in just nine major railroads serving North America—have combined with a virtual explosion of research-driven new technology and a generally improving national economy to produce an astounding advance in railroad traffic levels, efficiency, and profitability. Indeed, the railroad renaissance that was predicted around the time that the 1980 Staggers Rail Act was passed is in full force. It largely freed the industry from the stifling chains of government overregulation and enabled the industry to compete in the global transportation marketplace. Railroads that once spent their resources on rationalizing physical plant and cost cutting are now dealing with providing enough capacity to handle increasing demand for their services.

Revisions in this fifth edition reflect the trends that, along with major technical advances, are largely responsible for this renaissance. Throughout the past 30 years, the industry has witnessed the replacement or virtual extinction of a host of such railroading perennials as the Interstate Commerce Commission, cabooses, and paper train orders. These have been replaced by the Surface Transportation Board, end-of-train devices, and radio- or digitally transmitted track warrants, all of which continue to fulfill the critical service and safety functions of their predecessors. For perspective, this fifth edition retains some historical review of the development and significance of now-obsolete hardware and practices wherever they may be helpful in understanding today's thriving, growing, dynamic railroad industry.

William C. Vantuono

June 2008

Introduction:
How Today's Railroad
Network Evolved

Transportation exists to conquer space and time—to deliver people and goods where they are needed, when they are needed, and to deliver them in good condition.

In the beginning, transportation primarily was by water—across oceans and via inland waterways. It is no mystery why major cities sprang up and still flourish adjacent to ocean ports and rivers. In the United States, early settlement and development was east of the formidable Allegheny Mountains—primarily along the Atlantic coast. As transportation improved, civilization moved inland, following inland waterways, man-made canals and extending to the western shores of the Great Lakes. Early roads that were traversed by horse and wagon were crude and not well suited to the movement of people and goods. Indeed, overland transportation had remained static for millennia. Both Alexander the Great in 350 B.C., and the first Napoleon in 1800 A.D., used precisely the same form of horse-drawn transportation.

Railroad building in America began in the late 1820s—the Baltimore & Ohio, for example, just 13 miles long, opened for business in 1830. Its objective was to link the port city of Baltimore with the Ohio River and compete with New York's Hudson River and Erie Canal, which reached Buffalo and opened a connection to the Great Lakes and Midwest. The 130-mile South Carolina Canal & Rail Road—the longest in the world in 1833—connected the Savannah River at Augusta, Georgia, with the port of Charleston, South Carolina, in order to transport Georgia-grown cotton for export.

Early railroads were short lines, just a few miles long and serving but a handful of geographically close towns. Rarely did the tracks of early railroads connect, as their owners—highly suspect of neighboring communities, and ignorant of the benefits of free trade and regional specialization—sought to cultivate local commerce at the expense of rivals. In fact, these early railroads used an abundance of track gages (from as narrow as 2 ft to as wide as 6 ft) in order to frustrate physical interchange of freight and passenger cars in an attempt to gain a trade advantage over neighboring towns.

These early railroads were modest enterprises, designed to accommodate a local constituency, and largely supplemental to coastal, lake, and river transportation. They were powered by primitive steam-powered locomotives, constructed from scrap metal and melted-down gun barrels. The primitive locomotives pulled rickety wagons over a crudely assembled fixed guideway of wooden rails capped with half-inch-thick iron. The rails were placed in shallow trenches atop stone and granite blocks. As locomotive and freight car weight increased, wooden rails gave way to cast iron, and eventually, steel rails.

It was not until the Civil War that an interconnected network of railroads—with a standard gage permitting seamless interchange of passenger and freight cars—was recognized as an economic and military necessity. Union Army Gen. William Tecumseh Sherman and Confederate States President Jefferson Davis advocated a railroad of standard gage linking the Atlantic and Pacific coasts. Sherman called such a railroad "positively essential to the binding together of the republic."

To encourage the standard-gage rail network envisioned by 19th century progressive thinkers, Congress granted millions of acres of federal land (mostly west of the Mississippi River) to entrepreneurs who would sell the land to finance railroad construction. Initially, land-grant railroads carried immigrants west; then, the agricultural goods they produced were hauled east for consumption and export. By reducing passenger and freight rates to government, railroads more than repaid the value of those land grants.

From a modest beginning, later encouraged by federal land grants, America's railroads matured to an extensive North American mostly privately owned rail network that links major cities and ports and provides some of the most efficient, extensive, and cost-effective transportation on the globe.

By 1890, U.S. track-miles conforming to standard gage totaled about 95 percent, with the Interstate Commerce Commission observing: "Railroads of the United States are being welded, by the need of interchange of traffic, into a system ..." Standard gage helped to ease end-to-end unifications. Few railroads prior to the Civil War extended even 100 miles; by 1896, there were 44 railroads stretching at least 1,000 miles.

Population followed the railroad westward. Chicago became the metropolis of the Midwest because it was a major railroad junction that also enjoyed water access. A new generation of land-locked cities arose solely because railroad lines crossed or terminated at that particular point. So important were railroads that existing towns (with equally good geographic location) withered because main-line rail routes were located elsewhere. In agricultural regions, rail branch lines were constructed to permit a farmer to bring his grain by horse and wagon to a railhead and return home before dark. Branch lines connected to main lines.

Today, the standard gage throughout North America (Canada, the United States, and Mexico) is 4 ft 8½ in. And the network has become seamless, with a carload of freight able to move throughout North America without its contents being transferred until reaching the customer at destination.

The Railroad Advantage

Before the Civil War, transcontinental transportation consisted of a stagecoach or wagon journey along the Santa Fe Trail, requiring an entire summer. Such overland travel was considered even more hazardous than the ocean voyage around Cape Horn, which required 5 weeks. To transport a heavy load any distance was so time consuming and expensive as to be generally impractical.

In contrast to horse-drawn wagons, railroads could haul heavy loads over mountain ranges. Fixed guideway rails provided load stabilization and avoided the perils of wagon wheels on snow and ice. Headlights and whistles allowed trains to operate at night, and track switches made possible two-way operations that evolved into complex network operations.

Creation of classification yards contributed to near seamless network efficiencies—much like a relay team. One railroad originates one or many carloads of freight and transports them hundreds of miles to a classification yard, where they join scores of other cars from numerous other origin points. In the classification yard, the cars are sorted and put on trains to destinations in all directions where they continue the journey to destination. In some cases, the cars will travel through several classification yards, each time joining other cars with a similar destination.

In other cases, a single shipper (such as a Wyoming coal mine or a grain miller in Minneapolis) will load 100 or more cars on a single "unit" train that travels directly to a power plant or export point, avoiding classification yards.

Some Bumps, but Constant Progress

Competitive and political factors encouraged what soon became an overbuilding of rail lines in America. The inclusion of "Pacific" in the name of literally dozens of new railroads expressed the optimism of their owners to eventually reach the Pacific coast from the Midwest. Almost all failed to achieve their objective. Many early railroads failed financially, and their track was absorbed by successors through merger or acquisition of the bankrupt assets.

Union Pacific was the first railroad to link the Midwest with the Pacific Ocean—its golden spike driven on May 10, 1869, at Promontory, Utah. Soon after, railroads connected the Midwest with major Pacific coast points—Northern Pacific and Great Northern stretching to the Pacific Northwest; Atchison, Topeka & Santa Fe connecting with Southern Pacific to reach Southern California; and Southern Pacific linking New Orleans with central and Southern California.

Interestingly, there has never been a truly transcontinental railroad in the United States. Freight moving between the Atlantic and Pacific coasts, even today, must travel on at least two railroads.

The frenetic building of railroads during the late 19th and early 20th centuries produced winners and losers. The efficiency of economist Adam Smith's so-called invisible hand contributed to the creation of an interconnected rail network that became the envy of the world, and helped establish the United States as the world's dominant economic power. Wherever minerals, oil, seeds, and grains could be mined, extracted, or grown from the earth, they were assured efficient rail transportation to factories, milling, consuming points, and exporting points. Various manufactured goods could be moved long distances (at relatively low prices) for assembly, sale, and export.

As highways were improved and truck transportation grew, intermodalism was born. Intermodal describes freight loaded into a highway trailer or ocean container and being transported by more than one mode—in many cases, ocean, rail, and highway.

Today, goods from all points on the globe travel in intermodal transportation. Trailers and containers typically are moved from ports or North American factories over local roads to a railhead, loaded two-high aboard double-stack flatcars, and transported via train between cities. Then, the trailers and containers are unloaded from the flatcar for truck delivery nearby.

Fig. 1 illustrates early frenzied railroad construction, peaking in 1916 at more than 254,000 route-miles.

Railroads Come of Age

What distinguishes America's railroads from those railroads elsewhere in the world is that American railroads were constructed and owned by entrepreneurs. It was a rare American railroad that was owned by local or state government—exceptions being the Alaska Railroad (once federally owned, but now owned by the state), Amtrak (officially, the National Railroad Passenger Corp.), and Conrail (which was created out of numerous bankrupt railroads, but subsequently returned to the private sector and then divided between CSX Transportation and Norfolk Southern Corp.).

Railroads were America's first large corporations. Prior to the 20th century, when only 41 American manufacturing companies had capitalization of at least $250,000, the New York Central Railroad had invested $30 million in its rights-of-way, track, and rolling stock. In 1891, the Pennsylvania Railroad was the nation's largest single employer, with one-third more workers than the federal government. By 1894, the Pennsylvania Railroad's bonded debt exceeded $5 billion, while the national debt was but $1 billion. By 1906, some 85 percent of the bonds and 50 percent of the stocks traded on the New York Stock Exchange were those of railroad companies.

As railroad construction exploded during the mid- and latter 19th century, there were complaints of discrimination in rates and service, which allegedly benefited economically powerful shippers. Congress responded by passing, in 1887, the Interstate Commerce Act, which created the Interstate Commerce Commission (ICC), the nation's first federal regulatory agency (now the Surface Transportation Board).

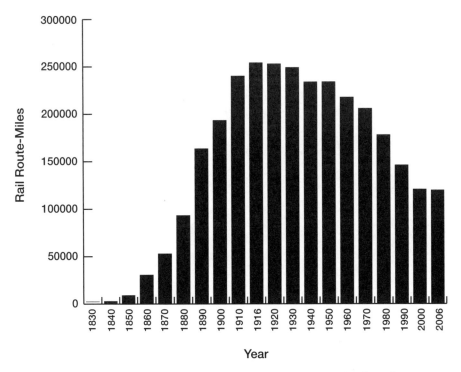

Fig. 1. Rail route-miles. Route-miles are the aggregate length of roadway, excluding yard tracks and sidings, and do not reflect the fact that a mile of road may include two, three, or even more parallel tracks.

Sources: Prior to 1890, Henry V. Poor, *Manual of the Railroads of the United States for 1890;* for 1890-1950, Interstate Commerce Commission, *Statistics of Railways in the United States;* for 1960-1990, Interstate Commerce Commission, *Transport Statistics in the United States;* for 2000 and 2006, Association of American Railroads, *Railroad Facts.*

The Interstate Commerce Act outlawed discrimination among shippers, required rates (prices for transportation) to be published and available for public inspection, and subjected railroad rates and service to oversight by the ICC, which could order rates to be lowered and discrimination against places, products, and shippers to be ended.

As government financing of road building accelerated, and trucks began competing with railroads, the frenzied railroad building of earlier years became an economic millstone for the industry. An example of early overbuilding and ruinous competition is seen between Buffalo, New York, and Cleveland, Ohio, where the tracks of New York, Chicago & St. Louis Railroad were laid almost directly alongside those of Lake Shore & Michigan Southern. By 1890, there were 20 separate railroad companies competing between Atlanta and St. Louis. Between New York City and Chicago, six separate railroad companies once competed.

Table 1. Number of railroads

Year	Total	Class I
1880	1,174	–
1890	1,797	–
1900	2,023	–
1910	2,196	–
1920	1,785	186
1930	1,497	156
1940	1,096	131
1950	785	127
1960	621	106
1970	518	71
1980	480	39
1990	530	14
2000	560	8
2006	561	7

Sources: Prior to 2000, Interstate Commerce Commission, various reports; and, for 2000 and 2006, Association of American Railroads. Prior to 1920, the ICC did not classify by size. See text under Modern Railroad Network, and in Figs. 4 and 5 for definition of Class I.

Involuntary bankruptcy and voluntary mergers and consolidations resulted in a reduction in the number of competing carriers, and also improved railroad productivity—reducing duplication of labor, streamlining operating practices, and simplifying pricing.

Table 1 shows the steady decline in the number of rail systems since 1880.

Prior to the government highway building and the growth of trucking, railroads dominated freight and passenger transportation in the United States. As trucks siphoned freight from railroads, jet aircraft and automobile travel along the 43,000-mile interstate system drained passengers from railroads. By 1975, the nation's rail mileage showed that 21 percent was being operated in bankruptcy.

Fig. 2 illustrates the decline in railroad market share and growth in market share of trucks over the years.

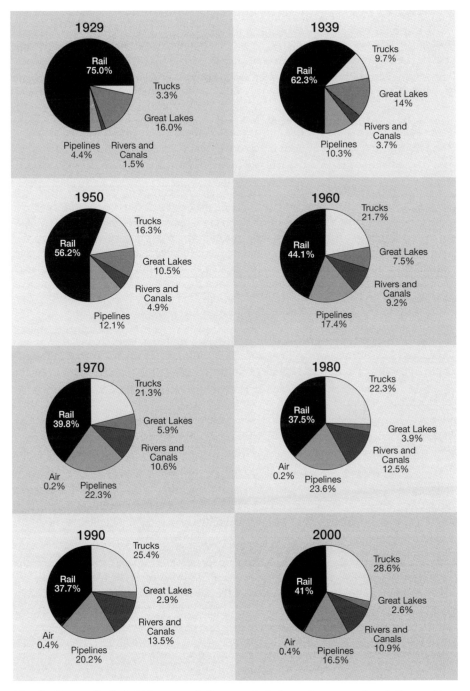

Fig. 2. Domestic freight transportation market share (in percentage). *Source:* Eno Foundation for Transportation.

To preserve America's private-sector rail network, Congress began (during the 1970s) to reduce economic regulation of railroads. The 1973 Regional Railroad Reorganization (3-R) Act and the 1976 Railroad Revitalization and Regulatory Reform (4-R) Act were precursors to the more expansive 1980 Staggers Rail Act, which partially deregulated railroads and allowed them greater freedom and flexibility to adjust rates based on market conditions, and to abandon uneconomic lines more rapidly.

Although trucks pay user charges (fuel and other excise taxes) to operate on highways, railroads contend that those user charges do not fully reflect the actual costs of pavement damage caused by heavy trucks. By contrast, railroads build and maintain their own privately owned routes and pay property and other taxes on the rail network.

In order to free railroads of the substantial economic burden of operating money-losing passenger trains, Congress, in 1970, created the National Railroad Passenger Corp., or Amtrak. Today, intercity rail-passenger service is operated by Amtrak over a 25,000-mile route structure. Although Amtrak (through the federal government) owns the Northeast Corridor linking Washington, D.C., with Philadelphia, New York City, and Boston, Amtrak service elsewhere in the United States operates over freight railroad tracks. Amtrak pays an access fee to the freight railroads, but uses its own locomotives and train crews to operate.

Following the Staggers Act, railroads commenced an accelerated consolidation movement. Where there were 39 individual Class I railroads in 1980, today there are seven Class I's (see list in paragraphs under "The Modern Railroad Network"). For example, Norfolk & Western and Southern Railway were merged into *Norfolk Southern;* Atchison, Topeka & Santa Fe, St. Louis & San Francisco, and Burlington Northern became *BNSF Railway;* Chicago & North Western, Denver, Rio Grande & Western, Missouri Pacific, Missouri-Kansas-Texas, Southern Pacific, and Western Pacific were merged into *Union Pacific;* and Chessie System and Seaboard System became *CSX Transportation.*

Merged railroads abandoned thousands of miles of redundant main-line track as well as lightly used and unprofitable secondary and branch-line track—almost 30,000 miles during the 1980s—allowing (in concert with improvements in technology) significant employee head-count reductions and increased traffic density on the fewer main lines.

Mergers also eliminated many costly classification yard operations where freight cars were transferred from one railroad to another. Microprocessor technology permitted trains to run faster, more closely spaced, and with fewer crew members. Since the 1970s, technology permitted elimination of the caboose, and a reduction in train-crew size from as many as five and six crew members for each train to, generally, just two by the 1990s.

The Modern Railroad Network

The 21st century North American rail network—some 170,000 miles of track in the United States alone—is characterized by seven major (Class I) railroad systems, dozens of smaller regional railroads, and hundreds of short lines. Many of the short lines have been created since 1980, after partial economic deregulation eased the ability of railroads to spin off marginal track to entrepreneurs with lower cost structures who operate those short lines largely as feeder railroads. Otherwise, the track likely would have been abandoned entirely.

Today, the Surface Transportation Board classifies railroads based on annual operating revenue. The largest are known as Class I, with annual revenue of at least $319.3 million (for 2005). The threshold is adjusted annually, based on an inflation index. The seven U.S. Class I railroads are: BNSF Railway; CSX Transportation; Grand Trunk Western (which includes Illinois Central, both subsidiaries of Canadian National); Kansas City Southern; Norfolk Southern; Soo Line (a subsidiary of Canadian Pacific); and Union Pacific. Most Class I railroads have annual revenues considerably higher than the threshold. In 2005, for example, Union Pacific's operating revenue exceeded $13 billion. See Table 2.

Table 2. Profile of Class I railroads (2006)

Class I Railroad	Route-miles	Operating Revenue	Employees
BNSF Railway	31,910	$14.8 billion	41,342
CSX Transportation	21,114	8.6 billion	31,318
Kansas City Southern	3,176	0.9 billion	2,909
Grand Trunk Western	6,737	2.2 billion	5,930
Norfolk Southern	21,141	9.4 billion	30,087
Soo Line	3,267	0.7 billion	2,683
Union Pacific	32,339	15.6 billion	53,312

Source: Association of American Railroads.

Regional railroads (smaller than Class I), have annual revenue between $25.5 million and $319.2 million. Railroads with annual revenue less than $25.5 million are known as local or short line railroads. See Table 3.

Table 3. Consist of industry (2006)

Railroad	Number	Miles	Employees	Revenue
Class I	7	94,801	167,581	$50.3 billion
Regional	33	16,713	7,742	1.7 billion
Short Line	519	28,415	11,634	2.0 billion

Source: Association of American Railroads.

Productivity improvements attracted freight back to the railroads. Trucking companies such as J. B. Hunt and United Parcel Service abandoned many of their over-the-highway operations and began giving their trailer and container loads of freight to the railroads for intercity movements. Steamship lines similarly abandoned trucking to enter into contracts with railroads for hauling cargo containers—stacked two-high on double-deck flatcars—between ports and inland points, and even coast to coast, eliminating longer ocean voyages from Asia to the U.S. East Coast. Instead, the containers are offloaded on the U.S. West Coast and moved by rail to population-dense East Coast markets.

Today's Network

Fig. 3 shows all rail routes within the contiguous United States over which rail freight could be routed. Lines do not differentiate between the main or branch lines.

Fig. 4 shows only main and secondary-main lines carrying at least 5 million gross tons (5 mgt) per year—roughly 40,000 revenue carloads annually, or 160 cars per business day.

The lighter traffic lines, not shown, which constitute more than one-quarter of the total mileage, generate less than one-twentieth of the ton-miles. These core lines are as important to the rail network as arteries are to the human body.

Frank N. Wilner is the author of four books on railroads, including "Railroad Mergers: History, Analysis, Insight"; "The Amtrak Story"; and "The Railway Labor Act & the Dilemma of Labor Relations," all published by Simmons-Boardman Books, Inc.; and "Comes Now the Interstate Commerce Practitioner."

Fig. 3. United States railroad freight lines (Courtesy of AAR and U.S. DOT/Bureau of Transportation Statistics)

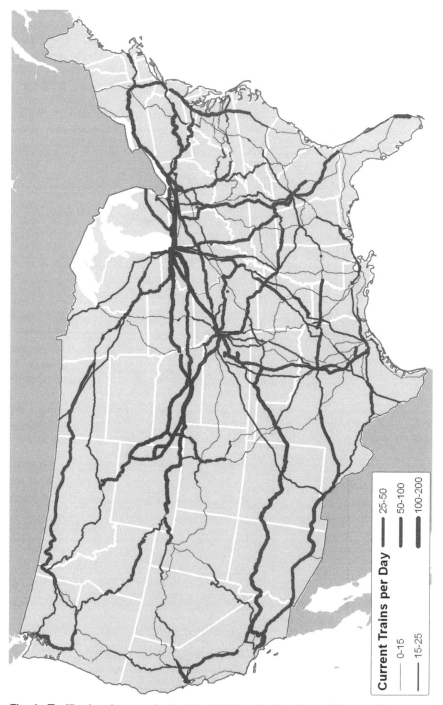

Fig. 4. Traffic density on principal freight lines in the United States (Courtesy of AAR and Cambridge Systematics, Inc. From Cambridge Systematics' final report on National Rail Freight Infrastructure Capacity and Investment Study prepared for AAR.)

Railroad Technology— The Tools of the Trade

A railroad is defined as a system of railroad track, including the land, stations, rolling stock (rail vehicles), and other related property. The railroad track consists of two steel rails that are held a fixed distance apart on a roadbed. The rolling stock (rail vehicles that are guided and supported by flanged steel wheels and connected into trains) is propelled on the rails as a means of transportation.

Key Inventions and Evolutions

Within that definition given above is a host of variations in the form of propulsion, details of track structure, train makeup or "consist," and dominant class of traffic. These variations are part of the term *railroad.* They are the essential features, and each is important for a very good reason.

Arguing whether the rail, the flanged wheel, or the train is the most vital feature is as futile as trying to decide which leg of a three-legged stool is most important. It is also not important whether the true ancestor of the railroad was grooved pavement on the island of Malta (dating from the time of the Roman Empire), a medieval German mine tramway, or one of the cast-iron "plateways" operating in South Wales in the 18th century. (See Fig. 1-1.)

The *system* that evolved from these beginnings, however, was the first phase of the most important transportation advance in all history: the application of heat energy from a machine to transcend the limitations of animal power. Therefore, it's worth taking a minute or two to see what's distinctive about it, as an introduction to a closer look at its principal parts as they exist today.

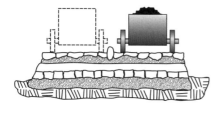

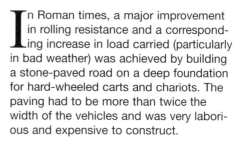

In Roman times, a major improvement in rolling resistance and a corresponding increase in load carried (particularly in bad weather) was achieved by building a stone-paved road on a deep foundation for hard-wheeled carts and chariots. The paving had to be more than twice the width of the vehicles and was very laborious and expensive to construct.

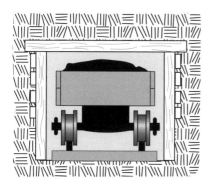

Some medieval miners had to push heavy loads through tunnels – extra width was costly, so carts guided by pulley-like wheels ran on a track of wood stringers nailed to crossmembers – thus "paving" only the essential strips of the roadway. Tracks later were extended outside the mines.

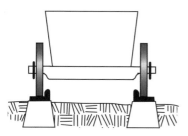

Eighteenth-century South Wales tramways used a single flange on the "plateway" – short segments of cast iron, usually mounted on stone blocks – to keep plain-wheeled carts on the track. Some of these plateways were 20 miles long; trackworkers in Britain are still called "platelayers." A major problem was keeping the track clear of debris.

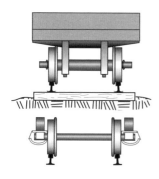

Single-flanged iron wheels running on the head of "I" or "T"-section iron rails held in gauge by wooden crossties rapidly proved to be a more satisfactory system – self-cleaning, readily crossed by roadways, relatively inexpensive, cushioned slightly by the wood's flexibility.

It was soon found that mounting the wheels rigidly on a rotating axle kept them in gage better, made efficient bearings and lubrication possible.

Fig. 1-1. Evolution of the flanged wheel and railway

The Cheap, Low-Friction Guideway

The railroad concept, in the first third of the 19th century, combined three critical factors:

1. It *reduced friction* to an extent that let a heavy steam engine not only move itself across the land but have enough power left over to move a good load at an unprecedented speed.

2. It *reduced the cost of a low-friction roadway,* making it possible for a railroad to penetrate any area of the country where raw materials were found or people lived and worked.

3. It *provided a guideway,* removing the limitation of transporting everything in single vehicles. This spread the cost of motive power and crew over a practical number of loads.

Monorail or Two-Rail System

Many basic decisions had to be made in developing any system that depended on and combined several separate inventions. Many false starts, misconceptions, and side issues were resolved by time and experience. Even such a fundamental question as the "right" number of rails re-emerges periodically; some recent studies of alternatives for urban transportation have used the term "bi-rail" (new term, same system) for the two-rail system—the best technical answer to the requirements is still the two-rail system. Fig. 1-2 discusses the reasons why the monorail remains a dream, useful only under extremely limited circumstances.

Saving half of the number of rails – and the job of keeping them level with each other and the right distance apart – has made the idea of the monorail a recurring dream. Its problem is that, like the bicycle, it is not a "statically stable" system – unless the "rail" is located *above* the vehicle's center of gravity.

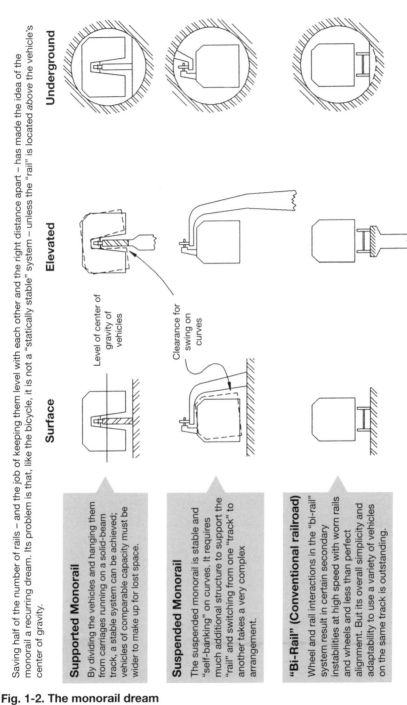

Surface **Elevated** **Underground**

Level of center of gravity of vehicles

Clearance for swing on curves

Supported Monorail

By dividing the vehicles and hanging them from carriages running on a solid-beam track, a stable system can be achieved; vehicles of comparable capacity must be wider to make up for lost space.

Suspended Monorail

The suspended monorail is stable and "self-banking" on curves. It requires much additional structure to support the "rail" and switching from one "track" to another takes a very complex arrangement.

"Bi-Rail" (Conventional railroad)

Wheel and rail interactions in the "bi-rail" system result in certain secondary instabilities at high speed with worn rails and wheels and less than perfect alignment. But its overall simplicity and adaptability to use a variety of vehicles on the same track is outstanding.

Any general-purpose transit system must be adaptable to surface, elevated, and underground location without too serious a cost penalty. As compared to "bi-rail" only the supported monorail in the elevated mode is somewhat cost competitive.

Fig. 1-2. The monorail dream

Where Does the Flange Belong?

Fig. 1-1 shows: (a) the way the *railroad* made reduced friction affordable, and (b) how the best way to keep the cars on the rails evolved. Almost from the first flanged metal wheels, 1 inch became the "standard" flange height, and no reason for any substantial change has ever been found.

Fig. 1-3 shows why the best place for the flange was found to be on the inner edge of the wheel tread.

Why Trains?

Once there is a guideway, cars can be hooked together into trains, with important savings in cost. One-car trains (the electric interurban railway and the streetcar, for example) proved relatively short-lived variations of the theme. But they have made a comeback under the name "LRV" (Light Rail Vehicle) in the form of articulated two-car units that can be combined into trains. Fig. 1-4 shows why combining the vehicles into trains is important in increasing the *capacity* of a narrow transportation corridor, particularly important in providing needed mobility without wasting vast areas of real estate.

The practical traffic-handling capacity of a track depends on an efficient signaling and control system. This system must assure vehicles at all times that there is no train closer than the stopping distance ahead. The actual vehicles-per-hour line capacities for the various consists and speeds will therefore always be lower than those shown in Fig. 1-4, but the ratios between them are representative.

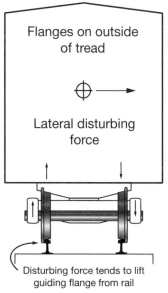

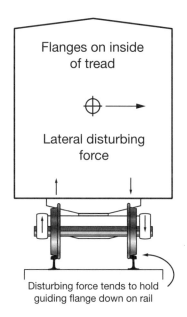

Fig. 1-3. Where should the flange be?

Apart from cost savings from having one operator controlling a larger amount of transportation capacity, hooking vehicles together into trains greatly increases the capability of a single "lane" of space to handle, safely, large amounts of traffic at any required maximum speed.

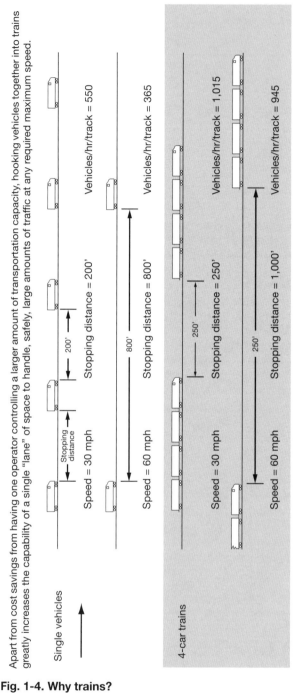

Single vehicles

Speed = 30 mph   Stopping distance = 200'   Vehicles/hr/track = 550

Speed = 60 mph   Stopping distance = 800'   Vehicles/hr/track = 365

4-car trains

Speed = 30 mph   Stopping distance = 250'   Vehicles/hr/track = 1,015

Speed = 60 mph   Stopping distance = 1,000'   Vehicles/hr/track = 945

Fig. 1-4. Why trains?

Stopping distance, which is the ultimate limit on how close together vehicles can safely travel, varies with the square of the speed; increasing the speed with vehicles traveling singly reduces the number of vehicles that one track can carry per hour. Even 4-car trains more than double the capacity of a single track to handle traffic at 60 mph, allowing for somewhat longer braking distance with a train (lower wind resistance, some delay in braking action).

For freight-length trains, capacity is much greater; even though the length of the train itself becomes the larger part of the "Track Occupancy Time." Trains of 7,000 ft length having 80 cars each, with 3,000 ft stopping distance, give a traffic capacity of 2,535 cars/hr at 60 mph.

A Hypothetical Railroad

R ather than use one of North America's existing Class I's as an example of a typical railroad, we've created the "East-West Railroad," a simplified, make-believe system, typical of any fairly large railroad that has been formed by the gradual merger, lease, and purchase of dozens of smaller railroads over many decades. Like real railroads in both the eastern and western parts of the continent, it has at least one major mountain range to overcome, and the location of its lines is greatly influenced by the presence of river valleys and the irregularities of the coastline. The system map (Fig. 2-1) is not drawn to scale, but the distance from A to J along the East-West's main line is about a thousand miles.

Connections and Competitors

Other railroads in the same area as the East-West (E-W) include the Northwest and Northeast (NW & NE), which taps territory generally north of the E-W and also reaches the ports at the metropolis of J and the industrial city of O; its main line goes to the port city of AA, which the E-W does not reach.

The Southwest and AA (SW & AA) extends from an inland area south of the E-W's western terminals to AA, crossing the E-W at several points in the process.

The Southeastern Railroad and the Peninsular Railroad are shorter lines that serve areas south of F & J, respectively, which are separated by an arm of the ocean.

Coming in from the Far West are the so-called "transcontinental" railroads, not truly coast to coast, but extending two-thirds of the way and connecting at gateway cities such as B and HH with the Eastern roads. Even on this simplified map, two points are clear:

- Many routes are from almost any point to any other.
- The larger rail systems *connect* with each other for traffic originating or terminating in their own territory and *compete* for through traffic.

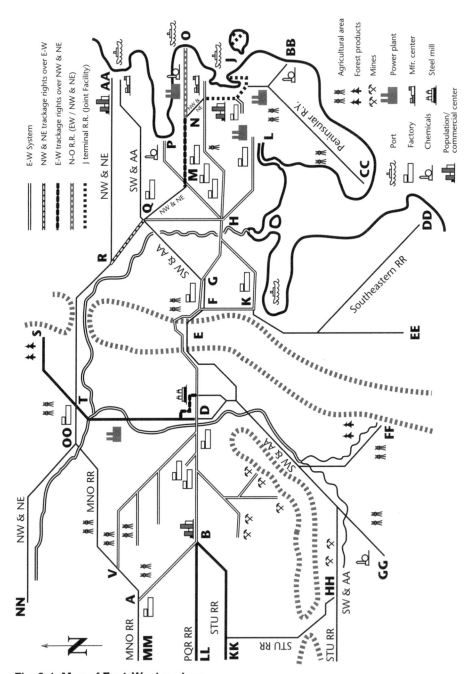

Fig. 2-1. Map of East-West system

From Point KK on the STU railroad, for example, shipment to AA could go south on the STU to the SW & AA connection and then directly to AA, involving only one interchange (or connecting point), or it could be routed STU to B, E-W to G, SW & AA to destination, a shorter route but with two interchanges.

The routing STU to B, E-W to T, NW & NE to destination is longer but does not take it up and over the mountain range between E and F.

Pulling the Map Together

For many commodities, the principal competition in recent decades is from three other modes of transportation: (1) common-carrier and unregulated contract trucks using the interstate highway system, (2) barge traffic on open waterways and those made navigable by the Army Corps of Engineers, and (3) pipelines. A more subtle form of competition is *decentralization*. Corporations that make and distribute products have the choice, over a period of time, of arranging their plants and distribution centers to reduce the amount of transportation involved in the whole process. The extra cost of producing goods in smaller plants is more than balanced by the reduced transportation costs—the smaller plants allow them to be closer to more customers.

Whenever possible, then, the individual railroad companies will combine, coordinate, or connect their tracks and other facilities to hold down overall costs. Several examples of this, common throughout the country, are found here.

Paired tracks. Both the E-W and the AA built their single-track lines through the only practical pass through the mountain range. The two lines are now "paired" between E and F; eastbound trains of both railroads use the SW & AA track, while all westbound trains go via the E-W line. Thus, each road gets the advantages of double track while maintaining only a single line.

Trackage rights. From R to Q, the NW & NE run its trains over the E-W's track, using its own crews and motive power, by paying a specified toll, often referred to as a "wheelage" charge because of its being based on the number of cars involved.

From M to N, the arrangement is the reverse. Trackage rights arrangements vary with circumstances. Usually, the owning line does not grant rights to its tenant line to receive or deliver freight to on-line customers.

Joint facilities. Between N and O, both E-W and NE & NW trains run over the N-O RR, a jointly owned company that is responsible for the operation of the line.

In the metropolitan area of J and its port, both lines connect with the Peninsular RR and reach many industries, terminals, and docks by way of the J Terminal RR, which is owned jointly by the line-haul railroads involved.

Detouring. All roads in the territory have standard detouring agreements with each other so that in an emergency the trouble spot may be bypassed by the best available route.

Interline terminology. In the United States, about 75 percent of all rail shipments involve at least two different railroads, so interchange of freight cars and the establishment of interline rates is an integral part of the business. Some of the terminology is illustrated in Fig. 2-2.

Haulage. In an arrangement that has become more common since the 1980s, the E-W pays the NW & NE to move its freight consists carrying traffic en route via B to or from E-W points in the vicinity of V. These trains operate with NW & NE crews. In this "haulage" arrangement, there is no interchange between the railroads and no division of the E-W's freight rate. Haulage is attractive to the E-W in this case, because it can offer better service and incurs less overall expense than it would in moving such traffic over its own more circuitous route via C, D, and U.

Which Way Is Best?

What is the "best" route for hauling coal between D and H (en route from the mines in the W area to the huge power plant at L)? Assume that the route that takes the *least total energy* to do the job is best. (This is not the whole story by any means, but energy is a major influence when hauling freight.)

The alternate routes. Fig. 2-3 shows the routes available. The direct route D-E-F-G-H via the E-W's main line is the shortest, but it takes you up 4,000 ft and back down again. The alternate D-T-R-Q-H route, aside from using "foreign" trackage from T to R, is downhill all the way for the coal, but 250 miles longer. Which is more important?

Train resistance. Train resistance may be divided into two main elements, *rolling resistance* (including the resistance to wheels rolling on the rail, friction in the journal [axle] bearings on the cars, and wind resistance) and *grade resistance*. The first is all friction, and once the energy is expended it is gone forever. Grade resistance results from the energy you must put into the train to lift it vertically. The energy is returned without loss when the train comes back down again.

On a gentle grade (one-third of 1 percent or less), all this energy can be recovered by letting the train roll along without applying the brakes; the locomotive has correspondingly less work to do in keeping the train moving at the desired speed. However, on a mountain grade (for example, 2 percent, or about 100 ft to the mile) almost all of this energy must be dissipated as heat, using the brakes to keep the train from exceeding the speed limit. A great deal of the energy put into reaching the top of the mountain is lost (except in electric traction with "regenerative braking," not currently in use in U.S. freight operations).

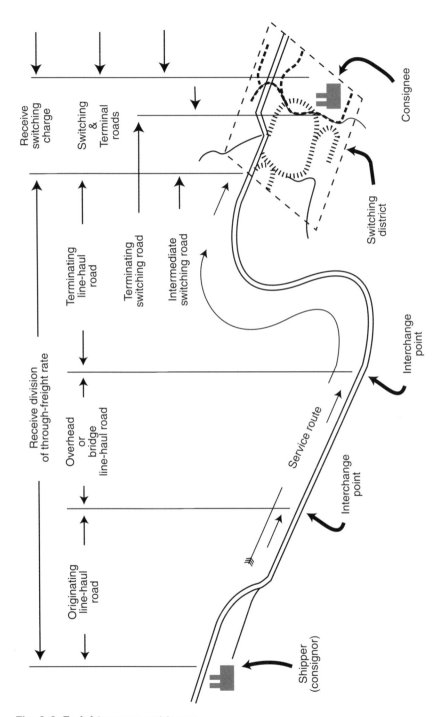

Fig. 2-2. Freight movement terms

Fig. 2-4 gives typical values for the rolling friction of cars of a type likely to be used to move trainloads of coal to a power plant, 100-ton capacity alloy-steel or aluminum-body gondolas weighing 25 tons empty. Rolling resistance varies with the weight of the car, being considerably more for a ton of empty than for a ton of load. It also increases gradually as the speed increases. We will use typical running speeds of 35 mph for the loaded train and 45 mph for returning the empties. The formulas usually used for estimating train resistance (Davis) gives 4.2 lbs *per ton* for the loaded car, and almost three times as much per ton for the empty. The graph in Fig. 2-5 fully illustrates this principle.

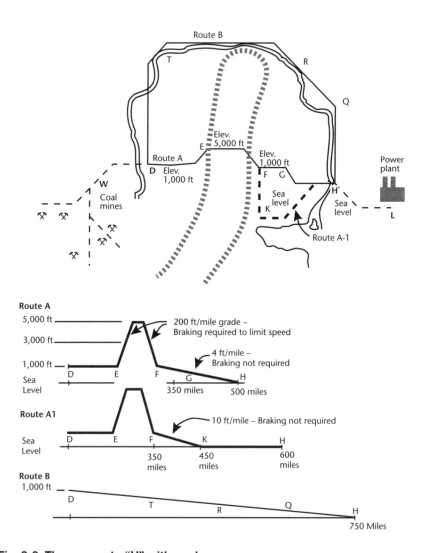

Fig. 2-3. Three ways to "H" with coal

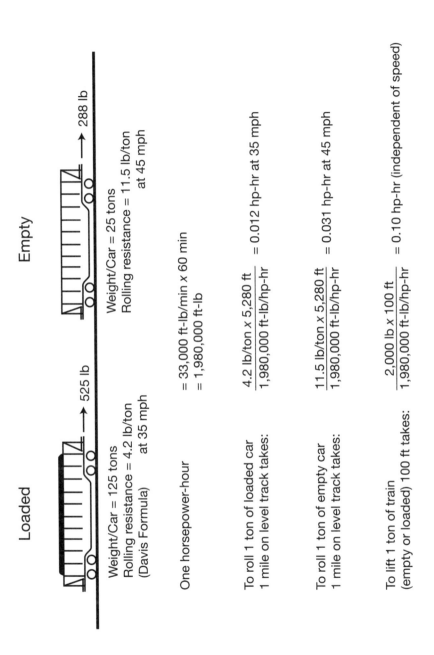

Loaded

⟶ 525 lb

Weight/Car = 125 tons
Rolling resistance = 4.2 lb/ton   at 35 mph
(Davis Formula)

Empty

⟶ 288 lb

Weight/Car = 25 tons
Rolling resistance = 11.5 lb/ton
at 45 mph

One horsepower-hour

= 33,000 ft-lb/min x 60 min
= 1,980,000 ft-lb

To roll 1 ton of loaded car
1 mile on level track takes:

$$\frac{4.2 \text{ lb/ton} \times 5,280 \text{ ft}}{1,980,000 \text{ ft-lb/hp-hr}} = 0.012 \text{ hp-hr at 35 mph}$$

To roll 1 ton of empty car
1 mile on level track takes:

$$\frac{11.5 \text{ lb/ton} \times 5,280 \text{ ft}}{1,980,000 \text{ ft-lb/hp-hr}} = 0.031 \text{ hp-hr at 45 mph}$$

To lift 1 ton of train
(empty or loaded) 100 ft takes:

$$\frac{2,000 \text{ lb} \times 100 \text{ ft}}{1,980,000 \text{ ft-lb/hp-hr}} = 0.10 \text{ hp-hr (independent of speed)}$$

Fig. 2-4. How much energy it takes to move a car

Grade resistance per ton is 20 pounds for every percent (1 ft rise in 100 ft of forward travel) of grade and doesn't vary with car weight or train speed. The energy it takes to lift a ton to the top of the mountain is entirely a matter of how high it is.

Adding Up the Horsepower-Hours

The mechanical energy or work we're concerned about here is the product of a *force* acting through a distance. The *rate* of applying energy to a job is *power*. Pulling twice as hard at the same speed or moving twice as fast while pulling with the same force represents twice the power. James Watt chose "horsepower" as the unit for rating his 18th-century steam pumping engines and defined it as 33,000 ft-lb of work (lifting pounds of water to a height in feet, for example) per minute; he chose a value somewhat above what any horse alive could keep on doing, presumably to avoid complaints. Today, power is often expressed in the unit named after James himself, the *watt,* and we pay

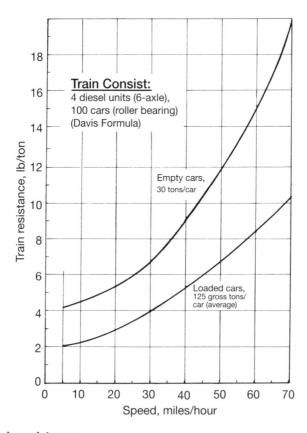

Fig. 2-5. Train resistance

electric bills on the basis of kilowatt-hours of energy. Since locomotives are still rated in horsepower, we'll stick with this unit; 746 watts (or three-quarters of a kilowatt) equals 1 horsepower (hp).

Fig. 2-4 proceeds to calculate the energy in horsepower-hours (hp-hr) that it takes to roll an empty and a loaded car 1 mile on level track and to lift it 100 ft in elevation. The *energy* it takes to overcome a given difference in elevation is the same if you do it via a 0.05 percent grade or straight up in an elevator. As we'll see in studying locomotive performance later on, grade *does* make a huge difference in the tractive force needed. Now we're ready to see which route uses the least total energy in moving a 100-ton car of coal from D to H and bringing the empty back for another load.

Route A. Fig. 2-6 adds up the two classes of resistance for loaded and empty trips by each route. Route A, going over the mountains, uses 750 hp-hr to lift the car over a 4,000 ft summit. Practically all this energy is lost because the train must descend the steep eastern slope under careful control of the brakes, converting the energy into heat. From F to H (Fig. 2-3), no brakes are needed on the gentle grade, and we have a net *input* of 125 hp-hr to boost the car up 5,000 ft, none of which we can get back on this trip. The total = 1,638 hp-hr per car, or 16.38 hp-hr per net ton of coal hauled.

Route B. The entire 750 miles of descending water-grade can be run without using the brakes, so 125 hp-hr needed to overcome 750 miles of rolling friction is provided by the change in elevation. We have to put some of that energy back in returning the empties: the total for Route B works out to 1,605 hp-hr, about 2 percent less than for Route A, in exchange for an extra 500 miles of wear on wheels and roller bearings.

Route BA. We notice that Route B was the overall winner, but Route A used less energy in getting the empties back (513 to 605 hp-hr). This is because of the greater effect of rolling friction over the longer route on the relatively hard-pulling empties. This suggests looking at a circle route, with the loads going east along the river and the empties coming back over the mountain, Route BA. Sure enough, this does the job for 1,513 hp-hr, 6 percent less than Route B. Mechanically, it would be a very practical routing since the same locomotives hauling the heavy loads east could probably get the empties over the mountain without a helper on the steep grade. But, overall, it might be more costly to operate because such one-way movement over long distances results in a lot of "deadhead" costs in getting the train crews back for their next trip.

Route A-1. The idea of hauling those cars empty all the way back suggests another look at Fig. 2-3. Suppose there is important iron ore that could come into the port at K and be hauled to the mills at D—this would mean an extra 100 miles in a side trip from H to F via K, but it's physically practical since the dense iron ore can be hauled as a partial load in the big coal cars (the reverse, of course, won't work). It turns out that the total energy *charged to the coal movement* is only 1,241 hp-hr. Energy used to lift the weight of the cars back up from K to the summit of the pass is part of the cost of the ore movement, which still has a favorable situation because the coal movement is now taking 23 percent less energy than via Route B. Again, whether this is the best arrangement depends on other factors. The car utilization may not be nearly as good if, for example, ore-ship arrival is irregular. And extra car-days cost money, as does diesel fuel.

Horsepower – Hours Per Car
(100 Tons of Coal)

		Eastbound (Loaded)	Westbound (Empty)	Total Energy (HP-HR)	Round-Trip Distance (Miles)
Route A: (Over the mountain)	Rolling Lifting	125 x .012 x 500 = 750 + 125 x .10 x 40 = 500 - 125 x .10 x 10 = -125 1,125	25 x .031 x 500 = 388 25 x .10 x 50 = 125 513	1,638	1,000
Route B: (Along the river)	Rolling Lifting	125 x .012 x 750 = 1,125 - 125 x .10 x 10 = -125 1,000	25 x .031 x 750 = 580 25 x .10 x 10 = 25 605	1,605	1,500
Route BA: (Circle route)		Eastbound Route B (Along the river) 1,000	Westbound Route A (Over the mountain) 513	1,513	1,250
Route A-1: (Side trip to pick up ore load)	Rolling Lifting	125 x .012 x 500 = 750 + 125 x .10 x 40 = 500 - 125 x .10 x 10 = -125 1,125	25 x .031 x 150 = 116 (H to K only-K to D with ore load) 116	1,241	1,100
Route BA-1: (Circle route with ore load on return)		Eastbound Route B (Along the river) 1,000	Westbound Route A-1 (Via K, to pick up ore load) 116	1,116	1,350

Fig. 2-6. Comparing the energy it takes to deliver the goods

Route BA-1. Finally the lowest energy routing turns out to be the "circle route" via the river eastbound with return through K to pick up the ore. A total of 1,116 hp-hr or 32 percent less energy is expended on the return through K than on Route A at a cost of a 35 percent increase in mileage, and with loaded car-miles 81 percent instead of 50 percent. Quite an incentive to the railroad to do whatever it can to develop the K-D ore traffic!

Overall Train Performance

This single-factor analysis omits many refinements and details that would have to be included in any real-life assessment, including the effects of track curvature, the relative energy, and other costs associated with various train speeds, comparative energy costs with local versus through-train haulage, and the equipment-ownership, fuel, crew, and competitiveness costs of line congestion.

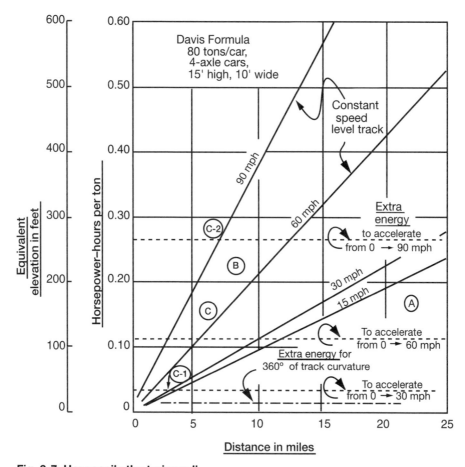

Fig. 2-7. How easily the trains roll

General Performance Factors

To give a little better feel for the ways speed, grade, curvature, and "stop and go" affect railroading, Fig. 2-7 puts these difference factors on one chart, based on cars loaded to 80 tons each (a typical average for the mix of loads and empties likely to be found in service). By looking at this graph, we can get some idea of just how easily the cars roll; later on, these matters will show up in the way tracks are laid out and locomotives are designed.

Grades and power versus distance. Considering the curve on the chart for 15 mph, for example, we see that the extra energy it takes to lift the train upgrade to an elevation of 200 ft would move it about *21 miles* at that speed if it were on level track (Point A). No wonder that trains can move the goods with little energy input and need good brakes on even the gentlest grades. The second set of figures on the vertical axis puts the same thing in terms of horsepower-hours per ton. Two-tenths of a horsepower-hour (running your lawnmower for 4 minutes) would move that ton of train the 21 miles!

Power versus speed. That same 0.20 hp-hr that moved the ton 21 miles at 15 mph would only take it about 9.5 miles at 60 mph (Point B), but at 30 mph it would make 18 miles. This shows that there is little to be gained by running a freight train on level at less than 30 to 35 mph, but that at 60 mph the extra resistance (primarily wind resistance) has begun to require significantly more energy.

Track curvature. Some extra friction occurs in hauling trains around curves, but the extra energy involved may not necessarily be large. As the line near the bottom of the graph shows, it adds about 0.014 hp-hr per ton (the equivalent of lifting the weight 14 ft) to go around curves that are equivalent to a full 360-degree circle. Since a railroad following a river in hilly country may have the equivalent of several complete circles, curves can show up in the fuel bill. Wear on wheels and rails is a more expensive result.

Stop and Go. Point C shows that the energy it takes to get a train up to 60 mph from a stop is equal to what it would take to roll it about 5.5 miles on the level at the same speed. The energy equivalent at 30 mph is about 3 miles (C-1) and 7 miles at 90 mph (C-2). This shows that stops and slowdowns take significant energy; a 60 mph train stopping every 10 miles will use about as much energy in accelerating as it will in covering the distance. Since it takes only one-third as much energy to go from 0 to 30 as it does from 30 to 60, a series of 30 mph speed restrictions is almost as much of a handicap.

Train Performance Analysis

The numbers in Fig. 2-7 are based on the "Davis Formulas," a set of equations assembled by W. A. Davis in 1927 to summarize the best available data on factors affecting the resistance of train consists and trackage typical of the era. (These factors include: journal bearing friction, rolling resistance, losses from impact and vibration, air resistance, and curvature.) The equation coefficients are based on changes in roadway, equipment, and operating practices, and the availability of new test data and analytical procedures over the years, yet they still provide the framework for constantly refining *train simulation models* now used for highly accurate computer predictions of in-train dynamic forces, schedule performance, and energy consumption for any train consist running over any specific route.

Beginning in 1989, the Train Operation and Energy Simulator (TOES) and related Train Energy Model (TEM) programs have been released in modules compatible with hardware of personal-computer capability. The TOES and TEM programs are refined continuously by the Association of American Railroads (AAR) to reflect analytical, laboratory, and test track and field data, which are measured in cooperation with the FRA, (Federal Railroad Administration) the railroads in the United States and Canada, and with inputs from railroad organizations worldwide. This has enabled railroad operating personnel to use them in such day-to-day matters as comparing the energy efficiency of alternate train-braking practices on a given run, as well as for longer range planning and costing operations.

System Operations Analyses

Along with these refined computations for the movement of individual trains, computerized *system* operational analyses seeks to optimize plant and scheduling. The system analysis studies the interactions among trains in moving traffic over a network of routes under various systems of train control—a major factor in railroad planning. The usefulness of such optimizations depends on how the items apply. For instance, the mathematical model relating individual axle loads to the degradation of track ballast particles is one item that is a factor included by AAR researchers in its TM (Track Maintenance) Cost program. A basic goal, then, in many ongoing industry research programs (on everything from the detection of bearing fatigue to the effect of rail lubrication on wear and resistance) is to validate increasingly sophisticated descriptive models after comparing field and laboratory test data. In particular, the AAR/FRA Heavy Axle Load Test program has provided critically important inputs.

C H A P T E R   3

The Track:
Alignment and Structure

The purpose of the railroad track structure is to support the loads of cars and locomotives and guide their movement. In order to perform this function, the track structure must withstand the loadings applied to it by both the vehicles and the environment.

Fig. 3-1 presents an overview of the track, which consists of two steel rails that are 56½ inches apart, supported by timber, concrete, or steel crossties, resting on rock ballast and subballast, which, in turn, rests on the original subgrade or foundation of the line. This track structure must support the loads generated by a modern heavy-haul freight train, which can weigh 14,000 tons or more and each wheel of which weighs 36,000 lbs or 18 tons.

With those heavy forces at work, it's easy to see that every item in the track has to be designed and maintained to do its part through conditions of high loads, heavy traffic density, and severe weather conditions that can range from extreme cold and snow to severe heat and rain.

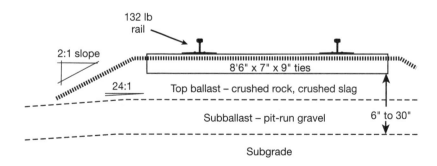

Fig. 3-1. Track overview

Track Alignment

Since railroad track must cross existing terrain that can include mountains, prairies, and rolling hills, trains are required to make numerous changes of direction, both vertical and horizontal. In the vertical direction, changes in the topography show up as grades or changes in elevation that can range from a fraction of 1 percent to over 4 percent, corresponding to a rise of 4 ft in height for every 100 ft of track traveled.

In the horizontal direction, track is divided into stretches of straight track (or *tangent track* as railroad engineers call it), and *curved track* where the track changes direction. Even though tangent track is used as much as possible because it is much easier to build and maintain, curves are a necessary part of the track layout and can be found with great frequency in hilly or mountainous terrain. In the United States, the sharpness of curved track is defined in terms of "degrees of curvature" or alternately, in terms of the curve's radius, in feet or meters. The relationship between degrees and radius is illustrated in Fig. 3-2, which also shows typical maximum speeds for some curves.

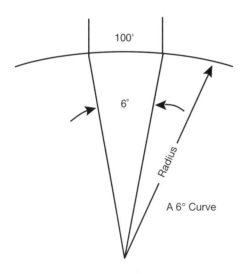

The degree or sharpness of a railroad curve is the angle through which the track curves in 100 ft.

$$\text{Radius in ft} = \frac{5,729}{\text{Degrees/100 ft}}$$

Degree of Curve	Radius Feet	Typical Max. Speed	Extra Curve Resistance, lb/ton	Equivalent Increase in Grade, %
1°	5,729	100 mph	0.8	0.04
5°	1,146	50 mph	4.0	0.20
10°	573	30 mph	8.0	0.40
15°	383	25 mph	12.0	0.60

Fig. 3-2. Track curvature

Railroad engineers generally prefer to keep curvature low, around 1 or 2 degrees, preferably. However, in hilly or mountainous territory, curvature is more severe, increasing to curves of 8 to 10 degrees or higher. Often railroad builders were faced with a choice of sharp curves or severe grades in order to go through mountain ranges. Since curves add significant drag to the train, where curves and grades occur together, a common practice is to compensate for curvature by reducing the grade on the curved track so that the combined resistance is the same for both tangent and curved segments of the grade.

Superelevation refers to the difference in elevation between the two rails on a curve. (The difference in elevation between the two rails on tangent track, which is usually undesirable, is referred to as *cross level*). To compensate for the effect of centrifugal force, the outer rail on a curve is often raised or *superelevated* to tip the cars inward (Fig. 3-3). The speed at which the superelevation fully compensates for the centrifugal force is referred to as the balance speed and is a function of the degree of curvature. The maximum superelevation ordinarily used on a standard-gage line carrying general traffic is 6 inches. However, because different trains will often operate at different speeds around a curve, under current railroad practice, track is often elevated less than that required for maximum speed. Current Federal Railroad Administration (FRA) regulations allow for operation at speeds above balance speed, usually limited to 3 inches of "cant deficiency." If heavy trains run over curves regularly at much less than the speed for which they are superelevated, however, the wheel flanges will ride the inner rail and wear it rapidly. Therefore, the maximum and minimum speeds on a given track cannot be too far apart on lines where there are many curves.

In order to allow for a smooth transition from tangent (and flat, i.e., no elevation) track to superelevated curved track, it is good practice to use a "spiral" or "easement" of gradually increasing curvature between each tangent and curved section of main-line trackage (Fig. 3-3). The spiral allows for a smooth transition in both curvature and elevation. The length of the spiral depends on the allowable speed and the amount of superelevation, and may be more than 600 ft in high-speed territory.

Track Gage

The most basic characteristic of track forming the North American rail network is its common "standard gage" of 4 ft 8½ in., which allows freight cars to freely roll from Canada to Mexico and from coast to coast. Fig. 3-4 shows how gage is measured.

This gage allows for a nominal clearance between the wheel flanges and the rail head on tangent track, though on curves, the wheel flange will frequently contact the side of the rail head, particularly on the outside or "high" rail of the curve. As the rail wears, the track gage increases. Excessive wear results in too wide a gage, requiring rail to be replaced or the track gage corrected.

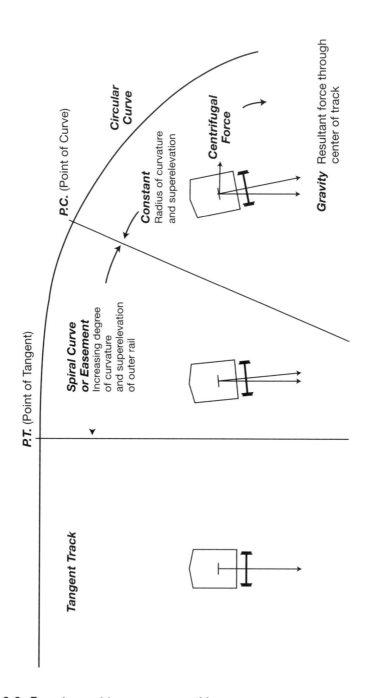

Fig. 3-3. From tangent to curve—smoothly

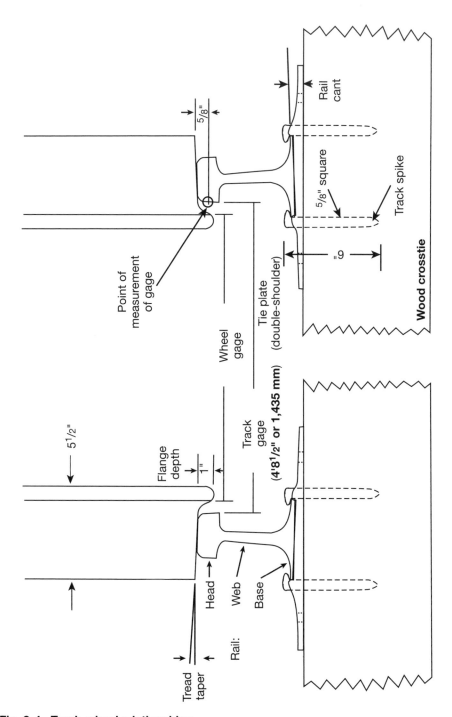

Fig. 3-4. Track-wheel relationships

25

Why Such an Odd Gage?

The current "standard" of 4 ft 8½ in. is the most commonly used gage in the world. It traces its origin back to early English tramways before the invention of the steam locomotive. Additionally, there is some basis for tracing this back to the cartwheel spacing of Roman stone gateways. George Stephenson and his son Robert, who were prominent promoters and engineers of railroad systems, adopted 4 ft 8½ in. as their standard. It is used throughout Europe, Asia, and North America with some exceptions such as the "Wide Gage" (5 ft or higher) systems in Russia, Spain, and Finland or the narrow gage (3 ft 6 in. or meter gage) used in parts of South America, Australia, and East Africa.

In the early years of United States railroading, several different gages were in use. In 1863, however, President Lincoln designated 4 ft 8½ in. as the gage for the railroad to be built to the Pacific Coast. This, then, became the standard to which all U.S. railroads conformed. Thus, the railroads south of the Potomac and Ohio Rivers that were mostly 5 ft gage until 1887 changed to standard virtually over a single weekend. By having a single common gage in North America, free transit is allowed between different railroads without the need for transferring loads or switching car trucks at "break-of-gage" points.

Loading of the Track Structure

The track structure's function is to transform the intense load of the wheel on the head of the rail to a moderate, distributed pressure that the foundation or subgrade

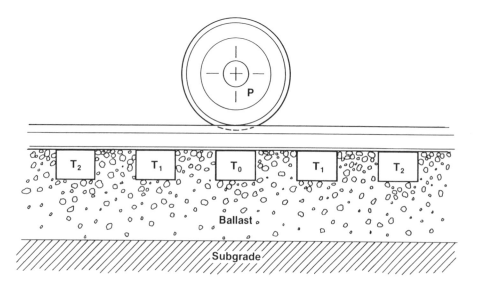

Fig. 3-5. Track overview showing distribution of loads

(i.e., the earth underneath the track) can sustain under all conditions without excessive settling or failure. This distribution capability is illustrated in Fig. 3-5.

Thus, the rail, which is the part of the track structure that contacts and supports the wheels of the railway vehicles, starts the process of load distribution by spreading each individual wheel load over a number of crossties. With wheel loads of 36,000 lbs and higher, the wheel-rail contact stresses generated can approach the strength of the rail steel. Each rail then distributes this load to between 6 and 10 crossties with tie plates used between the rail and the crossties to increase the bearing surface on the ties and reduce tie surface stresses. The tie, in turn, distributes this load to the top of the "rock" ballast layer, further reducing the level of stress. Finally the ballast (and subballast) layer finishes this stress reduction process, bringing the level of stress to a level that can be withstood by the parent soil or subgrade layer of the track. Fig. 3-6 illustrates this load distribution behavior as an inverse pyramid of stress reduction, with the corresponding American Railway Engineering and Maintenance-of-Way Association (AREMA) design limits defined for each component "layer."

This load that the track is subjected to comes from not only the locomotives and cars of the train but also from changes in the environment (such as variations in temperature, which directly affect the loading of the track structure). This includes vehicle-induced loadings in the vertical, lateral, and longitudinal planes (Fig. 3-7) as well as the thermal loading of the rails generated by changes in ambient temperature.

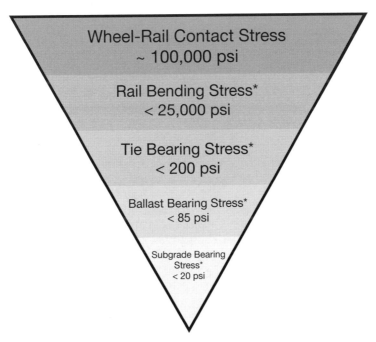

Fig. 3-6. Pyramid of bearing stresses (*AREMA design limits)

27

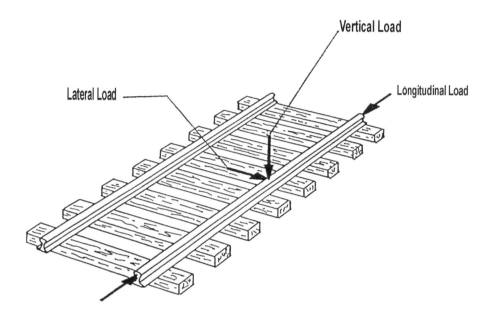

Fig. 3-7. Different loads applied to the track

The vertical loads include the weight of the vehicle itself, which can weigh as high as 39,000 lbs per wheel (Table 3-1), and the additional forces generated by the dynamic interaction of the moving vehicle on the track. Dynamic impact forces as high as three times the weight of the wheel itself have been measured under very severe service conditions.

Lateral loads, which are generated by the flanging of the locomotive or railcar wheels against the rail on curves or by dynamic hunting[1] of rail vehicles on tangent track, have been measured to be in the 15,000 lb range and even higher under severe service conditions.

Longitudinal forces are input into the track structure through two distinct mechanisms: mechanical forces through train action, and thermal forces through changes in ambient temperature. The mechanically induced longitudinal forces are directly related to train handling, and train acceleration, and braking and have been measured to be in the range of 20,000 lbs per rail and higher. Thermally induced longitudinal rail forces are present in continuous-welded rail and are caused by the change in temperature from the "neutral" temperature of the rail. These forces, which can be either tensile or compressive in nature, can reach levels of well over 100,000 lbs per rail, resulting in either buckling of the track (in hot weather) or a pull-apart of the rail (in cold weather).

---

[1] Dynamic side-to-side movement of railcars at high speed

Table 3.1 Static wheel loads—worldwide

Axle load	Gross weight of cars	
Axle load (in tons)	Gross weight of cars (in lbs)	Type
10	80,000	Light rail transit
15	120,000	Heavy rail transit
25	200,000	Passenger cars
25	200,000	Common European freight limit
27.5	220,000	United Kingdom and Select European limit
33	263,000	North American free interchange limit; limited international use (Sweden, South Africa, Brazil)
36	286,000	Current heavy-axle-load (HAL) weight for North American Class 1 railroads
39	315,000	Very limited use (Australia, North America); undergoing research tests

The Track Structure

The railroad track structure has been the subject of evolution and engineering for nearly 200 years through a combination of incremental improvements and technological innovation. A good example of this is the rail itself, which has evolved both in shape and in material composition. In Fig. 3-8, the rail section has evolved from a variety of early shapes to the modern self-supporting T-rail section, which is still in use today, though with larger rail sections of up to 141 lbs per yard. Matching the changes in shape are changes in the rail manufacturing process, and in rail metallurgy and treatment, with modern continuous-casting, rolling, alloying and heat-treatment techniques providing rail sections with significantly improved strength, hardness, and resistance to failure even under modern axle loadings and severe service environments.

This evolution of the railroad track, and its key components, has been paralleled by an evolution in railroad engineering. In the 19th century, railroad engineering focused on *building* the railroad (with a strong emphasis on construction techniques, bridge and tunnel engineering, and route alignment engineering). Modern railroad engineering is focusing on *improving the track structure's strength* and the ability to carry the ever increasing loads on the modern railway.

New technology continues to be introduced into the railroad industry (e.g., use of concrete, steel, or plastic crossties in addition to the wood crosstie), but the basic rail-

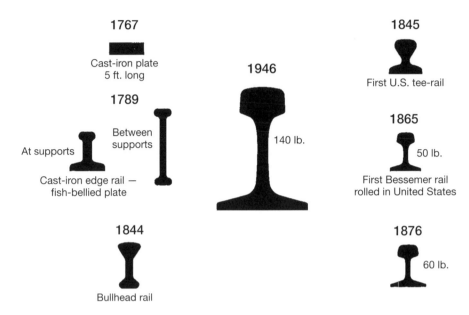

Fig. 3-8. The evolution of rail

tie-ballast system has continued to be used because it represents the most practical compromise among the conflicting requirements for high performance, minimal maintenance, and overall low cost.

The following sections examine each of the main parts of the track structure to see how each has developed and how each functions within the overall track requirement of guiding and supporting the trains.

Rail

Modern rail is a high-strength, low-carbon steel, which can support the high contact and bending stresses imposed by modern freight trains (Fig. 3-6) for dozens of years and longer on high-density lines. On tangent track, modern rail steel is expected to carry over 1 billion gross tons of traffic, corresponding to one 5,000-ton freight train every hour for 23 years. On sharp curves, special head-hardened rail is used to reduce the rate of side wear caused by the flanging of the wheels against the rail.

The shape of the rail, referred to as the rail section, varies in size and weight, to match the intended service environment. Since the cost of the rail is directly related to its weight, the heaviest (and most expensive) rail sections are reserved for the most severe tracks carrying the highest levels of traffic. Rail can vary in size from 90 lbs per yard (45 kg/m or kilogram/meter), which is used for light transit systems, to the heaviest modern rail section of 141 lbs/yd (70.5 kg/m), which is used on heavy-haul freight tracks. Most rail sections are rolled in accordance with the designs of AREMA and are designated by the initials RE that follow the section size. Thus, 136 RE rail, the most common rail in use on main-line tracks, is an AREMA-designed section with a weight of 136 lbs/yd (68 kg/m). Most new rail is of 115-, 132-, 136-, or the new 141-pound sections. Less than 10 percent of the rail in main track is lighter than 100 lbs, though light rail is common in transit systems. Modern rail stands from 6 to 8 inches high, and has a uniform base width of 5½ or 6 inches for compatibility with tie plates or other rail-tie fastening systems.

Rail is removed from main-line service based on either head wear or the development of defects at a rate indicating metal fatigue under today's heavy-axle loads. Fig. 3-9 shows that rail wears on both the top of the head, caused by normal passage of the wheel treads, and on the side of the head, due to the contact of the wheel flanges on sharp curves. Rail can last for over a billion gross tons on tangent track, but its life on curves can be one-third of that.

Lubrication is a technique that has become widely used to reduce rail wear on curves by applying a layer of petroleum-based lubricant or "grease" to the rail head. Automatic wayside rail lubricators are used in track to apply the lubricant to each wheel flange in the approach to sharp curves, thus spreading the lubricant across the curves and reducing rail wear. Improved wear resistance is also achieved by using harder premium rail, which uses alloy metallurgy or post-rolling heat treatment of the head to make this rail harder and more wear resistant than standard rail. The tradeoff between increased cost and extended rail life is such that premium rail is frequently specified for use on curves in high-density territory.

After removal from main-line service, rail is often re-laid onto secondary, branch, and yard tracks. In total, rail can last over 50 years, with corrosion being an issue over very extended periods of time or in very wet areas such as in tunnels and by the ocean.

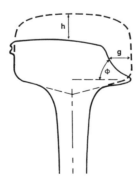

Fig. 3-9. Rail wear

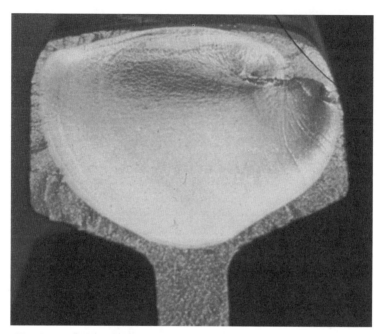

Fig. 3-10. Rail with transverse defect

In addition to wear, rail can accumulate fatigue damage caused by the high stresses from the passing of each individual wheel. This fatigue damage can result in the development of defects, illustrated in Fig. 3-10. When these fatigue defects develop at a high rate (such as 3 or 4 defects per mile each year), the rail is removed from main-line service.

The fatigue defects, generally starting as a small inclusion or defect inside the rail head, can grow under traffic until they break underneath a train. In order to find these defects before they grow to an excessive size that can cause failure, rail is tested using ultrasonic or magnetic testing techniques. Ultrasonic testing, the most common of the rail-inspection techniques, is accomplished using a special test vehicle that can test both rails of the track at speeds of up to 25 mph and find small defects in the rail head before they grow to a dangerous size. The section of rail with a found defect is then removed from the track and replaced with a short segment of good rail known as a rail "plug."

With the increase in rail head stress from heavy freight cars weighing as much as 286,000 lbs, rail fatigue has become a major reason for removal of rail, particularly from its original or first position. Although new rail manufacturing technologies such as vacuum degassing and continuous-casting are able to produce "cleaner" rail that contains fewer inclusions to act as defect initiation points, increasing loads on the rail continue to result in the development of fatigue defects. The use of modern inspection techniques such as ultrasonic testing and modern maintenance techniques (such as rail grinding) have become more commonplace to control the development of these defects.

Rail head grinding is a technique whereby a special contractor-owned rail-grinding train uses a large number of rotating grinding stones or wheels to correct the surface of the rail and establish a proper shape or contour to the rail head. With each grinding motor removing less than a thousandth of an inch of metal, large grinders with as many as 120 motors can remove defects on the head of the rail such as surface fatigue, rail corrugations, or engine burns. They can also reshape the rail to improve the contact between the wheels and the rail, resulting in reduced stresses at the surface of the rail and better interaction between the wheel and the rail. This, in turn, reduces the rate of fatigue defect development and wear. Rail grinding has been found to be particularly effective in reducing the rate of gage-corner defect formation, which commonly occurs on the outside rail in sharp curves and results in the rapid development and growth of fatigue defects in this area.

Continuous-Welded Rail (CWR)

Rail traditionally was rolled in 39 ft lengths, thus requiring that they be bolted together at the ends (Fig. 3-11). These connections or joints are traditionally staggered, resulting in one joint every 19 ft.

Joint bars connect the rail lengths together. The resulting gap, regulated to suit the temperature when the rail is laid so that it will just close on the hottest day, causes the rhythmic clickety-clack as a train moves along the track. Despite a great deal of design research, the joint is always less rigid than the rest of the rail and deflects enough to allow wear and battering of the rail ends. This can be corrected by building up the rail surface with weld metal and grinding it to its original contour, but it is an expensive and time-consuming process. In addition, the reduced stiffness at the joint also causes greater load on the ballast and subballast, resulting in "low joints" and rocking of certain freight cars at critical speeds, a phenomenon known as *rock-and-roll*. This loss of track surface likewise requires frequent and expensive maintenance of the track to tamp the joints back up to the level of the rest of the track.

Modern rail mills can now roll far longer lengths of rail, but the presence of joints still remains a high-maintenance cost area.

To eliminate these joints and reduce the cost of maintenance, rails can be welded together into continuous strings, known as continuous-welded rail, or CWR. This welding can either be accomplished in a plant (with the long strings, usually a quarter of a mile in length, being transported to the site and laid and fastened in place) or else welded on site using field-deployable welding systems. Electric flash butt welding techniques are used in the plant and (with specialized equipment) in the field for large field-welding operations. Thermite welding is a process used in the field for only a few welds. Even though electric flash butt welding produces the strongest welds, thermite welding is the more economical technique if only a few welds are required at any given location.

A major issue associated with CWR is the effects of expansion and contraction on the rail steel (Fig. 3-12). Rail steel normally expands when heated and contracts or shrinks when cooled. However, in CWR, the rail is not free to expand or contract, as is the case with bolted rail, and the restrained rail builds up forces internally. These longitudinal forces, which can be 100,000 lbs or higher, are compressive (can be pressed or squeezed together) in hot weather and tensile (can be stretched or extended) in cold weather.

Because of this temperature sensitivity, the laying of CWR is restricted to a narrow range of temperatures, often near the upper limit of those expected at the particular location. This can require the heating of the rail if the air temperature is cooler than the desired laying temperature. The goal is to keep the rail relatively unstressed or in tension. Otherwise, temperature-induced compressive forces can cause the track to buckle out. If the lateral stability of the track is disturbed (by maintenance of ties or ballast at times when high longitudinal stresses are present, such as in hot weather), the risk of

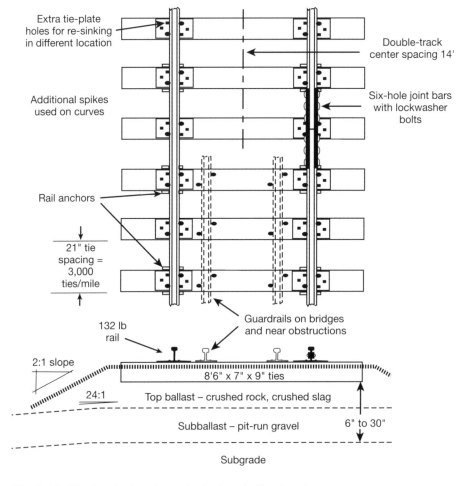

Fig. 3-11. The track structure—typical main-line track

buckling increases. Excessive tensile stresses can also be undesirable, however, resulting in *pull-aparts* in the rail, often at weak spots such as welds or joints. Although cold weather pull-aparts are usually considered a less serious problem than hot weather *sun kinks* or track buckling (because they do not usually result in a derailment and are normally detected by the track circuits), they still represent a maintenance problem. Selection of the proper rail-laying temperature must keep **both** factors in mind.

Track circuits for signaling require electrically insulated joints in the track. These joints use special electrically insulating material to isolate the individual rails and allow for track circuits. To approach the stiffness and endurance of the rail itself, these are commonly made with special permanently bolted angle bars encased and sealed with epoxy under controlled shop conditions within short "plugs" of rail. These are then field-welded into place.

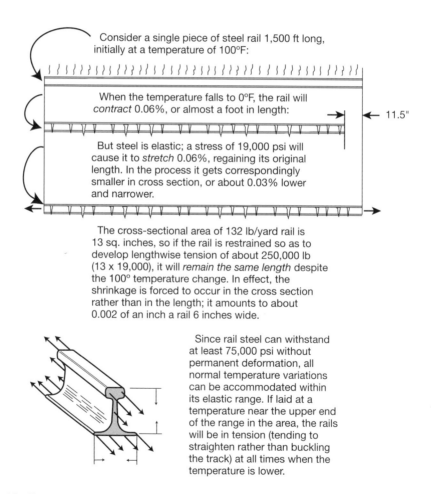

Consider a single piece of steel rail 1,500 ft long, initially at a temperature of 100°F:

When the temperature falls to 0°F, the rail will *contract* 0.06%, or almost a foot in length:

← 11.5"

But steel is elastic; a stress of 19,000 psi will cause it to *stretch* 0.06%, regaining its original length. In the process it gets correspondingly smaller in cross section, or about 0.03% lower and narrower.

The cross-sectional area of 132 lb/yard rail is 13 sq. inches, so if the rail is restrained so as to develop lengthwise tension of about 250,000 lb (13 x 19,000), it will *remain the same length* despite the 100° temperature change. In effect, the shrinkage is forced to occur in the cross section rather than in the length; it amounts to about 0.002 of an inch a rail 6 inches wide.

Since rail steel can withstand at least 75,000 psi without permanent deformation, all normal temperature variations can be accommodated within its elastic range. If laid at a temperature near the upper end of the range in the area, the rails will be in tension (tending to straighten rather than buckling the track) at all times when the temperature is lower.

Fig. 3-12. Expansion and contraction of rail with temperature

Crossties

In an effort to create a truly "permanent way," some of the earlier railroads mounted their rails on stone blocks bedded firmly in the ground. This construction was impressively expensive in comparison to the practice of spiking rails to wooden cross members or "ties" laid on the surface, but it turned out to be a lot less satisfactory. The lack of any cushioning between rail and stone resulted in a jarring ride that damaged both rail and vehicle, and the shifting of the blocks threw the track out of gage.

The use of wooden crossties, discussed earlier, allowed for a uniform transmission of the load from the rail to the ballast. Hardwood, which is the dominant material used in crossties in the United States and Canada, has good strength characteristics that provide gage holding, uniform distribution of the load to the ballast, and good support of the rail itself. It also provides for sufficient resiliency to cushion the impacts of wheels on rail, reducing the force of the dynamic loads applied to the track. Hardwood is also "nailable," allowing the simple and inexpensive method of fastening rail to tie, using cut spikes and large bearing area tie plates (Fig. 3-11). The cut spikes and large bearing area tie plates are used to spread the load of the rail over a large enough area to prevent local crushing and cutting of the wood.

In order to extend its life and prevent decay and insect infestation, wood crossties are pressure-impregnated with a creosote mixture (as much as 25 lbs of preservative are forced into a 200 lb tie). With these and other refinements, such as predrilled spike holes (which reduce fiber damage and improve the grip of the wood on the spike), the service life of first-quality ties has been extended to the range of 30 or more years.

Although timber remains the dominant material for crossties in modern railroad track in the United States and Canada, prestressed concrete ties have been used increasingly on severe service railroad environments to include high-speed passenger lines such as Amtrak's Northeast Corridor (Washington-Boston) and low-speed heavy-tonnage curved track. In other parts of the world, where timber is in short supply and is expensive, concrete ties are in widespread use.

Concrete ties are significantly heavier than their timber counterparts, ranging in weight from 650 to 800 lbs each compared to 200 lbs for timber. They also require a more complex fastening system, including *elastic clips* to hold the rail in place, *cast-in shoulders,* and *resilient pads* to replace the natural resiliency of the wood tie and avoid damage to the tie and rest of the track from wheel impacts on the rail. In signaled territory, separate insulators are also required for electrical isolation, since concrete does not have the natural electrical isolation properties of wood.

Concrete ties are highly uniform in design, since they are a manufactured product, and use pretensioned wires or post-tensioned rods to provide the resistance to tensile stresses that concrete does not normally possess. Because of the greater weight of the ties, concrete-tie track tends to be more stable; although they are usually spaced about 25 percent farther apart to take advantage of their uniformity and larger dimensions.

The overall relative economy of the two types of track will depend mostly on how long ties actually remain serviceable in practice.

In recent years, steel, plastic, and composite material ties have been introduced in limited numbers. Steel ties, which are inverted sections and thus require less ballast than wood or concrete ties, have been used in special applications such as tunnels and yards. Plastic and composite ties are new and have seen only limited service to date.

Rail Fasteners

Fastening systems keep the track together by securely attaching the rail to the crossties. In most track conditions, the rail remains upright and in place because the wheel forces acting on it (even on curves) are mostly downward rather than sideward and actually tend to keep the rail from turning over. In very sharp curves or locations of high lateral loading, however, it is the job of the fastening system to prevent the rail from overturning, In addition, the fastening system must keep the rail from shifting sideways. Tightly fastened rail also avoids some of the wear associated with movement between parts as passing wheels slam the rail and tie plate down against the tie.

In cut-spike track, which is the standard for tangent and shallow curves, cut-spike fasteners perform adequately and economically. As curvature increases, additional spikes, installed in the tie-plate holes provided, are used to hold the plate more firmly in place. Its shoulders then hold the rail from sliding.

In order to prevent the rail from moving lengthwise (a phenomenon known as *rail creep*), cut-spike track is equipped with rail anchors or anti-creepers. These are spring clips (Fig. 3-11) that snap onto the base of the rail and come up against the tie to restrain motion. As many as four per tie may be required in places where temperature changes, heavy grades, and train braking (particularly with loaded traffic in one direction) conspire to make the rail "run," forcing ties and switches out of line and developing stresses tending to make the track buckle sideways.

Elastic fastener systems, consisting of spring clips, cast-in-place shoulders, and resilient pads and insulators, represent an alternative to the cut-spike fastening system. Originally developed for concrete ties, these elastic rail-tie fastening systems have also been adapted, via a special tie plate, to wood crossties track. The result is a stronger track structure requiring no separate rail anchors. Also avoided is spike-killing, the damage from multiple respiking that may govern wood-tie life on curves where rail must be changed out repeatedly. Elastic fasteners on wood ties are more commonly being used to replace cut spikes on the most severe operating environments of heavy tonnage and severe curvature.

Ballast and Substructure

Ballast is the layer of crushed rock located under the crossties to further distribute and transmit the load down into the subgrade and parent material of the ground. Ballast also provides resistance to movement of the ties laterally (side to side) and longitudinally (along the length of the rail). It further permits drainage of rain or other water sources away from the track and allows for ease of maintenance of the track geometry by tamping or lining.

The ballast also provides resiliency to the overall track structure. Watch the wheels closely as they roll along the rail, and notice that even the heaviest, best-maintained track is not absolutely rigid—a "wave of deflection" moves along under each axle. The amount of this deflection is quantified by the track modulus, defined as the force required to depress the rail 1 inch for each inch of track length along which the load is considered to be applied. Track modulus values range from less than 2,000 lb/in. for the softest usable track to about 8,000 lb/in. for the heaviest main-line track on the best subgrade; corresponding deflections under the range of axle loads may range from 0.025 to 0.125 of an inch. By keeping this deflection uniform along the track, the smoothness of the ride is maintained. This deflection (and the *damping* of the ballast material that goes along with it) also provides a cushioning effect, both on the unsprung wheels and axles of rolling stock and on the upper parts of the track structure itself, the rails and the ties.

A key job of the ballast is to hold the ties in place, to prevent lateral deflections, and to spread out the load. The load ranges from around 85 psi underneath the tie to a pressure lower than the "endurance limit" of the subgrade, usually less than 20 psi (Fig. 3-6). For the modern ballast section, this requires 12 to 18 inches of ballast underneath the tie and an additional shoulder (off of the tie's end) of 12 to 18 inches.

In poor subgrade areas, additional depth of ballast may be needed. In problem areas such as swampy ground, it may be necessary to drive wood piles or even use concrete slabs to spread the load and provide a stable enough foundation to support the ballast and subballast (Fig. 3-11).

More than 80 percent of the weight of the track (above the subgrade) consists of ballast, so a primary requirement for ballast material is availability within a reasonable hauling distance. Crushed rock (granite, trap rock, or certain hard rock materials), hard-crushed furnace slags, and some forms of dense lava make the best ballast. For lighter duty, limestone or crushed washed gravel have been used. However, with today's prevalence of 33- and 36-ton axle-load freight cars on even secondary trackage, higher grade ballast is commonly used on virtually all lines.

In service, the ability of the ballast to resist degradation and continue to perform its most important function of draining rainwater freely is vital in achieving a low-maintenance, stable track structure. Fouled ballast (i.e., ballast with extensive fine particles that clog the ballast pores and block drainage) can result in rapid deterioration of the geometry of the track. Fouled ballast also freezes in winter, causing higher stresses in the rail and tie system from rough-riding equipment and track heaving when it thaws in the spring.

Overall, good track drainage is of paramount importance. In level country, track is usually laid on a low embankment with side ditches. Where subsoil conditions are good, ballast may be laid directly on the subgrade; in less favorable situations, a sub-ballast of smaller particle-size rock may be essential. At high-stress locations such as turnouts and grade crossings, the addition of a carefully chosen "geotextile" fabric to further spread the load and maintain clean ballast (by blocking the migration of sub-grade dirt) has become a common practice.

In high-density areas, tamping to correct the surface geometry of the track can be performed as frequently as every 2 to 3 years. In addition, techniques to clean the ballast (e.g., undercutting of the track or shoulder cleaning, performed every 10 to 15 years) can be used to extend the life of the ballast and avoid complete ballast replacement, an expensive and time-consuming process.

Turnouts, Crossings, and Track Work

Another key design feature of the track is the "turnout," which diverts the train from one track to another. This relatively simple arrangement (Fig. 3-13), which has only two moving parts, is built in various lengths to suit the speed required in operating through the diverging (curved) route. The turnout consists of the *switch* (the part of the turnout that moves the train from one track to another), the *frog* (the assembly that lets the flanged wheels cross over the opposite rail), and the *closure rails* (the rails that connect the switch and the frog—the two key parts of the turnout). Turnout sharpness is designated by the angle of the frog and determines the speed by which a train can go over the frog in the diverging movement. The longest turnout in common use is the No. 20 (some railroads go up to a No. 24), which is 152 ft long from point to frog and will allow a train to enter a passing track or branch line at speeds as high as 50 mph. *Equilateral* turnout arrangements that "split the difference" and divide the curvature between the two tracks allow speeds in excess of 50 mph at important junctions or in entering and leaving a section of double track.

To the operating department of the railroad, a turnout is always a "switch," presumably because the only moving parts are the points that divert the wheels from one set of rails to the other. Fig. 3-13 also defines some of the other parts of the turnout assembly.

Other important items of "track work" are the *crossing, crossover, double slip* and *ladder,* illustrated in Fig. 3-14.

Because of the complex geometry and the presence of up to four rails and a complex series of heavy components (such as the cast frog), significant dynamic impact forces are generated between the wheels and track elements. These occur most commonly at the switches, where the train is forced to change direction to take the diverging move, and at the frogs, which are stiff and generate high-impact forces in turnouts and cross-

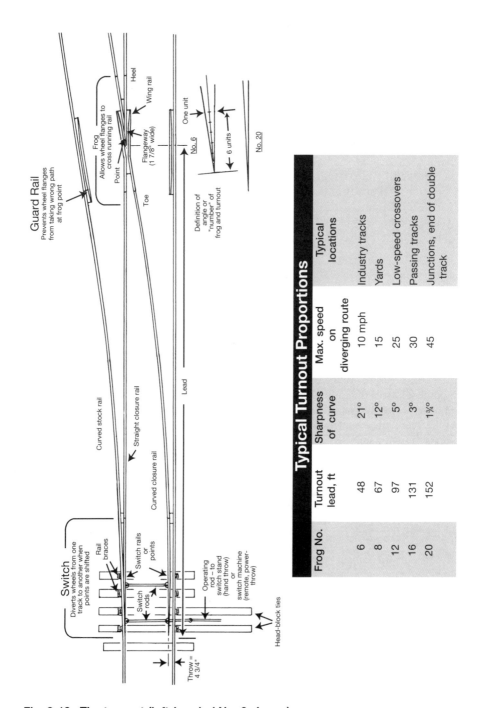

Typical Turnout Proportions

Frog No.	Turnout lead, ft	Sharpness of curve	Max. speed on diverging route	Typical locations
6	48	21°	10 mph	Industry tracks
8	67	12°	15	Yards
12	97	5°	25	Low-speed crossovers
16	131	3°	30	Passing tracks
20	152	1¾°	45	Junctions, end of double track

Fig. 3-13. The turnout (left-handed No. 6 shown)

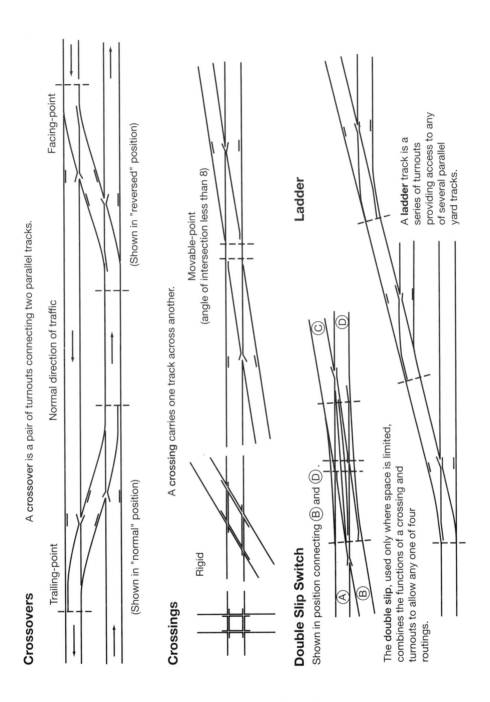

Crossovers

A crossover is a pair of turnouts connecting two parallel tracks.

Trailing-point

Normal direction of traffic

Facing-point

(Shown in "normal" position)

(Shown in "reversed" position)

Crossings

A crossing carries one track across another.

Rigid

Movable-point
(angle of intersection less than 8)

Double Slip Switch

Shown in position connecting Ⓑ and Ⓓ.

The **double slip**, used only where space is limited, combines the functions of a crossing and turnouts to allow any one of four routings.

Ladder

A **ladder** track is a series of turnouts providing access to any of several parallel yard tracks.

Fig. 3-14. Crossovers, crossings, and double slip switch

ings. In addition, special track work must accommodate both new and worn wheels as smoothly as possible. The result is a design that is generally complex and requires high levels of maintenance. Special features, such as high-manganese, work-hardening steel inserts in turnout and crossing frogs (often prehardened by detonating a sheet of explosive on the wearing surfaces), and stout rail braces to withstand the side thrust at switch points, are necessary to reduce wear and keep the rails in line without continual adjustment.

Because of effects on track geometry of the forces and impacts involved and the closer tolerances required for safe tracking, maintenance expenditures on such track work are high; in heavy-traffic territory, it is often many times that of conventional track.

Nevertheless, it is this simple and versatile system that can be designed to direct trains and cars through any pattern of trackage that made "conventional" railroads so flexible and practical.

Track Maintenance and Inspection

The key components of the track will wear out or degrade with traffic and time, so they must be replaced, either individually, or as a unit. In North America, track components are usually replaced individually. Rail is replaced when it is worn out or has excessive fatigue defects; ties are replaced when they begin to fail and are unable to support the track. In general, this replacement is limited, such as tie replacement where 800 to 1,000 out of the 3,250 ties in a mile are replaced. Complete track renewal where all of the track components are replaced together is a more common practice overseas, but it is not commonly done in the United States and Canada.

This replacement or renewal process does not vary in principle from that of a hundred years ago—worn rail is taken up and replaced; bad ties are identified, removed, and new ones are slid into place; new ballast is added. After a period of time, the entire track consists of new material, with a minimum of lost operational time and cost. On branch lines and short line railroads, the entire process can be handled by a small, well-trained track crew, equipped with relatively simple tools, often between trains or in limited maintenance "blocks" or "windows" of time.

On busy main-line tracks, however, where access time for maintenance is limited, the maintenance process relies on mechanization to minimize costs of replacement as well as occupancy time of the maintenance crews. To this end, large production crews equipped with major groups of specialized on-rail machines work systematically to accomplish the major maintenance programs: These production crews include:

- Rail crews, who install strings of CWR in place of the existing rail (CWR or jointed), and de-stress the rail as required. Long strings are further joined with field welds and insulated-joint plugs.

- Surfacing crews, who correct track geometry by adding new ballast. They align and smooth the track using laser-sight-controlled machines, and tamp, compact, and dress (reshape) the ballast.

- Tie crews, who replace hundreds of ties per mile on a production basis. Tie crews usually include a surfacing element as part of their equipment that aligns, tamps, compacts, and dresses the ballast. These are often referred to as Timber and Surfacing (T&S) Crews.

These large production crews are supplemented by smaller regional and division crews, who do similar functions but on a more limited scale, using fewer people and machines. These smaller crews do not have the same economic advantage that the large production crews have, but they are more versatile and can be used for smaller necessary maintenance work, in between the large production crews that cycle across the railroad on multi-year cycles.

These activities can be combined, if a major renovation activity is required. They can also be supplemented by additional equipment or activities, such as "sledding" or ballast-undercutting where the entire track is raised, old ballast is removed or cleaned and replaced, and the track is returned, realigned, tamped, compacted, and stabilized, reducing subsequent maintenance costs dramatically.

Other specialized maintenance activities include *rail grinding* (where large production grinding trains, usually contractor-operated, are used to correct and reshape the head of the rail), *rail welding* with portable flash butt welding equipment, and *shoulder and ditch cleaning* with shoulder and ditch cleaning trains.

In order to measure the condition of the track and help determine where maintenance is needed, specialized inspection equipment such as track geometry inspection cars and rail test cars are used. Modern track geometry cars measure each of the key track geometry parameters of gage, alignment, profile, cross level and twist at high speed, together with the shape and wear on the rail head, corrugations, and other necessary information about the condition of the track. Ultrasonic rail-testing vehicles inspect for internal flaws within the rail to detect rail defects and avoid broken rails.

This specialized inspection, coupled with regular once or twice a week visual inspection of the track and regular inspections of turnouts, crossings, and other track areas, provides a basis for short term repair and maintenance action as well for longer term track maintenance programs. The measured data are also transferred to computers within the railroad's maintenance-of-way department that maintain records of the track condition and use this information to forecast how quickly the track is degrading and when its components must be replaced.

Plate girder

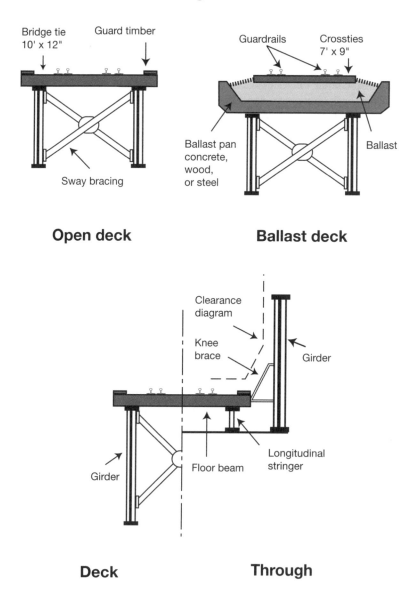

Open deck

Ballast deck

Deck

Through

Fig. 3-15. Some classifications of bridges

Bridges

On many rail routes, bridges represent an investment second in size only to the track structure itself; about 100,000 such structures exist on railroads in the United States, with an estimated replacement cost approaching $100 billion. With today's increasing axle loads, bridges are often a key factor in defining allowable load limits, with one major bridge potentially defining the weight limits on an entire line. Railroad bridges are long lived, with large numbers of active bridges originally built at the turn of the 20th century.

From a track standpoint, bridges may be categorized as open deck or ballast deck. In general, ballast deck is preferred, because the ballast layer provides many of the same advantages to the track on the bridge that it does for conventional track. From a ride-quality standpoint, it avoids the jolt from the sudden change in track stiffness entering and leaving the structure; from a maintenance standpoint, it allows continuing normal surfacing and lining procedures across the structure while minimizing the problem of matching rail head elevations between approaches and bridge as periodic reballasting raises the track. Open deck bridges, which do not use ballast and which attach the ties directly to the bridge structural elements, are more commonly used on secondary and branch lines.

The main bridges in use today are wood, concrete, and steel bridges. Steel bridges account for more than half of the railway bridges, including most of the very long and complex bridge structures. They progress in complexity from simple beam or girder bridges, to truss, arch, and cantilever designs, with increasing span lengths. Large multi-span structures often have a mixture of elements. Likewise, the spans may be of deck or through design (Fig. 3-15), depending on whether the strength members are beneath or beside the track. In general, the more complex and costly through spans are used where required over large rivers or chasms or to provide the clearance above a roadway, rail line, waterway, or watercourse.

Timber bridges remain a major category of railroad bridges. Timber trestles, which represent more than a quarter of the total of rail bridges, continue to accommodate mainline loads and speeds (often with concrete caps between vertical piles and longitudinal stringers) even though many miles of them have been replaced with reinforced concrete structures over the years. Concrete bridges are often the bridge design of choice for short new bridges or replacement bridges because of cost and maintainability.

The ability of a bridge to carry today's heavy-axle loads and heavy trains is a key to the viability of any line or route. Bridge Load Ratings are used to determine the capacity of the bridge and the resulting weight of car and train that it can carry. Some 19th-century solid stone arch structures remain that continue to carry loads of 21st-century proportions, thanks to the compressive strength of masonry, but the remaining bridges must have their load-carrying capacity continually assessed and assured.

Steel bridge load ratings are still commonly expressed in terms of the Cooper E system established early in the 20th century. Ranging from about 30 to 80, this rating expresses the calculated ability of the structure to carry a live load represented by double-headed steam locomotives hauling a train of uniformly loaded cars. An E-60 rating assumes that the locomotive driving-axle load is 60,000 lbs and the cars weigh 6,000 lbs per foot of length. To account for the effects of speed and "hammerblow" from the unbalanced reciprocating parts of the steam locomotive, the static load is multiplied by a generous "impact" factor. This impact factor has resulted in conservative bridge designs over the years, which accounts for the ability of even 70-year-old bridges to handle modern heavy-axle loads. Typical standards to which main-line bridges were designed progressed from E-50 early in the 20th century to E-80 and beyond for current bridges.

Since bridges are long-lived structures, the accumulation of "damage" over time can result in the development of fatigue, particularly in steel members and connections. This fatigue damage can result in the development and growth of cracks as the number of load cycles accumulates (determined by axles passing over the bridge). This requires regular inspection of the bridges with maintenance and even member replacement if fatigue defects develop. Warding off possible fatigue collapse under heavier traffic is critical and calls for a careful and comprehensive inspection program of each bridge element to detect early signs of distress.

FRA Standards

The Railroad Safety Act of 1970 for the first time gave the federal government (through the Federal Railroad Administration, or FRA) jurisdiction over track quality. This has resulted in the establishment of minimum safety standards for inspections, roadbed and track structure, geometry, and corresponding speed limits. Six classes of track were originally defined, ranging from Class 1 (10 mph freight, 15 mph passenger) to Class 6 (110 mph), with an additional high-speed "Class 7" standard for certifying 125 mph operation on specific Northeast Corridor segments. Changes introduced in 1998 and 2001 expanded these high-speed classes to include four high-speed classes (Class 6 through Class 9), representing speeds up to 200 mph. State and federal inspectors are empowered to suspend operation over substandard track. Civil monetary penalties are assessed for failure to correct reported deficiencies.

It is recognized that FRA standards do not necessarily cover all aspects of track structure that can affect safety. These standards have been developed to provide a practical framework relating objective measurements to the minimum track conditions that are necessary for the safe passage of trains (within the limits of available methods of measurement and understanding of vehicle-track dynamics). From a railroad operating standpoint, the safety standards generally do represent a minimum standard since most railroads find that track built and maintained to higher standards results in lower long-term maintenance-of-way and operating expenses. As a result, most railroads have their own set of maintenance standards. These standards are usually more restrictive than the FRA safety standards and provide an early warning to the railroad to take necessary maintenance, repair, or replacement actions before the track ever reaches the FRA safety standard limits.

Research and Development

Research and development has been a hallmark of the railroad industry since the 19th century when the railroad industry was a technology leader. In modern times, research is generated from several sources to include the railroad industry itself. Three of the sources are through the:

- Railroads' own R&D (Research and Development) activities and railroad-industry-funded research (through the Association of American Railroads and its subsidiaries)

- Supply-industry-funded research and development

- Government-sponsored research

Since the early 1980s, the FRA has funded research and development activities. And though the majority of these activities are directed toward safety aspects of railroad operations and maintenance, other areas have looked at high-speed train operation, improved train control, and improvements in the track structure and its components.

Joint railroad industry–government programs have led to improved understanding of the interaction between trains and the track structure (track-train dynamics), and to technological developments and improvements. One example is understanding the cumulative effects of a series of track irregularities (low joints) that rocked a car toward a wheel-lift derailment. This understanding resulted in improved track standards as well as better operating protocols in jointed track. It has also led to the development of performance-based standards, such as track strength measurements to replace visual tie inspections, and the technology to inspect the track in accordance with these standards. The modern track-loading inspection vehicles, developed through cooperative industry–government research efforts, are an example of a new generation inspection technology that allows for the monitoring of these types of performance standards.

Another example of joint industry–government cooperation in R&D is the development of long-term test capability to evaluate new track and vehicle-related technologies under controlled and accelerated conditions. One of the main obstacles to the development and widespread adoption of any "better" (i.e., more durable, economical, *and* safe) track and vehicle technology is the time it takes in normal service to wear out various components and thus get reliable "whole life cycle" cost comparisons. Since 1976, operations of a dedicated test loop (the Facility for Accelerated Service Testing or FAST track) have been addressing just this problem. The purpose of the FAST track is to test new track components and track designs under severe heavy-axle load operations, safely and quickly. Those components that prove themselves at FAST then graduate to real-life testing in main-line tracks.

The FAST track is located in the 52-square-mile Transportation Technology Center (TTC), located northeast of Pueblo, Colorado (Fig. 3-16). Established by the federal government as the High-Speed Ground Test Center in the 1960s and still FRA property, TTC has operated in recent years primarily to advance "conventional" railroad and rail transit technology; since 1984, it has been managed and staffed by the Association of

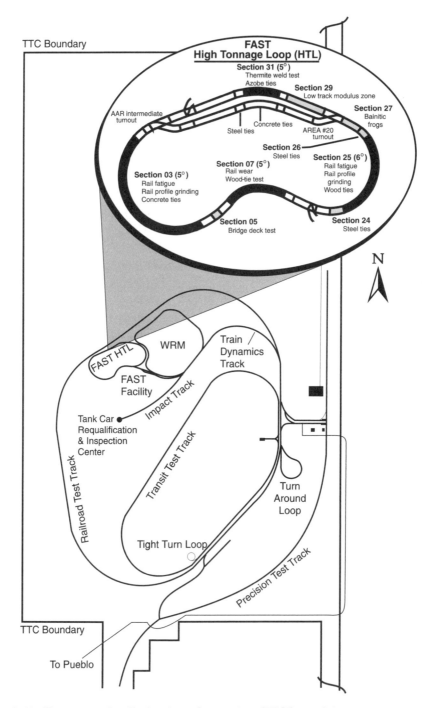

Fig. 3-16. Transportation Technology Center, Inc. (TTCI) track layout

American Railroads and its subsidiary Transportation Technology Center, Inc., (or TTCI) to carry out tests in support of association, government, individual railroad and industry supplier research and development programs. In addition to the FAST track, TTC has high-speed (electrified) railroad and transit track loops, specialized laboratory and test equipment, and other resources dedicated to testing new railroad technology.

Research at FAST and other locations have led to better understanding of the following important track behaviors as:

- Effects of track lubrication on wheel and rail wear

- Comparative curve wear of standard and premium (heat-treated and alloy steel) rail

- Effects of track structure and alignment on the development of rail-surface defects

- Life and stability of various materials, sizes, cross sections and treatments of ballast

- Benefits of operating improved suspension of freight car trucks

An important result of railroad research was that rail head lubrication significantly reduced friction between the wheel and the rail, thus reducing both wheel wear and fuel consumption on both tangent track and curves. Confirmed by subsequent over-the-road testing, this finding led to widespread increased use of rail lubrication.

Among the most significant tests have been the Heavy Axle Load (HAL) tests conducted to determine the cost and safety implications associated with general operation of very heavy-axle-load cars, the "125-ton" (39-ton axle-load) cars. The industry is still digesting the introduction of 36-ton axle-load cars in the late 1990s, but the economics of HAL operation, driven by the effect of these heavy loads on the track structure, may lead to the introduction of even heavier cars in the future. The information that is built up on how the track behaves under these loads will be critical to helping maintenance officers plan for and maintain their track under these loads.

Research and development is an ongoing activity with the railroad industry and its suppliers continuously trying to improve their track components with extended lives and reduced maintenance costs. Among the recent developments that have helped the industry are:

- Improved turnout components such as swing-nose (movable-point) frogs and tangential geometry turnouts. With turnouts representing a major high-cost maintenance area (with significant impact on speed and operations), improvements in the turnout designs to allow for faster operating speed and longer service lives are well received. Thus, the tangential geometry turnout design uses a longer and more gentle change in geometry to allow trains to move at a faster speed through the diverging leg of the turnout. Likewise, the movable-point frog provides continuous support for wheels crossing the opposing rail, reducing maintenance in extremely heavy-tonnage situations where the life of explosive-hardened manganese-steel frog inserts may be measured in months rather than years.

- Inspection and data collection technology to include laser-based measurement of rail wear, high-speed noncontact geometry measurement, track strength measurement, hand-held computer-based inspection of ties, track, and turnouts, and sophisticated computerized maintenance planning and forecasting systems.

- Continuous-action track machines, which maintain steady forward motion while their active components (tamping heads, for example) operate independently of the main chassis in stop-and-go fashion, and which are significantly increasing productivity in such major maintenance functions as track surfacing and rail renewal.

The Locomotive

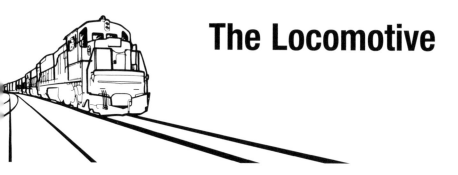

Development of a practical steam locomotive revolutionized land transportation, and the locomotive remains central to the concept of a railroad and its ability to transport cargo or passengers. Though the locomotive is a complex machine, a few fundamental factors (including tractive effort and horsepower) determine its ability to perform its job. The specific combinations of tractive effort and horsepower needed for any particular job determine the type and quantity of locomotives required to pull a train. The range of assignments required to operate a specific railroad will generally determine the makeup of that railroad's locomotive fleet.

Tractive Effort and Adhesion

The most basic element of locomotive performance is pulling capability—the ability for it to overcome resistance caused by the train consist, gravity, and the environment. Even on steel rails, every railway vehicle has a certain resistance to forward movement. At a starting condition, this resistance is mainly due to weight and the static friction in axles and bearings. The pull required to start movement of a single freight car may be as much as 15 or 20 lbs of force per ton; however, the actual value for rolling friction considered in calculations is typically 4 to 6 lbs of force per ton because the slack in the couplers and draft gear between cars allows the locomotive to start the train one car at a time (the cars already moving help to start the ones to the rear). With the very large tractive effort available with most diesel combinations, "taking slack" to start is not usually necessary.

Once in operation, a majority of the resistance working against a locomotive is caused by gravity. Trains working up a grade must overcome the force of gravity (approximately 20 lbs of force per ton for each percent of grade) to maintain forward movement. On small grades, the impact of gravity may only represent a fraction of the resistance force working against a locomotive. As grade increases, however, this percentage changes rapidly—grade resistance on a 1 percent grade represents a tenfold increase in total resistance when compared to resistance exhibited by the same train operating on level track. At very high speeds (typically higher speeds than anything seen in all but the fastest North American corridors), wind and environmental factors also begin to play a role and could contribute an additional 10 to 15 lbs of force per ton. This, along with the demand for a sleek, fast appearance, is why most passenger trains feature smooth, streamlined forms. It's not just for aesthetic reasons!

Resistance for a given vehicle type can be calculated by a series of well established resistance equations. Several variants exist, but all include similar terms representing rolling, bearing, flange, wind, and grade-curve resistance. *Rolling resistance* is constant, and *bearing resistance* is relative to the number of axles on the vehicle. *Flanging resistance* is tied to speed and *wind resistance* is tied to the vehicle cross-sectional area and the square of speed. *Grade and curve resistance* are related to percentage of grade and degree of curvature.

To overcome the resistance of a stopped or a moving train, the locomotive must produce a greater amount of horizontal tractive force at the wheel rim. Tractive effort is the amount of torque, in ft-lbs (foot-pounds), that the locomotive can exert at its wheel rims, converted to pounds of force. Developing the tractive effort required to move a train involves several variables. Fig. 4-1 provides an example of a tonnage chart, indicating the tractive effort needed to start and move a specific train with a given tonnage as it travels up various grades.

A locomotive's tractive effort capability is largely dependent on the following four factors:

• The locomotive's horsepower rating

• The mechanical design of the locomotive's traction system

• The electrical/thermal capability of the traction system

• The locomotive's adhesive capability

The successful interaction of these factors creates a locomotive's ability to successfully pull a train over a specific piece of track. At higher speeds (typically greater than 10 mph), tractive effort is linked to locomotive horsepower. All other systems being equal, a locomotive operating at a higher horsepower level can provide the same tractive effort at a higher speed than that of a lower horsepower capability. The other factors are more closely tied to operation in low-speed regimes.

Two of these factors, mechanical and electrical capability, are largely tied to the components designed into the locomotive's traction system. All locomotives in the North American fleet are of diesel-electric configuration, using a diesel engine–alternator set to create electrical energy for the traction motors located on each axle. The electric motor creates a force that is transmitted to the wheel-axle via mechanical gearing. Gear ratio and wheel size have a direct mechanical relationship on locomotive tractive effort and top speed capability. (Given a constant wheel size, a gearing change results in an inverse relationship between maximum tractive effort and top speed. Those geared for higher tractive effort typically have a lower maximum speed. Conversely, high-speed locomotives typically have much lower tractive effort capability.) Gearing

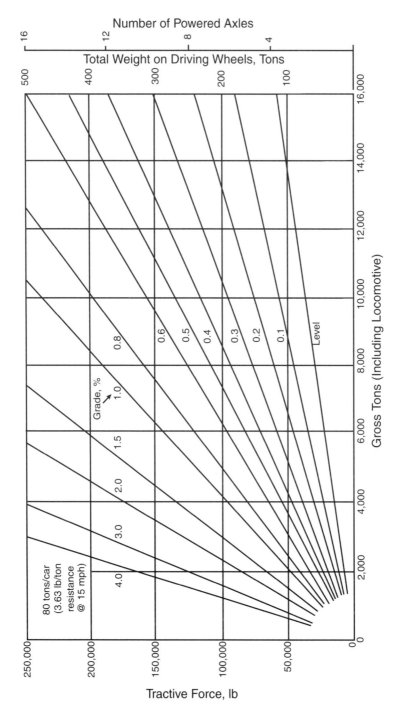

Fig. 4-1. Tractive force versus tonnage and grade

53

and wheel size is defined during locomotive design and is mainly driven by intended locomotive function, motor size, and any restrictions in locomotive height or under-body-rail clearance. Most modern locomotives are equipped with either 40- or 42-in. (new) wheels.

Traction motor type and size is determined by the desired service for the locomotive. In some cases, overall motor size is limited by the track gage or infrastructure weight limits. (North American trackage typically allows weight limits up to 72,000 lbs per axle, although in countries with less developed infrastructure, weight limits could be as low as 30,000 lbs per axle.) To counter these obstacles, builders have been improving traction motor designs for decades to achieve maximum capability out of smaller, more efficient machines. Like any motor, its capability is derived from its size, internal design, and the ventilation provided. Most of today's modern locomotives ventilate each motor with greater than 2,500 cfm (cubic feet per minute) of air during full-load operation. Under less demanding operation, ventilation is often reduced to conserve fuel through reduced auxiliary loads.

Traditionally, locomotives were thermally limited below a certain operating speed. Below this speed point, the minimum continuous speed (MCS), the locomotive could not provide sufficient ventilation to cool the motor, which was typically operating close to maximum capability. Consideration of the continuous tractive effort and MCS was critical during power assignment—mixing locomotives with different thermal capabilities could result in overheating of some units while others ran without concern. On older units, the decision of when to "stop and cool the motors" was solely under the discretion of the operator who used an ammeter and predefined "short term ratings" as the only guide.

Over the past 20 years, locomotive builders have worked to improve locomotive tractive effort capability while minimizing the risk of overheating equipment. To maximize performance under extreme conditions, motor thermal models are now regularly employed to monitor or calculate internal motor temperatures, allowing modern locomotives to exceed thermally continuous tractive effort limits for periods of time before automatic deration. This provides the maximum capability for the locomotive while preventing motor damage. Although the Continuous Tractive Effort (CTE)/MCS point remains on modern DC (direct current) locomotives, the locomotives automatically work beyond it, then protect themselves as required.

Use of AC (alternating current) traction systems has vastly changed the industry's locomotive evaluation and dispatch procedures. The increased capability of AC locomotives essentially eliminates the thermally continuous tractive effort restraint. Today's AC power, operating on good rail, can support tractive effort levels approaching their maximum starting limits almost indefinitely without thermal deration. Where once a coal train would have required helpers or multiple attempts to reach the summit, today's AC power can be left to grind up the hill at speeds of less than 5 mph for hours without risk to equipment damage. With the success of these AC systems not limited by thermal means, this leaves the last factor, adhesive capability, as the potentially limiting factor.

A locomotive's adhesive capability is its ability to grip the rail without slipping, an especially complicated task given that the contact patch between steel wheel and steel rail is approximately the size of a dime. The ability of a wheel to grip the rail does not vary much with the size of the wheel or with the weight it is carrying, but it varies significantly with external factors. The ability of each wheelset to maintain its grip is governed by:

- Weather conditions
- Contaminants on the rail (such as wet leaves or oil)
- Wear of the rail and the wheels
- The condition of the railroad infrastructure

The locomotive's adhesive capability also varies with the amount of creep (relative motion) between wheel and rail, being significantly higher when the tread is slipping slightly on the rail than when there is no slippage. Once rapid slippage *(wheel slip)* occurs, the coefficient of friction drops far below the static value, and power must be reduced to regain traction.

The amount of tractive effort that a locomotive can generate, at its maximum, is the product of the coefficient of friction between the wheels and the rails and the weight on the driving axles of the locomotive. This coefficient of friction, known to railroaders as the *adhesion coefficient* (or adhesion) can be as low as 10 percent on rail that is extensively contaminated, or can approach 50 percent on dry rail in good weather with sand. A locomotive can exert anywhere from 10 percent to almost half of its weight into pulling force, depending entirely on the conditions at the wheel-to-rail interface. Since there is a weight limit on each axle of a locomotive that is established by the railroad operating it, locomotive builders do their best to design the locomotive to generate high drawbar pull under "bad" rail conditions, and railroads do their best to try to maintain good rail conditions.

Adhesion control has improved dramatically over the last 20 years. The axle with the poorest rail condition (usually the lead axle) has historically governed the performance of the entire consist. One improvement results from connecting all motors in parallel, since this will tend to automatically reduce the power to an individual motor if it starts to overspeed in comparison to others. Advances in alternator and motor current and voltage ratings that allow the unit to develop full power over its operating range in permanent-parallel connection are now standard. Previous methods of detecting incipient wheel slip through comparison of the speed differential between axles have been supplemented with more sophisticated electronic computation of individual axle acceleration or differences between wheel rim and locomotive ground speed (as measured by a traction motor's reference speeds or a radar unit) in current automatic adhesion-control systems. These control instantaneous power levels to make full use of the wheel slip–adhesion relationship and replace manual control of the sanders in situations of significant traction loss. Control schemes are now employed that allow a locomotive to reallocate power to those motors with a reduced tendency to slip, based on real-time sensing of wheel-to-rail interface conditions. Also, in some conditions, wheel slip control schemes will rotate the wheel speeds slightly higher than the rail surface speed of the locomotive. This *wheel creep control* tends to increase friction in that the wheels tend to burn off contaminants, and "condition" the rail for following axles (and following locomotives), improving the adhesion.

Locomotives are also equipped with a sanding system that will spray sand onto the rail head immediately ahead of the wheelset that is tending to slip in order for that wheelset to maintain (or regain) traction. Since there is little indication in the cab when wheel slip is occurring somewhere in the locomotive consist, traditionally there was a "wheel slip" light in the control stand to warn of persistent loss of adhesion requiring the operator to reduce the throttle setting until conditions improve. On newer locomotives, most adhesion control is accomplished without the conscious intervention of the crew, and the operator is advised only if low adhesion cannot be corrected by the adhesion system.

With the adhesion-control systems used during most of the diesel era, many railroads traditionally settled on a dispatchable adhesion factor of 18 to 20 percent. In assigning motive power, this was a level expected to provide good assurance that the train would, under normal weather and other conditions, successfully surmount the ruling grades on its run. Recent advances, as noted above, make 30 percent or greater all-weather adhesion attainable. On AC locomotives with enhanced traction control, adhesion has been demonstrated well above 30 percent.

The right side of Fig. 4-1 shows the total locomotive weight needed for various amounts of tonnage and grade based on the traditional 18 percent dispatch factor. Since most modern diesels for main-line service carry about 60,000 to 70,000 lbs on each axle, there is another scale on the extreme right side of Fig. 4-1 that shows about how many powered locomotive axles it will take. The graph stops at 250,000 lbs because that is the point at which the possibility of coupler knuckle failure (minimum strength 350,000 lbs) begins to appear. With the advent of high-adhesion AC and DC traction locomotives (with substantially higher tractive effort and adhesive capability than predecessors), many railroads have been required to reclassify these new locomotives to represent a higher number of powered axles when dispatching locomotives. (For example, a six-axle high-adhesion locomotive may account for 8 "powered axles" when assigned to a consist.)

Horsepower

Horsepower is a measure of the rate of doing work. Horsepower was just discussed in connection with the amount of energy required to move trains by various routes (Fig. 2-4). At zero speed, horsepower is by definition also zero, but to move the train at any desired speed *above* that takes horsepower. Fig. 4-2 shows how much it takes to move 1 gross ton (locomotive, cars, and lading) at any speed, on level track, and on various grades. The curves on the graph are for straight track and cars averaging 50 tons of weight, so the exact figure representing the best estimate for a particular situation will vary with factors such as wind, roadbed quality, uncompensated curves, or heavier or lighter cars. The two lines represent horsepower available for traction and rail horse-power—the difference defined by losses in the locomotive's alternator, traction motors, and cabling. The generalities from these curves will give a feel for motive power requirements:

- Power requirements for overcoming rolling friction are moderate: a 3,000 hp locomotive can move more than 5,000 tons at 30 mph on level track.

- Grade, as noted previously, is highly significant for a heavy train. A train powered at 1.5 hp per trailing ton, capable of reaching 60 mph on level track, will slow to about 22 mph on a 1 percent grade and to 10 mph on a 2 percent grade. A train powered at 4 hp per ton has a "balancing speed" (at which power available just balances train resistance) of more than 90 mph. It can make 55 mph up a 1 percent grade or only 33 mph up a 2 percent grade.

Compared to the effects of grade, the increase in train resistance with speed is moderate. Below 30 mph or so, horsepower increases only slightly more than directly with speed—twice the power to do the same amount of work in *half* the time if speed is doubled. Even at 70 mph with a train of empty cars where most of the power goes to overcoming air drag, resistance is less than that from a 1 percent grade (Fig. 2-5). A freight

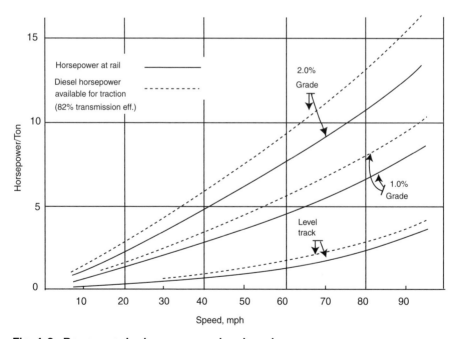

Fig. 4-2. Power required versus speed and grade

57

train has a small cross-sectional area in relation to its total weight. Because of this, and the fact that the train runs using steel wheels on steel rails, a freight train is very efficient in moving through the atmosphere, and its energy consumption rises much less rapidly with speed than that of a highway vehicle such as a truck. As a consequence, the fuel consumption of the locomotives of a train is much lower than that of any rubber-tired vehicle for the amount of tonnage moved.

Fig. 4-3 shows that not all of the gross engine capability is directly utilized to haul the train. The locomotive uses some engine output to power auxiliary devices that support operation and crew comfort. Further losses are experienced in locomotive propulsion devices and cabling as the mechanical power from the engine crankshaft is converted to electrical energy for use in the traction motors. Efficiency of the locomotive varies with traction system configuration (AC or DC), propulsion device type/design, and operating speed. Horsepower at the rail also includes gear losses.

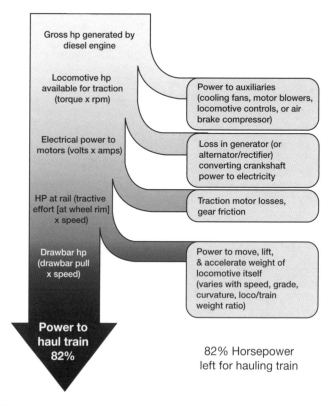

Fig. 4-3. Different horsepower ratings

Drawbar Horsepower

After some of the horsepower at the rail is used to move the locomotive itself, the majority remains useful horsepower at the rear coupler to move the train. No "typical" percentage goes into moving the locomotive because the percentage varies due to relative weight of the locomotive assigned and the weight of its train. If a 400-ton locomotive is hauling 8,000 tons, over 95 percent of the rail power is being used to haul the cars, but if it has only 400 tons in tow, it is using half its power to move itself! This is another reason why sizing the locomotive for its intended use is important for motive power application. Sizing a locomotive to a very specific application is not as common today, however, especially as railroads continue to eliminate locomotive models in a quest for fleet standardization.

Acceleration

The rate at which a train can gain speed is determined by the amount of tractive effort remaining after overcoming resistance of the train to motion. To provide the same tractive effort at twice the speed takes twice the horsepower, so gaining speed takes more and more locomotive power as speed increases. Fig. 4-4 shows a few of the innumerable combinations of acceleration rates and grade in terms of the horsepower per ton required at different speeds. At low speed, acceleration may be fairly rapid—up to 1.5 mph per second for a commuter train and up to 0.3 mph per second (mphps) for a fast freight. As the speed increases, horsepower has less of an effect. Even a "hotshot" freight train with 4.0 horsepower per ton can accelerate at only about 0.1 mph per second at 70 mph.

Railroading dispatching practices are developed so that, ideally, the number of times that a train is required to accelerate after slowdowns or a stop is minimized as time, distance, and more fuel is required to accelerate to operating speed after a slowdown. Most railroads apply enough power on each train, however, so that if a train is required to slow down or stop, the train can accelerate quickly in order to minimize the impact on following trains. On some corridors where train movements are less frequent (or of low priority), motive power planners may instead dispatch single-unit locomotive consists and accept lower train speeds and reduced ability to accelerate from stops or speed reductions.

Acceleration is absolutely critical in passenger and commuter operations where train schedules dictate frequent station stops and abbreviated spacing between trains. It is only somewhat important on most freight routes. Given that most passenger and commuter trains are small and light compared to freight consists, tractive effort becomes secondary to locomotive horsepower and engine load rate when specifying passenger locomotive requirements. A combination of these two factors in operation allows passenger locomotives to reach full engine power (full load) in a matter of seconds and accelerates the train as fast as possible toward its next stop. On heavily used passenger corridors, electric multiple-unit (EMU) or straight-electric locomotives are regularly employed in place of diesel locomotives. By design, these vehicles are capable of higher horsepower levels and rapid acceleration when compared to a diesel-electric locomotive of the same weight.

Locomotive History

The key invention that made the steam locomotive powerful enough to haul itself briskly and still have enough left over to haul a useful load was discovered by Richard Trevithick in 1803. He took the steam that was exhausted from the locomotive cylinders after it had pushed the pistons and directed it up the smokestack through a nozzle. The intermittent puffing action not only made the machine into a "choo choo" but sucked air so vigorously through the firebox that the boiler could generate steam at a rate many times greater than had been possible in a stationary engine of the same size and weight. The scheme was also self-regulating: The harder the locomotive worked, the more steam went out the stack, the faster the fuel burned, and the more steam was available, up to the maximum firing rate of the firebox and the capacity of the boiler.

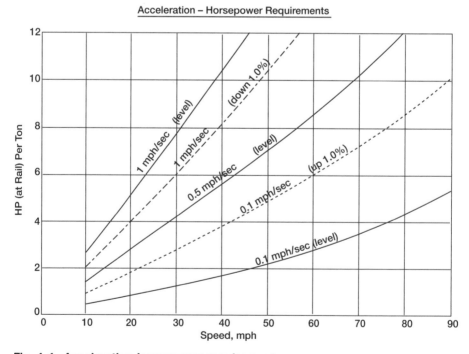

Fig. 4-4. Acceleration-horsepower requirements

Many other inventions, from equalizers (to keep the proper amount of weight on each wheel while going over rough track) to a headlight (to allow running trains at night on unfenced American routes), were needed to make the basic "iron horse" suitable for its work. However, for 125 years the reciprocating steam locomotive with its exhaust-stimulated white-hot fire represented the most effective way to get the necessary horsepower out of a machine no more than 11 ft wide, 16 ft high, short enough to swing around railroad curves at speed, and simple enough to be operated by two men. Numerous attempts to adapt more sophisticated and theoretically efficient steam-generating systems to locomotive requirements were made but none had any lasting success.

Those involved in locomotive engineering and design eventually turned to another energy-generating source—internal-combustion engines. The diesel engine was invented in 1901, at a time when the principles of electric railroad traction were fairly well understood. From the start, it was apparent that the diesel could be several times more efficient in converting the energy in fuel to mechanical power. But it was not until the 1930s that the weight and bulk of the diesel was reduced to the point where it could compete with steam in applications other than low-speed switching service. The key developments leading to the eventual shift to diesel power for all railroad services (completed in the mid-1950s) were made in the 1920s. These were primarily in the area of reliable controls to match the load of the electrical generating and propulsion systems to the fuel input and power output of the diesel engine.

Diesel Locomotive History

The American diesel-electric locomotive is now in its fourth generation of development, being a significant part of the motive power fleet for over 60 years and demonstrating a typical lifetime in heavy main-line service of over 20 years. During the early years of dieselization, five major builders established a North American presence—American Locomotive Co. (ALCO), Baldwin Locomotive, Fairbanks-Morse Corp., Electro-Motive Division of General Motors (EMD), and Lima-Hamilton. Three of the five (ALCO, Baldwin, and Lima) were former steam locomotive manufacturers that transitioned to diesel production between the mid-1930s and 1949. (General Electric was also a major locomotive builder. However, its products tended toward straight-electric, export, and industrial-mining applications until 1960.) A combination of fleet standardization, product reliability, and a cyclic locomotive demand resulted in the withdrawal of most minority builders by the late 1950s.

Since the mid-1960s, two major builders (General Electric and EMD), have produced over 90 percent of the locomotives now operating in North America. (EMD was sold by GM in 2005 and the firm is now known as Electro-Motive Diesel.) Essentially all freight locomotives now in service use technology or components developed by one of these two builders, and both builders have also heavily marketed their products to other nations. A number of other companies have entered the market over the last 20 years to rehabilitate or rebuild locomotives. A handful of these organizations have branched into constructing new locomotives for niche markets such as passenger, industrial, or, more recently, hybrid-genset yard switching. The production of new main-line freight diesel-electric locomotives, however, continues with EMD and GE.

Much of the first generation of diesel locomotives, developed between the mid-1930s and the mid-1950s, was targeted toward replacement of specific steam applications. This design approach resulted in a multitude of locomotive configurations (Fig. 4-5). Several are now virtually extinct or live on only in the form of components in "remanufactured" units. The vast majority of freight locomotives are of just two types (four- and six-axle "road switchers"), able to handle all assignments by being assembled into appropriate multiple-unit (MU) combinations under the control of a single operator.

Each of the two current builders catalogs a highly standardized six-axle, six-motor locomotive available with either DC or AC traction systems (Type 13). Today over 95 percent of new locomotives built for North American service are of this type. Tighter emissions regulations and an aging switching fleet has led to a resurgence of interest in switchers (Type 5 and 7/10), most specifically with hybrid battery or multiple high-speed engine/generator set configurations. Both major builders also offer additional customized designs for specific international applications. These designs often use diesel engine, traction, and control system technology from the North American de-signs repackaged for use in operations with more restrictive clearance and axle-loading requirements.

After remaining at a relatively constant 28,000 from the completion of dieselization in 1958 until 1982, Class I railroad diesel locomotive ownership declined steadily to slightly fewer than 20,000 by 1988 before rebounding to approximately 27,000 loco-motives today. A variety of model types are still employed by the Class I's, but railroads have extensively worked to standardize their fleets and reduce the number of active models. (For example, over two-thirds of Norfolk Southern's 3,800-unit locomotive fleet is represented by only four basic locomotive models.)

In broad terms, the North American Class I fleet can be categorized into four basic classifications:

- **Endcab switcher (Type 5):** Although easily recognized and well-known, the total number of endcab switchers has been steadily decreasing as railroads trans-fer switching assignments to larger four-axle (Type 7/10) locomotives. Today, the endcab switcher population represents only 5 percent of the total Class I fleet. Some railroads have been adopting hybrid and multiple-engine "genset" switch-ers, which are covered later in this chapter.

- **Four-axle road switcher (Type 7/10):** Ranging from 1,500 to 3,200 horsepow-er, the four-axle road switcher has taken on most switching and gathering duties for Class I railroads. Seen in a variety of applications, a majority of these loco-motives are over 20 years old but continue to remain in service because of their light duty operation and simplicity of maintenance. Today, 20 percent of the North America Class I fleet is made up of this locomotive type. Hundreds more are em-ployed on regional and short line railroads. In many cases, the 3,000-plus-horse-power units originally purchased for high-speed intermodal service have been

 Diagram	Type of Locomotive Unit	AAR-Std. Axle-Truck Designation (See Note)	Typical Horsepower (Per Unit) (Dates Built)
Diesel Engine Generator / **Powered Axle** / **Idler Axle** / **Train Heat**			
1	 Road Freight Cab (A-unit)	B-B	1,350-1,750 / 1941-1950
2 	Road Freight Booster (B-unit, hostler controls only)	B-B	1,350-1,750 / 1941-1950
3	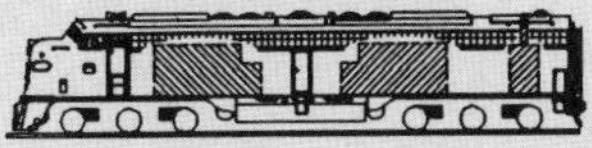 Passenger Cab Unit (B-units also built)	A1A-A1A	1,800-2,400 / 1937-1950
4	 Light-Duty/ Industrial Switchers "Commercial" diesel engines often radio controlled	B-B	300-350/1,000 / 1926-Date
5	 Medium/Heavy- Duty Switchers (100 & 125 ton units)	B-B	600/1,000- 1,000-1,500 / 1936-1980
6	 Loco + "Slug" Combination ("Powered Trailer" semipermanently coupled)	Various– B-B & B-B Illustrated	1,500-3,600 / Usually Rebuilds
7	 General-Purpose Road Switcher (Hood-type car body; steam boiler optional)	B-B	1,000-2,300 / 1940-Date
8	 Low-Axle-Load Road Switcher	A1A-A1A	1,000-1,800 / 1946-1950
9	 "Special-Duty" Six-Axle Road Switcher (Later models low nose)	C-C	2,400-4,000 / 1955-Date
10	 High-Horsepower Road Switcher (Low nose)	B-B	2,500-4,000 / 1961-1994
11	 Dual-Engine "Unit Reduction" Locomotive (Wide-cab hood car body)	D-D (Also built as B-B + B-B)	5,000-6,600 / 1964-1969
12	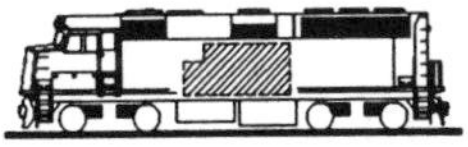 Cowl-Car Body Passenger 3ø 480V "Head-end power" For electric train heat/AC	B-B	3,000-4,000 / 1974-Date
13	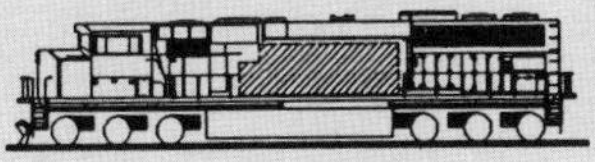 Wide ("Safety") Cab Freight (May also have cowl car body)	B-B and C-C	3,300-6,000 / 1984-Date

Fig. 4-5. Representative diesel-electric locomotive types

bumped into these secondary service roles as they are replaced by larger locomotives.

- **Six-axle medium horsepower road switcher (Type 9):** Once the pride of the main-line fleet, a majority of six-axle medium horsepower units have now accepted roles in secondary service or as part of on-demand surge fleets (Fig. 4-6). The best known unit from this classification, EMD's legendary SD40-2, is still rostered by all major railroads and continues to see use in some main-line service. This type of unit is also regularly applied in helper service and in heavy switching operations at major yards. Even though some have been retired or returned to leasing companies, this fleet (15 percent of the total Class I roster) continues to fill the gap between the smaller four-axle road switchers and today's high-horsepower road locomotives.

- **High-horsepower six-axle road switcher (Type 13):** Representing over 55 percent of the total Class I fleet, these locomotives are today's modern road power (Fig. 4-7). Ranging from 3,800 to 6,000 horsepower, these 15,000 locomotives are all heavy-haul, microprocessor-equipped machines designed by GE and EMD for main-line freight, coal, and intermodal service. All meet U.S. Environmental Protection Agency (EPA) Tier 0, Tier 1, or Tier 2 emissions regulations. This group is about 60 percent DC traction equipped and 40 percent AC traction equipped. A majority (95 percent-plus) are in the 3,800-4,400 horsepower range (only a few hundred are operating in the 5,000-6,000 horsepower range). Since the late 1990s, the nation's railroads have had traffic levels that exceed the traffic levels experienced in WWII, and they have been able to satisfactorily handle this traffic with very large fleets of high-horsepower six-axle, microprocessor-controlled locomotives with advanced traction systems and high locomotive reliability.

In addition to the locomotives operated by the Class I railroads, an estimated 2,500 to 3,000 units, mostly switching and general-purpose road locomotives of 600 to 3,000 horsepower, are on regional, local, and switching and terminal railroads.

Locomotive Configurations

Fig. 4-7 shows the general arrangement and principal components of a typical high-horsepower (4,400 hp) six-axle road locomotive built in 2008. The locomotive is an adaptation of the traditional "road switcher" design featuring external walkways and narrow engine hoods that afford excellent visibility to operators and easy access to the diesel engine and its support systems for maintenance. A diesel-electric locomotive operates equally well in either direction, allowing these road switcher designs maximum flexibility for operation. The term *road switcher* does not necessarily indicate a locomotive's function but refers to its body configuration, with a narrow hood (the *long* hood) enclosing the engine and other machinery and a short hood *(nose)* at the opposite end of the cab. These latest locomotives have expanded microprocessor control of engine and system functions, combined with an enhanced cooling system, in order to meet EPA emissions requirements.

Fig. 4-6. Six-axle medium horsepower road switcher – EMD SD40-2

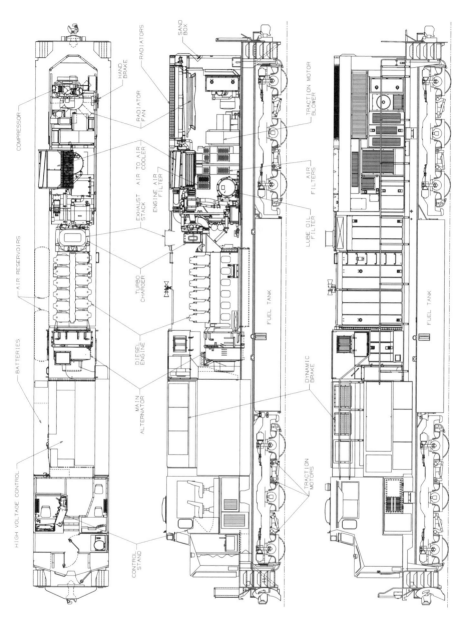

Fig. 4-7. GE ES44AC Evolution Series locomotive location of apparatus
[Courtesy of William R. Miller, GE Transportation]

Since the late 1980s, essentially all new locomotives have been equipped with a full-width nose and "safety cab" construction, providing improved crew safety and superior crew amenities and ergonomics. Also better accommodating the conductor and the paperwork in cabooseless consists, the sound-insulated, air-conditioned "comfort" cab is entered from the ground via the front platform, nose door, and a passageway through a heavily reinforced nose structure. The basics of this configuration had been employed by Canadian roads since the late 1960s, when specialized cabs or full-width car bodies were regularly used to lessen the crew exposure to harsh winter conditions.

The locomotive cab is equipped with either a desktop-style forward-facing control console or the traditional AAR-style upright control stand. After more than a decade of deliveries with desktop controls, most railroads have reverted to the AAR control stand to allow improved ergonomics and visibility for operating personnel. The full-width front windows (in accordance with FRA standards for anti-vandal vehicle glazing) must be capable of protecting occupants from specified-caliber bullets and cornerwise impact of a concrete block at 35 mph. The wide nose typically includes large crash posts, toilet facilities, and additional space for train control and cab signaling equipment.

To organize and coordinate an ever increasing number and variety of revisions and sophistication of cab displays, an AAR configuration standard is in effect. Traditional dials and gauges (speedometer, air pressure, motor current, train radio controls, and cab signal indications) are merged with the EOT (end-of-train) device and distributed-power monitors on console-mounted displays directly in front of the operator. These displays are provisioned for future train management systems now being developed by many railroads. On some locomotive designs, the displays themselves act as the Human-Machine Interface between crew and locomotive control, allowing crews to receive and reset diagnostic faults or perform functions such as traction motor cutout. The screens also provide system access points for maintenance personnel working to troubleshoot a locomotive.

Since 1995, FRA-mandated *ditch lights* have been provided on new locomotives. These lights, mounted to the front (and sometimes rear) of locomotives at platform level, improve the crew's view of the right-of-way. With the headlight (kept lighted by day since 1948), they also form a distinctive triangular pattern to augment motorist train awareness at highway crossings. Like the safety cab design, ditch lights were used in Canada prior to adoption in the United States.

Units intended mainly for yard switching duties (Fig. 4-8) have less horsepower, simpler trucks not suitable for road speeds, a lower long hood for 360-degree visibility, and, often, no toilet or provision for multiple-unit (MU) operations. Nevertheless, many of their components, from traction motors to cylinder assemblies, are interchangeable with those of road power—an important saving in everything from parts inventory to the training of machinists. The general principles of locomotive design and operation in present-day Type 5 units are similar to those in the Type 9 and 10 units.

Fig. 4-8. EMD/Wabtec GP15D 1,500 hp switcher [Courtesy of Wabtec]

The Prime Mover

The modern diesel engine, or *prime mover,* is a single V-type diesel that has 8 to 20 cylinders rated at about 125 hp per cylinder if "normally aspirated" or up to 390 hp per cylinder if turbocharged. Most current production is represented by EMD 16-cylinder 710-Series engines and GE 12-cylinder GEVO-Series engines, both rated at 4,500 gross horsepower. General Electric-built locomotives use four-cycle engines (one power stroke per two revolutions), while EMD (General Motors) engines have mainly used the two-cycle principle.

Today's diesel engines are equipped with electronic fuel injection systems designed to optimize fuel usage while maintaining performance and emissions requirements. This design change represents possibly the largest single contribution to diesel efficiency and lowered exhaust emissions in the past two decades. Combustion efficiency is improved because the systems employ advanced timing control as well as the ability to optimize fuel injection for each load and speed condition throughout the engine's operating range.

In accordance with North American practice, the diesel is a relatively low-speed machine, because of rugged design for extended life and low maintenance cost rather than for minimization of weight. Most idle at about 300 rpm (revolutions per minute) and develop full power at about 900-1,050 rpm. Even so, the diesel engine and its attached main generator represent less than 15 percent of the total locomotive weight. Many locomotives are "ballasted" (usually by addition of ballast boxes or by thickening steel underframe components) to provide improved adhesive capability.

High-horsepower units use a turbocharger driven by the diesel exhaust gases to ram extra air into the cylinders at each power stroke. Since the amount of fuel that can be burned is determined by how much air is available, this increases the power of the engine by up to about 50 percent without increasing its size or operating speed. The turbocharger is a compact but high-speed device requiring considerable maintenance, so many two-cycle locomotives used in switching or local services (where horsepower is less important) are built without turbocharging. Turbochargers as applied on most locomotive designs are either exhaust-gas driven or engaged via mechanical clutch.

The other part of the power plant is the alternator (or, on older units, the generator), which converts crankshaft motion into electrical energy (600-1,200 volts DC) for traction. The traction alternator (with slip rings on its rotor instead of a multi-segment commutator and brushes) is: (1) capable of greater power density when compared with a traction generator, (2) somewhat simpler and, most important, (3) smaller in diameter so that up to 6,000 horsepower can be developed in the space available. In the same scheme as now used in automobile electrical systems, AC produced by the alternator is immediately converted to DC by solid-state rectifiers. On locomotives with AC traction systems, the rectified DC voltage is then converted back into controlled AC using solid-state inverter devices. (On General Electric AC locomotives, one inverter system is provided per axle, while EMD has traditionally used one inverter per truck.)

The alternator typically includes a companion auxiliary alternator device to provide power for the numerous locomotive support systems including air compressor, locomotive control systems, 74 volt DC for battery charging, cooling system radiator fans and ventilation blowers for traction motors, alternator, and control devices. Most modern locomotive designs employ electrically driven auxiliary devices that allow controlled application of auxiliary loads, minimizing fuel usage. Many older designs still employ shaft- or belt-driven auxiliaries.

The diesel engine power plant is supported by extensive cooling, ventilation, and filtration systems designed to allow optimal performance and fuel efficiency while still meeting the requirements of EPA emissions regulations. The typical capacities for a 4,400 horsepower unit are: engine cooling water, 325 gal.; engine lube oil, 450 gal.; fuel, 5,000 gal.; and sand, 1.5 tons.

Emissions

In 1998, the U.S. EPA issued final exhaust emission standards for newly manufactured and remanufactured locomotives and locomotive engines. Initial regulations applied to locomotives manufactured after January 1, 1973, and included specific regulations for manufacture, remanufacture, maintenance, and testing of these locomotives. Multiple "Tier" levels of emissions compliance, including specific limits for oxides of nitrogen (NOx), hydrocarbons (HC), carbon monoxide (CO), particulate matter (PM) and smoke were defined, as shown in Table 4-1. The information also shows percent opacity of smoke and the emissions for NOx, CO, HC, and PM by gram/brake horse-power-hour (g/bhp-hr).

Tier 0 emissions are required for locomotives manufactured on or after January 1, 2001, and before January 1, 2002, and upgraded locomotives manufactured prior to January 1, 1973. Locomotives manufactured on, or after, January 1, 2002, and before January 1, 2005, are subject to the Tier 1 standards. Locomotives and engines used in locomotives manufactured on, or after, January 1, 2005, are subject to the Tier 2 standards. For each Tier level, the standards apply when such a locomotive or locomotive engine is manufactured, remanufactured, or imported on or after January 1, 2002.

Line-haul requirements are tied to a road-duty cycle with a higher percentage of time at full load. Yard locomotives of under 2,300 horsepower fall under the "switch" duty cycle, which includes very little time at full load but extensive time (60 percent) at idle.

In early 2008, the EPA released a new set of rules governing the future regulation of locomotive emissions. These emissions standards, 40 CFR Part 1033, affect both new and remanufactured locomotives. Key characteristics of the new regulations are provided below, although many nuances also exist that are not included here.

Tier 3 emissions limits will be required for new locomotives manufactured in 2012-2014. Tier 4 emissions limits apply to locomotives built in 2015 and beyond. Tier 3 is similar to the Tier 2 requirement with a further restriction of PM to 0.10 g/bhp-hr. Tier 4 regulations drastically curtail three components of the locomotive exhaust (NOx, 1.3 g/bhp-hr; PM, 0.03 g/bhp-hr; HC, 0.14 g/bhp-hr) and will likely drive significant design change into locomotives over the next 6 years. Smoke standards for Tier 3 have not changed from the Tier 2 limits. (For all previous and new EPA regulations, deterioration factors also apply. These factors dictate that a locomotive must meet the established standards for its entire useful life.)

For locomotives constructed with ratings less than 2,300 hp, a separate table of emissions limits apply that will not be covered in this text. Line-haul locomotives subject to Tier 0 through Tier 2 standards must also meet switch emissions standards of the same tier. Tier 3 line-haul locomotives must meet Tier 2 switch standards.

Additionally, the Part 1033 emissions regulations vastly change the emissions landscape for remanufactured locomotives. Previously, locomotives built between 1973 and 2001 were required to meet EPA Tier 0 emissions levels upon remanufacture. The new regulation dictates compliance with modified Tier 0 emissions levels for those locomotives built between 1973 and 1992 and a modified Tier 1 level for those built between 1993 and 2004. (These are commonly being referred to as "Tier 0 Plus" and "Tier 1 Plus.") Locomotives built between 1993 and 2001 that are not equipped with split-cooling systems are required only to modified Tier 0 status upon remanufacture. The application of these new standards for remanufactured locomotives will take place in a phased approach between 2008 and 2010 based on set percentages and the availability of emissions reduction kits. This change in both level and date range will force the application of emissions technology to much of the in-service fleet. For example,

Table 4-1. Emissions Compliance Tiers

Tier 0	Category	Line-Haul	Switch	
	HC	1.00	2.10	g/bhp-hr
	CO	5.0	8.0	
	NOx	9.5	14.0	
	PM	0.60	0.72	
	SS* smoke	30		percent opacity
	30-sec smoke	40		
	3-sec smoke	50		
Tier 1	**Category**	**Line-Haul**	**Switch**	
	HC	0.55	1.20	g/bhp-hr
	CO	2.2	2.5	
	NOx	7.4	11.0	
	PM	0.45	0.54	
	SS smoke	25		percent opacity
	30-sec smoke	40		
	3-sec smoke	50		
Tier 2	**Category**	**Line-Haul**	**Switch**	
	HC	0.30	0.60	g/bhp-hr
	CO	1.5	2.4	
	NOx	5.5	8.1	
	PM	0.20	0.24	
	SS smoke	20		percent opacity
	30-sec smoke	40		
	3-sec smoke	50		

* SS means "Steady State." Smoke is defined in EPA terms as either steady state (locomotive under load for extended period) or transient (upon notch up).

Note: Line-haul standards do not apply to Tier 0 switch locomotives.

a split-cooling-equipped locomotive originally built in 1995 without emissions controls may have since been updated to Tier 0 status based on the previous regulations. This latest 1033 regulation will now force the locomotive to a Tier 1+ status upon its next remanufacture.

DC Traction Systems

The series DC traction motor, universal in North American locomotive service until the early 1990s, remains in operation today on 80 percent of the North American fleet. A standard locomotive design uses two swiveling trucks (or bogies) per unit, each with two or three axles and traction motors. The traction motor is rated at 600-1,200 volts DC. Its magnetic field windings are connected in series with its armature to provide high starting torque. To adapt a common motor to all classes of service with the standard 40- or 42-inch-diameter driving wheels, different mechanical gear ratios are used.

Typical EMD gear ratios range from a 15-tooth pinion on the motor shaft engaging a 62-tooth gear on the axle (with a maximum speed of 71 mph) to a 57:20 ratio with a maximum speed of 102 mph. The most commonly employed gear ratio for GE locomotives is 83:20. For all ratios, the traction motor speed is kept to a predefined maximum rpm limit that varies somewhat based on specific motor design. For a given locomotive configuration, mechanical gearing provides an inverse relationship between top speed and maximum tractive effort. (Locomotives equipped with high-speed gearing will have less maximum tractive effort capability than a comparable locomotive equipped with a lower top speed gearing.) Most of the gearing employed on new locomotive production is designed for maximum operating speed between 65 and 75 mph.

The motors are arranged in the "nose-suspended" configuration illustrated in Fig. 4-9, exactly the same principle used in streetcars since 1890. This mounting is the simplest way to allow the wheels to move up and down over track irregularities while transmitting the motor torque to the spring-supported truck frame. About half of the nose-suspended motor's weight is supported by the axle and is, therefore, "unsprung" (subject to impact loads and, in turn, subjecting the track to similar forces). Track forces caused by unsprung mass are largely a factor of vehicle speed and play less of a role in the design of freight locomotives than those locomotives targeted for high-speed passenger operation. At speed ranges greater than 90 mph, track forces due to unsprung mass become more pronounced, forcing many high-speed locomotive designs to be of lightweight construction and equipped with frame-suspended traction motors that significantly reduce the unsprung mass contribution to track forces.

The wheels, axles, gears, gear case, and traction motor in the nose-suspended system constitute a single unit or "combo" that can be changed out for rebuilding with a minimum of out-of-service time. Traction motors are cooled by a flow of air supplied via flexible ducts from platform-mounted ventilation blowers. Improvements in motor insulation and design have allowed continuous power ratings to reach 1,000 hp per motor in a unit that will fit between the wheels and clear the roadbed.

At starting and low speed, the current required to generate full tractive effort creates more heat than the blowers can exhaust. DC traction system characteristics include a minimum continuous speed (MCS) where the motor heat generation is balanced against ventilation system capability. At speeds below this MCS, higher current levels cause the motors to increase in temperature. After extended time of operation below the MCS, the motors could overheat and burn out from the overload condition.

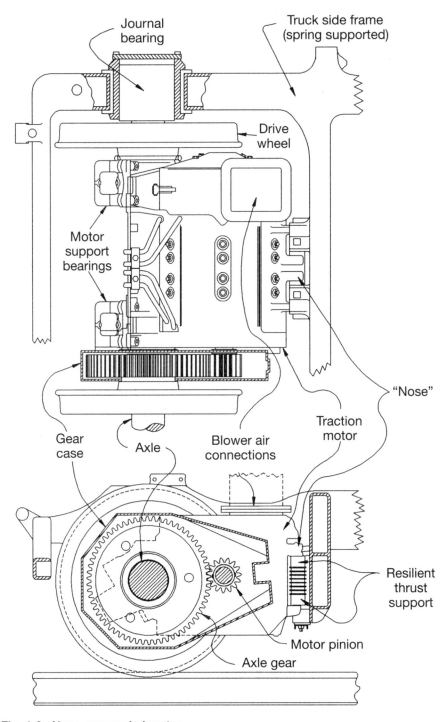

Fig. 4-9. Nose-suspended motor

In regular operation, most railroads dispatch trains with sufficient power to allow operation at speeds greater than the defined minimum continuous speed. If the combination of tonnage and grade is appropriate for the locomotive power and gear ratio, the train will reach the summit of the hill or attain a speed where blower cooling can keep up with the heat being generated before the motor windings reach a dangerous temperature. On modern microprocessor-controlled locomotives, a motor thermal map exists within the locomotive software so that the motors will automatically protect themselves before reaching their thermal limits without any conscious action by the operator. The speed of the train will decrease because of the reduced horsepower until the motors again are within their thermal limits. On older locomotives without this capability, the operator would stop and allow the motors to cool. In some applications, helper locomotives may be employed to allow the train to crest a grade at speeds greater than the MCS. On busy lines with steep grades, railroads often employ multiple main-line tracks and helper operations to keep operations at speeds that both protect the equipment and minimize operational congestion.

AC Traction Systems

Availability of solid-state inverters capable of converting direct current (or rectified AC) to three-phase VVVF (variable-voltage variable-frequency) power led in the late 1980s to the selection of AC traction motors for significant numbers of new or rebuilt rapid transit and commuter cars. Under microprocessor control, an extremely complex inversion/smoothing process generates three-phase power providing acceptable traction characteristics (including dynamic or regenerative braking down to a standstill) with relatively light weight "squirrel cage" traction motors and thus eliminate brush and commutator maintenance. GTO (gate turn-off) and IGBT (integrated gate bipolar transistor) devices are employed for this inversion process. This technology allows a relatively small control current to stop and start conduction in hockey-puck-size transistors capable of carrying locomotive-size currents.

Characteristics of DC and AC traction-motor counterparts affecting railroad use are presented in Fig. 4-10. The inherent speed-torque characteristics of the three-phase motor in combination with microprocessor control of the supplied frequency in relation to the wheel rotation raises "dispatchable" adhesion levels toward a new plateau, with numbers as high as 40 percent being reported. Inherent differences in AC traction system design permit higher torque performance and essentially no minimum continuous speed limitations that can handicap DC traction products in some applications. Further capitalizing on the capabilities of AC traction system design, some recent AC traction locomotives have included increased ballast and specialized software allowing a further increase in tractive effort capability over older AC designs.

Motors fed from a single inverter tend to move in "lock step," improving adhesion because an individual axle encountering poor rail conditions will automatically lose torque as it starts to slip—provided that all wheels are of very closely (¼ inch) matched diameter. If each motor is fed by its own inverter, wheel diameters need not be so close-

Rail Traction Motor Types – Characteristics

DC Series

Commutator/brush length subtracts from volume available for field and rotor copper and iron. Field and armature structures are complex.

Torque-speed characteristics match rail traction requirements – with maximum torque at starting. Feed-back or separate field-current control required for full use of available adhesion.

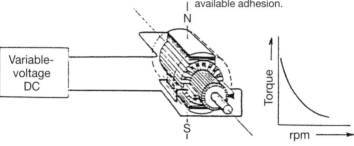

AC Induction

(Asynchronous, "squirrel cage") No mechanical commutation required. Entire length available for torque generation. Motor speed not limited by commutator/brush performance, flash-over voltage: totally enclosed, self-ventilated design feasible (with some weight penalty).

Supply frequency must be regulated with respect to vehicle speed to keep slip within high-torque region. Torque drop toward synchronous speed provides degree of adhesion control. Motors fed from common frequency source are electrically locked together. Will share load only if wheel diameters are closely matched.

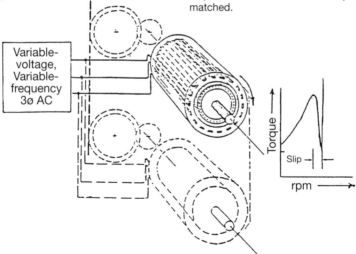

Fig. 4-10. Traction motor types, characteristics

ly matched but maximizing adhesion requires corresponding individual control of the frequency supplied. At this time, competing designs of the two major locomotive builders take opposite approaches: GE uses the inverter-per-axle approach, while EMD uses an inverter-per-truck.

Despite rather limited in-service experience, quantity production and introduction of AC-drive freight locomotives in North America began in the early 1990s, fostered by large-scale commitments to the new technology on the part of some major railroads. By late 1994, AC drive was present in the majority of new locomotives produced by both builders. The compactness of the motors and the improved adhesion levels being demonstrated resulted in commitments to provide units of 6,000 hp by 1997. In retrospect, most railroads could not effectively maximize the yield from their investment represented by 6,000 hp locomotives and have reverted to locomotive products with 4,000 to 4,400 hp.

The in-service performance of AC traction locomotives, particularly in heavy-haul/mineral-train service, has revolutionized the North American locomotive landscape. Today, of the eight large roads in North America, six have extensive AC traction locomotive rosters representing over 20 percent of the total North American fleet. Application of modern AC traction locomotives in heavy-haul service has allowed elimination of many helper districts and operational obstacles that once prevented regular operation of very heavy trains. Most AC locomotives are utilized in heavy-haul applications, however, some can also be found in intermodal and mixed freight service.

Steerable (Radial) Trucks

To accommodate three traction motors and transmit tractive effort from the wheel treads to the locomotive frame with a minimum of weight shift among its axles, the six-wheel truck designed for maximum adhesion has a relatively long wheelbase. This can generate extra flange wear and increased lateral rail forces on curved track, to the extent that six-axle locomotives were restricted (or even prohibited) on some secondary routes. As discussed in Chapter 5 in connection with the car-truck design, allowing the axles to "steer" themselves into the curve can be expected to improve vehicle curving performance significantly. Although the fore-and-aft motion in adjusting to an 8-degree curve (about the maximum through which full steering is practical) is small—one-half inch or so at the journal box—rather precise stiffness and damping relationships between the frame and wheelsets must be maintained if both radial action and freedom from hunting on tangent track are to be achieved. Since there is already no shortage of gear cases, blower ducts, and other equipment to fill up the interior of a power truck, accommodating the steering arms and diagonal linkage required in a radial truck (Fig. 4-11). in a maintainable configuration has been a challenging design task. Nevertheless, such a production six-wheel truck that entered service in 1994 has demonstrated significant reduction in wheel wear and lateral curving forces no higher than that of a standard four-wheel counterpart. Today, both major builders catalog self-steering trucks that accomplish reduced flange forces and lower wheel flange wear. While proven in service,

Fig. 4-11. Radial truck

the added first cost and subsequent maintenance costs for these trucks have caused some railroads to reconsider the benefits of the steerable trucks. Many have reverted to non-steerable truck designs on recent deliveries. In recent years, less than 25 percent of new locomotive deliveries were equipped with steerable trucks.

Locomotive Controls

Controls to use the locomotive's full capabilities are among the most complex parts of the machine. The control stand itself now has a minimum of levers, but each works through elaborate circuitry (now mostly solid state) to keep the diesel fuel supply and the electrical load on the alternator in step so that properly graduated power levels are applied to moving the train.

All new locomotives built today feature microprocessor control. First developed in the mid-1980s, the advent of microprocessor control logic has allowed maximum performance from the locomotive systems, minimizing fuel auxiliary device usage and maximizing diagnostics and troubleshooting capability. In most instances, locomotives can self-diagnose problems and provide some "get-home" functionality even under fault conditions. Gauges and switches have been replaced by operator display screens. Most third-party train-control devices such as cab signal, distributed power, end-of-train communication, event recorder, alerter, and air brake are now integrated (or at least closely tied) to the locomotive control system.

The locomotive electronic air brake control (not to be confused with the electro-pneumatic train brake discussed in Chapter 6) substitutes a microprocessor and electrically operated valves to replace the plumber's nightmare of piping within the control stand in quietly handling the complex functions of the modern air brake control logic. Essentially all locomotives delivered over the last 10 years have been equipped with electronic air brake.

The primary operator interfaces are the reverser handle (which determines the direction of travel), and the throttle/braking handles (which determine the power/braking effort applied). Today's throttle has eight positions (or notches) above Idle, each representing a higher horsepower output. Throttle, dynamic brake, and reverser controls are interlocked to prevent improper combinations. Organization and responsibilities of these handles varies slightly between desktop and AAR-style control stands as well as between GE and EMD products. Fig. 4-12 shows a GE control stand.

The primary throttle control now works through microprocessor logic to optimize diesel engine operation, including adjustments to the fuel injection control system of the diesel to maintain a specific rpm and horsepower for each notch, while minimizing emissions and fuel usage. At the same time, the magnetic field of the traction alternator is regulated so that the electrical power it is producing (and, therefore, the resistance

Fig. 4-12. General Electric ES44AC operator cab with AAR console [Courtesy of GE Transportation]

it offers to the turning of the crankshaft) just matches the horsepower the diesel can develop so the system is stable at the governed speed.

On some older locomotive designs, as the train speed increases, the traction motors generate more and more voltage ("back EMF") opposing the voltage they are receiving from the generator. At a certain speed, the net available generator voltage will become insufficient to develop full traction motor power. At this "transition" point, the motors, which have typically been connected in series to keep the low-speed motor current draw within limits, must be reconnected in parallel to put full generator voltage across them and let the train speed continue to increase. In early-model diesels, the transition (like shifting gears in an automobile) had to be made by the engineer. More recently, the locomotive control system would automatically transition without operator interaction. Modern locomotives have traction alternators sized with the capability to run the locomotive with all traction motors permanently connected in parallel. This permanent parallel motor connection scheme improves locomotive adhesion levels, and at the same time eliminates switchgear once required for transition.

On older locomotives, the engineman's principal guide to locomotive performance was the ammeter, which showed the current actually going through the motors and, therefore, the rate at which they were heating up. It was marked to indicate the maximum continuous current draw allowable and the time limits that must not be exceeded for various short term ratings. On microprocessor-controlled locomotives with thermal motor maps, there is no need for a separate ammeter since the locomotive is self-protecting. Locomotive tractive (or braking) effort is now available to the engineer on the operator display. Close observance of ammeter readings is still required for railroads that regularly mix locomotive models. Newer units in the consist will automatically protect, but older units still have the potential to overheat if not monitored.

Locomotive Performance

Fig. 4-13 shows what can be expected from a nonmicroprocessor 3,000 hp diesel-electric unit and compares the two versions available—the four-axle locomotive with its short-wheelbase trucks and the six-axle unit, weighing about 50 percent more, with its six traction motors but carrying the same diesel engine/alternator combination. Either can be equipped with different gear ratios for the desired maximum and minimum speed limits.

Why Six Axles Instead of Four?

The six-axle locomotive has two extra traction motors and gear sets to maintain, and its long-wheelbase trucks can be a problem on track with sharp curves. Over most of the speed range, tractive effort is limited by engine horsepower, and the curve is the

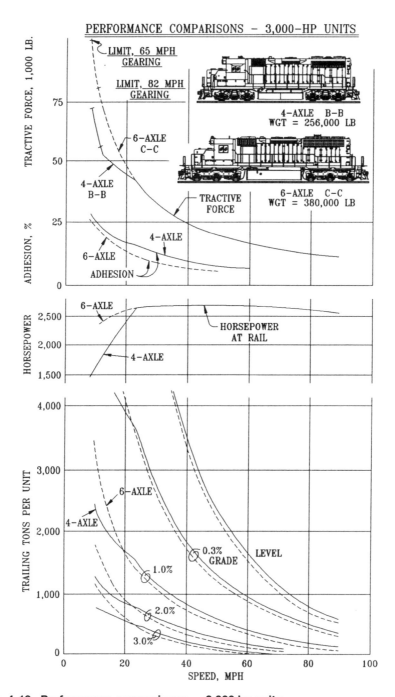

Fig. 4-13. Performance comparisons — 3,000 hp units

same for both types of units. The four-axle unit will actually haul a little more tonnage because it has some 55 tons less of its own weight to pull along.

The difference shows up below about 23 mph, where the adhesion required by the lighter unit to develop the tractive effort corresponding to its horsepower begins to reach the limit for reliable traction for non-microprocessor-equipped locomotives—16 to 18 percent. To keep the engine from being "slippery," its control circuitry is arranged to cut back its power at lower speeds. The six-axle unit, then, moves out in front in hauling capacity. With 50 percent more traction motor thermal capacity, the C-C unit can "lug" that much more tonnage up a grade where low-speed horsepower is needed.

As one would expect, six-axle units are prevalent on divisions where heavy trains must be hauled up long or steep grades, but scarce on lines whose loads are lighter and grades are such that all trains can get over them without dipping below 25 mph for more than brief periods. Over time, however, most North American train sizes have grown, forcing railroad operating departments to employ larger locomotives to haul them. Even most intermodal applications (once ruled by four-axle high-horsepower locomotives) have grown so much that large six-axle locomotives are now employed, freeing up older four-axle locomotives for secondary service.

Multiple-Unit Arrangements

On level track, a single locomotive could move an average freight train at about 35 to 40 mph. However, truly level track is a rarity for most railroads. Almost every line has at least some grades in the 0.3 percent range or greater where more than "drag" speeds must be maintained for practical schedules. Tonnage is likely to be assigned, in accordance with computer train performance analysis, on a horsepower per ton basis for the particular class of service, which results in more than one unit per train in most cases.

Units to be placed in multiple-unit (MU) consists are provided with four or five air hose connections controlling braking on all units and a standard 27-pin electrical connector controlling all other functions. It is possible to interconnect units of different makes, horsepower, and the number of motors, gear ratios, and brake-control equipment and still have the resulting lash-up function as one locomotive. If the units are not matched, the more capable units usually have some loss of performance. Maximum speed will be limited to that of the unit with the lowest gearing, for example. But the flexibility of being able to use any locomotives available while providing total power matched to the requirements of each train is a very important factor in achieving the best locomotive use possible.

Distributed Power/ECP

Where heavy trains must be moved up steep grades, additional tractive effort must be applied to overcome the added resistance caused by the grade—more locomotive pulling capability is required to offset the effect of gravity. Sometimes, locomotives can be added to the front of the train. However, in most situations, this added tractive effort could exceed coupler strength limits. Instead, railroads have come to employ two techniques: helper locomotives and distributed power (DP) consists.

On fairly short grades, helper locomotives run by another engineman are commonly used. Most often the units are attached to the rear of the train to prevent opportunities for coupler-drawbar failures and to minimize time lost switching the additional locomotives in and out of the consist. Occasionally, mid-train helper consists or multiple-helper consists may be used, although the amount of time required to add or remove the helpers is increased substantially.

Where there are several major grades scattered throughout a run, it is more economical to use distributed power units located at a point in the train where their tractive effort will result in the smoothest handling, typically at the rear or two-thirds of the way back in the consist. Through use of distributed power, the lead locomotive remotely controls these remote consists via radio signals. Commands between the lead and remote consists are similar to those being transmitted by jumper cable to MU'ed trailing units in the lead consist. Commands are transmitted so that other nearby DP consists do not recognize these commands.

All units equipped with distributed power equipment can be used in lead or remote positions. Each locomotive is equipped with a distributed power radio and antenna that is tied to distributed power control boxes. For most new locomotives, the distributed power control is integrated directly with the locomotive's control system and the electronic air brake system. Crews engage and monitor distributed power operations through the locomotive's display screens.

Use of older radio remote technology (including special repeaters and cars) has been abandoned in favor of modern distributed power. Today, thousands of locomotives are DP-equipped and most western railroads regularly employ DP in coal and heavy freight operation. Coincident with the introduction of DP into freight and intermodal operations, some railroads have elected to configure these locomotives with reduced tractive effort capability in order to optimize drawbar forces within the train. These locomotives have a "CTE" designation (for Controlled Tractive Effort), which can aid in train handling, especially for mixed freight or intermodal consists. When setting up for DP operation, crews can define whether locomotives are to be used with normal or controlled tractive effort modes.

Through 2008, the industry showed renewed interest in the application of electronically controlled pneumatic (ECP) braking to improve train handling and safety. ECP braking is an expansion of the traditional air brake system that uses an electronic link between locomotives and all cars to command brake operation simultaneously on all vehicles. (Traditional air brake systems use pressure changes in the train brake pipe to command brake action. Propagation of these pressure changes through a long train consist often takes several minutes.) The FRA issued a notice of proposed rulemaking regarding ECP, and several U.S. railroads are currently using or testing ECP in limited applications. It will be several years before enough cars and locomotives are equipped to allow full-scale implementation, such as in interchange service. Chapter 6 contains a more detailed discussion of ECP braking.

Dynamic Braking

Since a motor can act as a generator if its shaft is turned by an external source of power, the traction motors on most locomotives for over-the-road service are also used to provide braking, particularly on descending grades. In dynamic braking, the current generated is fed to resistance grids where the energy developed from retarding the train is dissipated as heat. On some locomotives, the energy recovered as electrical energy during dynamic braking can also be used to power the blowers that are used to cool the dynamic braking grids, thus saving fuel. In dynamic braking operation, the operator uses the same controls and display indications that are used during motoring. Modern dynamic braking systems can exert almost full braking effort to zero speed, and are extensively used during regular train handling to reduce the need for air braking and related brake shoe and wheel wear.

Slugs and Mates

Sometimes, the traditional locomotive setup is not capable of performing certain tasks. When it comes to pushing cars over the crest in a hump yard at a steady 2 to 4 mph, a single unit has plenty of horsepower but not enough tractive effort or traction motor cooling capacity. To remedy this situation, excess power is fed from the diesel unit's generator to a companion "slug" unit. The slug is a ballasted four- or six-axle unit having traction motors but no engine or generator. This homemade combination provides multi-unit, low-speed tractive effort with single-unit fuel consumption and engine maintenance. For some over-the-road services where particularly heavy loads must be handled at moderate speeds, "road slug" or "mate" units married to standard road locomotives also furnish that needed tractive effort.

Passenger Push-Pull

For commuter train service with its numerous short trips, a great deal of terminal switching is saved by providing a control cab in the rear passenger car, connected to the locomotive by trainline control cables, from which the engineman can run the train on the return runs.

Head-End Power

Passenger trains require "hotel" power for heating, lighting, and air conditioning. For many years, this power was obtained from axle-driven generators on the cars and steam-piped from a steam-generating boiler on the locomotive. (The earliest passenger car air conditioning systems used ice stored in bunkers beneath the cars, with fans blowing cold air into the car.) The HEP (Head-End Power) system now in practically universal use in the United States uses 480 volt, three-phase power trainlined from a passenger locomotive to provide all such power requirements.

Three basic systems have been developed to provide HEP. In most cases, an additional companion alternator (incorporated into the regular locomotive alternator) generates the power. Engine controls are programmed to "idle" at sufficient engine speed to develop the 60 Hz (hertz) HEP output even when no traction power is being produced. Typical HEP output is 500 kW (675 hp), which is subtracted from the diesel horsepower available for traction. On Amtrak, the high car demand required for dining and other services, and the need for extra power for longer passenger trains, has resulted in HEP systems with 800 kW (kilowatt) capability on its latest diesel-electric passenger locomotives.

On many commuter locomotives, a separate diesel engine "genset" (generator set) is provided on the locomotive, typically in the rear of the unit below the cooling system. This stand-alone system generates HEP with minimal involvement from the locomotive systems. For new locomotives, these gensets must also meet applicable EPA emissions requirements.

On AC traction locomotives, HEP can be provided via inverter. Typically, an additional traction inverter is added to the propulsion circuit and used solely for HEP. On some designs, a traction inverter is actually used for HEP, partially limiting the locomotive's traction system capability while operating in HEP mode.

Fuel Efficiency

A fundamental shift in locomotive design and operating goals occurred with the many-fold "oil shock" price increases of 1974 and 1979. In the latter year, fuel costs for the first time exceeded locomotive maintenance expenses and became (after labor) the second largest operating cost. Since then, fuel costs have continued to rise and continue to be one of the largest operating costs for any railroad.

Builders have committed to improvements in fuel efficiency for their products, even while complying with significant reductions in emissions as required by the EPA. A sampling of the variety of technical and operational changes have been employed.

Multi-microprocessor control systems in post-1986 locomotives have enhanced efficiency of the prime mover over the range of operating conditions and tailor the output of power-consuming auxiliaries such as cooling fans more closely to the demand.

Growth in computer-processing speed and power has enabled locomotive designers to more closely monitor traction and auxiliary loads to provide further reductions in fuel consumption and higher system efficiencies.

Electronic fuel injection has been incorporated into all new diesel locomotive deliveries to minimize fuel usage and improve emissions across the operating spectrum.

Trade-offs have been re-examined in basic engine, turbo, transmission, and auxiliaries design between fuel efficiency and mechanical, electrical, and aerodynamic refinement, first-cost, and complexity.

Engines and controls are adapted to lower idling speeds to minimize fuel usage, and according to new operating practices, units are regularly shut down rather than idled between runs. To further minimize idle time, builders have developed automatic start/stop systems that monitor locomotive characteristics and shut down the engine after only 5 or 10 minutes of idling. Engines are automatically restarted by the locomotive control system when any critical parameter goes out of predefined limits. Essentially all locomotives delivered are now equipped with these systems. Older locomotives have been

Fig. 4-14. General Electric Evolution Series locomotive [Courtesy of GE Transportation]

retrofitted with auto-start systems or standby heating and other provisions to facilitate safe shutdown and restarting in low ambient temperatures. (North American locomotives are not adapted to the use of antifreeze.)

Some railroads report fuel savings from MU controls that allow individual units in a consist to be idled during portions of a run where their power is not required to maintain schedule.

Due to recent developments in diesel engine technology, builders have been able to provide the power levels using 12-cylinder diesel engines that formerly required the use of 16-cylinder engines, with attendant reductions in both fuel consumption and in emissions levels.

Other Locomotive Types

Although 99 percent of all locomotive horsepower in the United States is generated by diesel-electric locomotives, a number of other types of motive power are also in use. Multiple-unit, self-propelled commuter and rapid transit train operations, which are discussed later, amount to several million horsepower. The other important form of locomotive is the straight-electric, usable, of course, only where overhead catenary or third rail power supply is available. Figs. 4-15 and 4-16 summarize the various types of motive power in use, including some hybrids developed to allow running across power-supply boundaries.

The Electric Locomotive

The straight-electric locomotive draws its power from an overhead conductor via a sliding shoe held against the wire by a pantograph. The important difference between the electric and diesel-electric is in the electric's ability to draw almost unlimited power from the wire while accelerating its train. Traditionally, the electric locomotive's traction motors had a continuous rating, the same as that on their diesel counterparts. But these units had a short-time rating (5 minutes, for example) that may have been almost double that rating. At low speed, the tractive effort is adhesion-limited (just as on the diesel), but as the speed increases, the extra horsepower can be used to keep the tractive effort at a high value. As Fig. 4-4 shows, the result is significantly improved. A six-axle electric with a continuous-duty rating of 6,000 diesel-equivalent horsepower (about 5,000 hp at the rail) loaded to 4 hp per ton could still be accelerating at 0.2 mph per second at 70 mph on level track and reach that speed well before the 5-minute rating period had been used up. Over an entire run involving many stops or speed restrictions, the time difference is considerable—an electric can be loaded considerably more heavily than an equivalent diesel and still make the same schedule. All recent electric locomotive deliveries have been AC traction designs that further minimize some of the traditional limitations of this design concept.

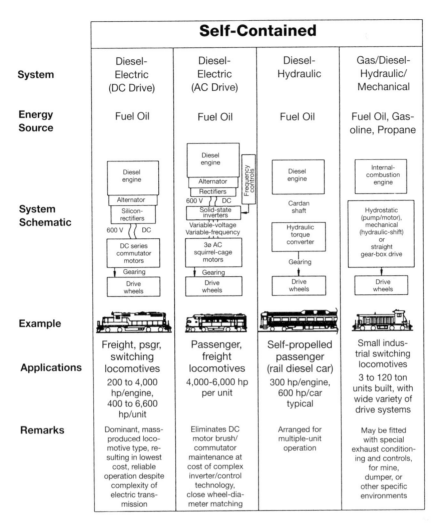

	Self-Contained			
System	Diesel-Electric (DC Drive)	Diesel-Electric (AC Drive)	Diesel-Hydraulic	Gas/Diesel-Hydraulic/Mechanical
Energy Source	Fuel Oil	Fuel Oil	Fuel Oil	Fuel Oil, Gasoline, Propane
System Schematic	Diesel engine → Alternator → Silicon-rectifiers → 600 V DC → DC series commutator motors → Gearing → Drive wheels	Diesel engine → Alternator → Rectifiers → 600 V DC / Frequency controls → Solid-state inverters → Variable-voltage Variable-frequency → 3ø AC squirrel-cage motors → Gearing → Drive wheels	Diesel engine → Cardan shaft → Hydraulic torque converter → Gearing → Drive wheels	Internal-combustion engine → Hydrostatic (pump/motor), mechanical (hydraulic-shift) or straight gear-box drive → Drive wheels
Applications	Freight, psgr, switching locomotives 200 to 4,000 hp/engine, 400 to 6,600 hp/unit	Passenger, freight locomotives 4,000-6,000 hp per unit	Self-propelled passenger (rail diesel car) 300 hp/engine, 600 hp/car typical	Small industrial switching locomotives 3 to 120 ton units built, with wide variety of drive systems
Remarks	Dominant, mass-produced locomotive type, resulting in lowest cost, reliable operation despite complexity of electric transmission	Eliminates DC motor brush/commutator maintenance at cost of complex inverter/control technology, close wheel-diameter matching	Arranged for multiple-unit operation	May be fitted with special exhaust conditioning and controls, for mine, dumper, or other specific environments

Fig. 4-15. Rail propulsion system (self-contained)

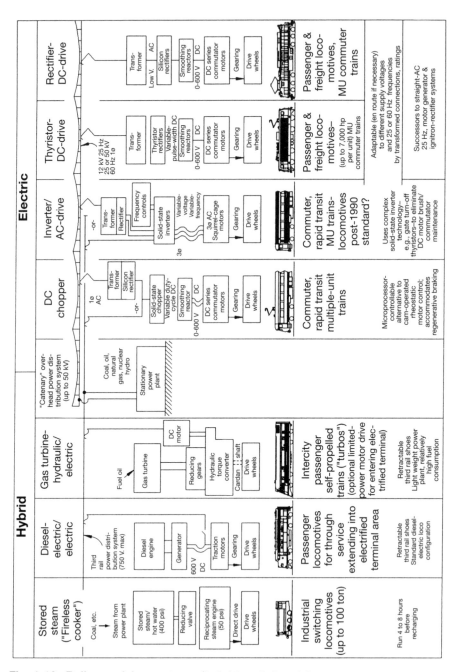

Fig. 4-16. Rail propulsion systems (hybrid and electric)

The electric locomotive cannot be considered apart from electrification, the process of providing the power distribution system. Recently built electric locomotives and MU cars (Fig. 4-16) are adaptable to high-voltage (25 or 50 kV) 60 Hz (commercial frequency) power, which can be provided by public utilities rather than railroad-sponsored power plants and picked up from relatively lightweight catenary. Some commuter rail lines in New Jersey and parts of the Northeast Corridor have been recently electrified or upgraded to newer electrification technology, but despite numerous economic studies, no main-line freight electrification remains in service in the United States or Canada. (Traditionally, most studies have shown the infrastructure costs of electrification do not allow sufficient return when compared to diesel locomotives applied in the existing infrastructure. Should fuel or other operational costs change, study results could change in the future.)

In addition to straight-electric designs, small fleets of "dual-mode" locomotives are employed in commuter operations around New York City. These units are diesel-electric locomotives with AC traction systems that are also equipped to accept power from the 650 volt DC third rail. Most operation is in diesel mode, but the locomotives operate using the third rail on approach to New York City terminals. They are designed to switch modes without stopping.

A recent development is the so-called "dual-power" locomotive, which is a combination diesel-electric/AC catenary unit. As of late 2007, several AC-electrified commuter railroads in the eastern United States and Canada were prepared to procure this type of unit, which would offer them the ability to operate through-trains in both diesel and AC catenary territory (and provide passengers with "one-seat" trips). Up until recently, this type of locomotive in main-line service had been considered impractical because of the combined weight of a diesel powerplant and an electric transformer being too heavy for the track structure (especially in curves at higher speeds). Recent advances in lightweight modular electric components as well as computerized engine control systems (for example, the possibility of running two lighter weight high-rpm diesel powerplants with shared duty cycles rather than a single, heavy prime mover) can make such a locomotive feasible.

Hybrid Locomotives

Over the past few years, interest has increased in applying hybrid technology to locomotives to further improve fuel efficiency or reduce emissions. For congested terminal operations, RailPower and several other builders have developed endcab yard switchers operating almost solely on hybrid capability. An engine genset is used to charge a bank of batteries that are used as the traction motor power source upon throttle demand. Through mid-2007, a number of these locomotives had entered service in yard and industrial applications throughout North America. Success in operation for this type of product is application specific—high-duty cycles may demand more power than available in the battery system, even with recharging. Long-term success for this type of product will be based on each builder's ability to adapt this technology to meet the wide range of locomotive performance required to cover all switching applications without negative life cycle cost, reliability, or durability implications.

General Electric has been investigating use of hybrid technology for another means: fuel efficiency improvements on large road locomotives. The GE system, which was under validation on a test locomotive as of 2007, recovers energy normally lost during dynamic braking. Instead of heat dissipation through the dynamic braking grid package, the energy is stored in onboard batteries for later use when in motoring mode. This allows reduced fuel consumption or increased available horsepower under certain operating conditions.

Multi-Engine Locomotives for Switching Service

To pre-emptively meet future restrictions in allowable emissions (EPA Tier 3 and beyond), several builders (National Railway Equipment Co., RailPower, Wabtec) have introduced multi-engine switching locomotives, mostly commonly known in the industry as *genset switchers* (Fig. 4-17). These small road switchers, mostly in the 1,400-2,100 hp range, use anywhere from one to three small high-speed diesel engines to provide power for the traction system. Each modular engine package includes an alternator and cooling system, allowing them to be brought on-line independently to meet locomotive power demand. Targeted to replace older endcab and road switcher designs, these locomotives have been tested mainly in yard and local duties since 2006. Long-term viability for this locomotive type (tied to operational performance and life-cycle costs) is now under evaluation by several Class I railroads.

Locomotive Maintenance

In recent years, many railroads have outsourced their locomotive maintenance operations to the locomotive builders or third parties. Given an increased push by the railroads for utilization (as well as the builders now having to maintain the products they have designed), the principal emphasis in recent locomotive design changes has been on improving reliability and reducing maintenance rather than simply increasing power. Concurrent with this effort has been the improvement of locomotive control diagnostics. Today's locomotive can:

• Recognize and diagnose onboard problems

• Take appropriate action for component protection (while minimizing impact to operation)

• Monitor the fault and report the situation, as necessary, to the crew or maintenance facility

Fig. 4-17. Triple-engine genset switcher, built for Union Pacific by National Railway Equipment Company [Courtesy of National Railway Equipment Co.]

To improve reliability, manufacturers have continually redesigned components for simplicity and maintainability. Where possible, total parts count has been reduced. One example, GE's recent GEVO engine design program, allowed introduction of a 12-cylinder engine with the same horsepower rating as the previous 16-cylinder engine. Further component consolidation has been achieved through integration of functions into microprocessor control system logic. Control systems themselves are regularly reinvented to consolidate architecture and make the best use of the latest available micro components. Most compartments housing electronics are pressurized with filtered air to minimize ingress of dirt and contamination that traditionally led to reliability concerns.

There is also a continuing battle to simplify the design of basic components to help compensate for the increased complexity that creeps in with each improvement in performance. One traditional example was the pressure-retaining 26L air brake control stand that allows trains to descend grades without having to stop to set up brake retainers on the freight cars. But the added features of this system did make air brake equipment more complicated, especially since it had to be compatible with older units not so equipped. In partial compensation for this, composition brake shoes with their higher coefficient of friction have made it possible to reduce the number of brake shoes per wheel on the locomotive from two to one, getting rid of considerable brake rigging in the process. On newer locomotives, electronic air brake systems have replaced the older style electropneumatic valves of previous systems, further improving maintainability.

The inherently higher reliability of the new systems, improved filtration systems, longer life oil packages and overall higher reliability of locomotive subsystems developed by locomotive manufacturers has resulted in an increase in the maintenance interval from 92 days to 184 days for many new locomotive models. This has further improved locomotive utilization.

Inspection and Running Repairs

One of the most obvious hazards of early railroading was a steam locomotive boiler explosion. The design, construction, inspection, and maintenance of steam locomotive boilers have been regulated by the federal government since 1911. By extension from the boiler inspection, power brake, and safety appliance acts and the Railroad Safety Act of 1970, locomotives and MU cars are subject to mandatory daily, 92-day, annual and biennial inspections, and tests of all components and adjustments that are considered to affect safety; compliance is subject to verification by FRA inspectors and enforcement by civil monetary penalties. The 92-day inspection requires such items as calibration of air gauges and putting the locomotive over a pit where the underside can be thoroughly examined. Due to advances in locomotive subsystems and safety systems technology that has resulted in higher component reliability, the maintenance interval of new locomotive equipment has been increased from 92 to 184 days.

Safety inspections are accompanied, as a matter of good maintenance practice, by increasingly refined diagnostic tests such as spectrographic analysis of the lube oil to detect early indications of unusual engine wear or internal leaks. A major advance in efficiently evaluating locomotive health after shopping is use of "self-load," the ability to test the diesel and electrical systems under load by running them with the full generated power being dissipated in the locomotive's own dynamic brake resistors. Newer diagnostics tools, including remote diagnostics and improved control system diagnostics and self-test, provide even greater capability on new locomotive designs.

Major Repairs

Most of the repairs and adjustments found necessary at periodic inspections can be taken care of with little time out of service. Modern diesel design is such that even major casualties to prime mover, auxiliary, or electrical components can be handled by quick exchange with spares in running-repair shops. Components removed are then remanufactured in a production line operation in railroad, contractor, or manufacturer shop facilities. Even so, after a certain amount of usage, a unit will be ready for a major overhaul. This could entail rebuilding trucks, replacing engine power assemblies, or other major work. The timeline between overhauls and the required work during the major overhaul has also changed, with many components now having extended design life that extend through several overhaul cycles. The timing of overhaul and components listed for changeout or repair vary by locomotive model and engine type, most typically driven by engine usage (total megawatt hours) or miles operated.

Remote Diagnostics and New Technologies

Modern microprocessor-controlled locomotives have extensive communications capabilities that are now used by the railroads to improve overall asset utilization. Many locomotives contain a global position receiver (GPS) that pinpoints each locomotive's exact location. When equipped with onboard systems that integrate with the control system, the locomotive can provide data on its location and current activities, as well as historical usage statistics. System reporting capability allows headquarters to understand where all locomotives are located with special notice for those that have not operated in a predefined time period.

Both builders (GE and EMD) have released remote diagnostics systems that allow locomotives to report operational and fault data to railroad dispatch centers and maintenance facilities. Messages are generated and prioritized on urgency and severity and sent for attention at the nearest (or next) terminal. The receipt of this information before locomotive arrival at the terminal allows maintenance facilities to plan work in advance and forecast shop loading based on inbound locomotives' schedules. In conjunction with these onboard systems, some railroads and maintenance teams have developed infrastructure to allow repairs at yard run-through and fueling facilities without a locomotive ever being removed from the train. As a result of the widespread use of these systems, the mission completion percentage of modern locomotives is extremely high and time in the shop has been reduced.

Onboard video camera monitoring systems have gained widespread acceptance over the last several years, mostly in response to the increased volume of lawsuits surrounding train-pedestrian and train-automobile accidents. Most new locomotives produced are now equipped with a forward-facing video camera that captures images onto an onboard hard drive device. Video images (and sound via microphone in the air rack) indicate that crossing gates and appropriate warning devices (horn or bell) were functioning properly at the time of accident. The video record is also used extensively in training and in a maintenance-of-way inspection function.

As of early 2007, railroads showed renewed interest in the application of ECP (Electronically Controlled Pneumatic) brake systems, although very few locomotives (and trainsets) are yet equipped for this functionality. Many new locomotive deliveries are being equipped with provisions for future installation of complete ECP systems.

Also under evaluation by many railroads are a variety of Train Management systems aimed at improved operational fluidity, improved fuel efficiency, or increased asset utilization. With a wide variety of products available (and under development), most applications of these systems to locomotives to date have been for test scenarios only.

Further discussion on these systems is considered in Chapter 7, Signals and Communications.

End of the Line?

The nominal life of a diesel-electric in its original form is typically 20 to 25 years, assuming that various components have received upgrades during the locomotive's life. At the end of this time, there are several options. Many locomotives are sold into secondhand markets for continued use by smaller railroads, short lines, short-term leasing companies or even tourist railroads! Subject to metals market demand, diesel locomotives are often coveted by scrappers (scrap metal dealers) who will resell major components then cut up the locomotive structure for scrap value.

Until the late 1980s, EMD and GE sought locomotive trade-ins as part of new locomotive sales. With a trade-in of a retired locomotive, the customer would receive a substantial credit on the new locomotive purchase price. At first this was in an attempt to re-use some trade-in components to keep new locomotive costs down. Later, the builders sought trade-ins, sometimes upward of a three-for-one ratio, to control the availability of secondhand power that could jeopardize new locomotive sales. With recent mass locomotive retirements and the simultaneous growth of the short line industry, trade-ins could not control the rapid growth of the secondhand market. Today, trade-ins on new locomotive deals are rare.

A multitude of smaller locomotive dealers have developed over the last 20 years, often acting as brokers between the larger railroads and smaller short line and industrial customers. In some cases, locomotives are sold "as-is" to short lines. However, in many cases, locomotives are purchased, remanufactured (or overhauled), then resold to these railroads. Remanufactured units of low or moderate horsepower (1,500 to 3,000) are likely to be the choice of local and regional railroads, which can make good use of locomotives cascaded out of Class I service. Until recently, a majority of these diesels were four-axle road switchers, although the recent growth of regional railroad traffic has caused larger numbers of six-axle road switchers to be chosen. In certain cases, Class I's have purchased or leased large groups of road switchers to fill voids in their fleet, sometimes getting back the same locomotives they previously retired and sold.

Some remanufacturing projects extend beyond "in-kind" repairs. Rebuilders have used older locomotive cores to develop vastly different locomotive-related products, including commuter locomotives, maintenance-of-way vehicles and remote control platforms. While once common, these types of projects are more unusual today. The recent pace of locomotive development makes it less likely that older locomotives may be economically upgraded and also less likely that older locomotives will share many common parts with new designs, principally due to new safety and environmental regulations.

The Railroad Car

Railroad cars, primarily, are designed to conveniently carry and protect their contents and to stay on the track as individual vehicles, but they also must serve as links in a very strong chain. Within the first few years of railroading in the United States in the mid-19th century, the basic durable car configuration evolved: a long car body built around a strong center sill and supported on two swiveling four-wheel trucks. This basic design hasn't fundamentally changed in over 150 years, though it has been refined continually.

The Basic Eight-Wheel Car

The basic eight-wheel car (Fig. 5-1) may not be the perfect design for railroad cars, but it has proven to be a solid performer. All of the hundreds of major and minor deviations from the basic design—four-wheel cars, guided trucks, six-wheel trucks, articulated (hinged) cars—seem to be less satisfactory and efficient based on an overall system cost. This has been borne out in all types of services, from high-tonnage ore hauling to high-speed passenger trains and in car lengths from 24 to 95 ft.

Early railroaders quickly found that it worked the best to employ *wheelsets*—wheels attached permanently and rigidly to an axle, with the entire assembly revolving in stationary metal bearings—in contrast to the previous horse-drawn carriage practice of wheels revolving independently on a stationary axle. The bearings could readily be provided with a continual source of lubrication by enclosing them in a "journal box" packed with oil-saturated wool fibers (waste). Once in motion, the so-called "friction bearing" actually carried its load on a film of oil, floating with a friction load equal to only about 2 lbs of pull to move a ton of weight. The total friction, including that of the wheel rolling on the rail, was about twice that. Friction bearings have been completely replaced in interchange service with sealed roller bearings that require no periodic lubrication and offer lower rolling resistance and far greater reliability. Fig. 5-2 shows several typical freight car wheelsets as well as some locomotive and transit vehicle applications.

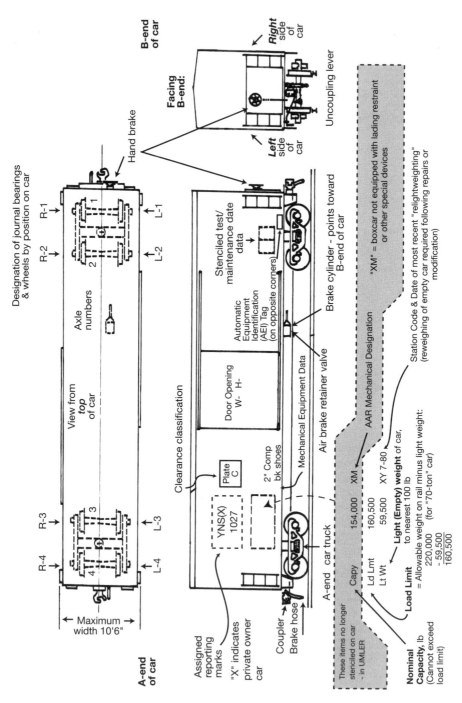

Fig. 5-1. The freight car

EMD locomotive set

New 100-ton
freight car set

Light rail
vehicle set

Plain bearing set

Heavy rail
vehicle set

Reprofiled freight
car set

Fig. 5-2. Wheelsets

Standardization and Interchange

Car design is a compromise between two conflicting goals—diversity to achieve the most efficient loading, transport, and unloading of a particular lading versus standardization on a minimum variety of general-purpose cars likely to cost less and achieve better use. Specific car types and designs for the principal classes of freight are illustrated in Chapter 9.

Most freight cars, specialized or general purpose, are interchanged between railroads and may be traveling in a train coupled to any of the other nearly 1.3 million cars making up the North American car fleet. In a continuation of the process started with the formation of the association of Master Car Builders in 1873 and now administered by the Association of American Railroads (AAR), the basic dimensions, design criteria, construction, and maintenance standards for the operating parts of a car making it suitable for interchange are rigidly specified.

Interchangeability and Evolution

The parts of a car subject to wear or damage in service must be as few in number and as interchangeable as possible, since they may need repair or replacement at repair-in-place ("rip") tracks or car shops anywhere on the North American network, including Mexico. Even cars in *captive* service on a single railroad en route are for the most part built to interchange requirements, since the cost of developing and building nonstandard designs usually outweighs other possible advantages.

Who Pays for Repairs?

Interchangeability of parts allows the approximately 1.3 million cars in existence to go just about anywhere, and be repaired just about anywhere. Interline repair billings of hundreds of millions of dollars are run up every year by cars operating in interchange service. These are charges for work done by a railroad on another company's car that was due for preventive maintenance or developed problems on-line (on the track). To avoid confusion and litigation, standards were set to determine who pays for which repairs. These standards are contained in the "bible" of the railroad industry, the *Field Manual of AAR Interchange Rules,* a pocket-size book of inspection standards, comparability of parts, repair and paperwork procedures, and responsibility rules. Pricing of all parts and repairs is determined by the *AAR Office Manual.*

Who Pays How Much for What?

In general, repairs are divided into those of a normal wear-and-tear nature, such as worn-out wheels and brake linings, and those associated with damage from treatment received (from railroad, freight shipper or receiver, act of God, or vandalism) on the handling line after it received and accepted the car at the interchange point. Wear and tear is the "owner's responsibility." The handling line pays for damage. Over the years, solutions to most of the thousands of common ("Who pays for the grease?") and questionable ("Who flattened the wheels?") problems have been determined. An arbitration board continues to decide new issues as they arise.

Car Capacity

Nominal car capacity is the basis for much of the rather remarkable degree of standardization in car repair parts. Wheels, axles, journal bearings, truck side frames, and many other components (whose size and strength is affected by the load they must carry) come in 30-, 40-, 50-, 70-, 100-, 110-, and 125-ton sizes. Practically all cars remaining in service today are the 110-ton variety—286,000 lbs total weight on rail, or gross rail load (GRL). The 125-ton cars are restricted to use by special interline agreements on roads and routes with track rated to support their 79,000 lb axle load (Table 5.1). Not all

Table 5-1. Nominal car capacity, gross rail load (GRL), and journal size

Nominal Car Capacity		Gross Rail Load (4-axle car)	Journals (diam. & length)	
30-ton	60,000 lbs	103,000 lbs	4¼x8 in.	(Class B)
40-ton	80,000	142,000	5x9	(Class C)
50-ton	110,000	177,000	5½x10	(Class D)
70-ton	154,000	220,000	6x11	(Class E)
100-ton	200,000	263,000	6½x12	(Class F)
110-ton	220,000	286,000	7x12	(Class G)*
110-ton	220,000	286,000	6½ x9	(Class K)*
125-ton	250,000	315,000	7x12	(Class G)*
125-ton	250,000	315,000	7x9	(Class M)*

*On the basis of economic studies in the late 1990s, most new freight cars are built with trucks and other components designed for a GRL of 286,000 lbs. The Association of American Railroads addressed some of the problems associated with the move to 286 and higher GRL cars by developing a new specification that took effect January 1, 2004. AAR Standard S-286, "Specification for 286,000 Pounds GRL Cars for Free/Unrestricted Interchange Cars," applies to all new four-axle freight cars built after December 31, 2003, that are designed and designated to carry a GRL greater than 268,000 lbs, up to and including 286,000 lbs. Existing freight cars and those rebuilt and newly designated for increased GRL or modified according to AAR Office Manual Rule 88 are qualified for free unrestricted interchange service provided they meet all S-286 requirements. S-286 requires roller bearings to be either Class K (6½x9), Class M (7x9), or Class G (7x12). On some 125-ton (315,000 lbs GRL) cars, the Class M can replace a Class G.

110-ton cars can carry exactly 220,000 lbs, however. *Total load on the rail is the governing force.*

Load Limit.

The *load limit* for a particular car, then, becomes the difference between its empty (light) weight and GRL. This varies depending upon commodity. For example, some 100-ton cars, such as hopper cars intended for a dense commodity (like rock that requires only a small cubic capacity) may weigh only 55,000 lbs empty and be able to carry 208,000 lbs. A 100-ton tank car built to carry relatively light liquefied petroleum gas and that must be built to take 350 psi pressure, on the other hand, may weigh over 100,000 lbs and thus have a load limit equal to only about 80 tons. Both cars will use the same size wheels, roller bearings, axles, and other weight-related parts.

Car Clearances

Overall car size is also standardized by AAR interchange regulations. A car fitting within the diagram Plate B can go anywhere. (Plate B requires 10 ft 8 in. wide by 15 ft 1 in. high, maximum, with further restrictions on width for extra-long cars so they will clear structures near sharp curves.) A 15 ft 6 in. high Plate C car, although listed as acceptable for limited interchange (the same as with higher cars), is restricted on less than 5 percent of all routes. Routes over which higher cars, such as the 17 ft 1 in. high-cube auto parts cars fitting within the dimensions of Plate F (1974) or the double-stack equipment built to carry 9 ft 6 in. high containers fitting beneath the 20 ft 2 in. limit of Plate H (1991) standards, are listed in *Railway Line Clearances,* an annual publication detailing allowable axle loads and the critical "top-corner" restriction (allowable width at each height in 3-inch increments) for each line segment of the railroad network.

For tracking quality reasons, overall car body length is limited to 89 ft (about 95 ft over the couplers). When the center of gravity of a loaded car exceeds 98 in. above the rail, "high-wide" handling is required, as detailed in Chapter 16.

Safety Appliances

The Federal Safety Appliance Act of 1893, which required automatic couplers and power brakes on railroad cars, also included standardization of the steps, ladders, grab irons, and running boards necessary for a brakeman to climb from car to car atop the train. A brakeman's original function was to control train speed with the hand brakes and, in the air brake era, to pass hand or lantern signals to the engine crew. Radio communication and remote-control yard locomotives have made it unnecessary for trainmen to traipse up and down the train; employees are now expressly forbidden to go atop cars in motion, and the ladders and running boards are being eliminated except where needed in connection with loading or unloading operations. The hand brake (now primarily a "parking" brake to keep stationary cars where they belong) has been relocated to a lower, safer position. For many years it has been of a geared design that can be set without using a "brakeman's club" to turn the brake wheel. Grab irons and steps for riding the cars during switching movements continue to be required, in standardized locations, so that an employee can count on a foot or handhold where expected, regardless of car age or ownership.

The Railroad Safety Act of 1970 extended FRA authority to all aspects of car design and maintenance, not just brakes, couplers, and safety appliances. The principal effect of this has been to give many requirements originally established for interchange purposes the force of law. After a period in the 1970s when what proved to be a very expensive program of periodic safety inspections and certifications of all freight cars was mandated, safety regulations were changed in 1980 to eliminate subsequent periodic inspection requirements. Inspection for defects judged critical for safe operation is required at the location where cars are placed in trains for road movement. Steep penalties of up to $7,500 for each offense may be assessed for any car subsequently found in service with such a defect. Cars developing defects must be tagged and moved for repair under restrictions determined by a qualified person.

Outlawed Designs and Components

Over the years a great many design improvements have become mandatory, and outmoded designs, whether single components or major aspects of design such as wooden underframes, outlawed. Passenger car structural design requirements are descended, for example, from Railway Main Service specifications developed in the process that required all RPO (Railway Post Office) cars be the equivalent of "all steel" construction.

Critical Car Components

With all these constraints, the job of the car designer in coming up with a vehicle that will make money is made possible only by the fact that there is considerable flexibility in using standard parts for the items where compatibility and interchangeability are required and then conceiving a car body and its specialty items that will meet the demands of traffic the best. From about 1962 on, there has been an increase of as much as 1.5 tons a year in the average freight car capacity, as new cars averaging over 80 tons capacity have replaced retired 40-, 50-, and even 70-ton cars. Wheel-rail stress levels are such that there is considerable question (studied quantitatively in a major 1988-1990 research program and ongoing in the AAR's Advanced Technology Safety Initiative) about the net benefits in raising car weight limits to the 125-ton level for general service over even the best of conventional trackage.

To the extent that handling much more than 100 tons as a single unit is desirable, it has been accomplished by grouping individual "platforms" of about the present size into permanently connected multi-unit "cars" by articulation (one four-wheel truck supporting each intermediate "joint") or with slackless drawbars. Such a configuration is employed in many intermodal cars, specifically, those consisting of three or five individual, articulated platforms.

The freight cars being built new today are bigger, lighter, stronger, require less maintenance and are a great deal more expensive (about five times the cost versus 30 years ago) than the ones they replace. Taking a closer look at the critical components that determine how the freight car does its job as a vehicle and a container will show how the freight car has become larger, better, and costlier.

Car Truck Design

Fig. 5-3 shows the standard freight car three-piece truck design now in use, with the established names for its components. The individual pieces undergo constant improvement and change, but the basic arrangement that allows quick disassembly and assembly in changing out worn parts has been around for generations. The whole 9,000 lb truck is held together only by gravity and the interlocking surfaces on the principal parts. Since it is equipped with roller bearings, wheel and axle assemblies are changed out simply by lifting the truck. Jacking up the bolster allows the spring group to be lifted off its seat in the side frame and taken out sidewise; the bolster can then be lowered, disengaging its gibs from the side frame. The entire truck is disassembled as simply as that.

Car Suspensions

Almost from the beginning it was apparent that some kind of system to isolate the car and its contents from the impacts of the unyielding metal wheels on the hard rails was needed. Also, since the wheel flanges are only an inch high, the vehicle must have enough flexibility to ensure that all its wheels are on the rails at all times. Although the theory underlying a "good ride" was not at all well understood at that time, the rough track typical of American railroading in the 19th century was a powerful incentive to develop effective suspension systems. Both passenger and freight car suspensions of a basic type that has proven hard to beat (steel coil or leaf springs) were in existence by the 1870s.

Unsprung Weight and Spring Deflection

The ability of the suspension to reduce shocks and vibrations at the wheel depends primarily upon two factors: (1) the smaller the portion of the car's weight that is "unsprung," (i.e., supported directly on the rail without intermediate cushioning by something flexible), and (2) the greater the deflection of the suspension under the weight of the car (the softer the springing), the better the ride can be. Obtaining a lasting and satisfactory ride in a simple, affordable system is a great challenge.

Freight Suspensions

The freight car truck has a single-stage suspension—one set of springs isolating the bolster (upon which the car body rests) from the side frames, which are supported directly from the wheels. The inventory of car springs is greatly reduced by the fact that anything from a 30- to a 125-ton truck is supported on the same springs, nesting inner and outer coils in different numbers and combinations to produce the total load capacity.

The softness of the suspension depends on the spring travel, the difference between the "free height" of the spring and its length when compressed by the weight of the car loaded to the limit. This travel ranges from 1⅝ inches in the D-1 spring (now rarely

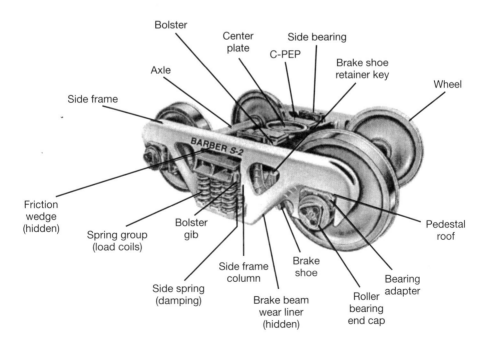

Fig. 5-3. Freight car truck—component nomenclature

103

used) to 4¼ inches in newer D-7s. Most cars have D-3, D-4, or D-5 springs with 2½ to 3¹¹⁄₁₆ inches of travel. The suspension cannot be softer than this in freight service because the difference in coupler height with a car empty and loaded would be too great and lead to breaks in the train. Long-travel springs not only provide a better ride but have greater reserve margin against "going solid" under severe track conditions and subjecting the car and its contents to very high loads.

Locomotive, Passenger Car, and Premium Freight Car Suspensions

The bolster and side frames of the three-piece freight car truck necessarily interlock somewhat loosely. The resulting assembly has limited resistance to going "out of square," which may allow development of severe lateral flange forces on curves and the onset of "hunting" (discussed later) at moderate speeds on tangent track. Passenger car trucks and locomotive trucks, on the other hand, have relatively rigid, one-piece frames to keep wheelsets parallel and in line.

Intercity and commuter passenger railcars, rapid transit cars, light rail vehicles, and road locomotives also have two-stage suspensions with one set of resilient elements between wheels and truck frame and a second set between truck frame and bolster (or its equivalent) on which the car body rests. This reduces unsprung weight, improving the ride and reducing track loads at high speeds. They also include *swing hangers* (Fig. 5-4) or equivalent elements that isolate the car body from lateral impacts and tend to keep it upright. Spring travel can total up to about 7 inches since there isn't much difference between empty and loaded weight. On some passenger cars, "air bag" suspensions, which use train air to adjust car-floor height with varying loads, are in use.

Premium freight car truck designs to provide some of these features at an acceptable cost (maintenance included) have long been an elusive goal for suppliers as discussed in connection with radial (self-steering) trucks. Radial trucks have been employed with great success in many six-axle locomotive designs.

Rock-and-Roll

Any single-stage suspension has a *resonant frequency*. Repeated jolts at or near this frequency, such as from "low joints" on bolted rail, will build up motion until something drastic happens unless there is damping to absorb energy. This was automatically provided in passenger cars by the use of leaf springs, which absorbed energy in friction between their leaves. Freight car suspensions now include one or another of various proprietary "snubber" arrangements, such as side bearings, that reliably generate an appropriate amount of friction between the bolster and side frame, preventing excessive vertical bounce of the car body at the resonant speed.

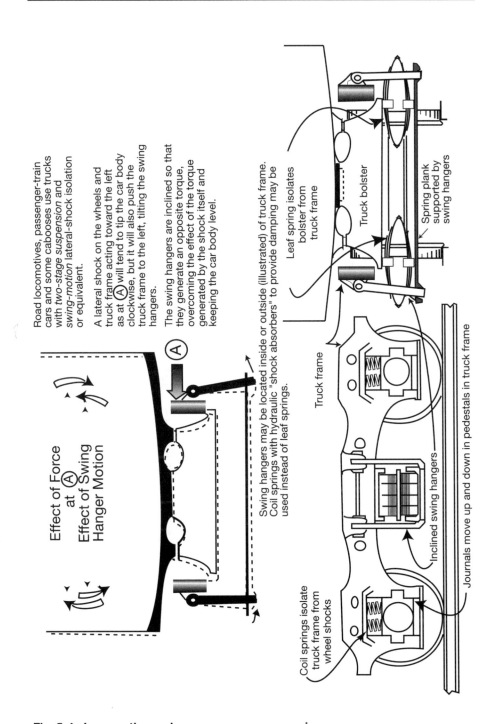

Road locomotives, passenger-train cars and some cabooses use trucks with *two-stage suspension* and *swing-motion* lateral-shock isolation or equivalent.

A lateral shock on the wheels and truck frame acting toward the left as at Ⓐ will tend to tip the car body clockwise, but it will also push the truck frame to the left, tilting the swing hangers.

The swing hangers are inclined so that they generate an opposite torque, overcoming the effect of the torque generated by the shock itself and keeping the car body level.

Effect of Force at Ⓐ
Effect of Swing Hanger Motion

Swing hangers may be located inside or outside (illustrated) of truck frame. Coil springs with hydraulic "shock absorbers" to provide damping may be used instead of leaf springs.

Truck bolster

Leaf spring isolates bolster from truck frame

Spring plank supported by swing hangers

Truck frame

Inclined swing hangers

Journals move up and down in pedestals in truck frame

Coil springs isolate truck frame from wheel shocks

Fig. 5-4. Locomotive and passenger car suspensions

Certain cars have a high center of gravity and truck spacing about the same as the 39 ft lengths of rail in jointed track. These cars can build up a resonant rocking motion to a point where wheels on one side lift off the rail. They can easily derail if on curved track at the time they go through the 15 to 25 mph speed range at which the resonance occurs. This rocking mode is harder to control because it happens at lower speed, and much more damping is required. The problem has been attacked with a combination of continuous-welded rail and improved snubbing arrangements.

Journal Bearings and Hotboxes

The overheated journal bearing or hotbox is one of the most hazardous aspects of railroad operation. If undetected, bearing malfunction rapidly results in friction heating of the end of the axle to a point where the steel is so weakened that the weight of the car breaks it off. This drops the truck frame to the roadbed, resulting in a potentially major derailment.

In the early 1960s, improvements and cost reduction in roller bearings (which had long before become standard for passenger cars) made their use in freight cars more practical. All cars built since 1963 have been required to have roller bearings; all cars operating in interchange service must have them.

The principal cost benefit of roller bearings is reduction in maintenance; plain (friction) bearings must be inspected by opening the journal box lid to verify the condition of bearing assembly, lubricator, and oil supply, whereas carefully monitored service measurements of grease consumption in latest-design roller bearings have allowed them to be certified to run the full 10 years before disassembly and refurbishing on an "NFL" (No Field Lubrication) basis. However, a roller bearing assembly that does fail can progress to disaster quickly and with little warning, so the detection of incipient trouble with specialized hotbox detectors is very important, discussed in Chapter 7, "Signals and Communication."

Axles

The rotating axle, which solved the problem of keeping the wheels in gage, also produces a bending stress that changes from compression to tension at any point in the axle every time the wheel revolves. This condition can result in metal fatigue, in which a crack develops progressively at a stress level below that which would cause any effect on a single steady application of load. The study of axle failures as far back as the 1850s was the first situation in which this condition was recognized. A recent development: the more durable raised wheel seat axle. This design lowers the concentrated stress in the axle at the inner face of the wheel that comes from the heavy force-fit used to keep the wheel in place. Today, axles are forged from medium carbon steel, machined all over to reduce surface fatigue possibilities, to weigh as much as 1,200 lbs, and to have a very low failure rate.

Wheels

Freight car wheels for cars of up to 70-ton capacity have been standardized at 33 in. diameter for many years. Larger wheels—36 in. for 100- and 110-ton cars and 38 in. for 125-ton cars—are used in high-capacity service to help spread out the concentrated load at the point of contact between wheel and rail head. A special 28 in. wheel is used on some intermodal flatcars to lower the deck 3 inches and help accommodate high truck trailers on routes where clearances are tight. All railroad wheels are made of steel, either cast or forged.

Iron wheels were economical and long-wearing but inadequate for the heavier loads that came along after World War II. When iron is cast into a metal mold, the sudden cooling produces a white "chilled iron" structure extending a half-inch or so from the surface and then blending into the soft "grey iron" of the rest of the casting. The chilled iron is extremely hard—so hard that it can't be machined. Until the 1930s, most wheels were made of iron, cast into a "chill ring" surrounding a sand mold so that the tread and flange were hard but the center was soft and reasonably tough. The axle hole could then be bored concentric with the rim and pressed onto the axle.

Wheel Thermal Loads

In addition to its functions of carrying the load and serving as the guiding element, the wheel tread must also survive the heat shock of serving as the brake drum and dissipating much of the heat energy resulting from descending grades and emergency stops. The locomotive dynamic brake is a big help, but the wheel tread temperature of 800 degrees Fahrenheit from a single high-speed emergency stop on a passenger car wheel is typical. The most severe stresses inside the wheel rim occur when the train has descended a long grade, raising it to a dull red heat; when these hot wheels are hit by the icy blasts of a blizzard, it takes a tough material to stand up to such torture.

Wheel material selection is a compromise between wear and thermal shock properties. Class A, B, and C heat-treated wheels are of increasingly higher carbon content, hardness, and wear resistance but of decreasing resistance to developing thermal cracks in service where extreme braking loads are frequent. Thus, a passenger train making frequent stops might require the use of the softer Class A wheels, while a heavily loaded unit-train car would get high wheel mileage from Class C wheels if its route did not involve long grades.

Wheels may also be overheated from a stuck or unreleased brake. Modern stress-analysis procedures led in the early 1970s to the development of designs with a curved *(deep dish)* plate contour between rim and hub that allows the tread to accommodate severe temperatures without generating dangerous stress levels in directions tending to cause catastrophic crack propagation. Under current rules, however, wheels with no detectable cracks but discolored to a depth of more than 4 inches from the rim must be scrapped. However, extensive destructive testing has established that thermal discoloration of heat-treated versions of low-stress wheels has no correlation with susceptibility to crack propagation. Since 1989, wheels of this class found discolored may remain in service, subject to certain route and service restrictions.

Wheel Wear and Profile

The exact contour of the tread and flange of the wheel (its *profile*) as it has been refined over the years is also a compromise. It's designed to ride well over its life and to last as long as possible before it begins to wear to a hazardous shape, either by developing a high flange with a vertical face that can climb the rail or a hollow tread with a "second flange" on the outside that can take the wrong route at a track switch. Wheel contour is one of the most closely gauged items in freight car inspection. After extensive analytical and field-test research, the "AAR1B" contour was adopted in 1989 as standard for new wheels. Visibly almost indistinguishable from the long-standard "AAR 1:20 taper" tread, subtle contour modifications reduce rolling resistance (and hence rail and wheel wear) by as much as 20 percent over the range of curvature and rail head shapes typical of main-line track while raising hunting-speed and wheel-climb thresholds throughout the wheel's service life.

In heavy service, the point at which 50 percent of a given lot of wheels have been changed should range from 200,000 to 350,000 miles. "Two-wear" wheels (popular for cars in "captive" service where the benefits of lower whole-life cost will be reaped by the owner who paid the initial-cost premium) are made with a thicker tread so that they may be machined once before becoming scrap. (*Machined* or *turned* refers to the wheels being guided by a computer program that minimizes metal removal in restoring tread and flange to a contour good for a second life.) With some 1.6 million wheels to be replaced or *turned* per year, the process of handling them (they weigh from 700 to 1,000 lbs each) is highly automated.

Car Body Structure

The car body structure for the most part is built around a center sill connecting the two trucks and the pockets for the draft gear and coupler assemblies that transmit pull *(draft)* and push *(buff)* loads associated with motion of the train as a whole.

Freight cars rely on gravity to hold the car body in place on its trucks; a standardized center plate from 12 to 16 inches in diameter (depending on car capacity) on the car body extends 1 inch into a corresponding center plate bowl on the truck bolster whose rim keeps the truck moving with the car body. Side bearings spaced 4 ft 2 in. apart are the other points of contact between truck and car body. To allow the car to keep all its wheels on the rail on warped track, the side bearings have some clearance or are resilient.

Trucks on passenger cars are connected to the center sill by a locked center pin that can only be released from within the car. Its design, stout enough to maintain the truck–car body relationship in the event of derailment, is intended to use the weight of the trucks to increase the probability that the car will remain upright.

Truck Hunting

The center plate–side bearing system has conflicting requirements. It should let the trucks swivel freely when entering curves to minimize friction and wheel wear, but it should also provide resistance to control truck hunting on tangent track. Truck hunting is a rapid oscillation occurring in empty cars at speeds of about 50 mph and above. At these speeds, the wheel flanges rapidly shift alternately from contact with one rail head to the other, with bad effects on both and generating damaging forces and wear in trucks and car body. As a result of this problem, a number of proprietary designs have been developed for resilient side bearings, center plate extensions, and bolster–side frame elements that are intended to delay the onset of hunting as speed increases; some also fight rock-and-roll. Not one of these designs has been universally accepted as fully meeting requirements for all classes of service at a satisfactory price.

The speed at which truck hunting may begin is lower in empty cars, with worn (hollow tread) wheels and with truck-bolster looseness allowing "out-of-square" oscillations.

Radial and Premium Trucks

In standard truck designs, the two axles remain parallel as the train goes around curves. If they could move within the truck so that each remains radial with respect to the curve, wheel treads with the proper angle of "conicity" could steer the truck around the curve without flange contact or wheel slippage, reducing friction, wear, and lateral forces. Angularity of the axles must be linked to secure the proper radial orientation and yaw motions must be correctly damped to prevent hunting on tangent track.

A few hundred carsets representing competing designs were placed in service in the 1980s. The competing designs were aimed at providing significant radial action on curves of up to about 8 degrees without unacceptably increasing truck complexity, weight, cost, and maintenance. Over routes with a high proportion of curved track, data from TTCI's FAST (Facility for Accelerated Service Testing) and field-service tests indicated that, under cars in very high-mileage service, an investment in radial trucks may earn a satisfactory return. Savings in the same fuel and wear elements from extending rail head lubrication to tangent track (widespread as a result of similar tests in the late 1980s) tend to narrow the range of profitable radial truck applications.

Suspensions have always provided a degree of radial action in the single-axle trucks that support light weight intermodal platforms (see Chapter 15) that have recently achieved some degree of acceptance in North American service for the four-wheel car. Sufficient to achieve full radial action only on the gentlest curvature (with proper damping), this action does significantly improve overall performance in these vehicles where accommodating 48 ft trailers requires a wheelbase of over 30 ft.

Some less complex designs providing improved performance—particularly, higher hunting-threshold speeds—have achieved wider acceptance, especially in intermodal service. The frame-braced truck adds bolted-on diagonal cross-struts to maintain truck squareness. A heavy-duty version of the Swing Motion truck uses the side frames as swing hangers to provide lateral cushioning and a transom-bolster combination increasing truck-frame rigidity.

The Rolling Bridge

The car body also must serve as a bridge holding up a load supported only at the truck center. The load is always heavy; it may be concentrated in a short part of the car length, or it may be dumped into the car. To do this job with as little weight as possible, the car body is designed as a unit with the center sill. This is why a boxcar may actually be lighter than a flatcar of the same length and capacity—its sides, roof, and underframe form a box structure that is quite efficient structurally in comparison to the deck of a flatcar, which is designed to be as shallow as possible.

Critical parts of the car must be strong enough to take incidental loads that make it a more efficient carrier of freight, such as wheel loads of as much as 50,000 lbs from forklift trucks on boxcar floors and clamp loads from rotary dumpers that empty gondola cars by simply overturning them.

Car Body Materials

The body must also withstand the lading itself, which may be corrosive, abrasive, contaminating or flammable. As a result, most car bodies are built with many parts of copper-bearing low-alloy high-tensile steels; the extra cost of the premium material is counterbalanced not only by longer life and reduced cost of hauling dead weight but also by the smaller quantity required to do the structural job. Aluminum alloy car bodies are used in specific services (such as coal) where their corrosion resistance to a particular lading together with the extra load permitted by the weight saving will justify the extra cost.

Car Cost and Maintenance

Freight car purchases and construction (in past decades influenced far more by tax considerations and regulated car-hire rates than traffic considerations) fluctuate so much that both new-car price and average-life calculations based on year-to-year figures are meaningless; a car-buying binge in the late 1970s in which investors pumped as many as 95,000 cars a year onto the rails was followed by a decade in which traffic expanded but car installation fell to as low as 6,000 a year. Another climb in railcar building occurred in the late 1990s when operating inefficiencies from railroad mergers created an artificially high demand for new cars. Following a fall-off to about 15,000 cars in 2000, car building rates leveled off to about 60,000 to 70,000 annual units in 2007 and were expected to remain steady through around 2012, driven mainly by the need to replace many older cars.

Based on the long-term replacement history, the average life of a freight car is about 22 years, during which it will have had at least one major overhaul. Since components representing a major fraction of car cost (trucks, for example) are interchangeable, and fleet size to handle a given volume of traffic has been declining as use has improved, rebuilding including cannibalization (in railroad, owner, or contract shops) has been effectively used to avoid or postpone purchases while coping with shifts in demand for specific car types. Examples include the conversion of boxcars to skeleton intermodal units carrying 53 ft trailers and the application of enclosed multilevel autoracks to 85 ft piggyback flatcars not readily convertible to handle a pair of 45 ft trailers. Major overhauls also include upgrading to current component (safety appliance, brake, coupler, strength) standards. However, AAR regulations now prohibit unrestricted interchange of cars over 40 years old regardless of whether it follows all other requirements.

Interchange and Inspections

Current FRA rules allow a train to operate a maximum of 1,000 miles between car inspections and brake performance tests provided that there is no change in the consist of the entire train. Establishment of responsibility for repairs and other aspects of operation requires inspection and acceptance of cars and their loads at the point where they are interchanged between railroads in an interline movement; for unit trains (Chapter 14), agreements are in force allowing interchange on the basis of inspections only at the point of train origin and as required by the 1,000-mile rule.

Periodic work legally required includes in-date tests of air brake performance and "COT&S" (Clean, Oil, Test, and Stencil) disassembly and rework as necessary of the brake valve assemblies. For the current ABDW design, the interval (based on demonstrated reliability in service) of 144 months is long enough to take the car to its likely first major overhaul.

CHAPTER 6

The Train

The business of the railroad is the selling and delivery of transportation. From an economic standpoint, it's the ability to assemble and move a large number of coupled cars as a unit that distinguishes rail systems, so the real name of the game is running *trains*. The rails and the flanged wheels guide the individual cars and let them roll with minimum friction, but action of the train as a whole is considerably more complicated than just the sum of the actions of its parts.

What's a Train?

The track is not clear until all of a train has passed, so it's extremely important for safety's sake to identify each train and be sure that it's intact and clear of the track. For operating purposes, the Book of Rules defines a train very specifically as "an engine or more than one engine coupled, with or without cars, *displaying markers*." Basic markers are a headlight or other white light on the front of the consist and (in freight service) the blinking red light of the EOT (end-of-train) device attached to the rear coupler of the last car.

Couplers

In order to have a train, the cars and locomotives must be coupled together. The Federal Safety Appliance Act of 1893 required the adoption of automatic couplers that would permit cars to be connected and disconnected without requiring a person to go between them. Of the thousands of patented devices designed to do this, the swinging-knuckle design of Major Eli H. Janney was selected for standardization and, except for specialized applications like drawbar-connected cars in a unit train or articulated intermodal platforms, is used on all North American cars and locomotives.

Es and Fs

The current standard coupler for general freight service is the Type E shown in Fig. 6-1. Like all Janney couplers, it works on the "clasped-hand" principle. To couple automatically, one or both of the knuckles must be open when the cars are pushed together; the knuckle swings to the closed position and a lock drops in place and holds it closed. Various internal features prevent the knuckle lock from jiggling or bouncing open under shock and vibration. To uncouple, the cars are pushed together enough to take the load off the coupler (the slack is taken in) and the "cut" or uncoupling lever is turned by hand, lifting the lock pin. One knuckle opens as the cars move apart, and uncoupling has taken place.

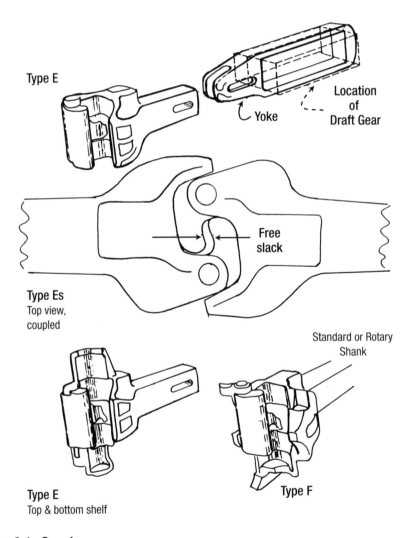

Fig. 6-1. Couplers

The Type E coupler does not interlock in the vertical direction. Coupler height is maintained between 31½ and 34½ inches above the rail with the car either loaded or empty. The coupler knuckles are 11 inches high, so there is always a nominal engagement of at least 8 inches. Under extreme conditions, it is possible for couplers to "slip by" in a moving train.

Interlocking Couplers

Passenger cars, hazardous-material tank cars, and many other freight cars are now equipped with couplers that also interlock in the vertical direction. Fig. 6-1 shows some of these. The passenger Type H "Tite-lock" is similar to the Type F freight coupler but uses some machined parts to restrict free slack between mating surfaces to a minimum. F and H couplers do not allow the knuckles to slide vertically on each other and so must be hinged in the vertical plane to allow some up-and-down swiveling as cars move over vertical curves in the track; coupler carriers must allow vertical motion as well.

Type E shelf couplers, like Fs and Hs, will tend in a derailment to reduce the severity of the accident by preventing the cars from disengaging, reducing jackknifing and the possibility of puncturing cars of hazardous materials. Shelf clearance is enough, though, to eliminate the vertical-swiveling complication. Also, if the shank of an E coupler mated to a shelf coupler should be pulled out, it will be prevented from dropping to the track and perhaps causing a derailment.

Rotary-shank couplers that allow a car to be rotated 180 degrees to dump its contents without uncoupling are an important feature of cars for unit-train service where this form of unloading is used. They must be of interlocking design.

Couplers for long cars, such as 89 ft piggyback flats, must have extra long (60 in.) shanks and wide coupler pockets to allow enough coupler swing for sharp curves. On these cars in particular, it may be necessary to line up the couplers manually so they will couple.

Draft Gear

Even before the automatic coupler was invented it became clear that some controlled "give" between the drawhead and the car body could greatly reduce shock and strain on the cars. The importance of *draft gear* and the difficulty of meeting all its requirements is well illustrated by the fact that over 21,000 U.S. patents have been issued in this field. At first, a stout spring was used, but soon an arrangement that would dissipate the energy of a starting, stopping, or coupling impact in *friction* between its internal parts rather than springing back was found to be far better. Another essential feature of the draft gear was to provide relative motion or "slack" between the cars to help the locomotive start a heavy load. With high-tractive-force, multi-unit diesel power, this has become less important.

Impact Protection

The role of draft gear in protecting cars and lading remains, and indeed has become, more significant as train weight has increased. There is about ¾ in. "free slack" between a pair of Es and half that between two Fs; there is a total of somewhat over 6 inches of stretch per car in the head end of a heavy train being started. Management of this slack to avoid breaking the train in two is one of the biggest challenges to the engineer's skill.

Draft Gear Capacity

The space into which draft gear must fit has been standardized; most cars have draft gear pockets 24⅝ in. long, with total coupler travel of 5½ in. draft (pull) and buff (compression). In 1956, an alternate standard pocket of 36 in. long was established, with maximum travel of 9½ in. The impact energy that can be absorbed at any given level of maximum force is directly proportional to the distance over which the impact can be spread out; improved rubber (or elastomeric) friction or friction-hydraulic draft gears fitting in these pockets can keep car impact forces within the 500,000 lbs limit in loaded cars striking at about 4 mph. Car center sills now have a compressive strength without serious distress of about 1.25 million lbs. The cars may take the punishment, but merchandise within may not, even if held in place with rugged load-restraining devices to prevent damage from internal impacts in the lading.

Cushioned Cars

About 20 percent of all freight cars are equipped with longer travel end-of-car cushioning systems (Fig. 6-2). Some older cars are equipped with sliding center sills, also known as "cushioned underframes," but they have largely been phased out. Fig. 6-3 shows typical maximum-force curves for different lengths of travel as impact speed increases. Nobody *wants* to bang cars together this vigorously, but impacts in the range above the "safe coupling" limit of 4 mph do occur often enough to make the extra complication and cost of the cushioning device a reasonable investment for carrying sensitive freight and avoiding loss-and-damage charges. A typical application for an end-of-car cushioning unit is an autorack car. End-of-car cushioning devices have up to 15 in. of travel. Thus, acting like very-long-travel draft gears, they may let each car shorten by more than 2 ft.

Cushioning unit technology has undergone an evolution, driven mainly by shipper demands for damage-free transport and the railroads' desire to reduce loss-and-damage payout. Older units provided for lading protection during coupling but did little to reduce in-train buff and draft forces experienced while a train is in motion. Research conducted in the late 1980s indicated that the devices in use at the time provided good buff protection but offered little resistance to in-train draft action, actually contributing to higher intercar velocities and, in turn, causing lading shift or damage, coupler knuckle breakage, or, in extreme cases, derailment. Initial improvements validated the advantages of preload cushioning, also known as *passive draft*. Preload, in which the device remains partially compressed and allows no more than 10,000 lbs of in-train buff forces, provides better draft shock protection than devices that return to their fully extended neutral position. A more recent development in cushioning devices is active draft (protection against both buff and draft forces). With *active draft,* a cushioning device offers cushioning travel in both directions. Upon relief of buff forces, the unit returns to a normal position that prepares it for a potential draft shock.

Draft System Strength

As trains have become heavier and locomotives more powerful, all parts of the system, knuckles, coupler shanks, yokes (holding coupler to draft gear), draft gear parts, center sill lugs (against which the draft gear acts), and the center sills themselves have been strengthened. This has been done by increasing the size of parts where interchangeability is not affected and by using stronger alloys and heat treatment. However, the knuckle is deliberately kept weaker than the coupler shank, the shank weaker than the yoke, and so on. Thus, in case of failure out on the road, it will usually be the knuckle that breaks. It can be readily replaced by the crew, and the likelihood of something serious such as a buckled center sill is remote.

Accordingly, coupler knuckles for general service are made of Grade B steel and have a strength of 350,000 lbs. For *captive* service where all cars in the train will be designed to the latest and strongest standards, Grade E knuckles with an ultimate strength of 650,000 lbs are available, giving the railroad much more leeway in adding tractive force on the head end.

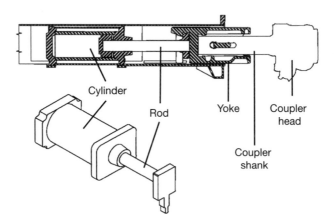

Cylinder

Rod

Yoke

Coupler head

Coupler shank

Fig. 6-2. End-of-car (EOC) cushioning unit

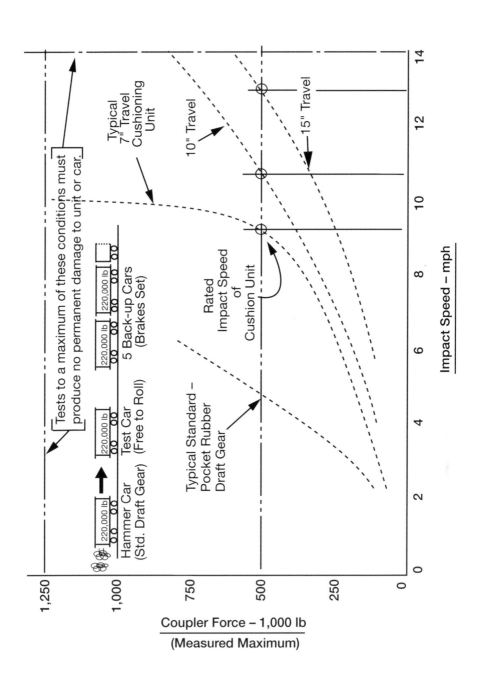

Fig. 6-3. Hydraulic cushioning performance and requirements

Power to Stop

In moving traffic over a railroad, *power to stop* can be more important than tractive force, heavy cars, or strong couplers. If the motive power can handle only a few cars at a time, more trains can be run until the job is done, provided that a steady procession of them can move at reasonable speed without running into each other. That takes reliable braking power.

Before any train leaves its terminal, its crew must follow a specified test procedure to verify that: (1) pressure at the rear end is within 15 psi of that being fed into its trainline by the locomotive; (2) system leakage with brakes applied does not exceed 5 psi per minute; and (3) brakes on each car have applied and released properly.

The Air Brake

Since 1900, the common factor on all trains in American railroading has been the air brake—the most complex set of equipment on the freight car fleet, and the only one that has some components that could possibly be called "delicate."

Like wheel and coupler contours, air brake components have had to be standardized throughout the system. Despite the restriction of having to ensure that each innovation would work satisfactorily in a train with its predecessors, brake performance has continued to improve in major respects as the various systems have been invented, developed, tested, phased in, and phased out. Each of the features of the ABD and newer ABDW freight brake system has come about as a result of some limitation in earlier equipment that became enough of a problem to require improvements.

Brake Pipe Pressure

The chief function of the air brake system is to provide adequate, uninterrupted pressure from car to car. With the train assembled in the departure yard, the single air hose at the end of each car is manually connected to its neighbor, with all the angle cocks (shut-off valves) in open position, except at each end of the train. (Automatic coupler assemblies that also make the air connection have been perfected and are widely used in rapid transit and light rail service only because they are not compatible with any other system.)

The brake system is charged, either by the air compressors on the locomotives or from a yard air supply (usually quicker), if available. Maximum braking power varies, within limits, simply by adjusting the feed valve on the locomotive. On a solid train of empties headed for a relatively level run, pressure would probably be set at a value near the lower legal limit of 70 psi, providing adequate braking with minimum chance of sliding any wheels flat. More demanding conditions would call for trainline pressure up to the maximum (90 psi) for normal freight train operation. Passenger-train pressure is 110 psi.

Brake Pipe Gradient and Leakage

When the pressure throughout the train has built up, the brake valve on each car is in the "release" position (Fig. 6-4), with the brake pipe connected to the reservoirs and the brake cylinder exhaust connected to the atmosphere (via a special "wasp excluder" fitting that ensures that nest-building insects can't frustrate brake action). There will always be some leakage, resulting in lower pressure at the rear end of the train. But the actual pressure in the reservoirs on each car is the system's reference, and its response to *change* in brake pipe pressure is unaffected.

By law, a train cannot leave its terminal unless measured brake pipe gradient is less than 15 psi. Leakage, with air supply cut off, must also be less than 5 psi per minute; air flow into the brake pipe of less than 60 cfm (as measured by a calibrated flow meter in the cab) has been accepted, subject to specific FRA conditions, as an alternate to the leakage test.

The End-of-Train (EOT) Device

Since elimination of the caboose on freight trains in the late 1980s, the end-of-train (EOT) device (in addition to serving as the rear marker) continuously displays the brake pipe pressure in the locomotive cab via radio link. It not only allows required brake tests to be performed without a long walk from the head end to the rear of the train, but also verifies proper transmission of the desired pressure reduction throughout the consist whenever train brakes are applied during the run. Most EOT devices also contain a motion sensor (pendulum or simple radar) to signal that "the rear end is moving" and to advise the engineer that the slack has been taken out and full power can be applied to accelerate the train.

If equipped with a two-way radio link, the EOT device can be used to initiate an emergency brake application from the rear end, a vital consideration in the rare event that some blockage in the brake pipe (behind which a brake application from the cab will be ineffective) has occurred subsequent to the last use or test of the train brake. This feature has been phased in as a requirement in any train service involving speeds and grades in which such a situation could be hazardous.

Passenger cars are equipped with a "conductor's brake valve" that can be opened to apply the train air brakes, primarily for use in emergency situations.

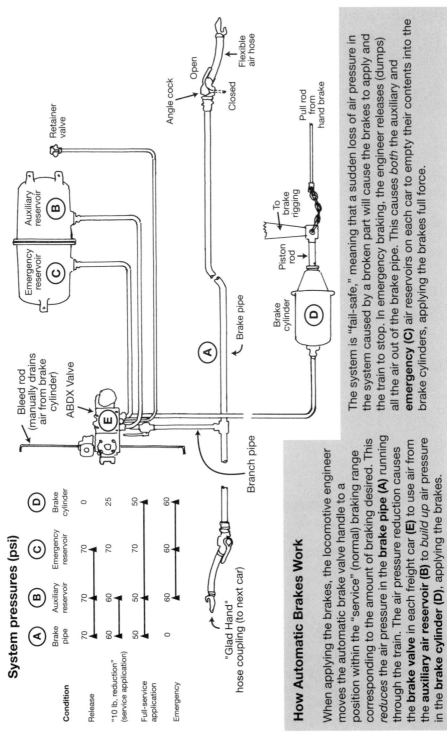

System pressures (psi)

Condition	(A) Brake pipe	(B) Auxiliary reservoir	(C) Emergency reservoir	(D) Brake cylinder
Release	70	70	70	0
"10 lb. reduction" (service application)	60	60	70	25
Full-service application	50	50	70	50
Emergency	0	60	60	60

"Glad Hand" hose coupling (to next car)

Bleed rod (manually drains air from brake cylinder)

ABDX Valve

Retainer valve

Auxiliary reservoir (B)

Emergency reservoir (C)

Open

Angle cock

Closed

Flexible air hose

Brake pipe

(A)

Branch pipe

(E)

To brake rigging

Pull rod from hand brake

Piston rod

Brake cylinder (D)

How Automatic Brakes Work

When applying the brakes, the locomotive engineer moves the automatic brake valve handle to a position within the "service" (normal) braking range corresponding to the amount of braking desired. This *reduces* the air pressure in the **brake pipe (A)** running through the train. The air pressure reduction causes the **brake valve** in each freight car **(E)** to use air from the **auxiliary air reservoir (B)** to *build up* air pressure in the **brake cylinder (D)**, applying the brakes.

The system is "fail-safe," meaning that a sudden loss of air pressure in the system caused by a broken part will cause the brakes to apply and the train to stop. In emergency braking, the engineer releases (dumps) all the air out of the brake pipe. This causes *both* the auxiliary and **emergency (C)** air reservoirs on each car to empty their contents into the brake cylinders, applying the brakes full force.

Fig. 6-4. The automatic air brake

121

The Fail-Safe Principle

When braking is required, the engineer moves the automatic brake valve handle to a position within the "service" range corresponding to the amount of retardation desired. This *reduces* pressure in the brake pipe leading back through the train, at a controlled rate. This reduction causes the ABD valve on each car to use air from the auxiliary reservoir to *build up* pressure in the brake cylinder, applying the brakes.

This fail-safe, reverse action is the basis for the whole technology of the automatic air brake as it has developed from George Westinghouse's invention of 1872. With a supply of air on each car, a train break-in-two, a burst air hose, an air compressor failure, or any other situation causing loss of pressure will bring the train to a stop. The scores of improvements that have been, and still are being, incorporated into the system work to speed up, smooth out, fine-tune, and otherwise improve braking action throughout the train.

Service Application

For each pound of reduction in brake pipe pressure, the valve will build up 2½ psi in the brake cylinder, until a "full-service" reduction of 20 psi from the 70 psi brake pipe pressure produces a full-service application of 50 psi cylinder pressure (Fig. 6-4). At this point, the pressures in reservoir and cylinder are equal, and any further reduction in the pipe pressure will have no further effect.

Slack Action Control

In the days of hand brakes, in an emergency the engineer could only set the steam brake on the locomotive drivers (or put the engine in reverse), whistle "down brakes" to signal the brakemen to start turning hand brake wheels on the cars, and hope for the best. The locomotive would start to slow down, and then the cars would run into it, one by one. The crude draft gear of the time was probably enough to keep the impacts from throwing cars off the track, since the engine didn't have much braking power anyway, but it was not a graceful process.

With the first version of the automatic air brake, the brake on each car would begin to apply only after there had been time for the air in its section of the brake pipe to flow up toward the opening to atmosphere in the locomotive brake valve. This took time, time enough for the slack to run-in before the brakes of the rear of a long train even began to take hold. With good braking power on the head end of the train, the result was quite violent—sometimes enough to buckle the train. The remedy was to add a *serial action* feature to the brake valve on each car. As the valve sensed the reduced pressure, it not only applied pressure to its own brake cylinder but also vented brake pipe air. This would, in turn, speed up the pressure reduction in the brake pipe of the next car. Modern valves use this basic idea in a variety of ways to move air among the various reservoir, brake pipe and brake cylinder volumes, and the atmosphere, not only to speed up and improve the certainty of brake applications but to speed up release as well.

Emergency Braking

For an emergency application, the brake valve opens the brake pipe wide (the "big hole" position). The resulting rapid rate of brake pipe pressure reduction causes the car valves to dump the contents of both auxiliary and emergency reservoirs into the brake cylinder (Fig. 6-4). This builds up a brake cylinder pressure equal to about 85 percent of brake pipe pressure (as compared to about 70 percent for full service). The rate of application back through the train is as fast as 900 ft per second, rather impressive considering that the speed of sound in air is only 1,100 ft per second, and that is the theoretical absolute maximum rate of "passing the word" pneumatically.

Brake Rigging and Braking Ratio

Braking ratio is the relation of the weight of the car or locomotive to the braking force; that is, the percentage obtained by dividing the braking force by the weight of the car or locomotive. Brake cylinder pressure is translated into stopping power at the wheel treads by the brake rigging and brake shoes. Most freight cars use a single cylinder on the car body, connected by levers and rods to one brake shoe per wheel. There is a single rod connection to the brake gear on each truck, and this is the only disconnection to be made in separating truck from car. The same rigging is actuated by a connecting chain from the geared hand brake, now used only in switching individual cars and to keep "parked" equipment from moving. An alternative to this standard "foundation" brake rigging used particularly on cars whose car body design would complicate the rigging (such as large-diameter tank cars where the tank serves as the car's "centersill" structural element) is the use of two smaller brake cylinders on each truck that apply force directly to the brake beams.

The brake ratio is calculated by the following formula:

$$\frac{P \times L \times A \times N}{\text{Weight in lb}}$$

where,

     P = Brake cylinder pressure (50 lbs)
     L = Ratio of brake levers
     A = Area in square inches of brake cylinder piston
     N = Number of brake cylinders

As an example, let's take a boxcar that weighs about 80,000 lbs and has a gross rail load of 220,000 lbs. This car has a brake lever ratio of 12.2:1, a piston area of 78.54 in., and one brake cylinder. Using the formula from above, we can determine the light weight ratio:

$$\frac{50 \times 12.2 \times 78.54 \times 1 \times 100}{80,000} = 59.89\%$$

For the gross rail load, we get the following formula:

$$\frac{50 \times 12.2 \times 78.54 \times 1 \times 100}{220,000} = 21.77\%$$

The calculated ratio is strictly theoretical, as it does not take into account such items as the force of the return spring in the brake cylinder and friction in the brake rigging from angularity or dirt. The actual brake shoe force measurement is called the Golden Shoe ratio, and is usually about 65 percent of the calculated measurement. The Golden Shoe ratios are determined by a test mechanism that is substituted for the shoes on a car. The device has a digital display that gives a direct reading in pounds of brake force when air pressure is put into the brake cylinder.

AAR standards call for the following calculated ratio:

Composition shoes 6.5% (gross rail load)
30.0% (light weight)

Slack Adjustment

The distance that the brake cylinder piston must travel to move the shoes against the wheels depends on the wear of all the parts of the rigging and particularly on the remaining thickness of the brake shoes. The longer the travel, the greater the volume of the brake cylinder and the lower the equalizing pressure in a full-service or emergency brake application. All cars are now required to have automatic brake slack adjusters that keep piston travel within limits.

Brake Force Ratios

The braking force applied to the brake shoes (expressed as its ratio to the car weight) results in a retarding effect that is quite low at high speed (say, 65 mph and above) but becomes as much as 2½ times higher as the train speed is reduced. The friction attainable between wheel and rail to slow the train also varies in the same direction with speed, but to a much smaller degree. In practice, the braking ratio could be about 150 percent for an emergency passenger-train application and no more than 70 to 80 percent for any empty freight car in full service. Otherwise, there would be too much likelihood of sliding wheels flat. This causes two problems.

Empty-and-Load Brakes

In freight service, the difference in weight between a loaded and empty car is now as much as 4 to 1. The same braking power for a loaded car will thus result in only one-quarter the stopping rate of the empty. At higher speeds, the stopping distance will become very long; the most economical operating speed for a loaded train, considering the cost of energy against the cost of equipment time, may not be practical because stopping distance becomes too long for the signaling system.

If the loaded-to-empty weight ratio of a car with composition shoes is greater than 4.6 to 1 (30 percent divided by 6.5 percent), the required minimum (loaded) and maximum (empty) braking ratios above can only be met by adding an "empty-and-load" braking function to change the brake force to match the light or loaded car weight. Any 100-ton car with a light weight of less than 57,000 lbs is thus required to be so equipped. Automatic empty-load systems have been available for decades, though only more recently in simplified and relatively less expensive versions; with more efficient car body designs (particularly, costlier but more productive aluminum-body coal cars), this refinement is now commonplace.

High-Speed Braking

Early passenger trains had to use elaborate speed-governor-controlled brake systems to allow very high braking ratios during the high-speed portion of a stop, progressively reducing it as the brake shoe friction increased. Today, individual microprocessor-based wheel slip controls, similar to those on locomotive driving axles, act to momentarily reduce braking on an axle that starts to slide, avoiding the need for a reduced average braking force to take care of local rail-wheel adhesion problems.

Composition Brake Shoes

Many problem areas have been mitigated considerably by the development of composition brake shoes, first used extensively in the early 1960s. These have both a higher coefficient of friction (simplifying brake rigging and reducing the force it must generate) and one whose variation with speed better matches rail-wheel adhesion.

Release, Runaways, and Retainers

Freight train brake systems can *apply* braking power in steps but do not have the *graduated release* capability practical in relatively short trains and provided in passenger brake systems so that the engineer can make accurate station stops and come to rest without a "stonewall" effect.

In freight trains, once release is initiated by increasing brake pipe pressure, the brake valve completely exhausts the brake cylinder while recharging the reservoirs. The only way to reduce braking is to release the brakes completely and then reapply them at a lower level. With earlier systems, this could take a matter of minutes in a long train. If brake application was made at less than 30 mph in a long train, it was necessary to stop completely and allow all the brakes on the rear end to release before starting again. The ABD system largely eliminates this problem by its accelerated release (450 ft/second) and relatively rapid reapplication capabilities.

Retainers and Pressure Maintaining

When air brakes were still in the early stages of development, there was always the chance that the train could run away while the brakes were being released prior to being recharged to make up for the gradual leakage that eventually reduces brake cylinder pressure. This was initially overcome by the *retainer,* a valve on each car (manually turned up at the top of a descending grade) that retained some pressure in the brake cylinders after release. At the foot of the grade, the train would have to stop again while retainers were turned down.

In most cases, use of retainers have been eliminated by the *pressure-maintaining* feature of the 26L locomotive brake valve. This maintains brake pipe pressure at a level that gives the desired degree of braking, making up for leakage by feeding air into the brake pipe. With the dynamic brake on the locomotive adjusting for differences in train action (e.g., curves), it is usually possible to hold the train at the desired speed throughout a descent. Occasionally, retainers are still useful in holding heavy-tonnage trains on grades while recharging after a stop, where the independent brake alone would not hold the train.

Braking Horsepower, Dynamic Brakes, and Hot Wheels

Since it's effective on all the wheels of the train, air braking horsepower can greatly exceed locomotive horsepower. A 13,000-ton train going down a 2 percent grade must dissipate 83,000 hp in heat to remain at a steady speed of 30 mph. Dynamic-brake horsepower may be about equal to the traction horsepower rating of the locomotive, perhaps 12,000 to 18,000 hp in this case. Every bit helps save brake shoes, which is why you'll see "helper" locomotives attached to trains going *downhill,* to contribute to dynamic braking capacity (though all railroads do not agree on this practice). In trains of less than 100 tons per operative brake, downhill dynamic brake helpers can cause undesired slack status changes. On a grade this steep, though, most of the work will have to be done by the brake shoes. If the grade is long, it may be necessary to stop and cool the wheels.

Since the brake heating environment is a wheel's toughest test, why not use a disc brake in which the thermal load has been taken off the wheel tread? Disc brakes are used widely in passenger service, but the relative simplicity, wheel-cleaning characteristics, minimum weight, and minimum cost of tread brakes has so far made them the most cost-effective system for general freight service. Even though brake shoe replacement is by far the most frequent item of maintenance on the freight car, it's also one of the easiest and quickest.

The Independent Brake

Brakes on the locomotive units themselves are controlled by the separate *independent* brake valve. This is a *straight-air* system in which braking force can be applied and released to any desired degree without delay. It is used in switching cars when their brakes are not connected and is very important in train handling, allowing the engineer to gently bunch the slack, for example, before applying the train brake. Since retarding forces of independent and dynamic braking would be compounded and applied to the same wheels, they should not be used at the same time because the wheels would slide.

Two-Pipe Systems

For special situations involving operation of loaded trains down steep grades, the addition of a second brake pipe can eliminate stops to set up and turn down retainers and may be worth the extra cost on unit trains used intensively in a specific service. One option is to use pressure in the second brake pipe to set the retainers from the locomotive cab. In another system, the second brake pipe is connected to the brake cylinders on each car by way of a simple differential pressure valve that allows pressure from the regular brake system or the second pipe, whichever is higher, to enter the cylinder. The second pipe thus functions as a *straight-air* system in which the engineer controls retardation directly. Since reducing pressure in this system will *reduce* braking, graduated release is provided and precise control during the descent is possible; at the same time, the standard automatic air brake system is fully charged and is available at all times should the straight-air system fail.

Electronically Controlled Pneumatic Braking

The speed of sound in air at normal temperature is about 1,100 ft per second; this is the maximum possible velocity at which the pressure reduction in the trainline calling for a brake application can travel back from the cab. Although a service application in the latest ABD system is propagated at somewhat more than half this speed, in a long train, the delay in braking at the rear end is many, many seconds. Furthermore, in a service application the rate of brake cylinder pressure buildup must be limited so that brakes at the rear have begun to apply before the head end has slowed enough to cause a destructive run-in of slack. At any particular train speed, the resulting extended stopping distance elongates the necessary spacing between trains, limiting line capacity.

George Westinghouse himself felt at one point in the 1880s that only an electrically controlled brake transmitting the word at the speed of light instead of the speed of sound would be usable in long trains. He went ahead, however, and improved the quick-service feature of his brake to the extent that it has served faithfully in general freight service for over a century, postponing the complication of providing, maintaining, and hooking up reliable electrical connections between all the cars in a fleet numbering over one million.

In rapid transit and commuter railroad multiple-unit (MU) train service, where electrical connections between cars are required anyway, the electronically controlled pneumatic (ECP) brake has been in use in various forms since the early years of the 20th century. Freight trains are an entirely different story!

Availability of reliable, high-capacity two-wire communication technology has shifted the cost balance of ECP versus traditional air brakes to the point that one of the most significant advances in train performance in recent history is taking place: standardization of an ECP brake system for North American service and its gradual implementation across the interchange freight car fleet.

The ECP brake system, in accordance with performance and physical compatibility standards coordinated and established by the AAR, incorporates a two-wire trainline paralleling the existing trainline, which then becomes basically an air supply line for the service and emergency reservoirs on each car that continue to contain the muscle to control train speed (Fig. 6-5). An electronic control unit on each car, including battery backup, takes over all braking control functions in accordance with digitally coded signals transmitted over the 230 volt DC trainline from the locomotive cab. The intercar connector, a standardized design approved by the AAR, looks and functions similar to an air hose "glad hand" connector in that it can be connected quickly and separates automatically when cars are uncoupled.

ECP brake systems have consistently demonstrated reductions in stopping distance, depending on load and gradient, of 40 to as much as 70 percent. In conventional automatic air braking, once the brake pipe reduction triggers the brake application car by car, the buildup of brake cylinder pressure must be at a controlled rate to allow braking to the rear the time to take hold and soften the slack run-in. With ECP and its simulta-

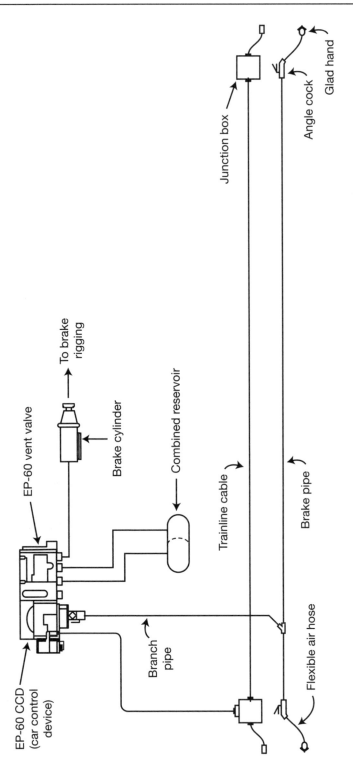

Fig. 6-5. Typical EP-60 arrangement [Courtesy of New York Air Brake]

neous electronic braking throughout the consist, the brake cylinder pressure buildup can be unrestricted.

ECP brakes also provide graduated release (and application) and release throughout the range of service braking because it is the electronic signal rather than the brake pipe pressure that is controlling the applied braking force. Since release can be stopped at any point, retainer valves are not needed. Brake pipe pressure is available at all times to recharge the reservoirs and compensate for brake pipe and cylinder leakage. Circuit integrity throughout the length of the train is monitored every second; in the event of loss of signal (through break-in-two or whatever), each car goes into emergency. Malfunction of the control unit on an individual car, on the other hand, results in that car alone ceasing all braking activity, sending a diagnostic signal to the cab advising the engineer of the loss of that portion of the train's braking capacity.

Initial testing of ECP brakes in revenue service took place on unit coal, solid double-stack and other captive-equipment trains that could be equipped and operated a train at a time. In such service, ECP's benefits in safety, increased allowable speed, reduced slack action, reduced wheelset casualties (e.g., freedom from stuck brakes and shelled or slid-flat wheels) and costs were assessed without regard to compatibility for fleetwide application. (One example of costs could possibly be some increased brake shoe wear when engineers find train handling with the train brake is smoother than with the locomotive's dynamic brake.) Up until 2006, charting an optimum path—whether selective, voluntary, or mandated—toward general-service adoption of ECP brakes constituted a challenge. One reason was that differences in performance between the two systems are so great that operation of mixed consists (nonequipped cars on the rear) during a transition was not considered feasible.

In 2007, following an exhaustive cost-benefit analysis, the Federal Railroad Administration embarked on a rulemaking proceeding with the intent of providing the railroads and their suppliers the means to move forward with fleetwide application of ECP brakes—a process that is expected to take 10 to 15 years. The FRA's strategy, developed jointly with railroads and suppliers, calls for ECP implementation to begin with unit coal trains in captive-fleet service, progress to intermodal trains, and conclude with merchandise cars in general interchange service. The FRA's granting of waivers to the established Code of Federal Regulations, such as permitting trains equipped with ECP brakes to travel up to 3,500 miles between routine brake tests—more than double the current minimum distance—to individual railroads for specific operations, are part of this process.

Track-Train Dynamics

A 150-car train of mixed loads and empties stretches more than a mile and a half. When starting up, the locomotive will move about 75 ft before the last car even quivers. Drawbar pull in moving the weight of, for example, 9,500 tons on level track is about 25 tons, more than the weight of some of the cars in the train. Most track is not level, however, but is a series of ups and downs. When the rear of the train is on a 1.0 percent downgrade and the forward half is headed uphill at the same rate, there will be a net compression at mid-train of about 30 tons, pushing the slack in and compressing the draft gears. This compressed section of train must shift along the consist as it moves over grades. Add in the effects of curves, braking time lags, cars of different weight and with short- or long-travel cushioning, and the dynamics of this enormous snake becomes most complex. This is, of course, an extreme situation. When proper train-handling methods are observed, when long car–short car coupling locations are regulated, and extreme "loads-rear, empties-forward" situations are avoided, then track-train dynamics problems can be minimized.

Ideally, trainmasters would like to make up trains according to where the cars are going, rather than by where they must go in the consist to stay on the track. They would also like every engineer to have the experience and skill to be able to run any train smoothly, safely, and quickly over the division.

Train-Dynamics Analysis

Fortunately, it is now practical to study by computer analysis the effects of train makeup and handling by calculating the forces developed and absorbed by the components of each car as it moves along a representation of the grades and curves on any specific rail route. In-train forces developed can be determined with good accuracy, and the limits of train-handling technique in minimizing run-in and run-out forces can be worked out for favorable and unfavorable arrangements of light and heavy, short and long cars within the train. Using test data on individual car behavior in TTCI (Transportation Technology Center, Inc.) experiments with instrumented cars subjected to pull and buff forces up to 250,000 lbs between multiple-unit locomotives while on curves and grades, the train forces can be interpreted in terms of the margin of safety against derailment.

The L/V Ratio

The key factor is the ratio of lateral forces on each wheel to the vertical load holding it down to the rail. This value reflects the combination of: the weight of the car; the bounce, rock, and other dynamic effects on the truck suspension; weight shifts between axles from braking and train forces; brake shoe reactions; and (usually most important) the effects of lateral coupler forces as affected by the angle of the coupler shanks through which pull and buff forces must reach the car. Fig. 6-6 shows some examples of critical L/V ratios for a car with a high (98 in.) center of gravity. The rail-overturn figure is conservative since it assumes the rail has no stiffness against twisting (which would let the weight of other wheels help keep it upright).

With respect to rail climb, limits can be more closely determined under a variety of wheel and rail contour conditions with the AAR TLV (Track Loading Vehicle). This research car, riding safely on its two trucks, has a central wheelset that can be loaded to any desired combination of lateral and vertical loads to find the ratio at which it actually does leave the rail.

Vehicle/Track Dynamics—On the Road

To cope with increasingly severe train-dynamics problems associated with major increases in locomotive power and train tonnage associated with the general adoption of the 100-ton car in the early 1970s, a Train Track Dynamics Program coordinated by rail industry, supplier, and regulatory organizations in the United States and Canada developed train makeup and handling principles and practices based on state-of-the-art analyses, ongoing test programs, and the distilled experience of participating railroads.

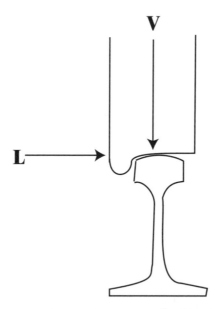

Effect	Lateral to vertical wheel force ratio
Incipient wheel climb (new rail)	1.29
Incipient wheel climb (worn rail)	0.75
Rail overturn	0.64
Wheel lift (zero speed on superelevation)	0.82

Fig. 6-6. The L/V ratio

These were widely disseminated and applied through "implementation officers" on individual railroads, often resulting in dramatic reductions in break-in-twos, derailments, and other incidents. Since 1987, industry-government research into this performance-critical matter of understanding and controlling interactions between train and roadway has continued under TTCI's Vehicle Track Systems program.

Such programs proved extremely important in developing throttle and brake-handling procedures compatible with the reduction or elimination of the *stretch braking* procedure long used to control train slack and prevent break-in-twos over difficult (undulating) track profiles. Applying locomotive power and train brakes simultaneously, often over a considerable portion of a run, obviously could rub away a lot of brake shoe material, as well as burn up an amount of fuel totally unacceptable once the price per gallon increased sharply. Working out ways to get over the railroad in one piece without stretch braking was much more a matter of computation than full-scale trial and error. With the aid of simulators for training, some modifications in train makeup, aids such as consist tonnage–distribution printouts or displays, and detailed procedures for anticipating and minimizing slack action, many railroads were able to virtually eliminate stretch braking by the early 1980s.

An increasingly infrequent but still important use for the latest in-train performance programs is derailment analysis, a powerful supplement to track and wreckage inspection in assessing in-train forces and achieving probable-cause determinations precise enough to lead to effective preventive operating and maintenance practices.

Simulators

A sophisticated descendent of the relatively limited-performance simulators used by an increasing number of railroads since the middle 1960s to supplement road experience in locomotive engineer training is the FRA-financed RALES (Research and Locomotive Evaluator/Simulator) at the Illinois Institute of Technology Research Institute in Chicago. Built to be capable of conducting research on crew performance under fatigue and stress factors characteristic of a full over-the-road tour of duty, it supplements front/side/roadway cab-view displays with continuously programmable multi-axis cab motion and noise environment. It (and simpler versions incorporating route and signal displays based on more economical new technology such as digital video) is being kept busy training and retraining engineers in routine and emergency train handling with consists and over routes realistically representative of any over which they may be called upon to drive trains. Several railroads now employ training simulators of their own.

Locomotive Cab Displays

Many railroads have been providing locomotive engineers with a printout graphically profiling car-by-car weights along with consist length and tonnage figures affecting train handling. In common with the increasingly prevalent use of onboard microprocessors in conjunction with locomotive power control, diagnostics, and PTC (Positive Train Control), various computerized cab displays intended to enhance the engineer's ability to get over the road swiftly but smoothly and safely have been introduced. Several types continuously display the consist as it moves across a profile of the railroad, helping to prevent track authority and speed limit violations and unauthorized entry into work zones. PTC systems monitor and enforce train-crew compliance with operating instructions. Using an onboard geographic database and GPS (global positioning system) data, such systems can continuously calculate warning and braking curves based on speed, location, movement authority, speed restrictions, work zones, and consist restrictions. One has been developed to provide data on train acceleration/deceleration and predicted braking pressure and draft gear forces throughout the consist.

Signals and Communication

The railroad is classified as a "single degree of freedom" mode of transport, that is, rail vehicles can only go back and forth along the "guideway." With only this one degree of freedom in which to maneuver, attaining high-unit capacity and safety in all types of weather depends on a control system that keeps its vehicles in proper relation to each other. If paths cross or vehicles overtake each other from the same or opposite directions, a collision is inevitable.

The steam railroad was the first system where speeds could be high enough for stopping distance to exceed sighting distance; therefore, a clear track had to be assured by some means other than an alert driver. The railroad pioneered the development of several principles and techniques that today form the basis for all successful traffic control systems.

Scheduling and Dispatching

In the 19th century, American railroads quickly evolved to operation by timetable. Many of the lines were single track, so meeting points had to be established at stations where there were sidings, and the short trains of the time meant that traffic was rather dense in terms of number of trips per day. Delaying one train essentially paralyzed the line, since a train had no alternative but to wait until the train it was required to meet eventually showed up. In turn, it would delay all the following trains, which couldn't move until it came through.

Timetable and Train-Order Operation (T&TO)

In 1851, Superintendent Charles Minot of the Erie used his recently installed telegraph line to issue the first train order—a message changing the meeting point between

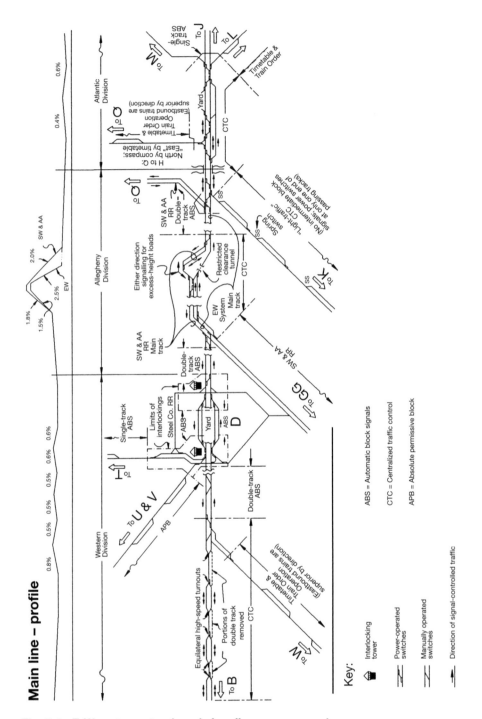

Fig. 7-1. E-W system—track and signaling arrangement

two trains, to the benefit of both, but doing it safely by first determining that the train being held at the meeting point had in fact "got the word." Minot had to run the train himself, since the engineer would have no part of disobeying the timetable. This organized system of train dispatching by "timetable and train order" (T&TO) was rapidly adopted due to the significant benefits. Procedures were standardized by committees of the Standard Rules Convention, forerunner of today's Association of American Railroads (AAR).

Train Orders—Revisited

In common with most railroads in the United States since the mid-1980s, our hypothetical East-West Railroad (E-W) has dispensed with train orders and now dispatches trains by Track Warrant Control (TWC) or Direct Train Control (DTC) rules on lines not equipped with Centralized Traffic Control (CTC). A bit of background in the principles underlying T&TO and manual block signaling is necessary in understanding how these new systems work.

Rules were developed over the years to specify the form of train orders and eliminate any uncertainty about their meaning while ensuring accurate transmission, delivery, and observance. Train movements are authorized only by the current employees' timetable and orders issued by the train dispatcher. T&TO is safe but time consuming; it takes about 35 pages in the Book of Rules to define the process, which until 1985 satisfied the E-W for moving a few heavy trains per day over its single-track line from W to C (Fig. 7-1).

Superiority by Direction

Many of the rules governing T&TO operation must relate to "superiority of trains" (mainly, which train will take siding at a meeting point). Misinterpretation of these rules can be a source of either hazard or delay. The employee's timetable specifies the class of each train (first, second, and so on) and which direction (eastbound or westbound, for example) is superior to the other when trains of the same class meet.

Time Spacing

For trains following each other, T&TO operation must rely upon time spacing and flag protection to keep each train off the back of its predecessor. A train may not leave a station less than 5 minutes after the preceding train has departed. There's no assurance that this spacing will be retained as the trains move along the line, so the flagman (rear brakeman) of a train slowing down or stopping will light and throw off a 5-minute red flare *(fusee),* which may not be passed by the next train. If the train has to stop, the flagman must trot back with a red flag or a lantern for a sufficient distance to protect the train, remaining there until the train is ready to move. The flagman was called back (in preradio days) by whistle signal—four long blasts to return from west or south, five from east or north, plus one toot per track number if in multiple-track territory, to be sure only the right flag came in.

A fusee and two track torpedoes provide protection as the flagman scrambles back and the train resumes speed. The system works, but it depends on a series of human activities and is no fun in bad weather.

Safety and Capacity—Block Signaling

It is perfectly possible to operate a railroad safely without signals, and about half of the route-miles in the United States make do without them. Most of this mileage, of course, represents branch-line trackage, usually occupied by only one train at a time. The purpose of signal systems is not so much to increase safety as it is to step up the efficiency and capacity of a line in handling traffic. Nevertheless, it's convenient to discuss signal system principles in terms of the three types of collisions they must prevent—rear-end, side-on, and head-on.

Manual Block Signaling

Block signal systems prevent a train from ramming the train ahead by dividing the main line into segments *(blocks)* and allowing only one train in a block at a time, with block signals indicating whether or not the block ahead is occupied. In very early applications, a human operator controlled each signal, and the system was called *manual block.* Great reliance was placed on three things: (1) the operators, (2) clear communication with adjacent operators, and (3) accurate record keeping. Minimum train spacing was dependent on the spacing of block stations. One advantage was that additional temporary block stations could be added fairly easily to handle heavy seasonal traffic, but the system is labor intensive and subject to human error.

Nevertheless, manual block does afford a high degree of safety, and federal rules allow a maximum speed of 79 mph in manual-block territory, compared to 59 mph for passenger trains and 49 mph for freight trains, in *dark* (no signals) territory. Our E-W Railroad operated the line from V and U to D based on those speeds. This route, which is usually not very busy, experiences seasonal traffic "rushes," during which additional block stations were assigned operators to keep things moving.

Automatic Block Signaling (ABS)

The block signaling that does the most for increasing line capacity is automatic block signals, in which the trains control the signals. The presence or absence of a train is determined by the track circuit. Invented by Dr. William Robinson in 1872, the track circuit's key feature is that it is *fail safe*. If the battery or any wire connections fail, or if a rail is broken, the relay can't pick up, and a clear signal will not be displayed (Fig. 7-2). The relatively simple ABS works well when trains operate in only one direction on a track, but ABS requires double track to move trains in both directions. Other operating methods can be used if trains have to run "against the normal direction," especially in emergencies, but a better solution was developed around 1918.

Absolute Permissive Block (APB)

APB is an ingenious arrangement of circuit functions among individual automatic block signals between passing tracks for signaling in both directions. These circuits can determine the direction in which a train is moving and act to put all opposing signals from one passing track to the next at red as soon as a train heads out onto single track. At the same time, they will allow signals behind the train to clear as it passes from block to block, allowing following trains to move along without delay. The name is from the system design using *absolute* (stop) signals controlling trains leaving sidings, and *permissive* (stop-and-proceed) signals in between. This system is used in areas with single track and passing sidings, such as between D and V.

Vital Circuits

The track circuit is also an example of what is designated in railway signaling practice as a *vital circuit,* one that must operate properly to prevent an unsafe indication even if some of its components malfunction in certain ways. The track circuit is fail safe, but it could still give a "false-clear" indication should its relay stick in the closed or "picked up" position. Vital-circuit relays, therefore, are built to very stringent standards: they are large devices; they rely only on gravity (no springs) to drop the armature; and they use special nonwelding contacts that will not stick together if hit by a large surge of current (as from nearby lightning).

Track Circuit Adjustment

Getting a track circuit to be absolutely reliable is not a simple matter. The electrical leakage between the rails is considerable and varies greatly with the seasons of the year and the weather. The joints in bolted-rail track are bypassed with bond wires to ensure

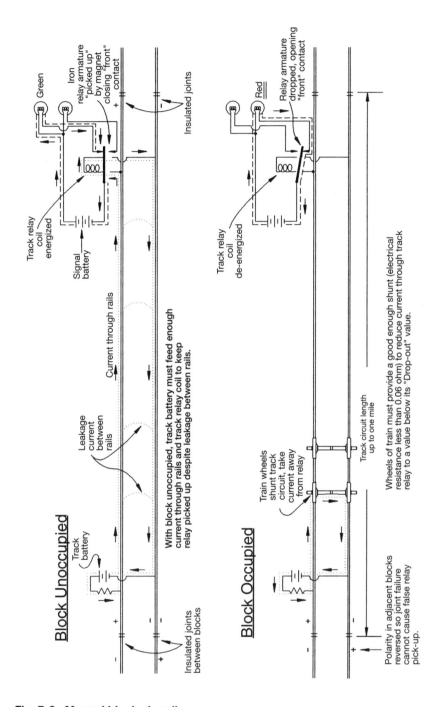

Fig. 7-2. Manual block signaling

low resistance at all times, but total resistance still varies. It is lower, for example, when cold weather shrinks the rails, and they pull tightly on the track bolts or when hot weather expands the rail to force the ends together tightly.

Battery voltage is limited to 1 to 2 volts, requiring a fairly sensitive relay. Despite this, the direct current track circuit can be adjusted to do an excellent job, and false-clear indications are extremely rare.

The principal improvement in the basic circuit has been to use slowly pulsed DC so that the relay drops out and must be picked up again continually when the block is un-occupied. This allows use of a more sensitive relay that will detect a train but additionally work in track circuits twice as long (about 2 miles) before leakage between the rails begins to threaten reliable relay operation.

Insulated Joints

The insulated joints defining block limits (usually used in dual sets in case one should get leaky) must be of rugged construction and are now frequently bonded with the toughest plastic adhesives available in addition to being secured with permanently crimped bolts. An alternative is the use of tuned audio-frequency track circuits that can do the job without insulated joints, which will be discussed later.

Signal and Train Spacing

Fig. 7-3 shows the situations determining the minimum block length for the standard "two-block, three-indication" ABS system. Since a train may stop with its rear car just inside the rear boundary of a block, a following train will first receive warning just one block-length away. By law, no allowance may be made for how far the signal indication is seen by the engineer. So the block must be as long as the longest stopping distance (with a service application, *not* an emergency brake application) for any train on the route, traveling at its maximum authorized speed.

Track Capacity

From this standpoint, it is important to allow trains to move along without receiving any *approach* indications that will force them to slow down. This requires a train spacing of two block lengths—twice the stopping distance—since the signal can't clear until the train ahead is completely out of the second block. If heavily loaded trains running at high speeds (with their long stopping distances) are in the picture, block lengths must be long, and it may not be possible to get enough trains over the line to produce appropriate revenue.

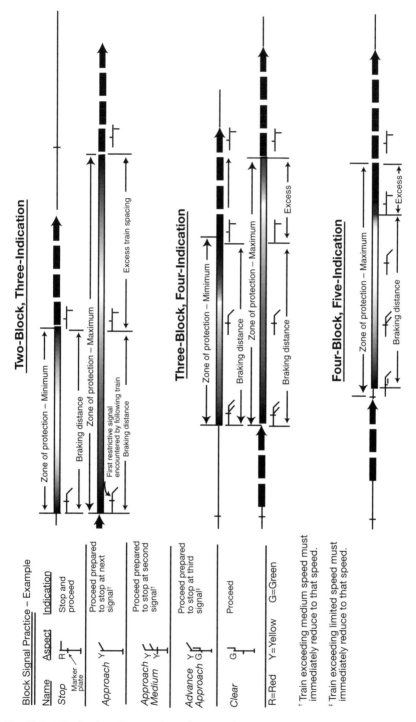

Fig. 7-3. Block signaling and track capacity

Multi-Aspect Signaling

The "three-block, four-indication" signaling (Fig. 7-3) reduces the "excess" train spacing by 50 percent. With warning two blocks to the rear, signal spacing needs to be only half the braking distance. In particularly congested areas, such as downgrades where stopping distances are long and trains are likely to bunch up, four-block, five-indication signaling may be provided. *Advance approach, approach medium,* and *approach and stop* indications give a minimum of three-block warning, allowing further block shortening, and keep things moving.

Signal Aspects and Indications

Fig. 7-4 uses symbols based on *upper-quadrant* semaphores to illustrate block signaling. These signals, with the blade rising 90 degrees to give the clear indication, began to replace the *lower-quadrant* semaphores in the early 1900s and are still used in diagrams to show available aspects on each signal head. Since World War I, when electric lamps and lens systems bright enough to be seen against the sun were developed, most new wayside signals have used lamps displaying the same aspects day and night, avoiding the maintenance of the moving semaphore arm that still had to be supplemented with lamps and lenses at night.

Fig. 7-4 shows some of the signal aspects developed by different railroads. The aspect is the appearance of a signal (the color used and the position of the colors); each aspect tells the train engineer exactly one thing—the indication. Within the general rules discussed below, a railroad is free to establish the simplest and most easily maintained system of aspects and indications that will keep traffic moving safely and meet any special requirements due to geography, traffic pattern, or equipment.

Aspects such as flashing yellow for *approach medium,* for example, may be used to provide an extra indication without an extra signal head. This is safe because a stuck flasher will result either in a steady-yellow *approach* or the more restrictive light-out aspect.

Special Aspects

Systemwide aspects are illustrated in the Book of Rules. The signal-system rules in effect on each segment of line and each track (shown in Fig. 7-1), along with rules for any special signal indications at particular locations, are established by the Employees' Timetable and are decided for each division. The important thing, of course, is that there be no uncertainty whatsoever about the meaning of a signal.

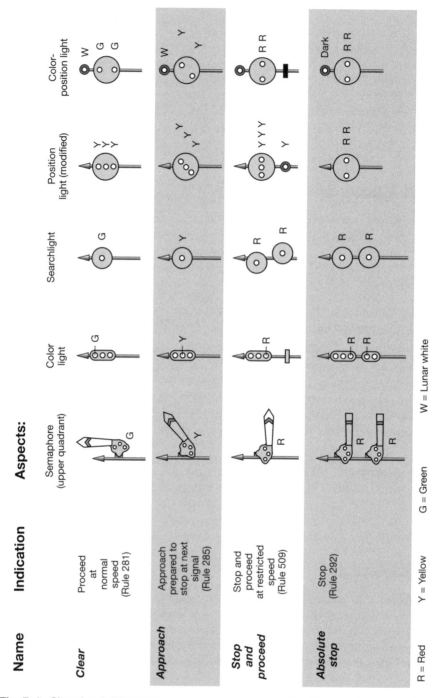

Fig. 7-4. Signals of different types — examples of indications and aspects, interlocking and automatic block signal rules

General Design Rules

Some rules regarding signaling practices are established and enforced by the FRA as law. An example is prohibiting the use of white as a *clear* aspect—a missing colored lens would give a false indication. Other recommended practices come from the work of the Signal Section of the AAR (now AREMA Communications & Signals). To abide by the "fail-safe" rule, most two-light aspects are arranged so that the absence of either light will result in a more restrictive indication; if this is not the case, a filament-checking circuit must be used so that a burned-out bulb will either cause the signal to "go red" or be completely extinguished. By rule, a dark signal must be regarded as being at the most restrictive aspect possible.

Absolute and Permissive Signals

Automatic block signals, whose purpose is to prevent rear-end collisions, have as their most restrictive indication *stop and proceed.* Once the train has come to a stop, it is permitted to proceed at restricted speed (usually 15 mph maximum) but must be prepared to stop short of any obstruction (a train, broken rail, or open switch) that has caused the red signal to be displayed. The permissive nature of a signal must be identified by the presence of a number plate on the mast or a second marker light in a staggered position (Fig. 7-4). A marker light or second signal head in vertical position with respect to the main signal is an "absolute" signal, such as at a junction or at the end of a passing track, which indicates that a conflicting movement has been authorized and requires that an approaching train stop and *stay* stopped. Only the authority of a specific train order can pass such a "stop and stay" signal.

Grade Signals

On an ascending grade, a tonnage train (one carrying its full rated load) will have a difficult time starting again if it's stopped by a block signal. Since its stopping distance on the grade is short, it can safely be allowed to proceed past a "stop and proceed" signal at restricted speed without a stop. Signals where this is the case are marked, usually with a "P" (for permissive) or "G" (for grade).

Cab Signaling

The earliest industrial use of electronics outside of communication systems was in the early 1920s in the form of cab signaling of "steam" railroads. By using a slow-pulsed AC, it was possible for the signal system to send a continuous message through the rails to a receiver-amplifier on the locomotive. Bringing the signal indication inside the cab where it cannot be obscured by fog and providing an audible alarm to further alert the engine crew to a restrictive indication increases the safety factor. The most attractive feature is that it allows a train to resume speed promptly when a block is cleared, even though the signal may not become visible for some distance. Subsequent improvements in electronic technology have allowed use of DC or audio-frequency transmission through the rails.

Automatic Train Stop (ATS)

Systems for automatically stopping the trains were a popular subject for inventors even before reliable train brakes had gone into general use. Systems using a mechanical trip that hits a brake actuator on the train are successfully used in rapid transit systems *when* all the equipment is alike, the right-of-way is protected, and ice is not a problem. In these systems, the mechanical trip moves out of the way only when the signal is clear. The first relatively satisfactory ATS for steam railroading was the intermittent inductive system of the late 1920s. In this scheme, a magnetic device on the locomotive passes near and is actuated by an iron lineside "inductor," unless the effect of the inductor is nullified by an electromagnet inside. The magnet is energized only if the block signal is clear. Since ATS provides only an on-off control, it must take effect at the first restrictive signal, where there is still stopping distance. Before passing the restrictive signal, the engineer has a few seconds to retain control of the brakes by operating a "forestalling" lever. If the engineer fails to do so, or if the forestalling lever is held down more than 15 seconds, a "penalty application" of the air brakes will occur.

Automatic Train Control (ATC)

More precise automatic supervision of train operation is available with continuous-coded automatic train control in which pulses at various repetitive rates in the rails are decoded by a receiver on the train and used to ensure that train speed is brought into accord with *approach-medium, approach,* or *stop* indications. ATC systems, usually in combination with cab signaling, are in use on several thousand miles of the most heavily traveled routes, such as Amtrak's Boston–New York–Washington Northeast Corridor. By an ICC (now FRA) order of 1951, train speeds in excess of 79 mph are permitted only where ATS, ATC, or cab signals are in use.

Interlocking

So far, we have considered signal systems designed to prevent rear-end collisions. Once turnouts and crossings were developed so that tracks could branch from or across each other, it became apparent that some way of assuring a clear route was needed if trains were to take advantage of their speed capabilities. The answer was developed as early as 1857, to prevent side-on and some types of head-on collisions.

Railroad Crossings at Grade

At places where two (or more) railroad tracks cross each other at the same level, the law requires a "statutory stop" to verify that the way is clear before a train can proceed, unless the crossing is protected by an "interlocking plant." Operation was originally completely mechanical, with the levers in the control tower connected by long runs of "rodding" (actually pipe) to cranks that worked the signal arms and track switches. Later systems used pneumatics that were easier to operate. In the "interlocking machine" (some of which are still in use), "tappets" and "dogs" on locking bars between the levers make it physically impossible to work the levers in clearing a route in anything but the proper sequence; signals must be at stop and derails open on the conflicting routes before the signal can be moved to "clear" from its normal stop position. Throwing a track switch under a train had to be avoided, so a complex arrangement of detector bars was included that, when held down by the presence of wheels, impeded the movement of the levers. As soon as reliable track circuits became available, they replaced the detector bars for this occupancy-locking purpose.

Electric and Microprocessor Interlocking

Interlocking functions are now generally performed electrically by vital-circuit relays controlling power switches and signals, but the functions remain the same. To prevent all possible accidents, a number of distinct types of locking are required. For example, the system must also assure that any train approaching at maximum speed has had time to stop clear of the route being set up before it can be changed. This is handled by time or approach locking requiring an appropriate delay (typically up to 5 minutes) after a signal is placed at stop before any signal can allow changes in routes. Since microprocessors can perform the logic functions of an interlocking at lower cost and in a minute fraction of the space required for relay systems, demonstrating that they can be at least equally safe in such vital functions has been a long-time goal of signal suppliers. Continuous, enormously complex self-checking routines are required to ensure that no failure mode, including power loss and lightning surges, can allow the system to fail to "remember" the presence and status of every train, switch, and signal. The first vital microprocessor application was in a basic time-delay relay, and the first complete "microprocessor" interlockings went into service in 1985. Microprocessor interlockings do include one vital relay to implement system fail-safe by cutting off all power to signals and switches when any of the digital logic checking turns up a discrepancy.

Junctions

To take care of junctions where trains are diverted from one route to another, the signals must control train speed. A train traveling straight through must be able to travel at full speed. Diverging routes will require some limit, depending on the turnout numbers (Fig. 3-13) and the track curvature, and the signals must control train speed to match.

Route or Speed Signaling?

One approach would be to have signals indicate which route has been set up and cleared for the train. American practice is to use speed signaling, in which the signal indicates not where the train is going but rather what speed is allowed through the interlocking. If this is less than normal speed, distant signals must also give warning so that the train can be brought down to this speed in time. Fig. 7-5 shows typical signal aspects and indications as they would appear to an engineer on the E-W approaching H from the west. Once a route is established and the signal cleared, route locking must ensure that nothing can be changed to reduce the route's speed capability from the time that the train approaching it is committed to enter until the train has cleared the last switch. Additional refinements to the basic system to speed up handling trains in rapid sequence include sectional route locking, which unlocks portions of the route as soon as the train has cleared so that other routes can be set up promptly. Interlocking signals also function as block signals to provide rear-end protection.

Automatic and Route Interlocking

At isolated crossings of two railroads at grade, an automatic interlocking can respond to the approach of a train by clearing its route, if there are no opposing movements cleared or in progress. Automatic interlocking returns everything to stop after the train has passed. Busy, complex interlockings, such as at the throat of a busy commuter train terminal, may be handled by automated route interlocking, allowing one operator to take care of traffic that would require several levermen and a supervisor, if each switch and signal had to be thrown individually. Pushing a button at the entrance and another at the exit of a route causes the machine to locate the best (highest speed) path that's available, to set up all switches in that route, and to clear the signal. Other situations that must include interlocking protection if trains are to proceed without statutory stops or flag protection include drawbridges and "gantlets" (sections of double track on bridges or in tunnels where the two lines overlap or are so close together that only one train can pass at a time).

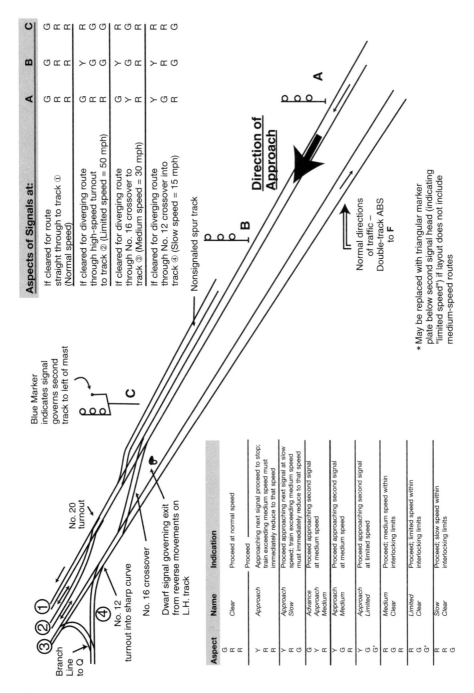

Fig. 7-5. Example of speed signaling in approach to a junction (East-West system, eastbound at west end of H)

Train Operation by Signal Indication

Where all trackage in a territory is controlled by block signals and interlockings, it is common practice to institute operation by signal indication, superseding the superiority of trains and eliminating the necessity for train orders in moving trains on designated tracks in the same direction (Rule 251) or in both directions (Rule 261). In effect, all trains become "extras," and instructions for their movement are conveyed directly by the signal system as supervised by the dispatcher, directly or through the block and interlocking station operators.

Centralized Traffic Control

When a system is so arranged that the dispatcher controls the throwing of switches and the clearing of signals for train operation by signal indication from a machine in the office, the terms TCS (Traffic Control System) and CTC (Centralized Traffic Control) are used to describe the system. On many sections of double track where trains move along under block-signal protection with few stops and rarely pass each other or encounter other interruptions, timetable and train order operation is satisfactory in moving heavy traffic without serious delay; in practice, only occasional train orders are needed. Such a section of the E-W as that from C to E (Fig. 7-1) continues to be operated under double-track and block-signal and interlocking rules. Most trains travel in the "normal direction of traffic" on the right-hand track; train orders are issued when track work or serious delay requires a left-hand movement. For heavily traveled single-track lines or congested sections of multi-track routes, however, CTC is usually the answer.

Single track with CTC is considered to have about 70 percent of the traffic-handling capability of ABS double track, so the E-W line between B and C, like thousands of miles of other main line in the United States, has been so converted. Pulling up some of the second track but leaving long "passing track" sections connected with high-speed turnouts reduces track investment, maintenance, and taxes while improving the flexibility of handling traffic that must move at much different speeds in the same direction (piggyback trains versus ore extras). About 50,000 miles of line on U.S. railroads are so controlled.

CTC Controls

Controls for an extensive section of line are located on a panel with a diagram of the trackage. The dispatcher plans the moves based on lights that show the locations of all trains. The orders are implemented by sending instructions to what are, in effect, interlocking plants at the ends of each passing siding. The dispatcher gives instructions by turning a knob and pushing a button; when the switch points have shifted or the signal has cleared dozens or hundreds of miles away, a message is received that the action is complete.

Vital and Nonvital Circuits

CTC was originally made economically feasible, starting about 1930, by pulse-code technology making it practical to control all the signals and switches in an extended territory over only two line wires; today much CTC control goes by microwave. These are "nonvital" circuits that can use up-to-date electronics to speed up, simplify, and reduce the cost of transmitting information because safety is not involved. The vital-circuit relays that are out in the field control and interlock switches, signals, and track circuits so that the points cannot be thrown in the face of an approaching train, and the signal indications correspond to the route lined up, and so on. The CTC machine is arranged so that it cannot send out conflicting messages, such as trying to clear signals in both directions on the same track. Should any such instructions get through, the local APB circuitry would prevent conflicting messages from affecting safety.

Control Centers

A logical (though not universally chosen) extension of CTC is to consolidate installations to the point where the entire railroad is dispatched from one room. In Fig. 7-6 such a center is shown built "from scratch" to control all trains operating on more than 25,000 route-miles of railroad, including both CTC and "dark" territory (see DTC/TWC under "Radio-Based Manual Block Control"). Its assigned personnel, computers, and communications systems also handle virtually all related operations-department functions such as crew calling and motive power assignment. In common with modern CTC practice, the "big picture" of traffic throughout the railroad is displayed where all dispatchers and managers can see it, with detailed displays and controls for individual sections of line called up on each dispatcher's monitors for action as required. (Modern CTC practice is where the nonvital "office" functions of maintaining control displays, generating commands, and communicating with the field interlockings have always used electronic technology of the current generation—from individual transistors through microcircuits to touch-control panels, microprocessors, and projection TV.)

Computer-Aided Dispatching

With the advent of digital minicomputers of lowered cost but steadily increasing computing speed and memory capacity, varying degrees of computer-aided dispatching have become commonplace. The CTC system may, for example, recognize the need for a meet between two opposing trains, calculate the best meeting point from the

Fig. 7-6. Union Pacific's Harriman Control Center

trains' anticipated performance (based on horsepower per ton and route characteristics), check progress as the trains approach each other, and (subject to override by the dispatcher at any point) send switch and signal instructions to the field to execute the meet. The computer may also free up dispatcher time for overall planning by taking care of much record keeping and paperwork, such as generating the "train sheet" (OS) record of all movements required by law.

Computer Control

For rapid transit systems where trains making many stops are operated on extremely close headway, various degrees of "computer control" have been developed. Supervision of overall system performance, including regulation of the speeds and station-stop times of individual trains, may be provided, along with automatic spotting of the train at platforms, station announcements and so on, leaving the onboard operator in a monitoring and emergency manual control role. However, all successful systems of this type still separate the functions of automatic train operation (ATO) from those of ATC; that is, the computer-controlled ATO tells the train how to proceed, but it will only do so to the extent that the vital-circuit ATC has independently assured the computer that it is safe to do so.

Communications

From the very beginning of railroading, communication has been recognized as a key element. Superintendent Charles Minot was so sure that Morse's new telegraph would be crucial in running his railroad that he had already put up poles and strung wire alongside the Erie and was prepared to make his own illegal instruments if necessary, before he reached agreement with the inventor on providing service. The advent of telephone communication helped make operations a great deal more flexible; train crews could communicate with the dispatcher from wayside phone sheds without knowing Morse code. Allocation of VHF FM frequencies for railroad use after World War II and the development of portable radio equipment that could remain reliable under rugged conditions caused a rapid systemwide increase in radio communication between engine and caboose, and train and base stations.

Radio-Based Manual Block Control

Apart from the intermittent refinement in train-crew language caused by the need to observe FCC rules, use of radio has required great care in establishing procedures for its safe use. The dispatcher can plan meets much better by determining up-to-date positions and progress of a train from its crew rather than by calculations based only on the time reported at its last OS (train passing recorded "on sheet") point, but precluding disastrous actions based on mistaken identity or wrong assumptions from overheard conversations requires rigid rules.

Under proper safeguards established in the mid-1980s by individual railroads and subsequently standardized through the efforts of the AAR and interrailroad rulebook coordination organizations, new forms of manual-block control based on direct radio communication between dispatcher and train crew are in effect on most non-CTC trackage. As in the case of T&TO operation, in ABS-equipped territory, the signals are a safety overlay to the dispatching system.

Direct Train Control (DTC): In DTC, fixed blocks (marked by wayside signs and often extending from one passing track to the next) are established. Train crews receive exclusive authority to occupy one or more blocks by radio in a standard-format transmission recorded by a check mark on a pad form (Fig. 7-7); this authority takes effect only after being repeated back to and verified (names and numbers spelled out) by the dispatcher. Upon leaving the block, the crew releases it by a similar radio protocol.

Track Warrant Control (TWC): Under the TWC system, in designated territories, crews (including work crews and track inspection personnel in hi-rail vehicles) similarly can occupy main tracks only by possessing a "track warrant" or "movement authority" covering a precisely defined (by milepost, siding switch, or designated "control point") track segment of any length—often, to the next expected meeting point. Recently, new systems have been developed for crews and inspectors to request, and dispatchers to issue, such warrants or authorities electronically.

Advanced Train Control Systems (ATCS)

In the late 1980s, the Railway Association of Canada and the AAR coordinated an effort to inspire the use of new technology to enhance train-control capabilities across the spectrum of traffic densities while reducing system capital and maintenance costs. A team of railroad signal officers undertook the development of performance specifications for building blocks —hoping to attract competing suppliers' implementation ideas—from which advanced train-control systems (ATCS), matched to the needs of any route, could be assembled. Subsequently, installations in service on individual railroads have tended to veer off toward functions of particular interest, such as reporting detailed locomotive diagnostics or coordinating local-freight work orders, items not usually considered part of C&S (Communications and Signals).

Although the march of technology—especially, computer power—has accelerated, and performance specifications that guide important functions are in effect, no extensive installations exactly in line with any one of the contemplated ATCS systems were in service as of 2007. Important functions guided by performance specifications include integrating the ever expanding array of electronic controls and displays in the locomotive cab and standardizing lineside radio communication protocol to facilitate its substitution for more costly line wires or buried cable. Some systems have been placed in partial revenue service, some are still under test, and at least one project seems to have been canceled.

A location determination system on the locomotive is a common basis for versions of ATCS currently under test or being deployed in various locations under a variety of names (all subject to change) and various railroad, industry, or government sponsor-

TRACK WARRANT E W EAST-WEST R. R

No. 132 July 9 19XX

To: Extra 8172 West At: Elmore Yard

1. ☐ Track warrant number ______ is void.

2. ☒ Proceed from Elmore Yard To Lansford On ______ track.

3. ☐ Proceed from ______ To ______ On ______ track.

4. ☐ Work between ______ And ______ On ______ track.

5. ☐ Not in effect until ______ M.

6. ☐ This authority expires at ______ M.

7. ☐ Not in effect until after arrival of ______ at ______.

8. ☐ Hold main track at last named point.

9. ☐ Do not foul limits ahead of ______.

10. ☒ Clear main track at last named point.

11. ☐ Between ______ and ______

make all movements at restricted speed. Limits occupied by train or engine.

12. ☐ Between ______ and ______

make all movements at restricted speed and stop short of men or machines fouling track.

13. ☐ Do not exceed ______ MPH between ______ and ______.

14. ☐ Do not exceed ______ MPH between ______ and ______.

15. ☒ Protection as prescribed by Rule 99 not required.

16. ☐ Track bulletins in effect ______, ______, ______, ______, ______, ______, ______, ______, ______, ______, ______, ______.

17. ☐ Other specific instructions: ______

OK 2108 M Dispatcher EWK.

Relayed to ______ Copied by D. E. Brainz.

Limits reported clear at ______ M By ______.

(Mark X in box for each item instructed.)

Fig. 7-7. Track warrant — direct communication by radio from dispatcher to conductor

ships. Without requiring a flow of information from the dispatching center, this "black box" must know, continuously, where it is with respect to key locations, characteristics, and circumstances on the line (passing tracks, permanent and temporary speed restrictions, and maintenance work) affecting the authority of the train's movement to be displayed to the engineer. It must report this information to the dispatching center frequently, though not so often that it clogs up the radio link. To do its job, it must have in memory all details (track arrangements, curves, and grades) of the railroad line; with today's cheap gigabytes, this is no problem.

Selecting and perfecting an affordable system to do this is the nub of the development. Continuing reductions in GPS (Global Positioning System) transponders that are expected to locate the train within as little as 50 feet (still not precise enough to tell which track it's on) make this satellite-based technology a strong competitor when teamed with locomotive interrogation of fixed lineside transponders or even inertial sensors that can "feel" which direction the train has taken at a switch. An onboard odometer periodically zeroed by similar interrogator/transponder inputs to maintain the required locational precision is a more down-to-earth alternative.

Positive Train Control (PTC) and Communication-Based Train Control: These are names for similar systems in which various other features may be added to exploit the potential economic advantages of the continuous, precise train-location information provided in PTC. For example, in dark (unsignaled) territory, the number of track-warrant segments can be increased, shortening them to ABS proportions and safely increasing line capacity without the expense of track circuits—one of the original goals of the ATCS program.

Positive Train Separation (PTS): The dispatcher uses the computer to send the track-warrant authority to the locomotive's computer. After the engineer acknowledges it, the warrant is read back (as in the case of any train order) to verify receipt and correctness; it then takes effect. Failure to observe any speed restriction or the limit of authority results in a brake application. Another name for this class of system is *Electronic Track Warrant.*

Railroad Communication Networks

Like any business geographically far-flung, serving many customers, the railroad has a seemingly insatiable need for communication, which has been augmented within the last two decades by the use of centralized digital computation for both operational and business aspects. Large railroads now find their long-haul communication load heavily weighted toward digital data traffic. The heaviest routes may equate to 1,200 simultaneous voice circuits, a minor load in terms of the capacity of the communications-company-owned fiber-optic cables now located on tens of thousands of miles of railroad right-of-way. The economic advantages of railroad-owned microwave systems for long-haul communications may have eroded (particularly where some of the cable right-of-way rental has a large transmission capacity), but they may retain value for local traffic. Because of the remote locations of some relay and signal installations, railroads have pioneered the use of solar-panel power sources.

Other Signal Devices

Other devices or systems whose electrical or electronic nature places them under the responsibility of the Signal and Communications Department on most railroads include:

- Highway grade crossing warning flashers and gates
- Hotbox, hot wheel, and dragging equipment detectors
- Wheel impact load detectors (WILD)
- Truck performance detectors (TPD)
- Automatic Equipment Identification (AEI) readers

For maintenance of freight cars and track, an emerging philosophy in North America is to use actual test and detector results to determine when to remove faulty cars that damage the track and how to identify and correct poor track conditions that cause undesirable vehicle performance. The evolution of this philosophy can be attributed to the growing availability of such detection and testing technologies developed to measure and quantify vehicle-track interaction performance TPDs and WILDs. The AAR has developed the Advanced Technology Safety Initiative (ATSI) to optimize car maintenance. The "don't fix it until it's broke" reactive approach to freight car maintenance is rapidly being replaced by so-called "predictive" or "condition-based" maintenance, a *pro*active approach. Driven by the growing availability of these new detection and information exchange technologies, the AAR established ATSI in 2002 to develop new processes and systems for condition-based maintenance to reduce the dynamic forces that vehicles impose on track and structures, thus reducing maintenance and replacement costs.

Grade crossing warning flashers and gates. Except for the absolute safety of an underpass or overpass, flashing signals with automatic crossing gates provide the best available assurance against rail-highway collisions and continue to be added or updated at a rate of 1,500 or more per year. These installations require sophisticated circuitry to initiate the warning action sequence a safe distance ahead of the train but halt the sequence when the train has cleared the crossing. If nearby switching movements are common, manual controls are also needed to let the train crew start or release the warning and preserve their credibility and acceptability with the public. With the widespread use of welded track, the DC track-circuit installation requirement of four pairs of insulated joints has become an undesirable break in rail continuity. "Frequency Shift Overlay" circuits, operating in the low audio range around 1,000 Hz, may now be used. Since current at these frequencies will travel only a short, predictable distance along the rails before fading out, and since different frequencies can be used to cause a receiving relay to pick up only in response to current from one source, these systems can do the

Fig. 7-8. Wayside hotbox detector

job with uninterrupted rails. They can also detect the rate at which a train is approaching by how fast the current is being shunted by its wheels. A grade crossing predictor that lowers the gates a relatively constant time ahead of the arrival of trains traveling at widely different speeds is thus possible and now widely used. This technique is known as *constant warning time.*

Hotbox, hot wheel, and dragging equipment detectors. Fig. 7-8 shows a wayside infrared hotbox detector that scans the journal bearings of trains passing at any speed. Such detectors are typically maintained at intervals of 20 to 50 miles on main lines. The heat profile of each bearing (compensated for ambient temperature) is measured, with such techniques as comparison with the opposite bearing on the same axle used to determine if a bearing is dangerous. Also under development are acoustic defect detectors based on analysis of the sound spectrum emanating from the bearing, which typically will get noisy as failure approaches. If defects are detected, predominant current practice is to have the detector automatically radio a message to the passing train identifying axle numbers and side, a notification method compatible with cabooseless operation. Reliability of detection with these devices is generally high, with false alarms more of a problem than missed hot bearings; complete protection is not economically feasible with wayside detectors because the cost (typically $35,000 to $100,000 per installation) precludes spacing them so closely that a disastrous failure cannot occur within the time between detectors. Sound-spectrum analysis of roller bearings approaching failure suggests that an acoustic approach, considering current advances in real-time data processing, may ultimately lead to a solution.

Hot wheels (statistically much more frequent than hotboxes) result from stuck or unreleased brakes and can be similarly detected and reported. They are a hazard because of their potential for subsequent broken wheels,

Dragging equipment detectors are located ahead of major bridges and interlocking plants where the potential cost of any resulting accident is high. Rockslide detector fences alongside (and even overhead in vulnerable cuts) are connected to the block signal system to provide advance warning. High-water, earthquake-motion, shifted-load and high-car detectors are used in particular situations where the potential for hazard is high.

Wheel impact load detectors (WILD). Research has indicated that wheel-tread defects are highly damaging to the track structure, particularly if concrete ties are involved. (Wheel-tread defects include not only slid-flat wheels readily detected by inspection but also wheels with built-up or otherwise out-of-round contours resulting in even greater impact loads.) Microprocessor analysis of impact force data from strain gages mounted on the rail can detect such axles; transmission of this data to the next inspection point is a required link in the chain leading to a reduced population of such mavericks.

Truck performance detectors (TPD). A recent development, TPDs are capable of detecting excessive lateral *(hunting)* and vertical motion of a freight car truck.

Automatic Equipment Identification (AEI). Keeping track of millions of freight cars in interchange service has always been an expensive problem, basically handled

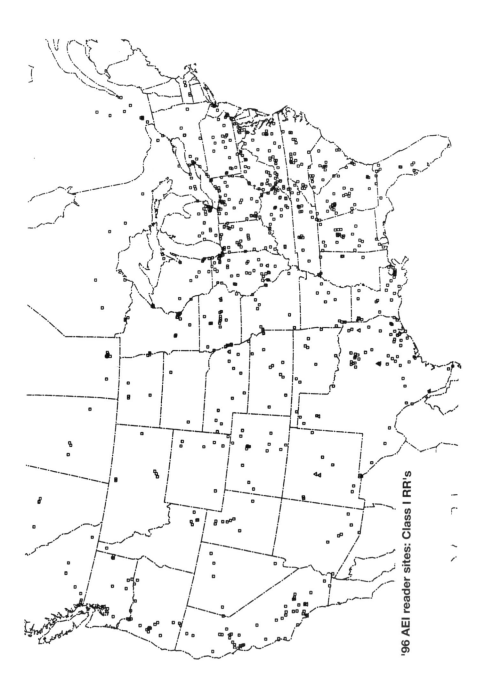

'96 AEI reader sites: Class I RR's

Fig. 7-9. Automatic Equipment Identification (AEI) reader sites

for the first 150-plus years of railroading by clerks walking yard tracks with clipboards, a process in later years sometimes moved out of the weather and into the yard office by closed-circuit monitoring of illuminated incoming consists creeping by a TV scanner. A 1960s AAR Automatic Car Identification (ACI) program mandated tagging of all cars in interchange with relatively inexpensive multicolor bar-code labels. Provided the car labels were kept reasonably clean, the optical scanning system, state of the art at the time, functioned reliably. The comparatively high cost of reader installations, however, resulted in less than universal use among major railroads. The label requirement was dropped and general railroad use of the optical system faded away in the early 1970s.

With the development of inert-transponder radio-frequency identification systems unaffected by grime and with the capability of reporting information in addition to reporting marks and car numbers, mandatory ACI tagging was reinstituted in 1992 as Automatic Equipment Identification (AEI) and was essentially completed on the existing freight car fleet within 3 years. With readers in service at more than 1,500 sites (Fig. 7-9) that are keeping tabs on locomotive units, end-of-train devices, and some intermodal equipment (in addition to freight cars), AEI is also being used to check equipment in and out of repair facilities and to update train consists and expedite interchange reporting. To reduce costs, readers are often co-located at defect-detector sites.

Railroad Operation— Moving From Here to There

Moving goods from here to there involves the transfer of cars from one road to another at a common junction point. This is called *interchange* or *interchange service*. If offered in interchange, a car complying with all interchange requirements must be accepted by an operating railroad.

During every business day, approximately 160,000 freight cars are loaded in the United States, Canada, and Mexico. Some are loaded with bulk commodities while in motion and without being uncoupled from their trains, and others have their loads placed aboard in piggyback trailers or in sealed containers that started their journey by highway or water. Somewhat more than half of these carloadings, however, are represented by shipments of an individual car or a small group of cars, loaded at a specific point where the contents were produced or processed, and destined for a consignee hundreds or thousands of miles away. The shipment may start its journey alone or coupled to other cars that are loaded at the same time or place but headed in other directions; the shipment will finish its trip at an unloading point where the contents will be consumed, processed, distributed, or sold.

With the rapid increase of regional and short line spinoffs of important secondary and branch lines, interchange service between railroads will remain typical of many shipments. Numerous mergers since 1980 have consolidated more and more long-haul traffic onto nine major systems in North America. As of 2007, the nine major systems are: BNSF Railway, CN, CP Rail, CSX, Ferromex, Kansas City Southern and its Mexican subsidiary, KCS de Mexico, Norfolk Southern and Union Pacific. As of 2005, an estimated 20 percent of all carloads (producing almost 50 percent of rail freight revenues) traveled over more than one company's lines. Frequently, a shipment will travel in a car belonging to none of the railroads over which it is routed.

The "Average" Freight Train

Statistics for the average freight train, of course, doesn't begin to describe the variety of operations involved in railroad freight movements. Consider the following freight train statistics: 69 cars carried 3,115 tons at an average speed (including all terminal and en route delays) of 18.6 mph to produce 58,000 net ton miles on Class I roads in 2005. Unit trains carrying 12,000 net tons in 110 cars may travel over 1,500 miles without a change in consist; intermodal trains may run at allowed speeds up to 70 mph over connecting railroads, stopping only at hub terminals to pick up and set out large blocks of cars. On the other hand, a car in a local freight may travel only a few miles at a jump and start out as the entire train consist. A large part of the railroad system's profitability depends upon arranging its operations so that most of the travel of individual shipments (average haul is 894 miles) is in trains of average or better proportions and performance.

Obviously, the labor and energy involved in a specific shipment will vary with the tonnage, distance, route, and handling involved. On the average in 2005, earning the carload's $1,500 in gross revenue required the expenditure of 13.6 hours of railroad-employee time in total—including maintenance-of-way and equipment, bringing back the empties, debugging computer programs, quoting freight rates, and so on. Total diesel fuel consumption for all movements (switching and road) amounted to 132 gallons for that hypothetical average revenue carload.

Follow One Carload

To get some idea of how this task of moving freight is accomplished year in and year out, we can examine in sequence the process of handling a carload from receipt to delivery, and later discuss rules and practices common to earlier regulatory circumstances and other classes of traffic.

Contract Rates

Notice that in keeping with partial deregulation of railroad traffic in the 1980s, roughly 70 percent of freight now moves under rates and terms set by contract between the railroad and shipper rather than on the pre-1980 basis of published tariffs and conditions proposed by railroad rate bureaus and approved or set by the Interstate Commerce Commission. Since the terms of a contract still need to cover the same matters as a tariff (exactly who will do what for whom for how much and when), the functions remain, although the terminology may be different. (The terms of a contract are not public information, except that summaries of the terms for those covering agricultural commodities must continue to be published.) By the terms of the ICC Termination Act of 1995, remaining regulatory aspects of rate setting and tariff publication for nonagricultural commodities were eliminated. Authority for review of the competitive consequences of, and setting conditions for, railroad merger proposals was retained by the Surface Transportation Board, which succeeded the ICC as an independent agency and is housed within the Department of Transportation.

Consequences of a century of regulation aimed at enforcing common-carrier access and equal treatment of small and large shippers tend to live on in the form of business practices that may seem archaic. These consequences include rigid prohibitions regarding the extension of credit or anything else that could look like a railroad "rebate" to a favored customer. The ancestry of some of these will be traced later as historical background.

The Paperwork Path; EDI

Tracing a single carload from origin to destination should provide some feeling for the "paperwork" that must accompany the physical transportation of the goods as well as some appreciation for the degree to which it may now be represented by computer displays and printouts rather than by typed forms. Much of the process described here has already been superseded by later technology (the twilight of the "IBM card") and references to local agents should be interpreted to refer to centralized customer service centers, since the function is now more likely to be accomplished remotely by data network, fax, or the Internet.

As was the case in the 19th century in the establishment of the system of Standard Time Zones, the railroad industry was a leader in the development and use of Electronic Data Interchange (EDI) standards for transmitting data from computer to computer, a protocol that has been widely adopted throughout the nation's commercial establishment.

On our hypothetical East-West Railroad (E-W), Jones Cannery is located on the E-W at city B (see system map, Fig. 2-1). Jones contacts the E-W's centralized customer service center or electronically transmits a request for a car to ship 100,000 lbs of canned goods to its customer, Smith Company, in the port city of AA. The E-W's Car Service Division will then pick out the appropriate car for placement at Jones Cannery's railroad siding. With a west to east shipment such as this, the Car Service Division will adhere to published car service rules and will most likely select an eastern line car so that the car will be heading back toward its home railroad.

They select a boxcar (identified as PR 123456) belonging to the Peninsular Railway because AA is in the same general direction as Peninsular trackage. While the E-W is using this particular boxcar, it is paying car hire (rent) to the Peninsular in the form of mileage and per diem charges, much the same as one would pay when renting an automobile.

After the car is obtained and inspected by the mechanical department to see if it's mechanically fit for loading, the car is then spotted by the switching crew to Jones' siding (more about switching in Chapter 11). On the E-W, the car is processed through the yard by the continuous automated inventory car location system and displayed on computer monitors.

Demurrage

Once the car has been delivered to Jones, it is subject to the demurrage rules. Demurrage is a tariff established and assessed by individual railroads to encourage shippers to load and unload quickly to get the cars back in revenue service. The customer generally has 24 hours to load and 48 hours to unload. The amount of time varies according to commodities, rate, and tariff applications. After the allotted time has expired, the customer is subject to a demurrage charge. The demurrage bill is issued by the centralized customer service center to the customer and is paid at that point.

Bill of Lading

Following receipt and loading of the car, Jones presents to the railroad a straight bill of lading. The bill of lading is a contract of carriage between Jones and the E-W. It is also Jones' receipt that states the customer has issued the railroad a carload of goods and a bill of lading. In most cases, the shipper pays the freight charges, so the bill of lading is marked "Prepaid." If the consignee is to pay the freight bill, the bill of lading is to be marked "Collect." Once the bill of lading is tendered by the shipper and received by the railroad, it is a legal contract, admissible in a court of law, in the event of any contention about the shipment. The legalities concerning bills of lading and agreements between shippers and transporters are spelled out in the law of bailments, often summarized in the "fine print" of most bills of lading.

There are several different types of bills of lading, but they all fall into one of two categories, *open* or *straight* and *order.* The open bill of lading is used for most collect and prepaid shipments. The order bill of lading comes into use when the shipper wants to be paid for his goods before the shipment is released to the consignee. The finances are taken care of by the shipper's and consignee's respective banks. Freight charges may be prepaid or collect. Other types of bills of lading include individualized forms used by the federal government and some private industries and export bills of lading.

Rating the Shipment

If the shipment is to be transported under a contract between railroad and shipper, its terms will determine the rate charged. In other cases, where deregulation means that a published, STB-approved tariff is not involved, if it is to do business, the railroad must establish and provide equivalent price information. This is most likely to be made available through the centralized, computerized REN (Rate EDI Network), which can be accessed by anyone with EDI data exchange capability. As discussed in this chapter under "Tariffs," determining the cost of a shipment is still not necessarily a simple matter.

Compiling a Waybill

When the E-W receives the bill of lading from Jones, the E-W rating system will rate the shipment, that is, the system will check the various tariff documents to find out the actual rate for the products Jones is shipping. From all the information received and determined to this point, the E-W makes up a waybill to help keep track of the car and shipment and to inform the rest of the railroad that the shipment is moving on the E-W system. A waybill contains, at a minimum, the following information:

- Car initial and number
- Waybill number, which is assigned to the freight agent by the railroad
- Waybill date
- Origin station
- Name of shipper
- Consignee, or customer at destination
- Destination city
- The route the car will travel
- The Standard Transportation Commodity Code, a seven-digit number assigned by the STB to a particular commodity
- Physical description of articles
- Weight of shipment
- Applicable rate
- Total freight charges (weight x rate = freight charges)
- Prepaid or collect
- Whether the shipment is perishable; if so, perishable instructions to be included

All of this information is fed into the E-W's computer in headquarters, which keeps track of all cars on the system, the freight being carried, and its destination.

The waybill is a contract between the railroads that are moving the shipment. The junction designations applied to the waybill (as it travels between carriers) determine the divisions of revenue that will apply and provide the basis for routing between carriers. The last handling road-haul carrier takes the waybill into account and is responsible for collecting the freight charge and allocating it among the handling lines. The handling lines match up waybill numbers in interline settlements to assure that they

167

have not been left out of the payments for any car they handled on a roadhaul. Thus, the waybill is a great deal more than a simple movement instruction.

The original waybill will travel electronically with the car from its origin to destination. All additional processes requiring information contained on the waybill will be accessed electronically by the appropriate departments. Under the Interchange Settlement System (ISS), an AAR procedure put into effect in 1996, any waybill involving interchange is entered electronically into a central file, where it is assigned a unique identification number; copies are automatically sent to all carriers on the shipment's route.

Other Computer Operations

Several steps involving the use of the continuous inventory car location system and the railroad's computer operating database follow the preparation of the waybill. These procedures vary from railroad to railroad in their details, but in most cases, several events will be reported to the computer plus changes made in the continuous car inventory in the form of data entry into the carriers' information systems. These events include the set, release, and pull of the car, any bad orders (cars that have defects that may prevent their safe movement over the railroad), weighing or inspection movements, and holding for billings. The car inventory system produces the switch lists used in picking up and in classifying the outbound load.

Subsequent to the electronic receipt of forwarding instructions from the customer, a switch crew goes to Jones' siding to pick up the car and take it to the classification yard, where the car will be switched into the proper outbound train. All the waybill data for the particular train are compiled, and a wheel report is prepared for the conductor. The wheel report is a list of cars in a train showing destination, weight, and load or empty status for each car. The conductor updates this list as the train picks up or sets out cars en route. The wheel report is used by the conductor for the haul over their territory, in this case from city B to city C. At city C, the wheel report is turned over to the conductor on the haul from C to D, and so on. Wheel reports are turned into headquarters and are sometimes used to figure mileage on the cars.

Many roads no longer use the conductor's wheel report to figure mileage, but rely on computer-generated wheel reports and computation programs. The mileage calculations are for interline settlements of the mileage charges on cars that the railroads are "renting" from each other.

The next report entered in the computer, just prior to train departure, is the consist report. This report now lists only time, date, location, and car numbers, since on any sophisticated system, the waybill data was previously entered, and train symbol itinerary is already established in the computer. The division point will now be aware of what train is coming in, what's on it, and whether they will have to add or cut out cars. When the new crew comes on at the division point, the old crew hands over the wheel report.

Interchange

In order to get Jones' shipment to Smith in city AA, the car must be turned over to the SW & AA Railroad at city G. Before the train gets to G, the E-W yardmaster in G has already received a consist report from the computer. From this report, he makes up a switch list for his switching crews so that they will know whether each car stays with the train, stays in the area for local delivery, or as in this case, interchanges (cars are moved from one road to another at a common junction point) to the SW & AA Railroad to continue on to city AA.

The switching crew brings car PR 123456 and any other cars being interchanged to the SW & AA yard to be made up into a train heading for city AA. The E-W personnel must enter into the computer an interchange delivery report, which confirms that the cars have been turned over to the SW & AA. The report includes the initial and number of the car, its contents, destination, and the time and date it was delivered to the SW & AA. As soon as the car is turned over, the E-W's car hire (per diem and mileage) charges end, and the SW & AA's charges begin.

The waybill information that was originally entered by E-W Railroad has been electronically forwarded to all carriers in the route. Because the carriers participating in the movement of this shipment have received advanced information, they are able to use the information to support their own systems and processes.

Arriving at Destination

The SW & AA train then continues on to city AA. When the centralized customer service center is electronically notified that the shipment has arrived in city AA, the customer service representative will notify Smith Company that the car containing their shipment of canned goods has arrived. Smith will either order the car to be sent to their siding as soon as feasible or will order it in by number (i.e., a specific sequence of cars). The SW & AA switch crew will then bring the car to Smith.

Car PR 123456 then goes on to Smith's demurrage. Smith has an allotted amount of time to unload the shipment and notify the SW & AA to pick up the car. If Smith goes over the allotted time, then the SW & AA charges and collects the demurrage fee.

A freight bill is prepared for the designated payer or consignee, which is made up from the information on the waybill. Smith remits its check for these charges to the SW & AA Railroad, unless the charges have been prepaid.

Order Bill of Lading

If the shipment carries an order bill of lading, the last road-haul line cannot turn over the shipment to the consignee or to the switching company, making final delivery, until it has proof that the goods have been paid for. Proof of payment includes: order bill handed over by the bank that has made payment; a consignee bond that is on file with the railroad's credit and collection department; or a certified check of 125 percent of the value of the shipment. Mistakes can sometimes happen. Improper communication between railroad employees may allow the shipment to be delivered before proof of payment is received. Should something go awry, and the consignee cannot pay for the goods, the last road-haul company is responsible for the cost of the merchandise.

Regardless of who pays the freight charges, the company has 120 hours (not including weekends and holidays) to pay the charges. U.S. government agencies have 30 days to pay. If the railroad does not show evidence of attempting to collect, it could be found in violation of the Elkins Act. The railroad may also be liable to fines if it unduly denies credit to shippers. Credit regulations are spelled out in Section 1320 of the ICC Act.

Rate clerks are entrusted to accurately rate shipments and supply the proper data for freight bills. In the event of undercharges or overcharges due to errors on the bill, the railroad is not absolved of the responsibility of refunding the overcharges, nor is the shipper excused from paying to the railroad the difference between the undercharge and actual charge. The originating carrier must make the refund or collect the difference when the shipment is prepaid. For collect shipments, it's the delivering line's responsibility. The payee has 30 days to make payment to the railroad after being notified of undercharges.

The Complexities of Switching

The road-haul freight that brings a car into town usually doesn't deliver it to the consignee's siding but must rely on switching to get the car to its final destination. Basically, there are three types of switches—intraplant, intraterminal, and interterminal. *Intraplant switching* involves the movement from one track to another or between two points on the same track within the same plant or industry. *Intraterminal switching* is the movement from a track, industry, or firm to another track, industry, or firm on the same road within the same district. *Interterminal switching* covers movements from a track of one road to a track of another road within the same district.

When an interterminal switch is called for, things can get complicated. Interterminal switching involves complex agreements between the railroads in every city. Each railroad establishes a switching district (see Chapter 11) in which it will arrange to have a car delivered, regardless of whose tracks the siding is located on. Railroads establish reciprocal agreements ("we'll switch your cars, if you'll switch ours") to ensure that cars are delivered.

Switching Charges

The road handling the switch will be paid a switching charge that is determined by each railroad within each switching district. These charges are computed via careful analysis of crew time, fuel cost, and so on. The rates are then published and usually approved by the STB. They can be determined by any basis the railroad selects—commodity, weight, distance, type of car, or any combination.

Settlement of charges among railroads is taken care of by monthly switching settlement statements based on lists provided by the freight agent. The accounting department arranges for settlement of charges via a process similar to interline settlements.

Interline Settlements

In order for the E-W Railroad to collect its share (division) of revenue from the shipment, it must get its money from the SW & AA Railroad, which collected the freight charges from Smith. Under ISS, the central computer advises each railroad in the route of its share; each has an opportunity to approve or question its share electronically. If all concur, that's it and the customer is billed; any railroad's objections must be resolved by negotiation within a fixed time frame or the matter will be settled arbitrarily. Once a month, the participating railroads settle their net balances with each other by transfer of funds.

Railroad Regulation—Some History

Since it would be virtually impossible to obtain a right-of-way through settled country without the backup capability of invoking the government's power of eminent domain to set a reasonable price, railroads must, in practice, be chartered by public authority. These charters, in turn, require that railroads operate as common carriers. Since the railroad by its very nature can carry just about anything that's worth transporting, this isn't just an academic matter. Most of the federal regulation of railroads in the United States is based on the Interstate Commerce Act of 1887 and subsequent extensions; these, in general, were established at a time when railroads were in a monopoly situation in land transport and had the primary thrust of keeping the overall level of rates low and equalizing access to regulated transportation among shippers and consignees in different locations and situations. Railroads are exempt from the antitrust provisions of the Clayton Act and are allowed to propose rates and establish standardized tariff provision (and formats) collectively through the workings of rate bureaus.

The steady growth of the state and, later, federally financed highway systems and the federally constructed (and maintained) internal and coastal waterways systems have made the monopoly aspects of rail transportation a thing of the past for most commodities. The regulation of railroads, however, continued in full flower until the passage of significant deregulation legislation in 1980—the Staggers Act of 1980. (Common-carrier trucking was also regulated—except for any commodities however remotely related to agriculture, which were exempt.)

Full effects of the Staggers Act (which followed the "4R" Railroad Revitalization and Regulatory Reform Act of 1976, a less far-reaching piece of legislation whose effects were largely postponed by ICC interpretations) can only be assessed with the passage of time as they are interpreted by litigation, and as the thought patterns and habits of railroaders, shippers, and regulators ingrained over the years adapt to the shifts in philosophy implied. A few of the provisions of the Staggers Act are:

- Railroad pricing is subject to antitrust law; rate-bureau functions are severely limited, with only the railroads participating in an interline (joint) rate allowed to vote in establishing its level.

- Within broad limits, especially on traffic for which other modes of transport provide an alternative to the shipper, individual rail rates may be raised and lowered rapidly in response to the competitive situation from unregulated carriers, seasonal factors, and other service and cost effects. Intermodal (piggyback) and some boxcar traffic has been totally deregulated.

- "Blanket rate" changes under the ex parte procedures were phased out, except for limited changes directly related to specific cost increases.

- Contract rates between railroad and shipper guaranteeing a rate basis for a specified volume or proportion of the shipper's business over a specified period of time under agreed-upon conditions are specifically made legal (subject to antitrust law); not all aspects of the contract are public information.

- Surcharges may be applied by a railroad to a specific commodity or route or to its division of a joint rate to bring revenue up to the cost of handling the shipment, potentially eliminating the cross-subsidization of unprofitable traffic associated with the regulated rate structure evolved over the years.

In general, the major effects of the first 25-plus years of this partial deregulation has been a dramatic improvement in railroad stability and profitability (though the industry's "return on investment" has not reached "cost of capital" levels), virtual elimination of such historically important ratemaking principles as "processing in transit" and—with continuing competitive pressures such as those associated with private trucking—a broad lowering of constant-dollar rail rates (in some commodities, exceeding the rate of inflation).

Though now likely to be reflected primarily in the provisions of rate contracts rather than rulings and tariffs, legacies of the regulated years nevertheless live on, showing up intercommunity (especially interseaport) conflicts and pressures for legislative adjustments to the extent that a discussion of some of these historical factors is included.

Equal Access

Since most rail shipments now represent fairly regular movements from quantity producers to their customers, they usually originate at private sidetracks. As common carriers, railroads are required to provide a track connection to any customer who wants it, unless it can be shown that it is physically impractical. The railroad can require financial arrangements appropriate for the volume of business involved, but the same rules must apply to all. The railroad will place a car for loading and pick it up as part of the freight charge, but since equal service to all is the rule, intraplant movements require a charge, specified by the tariff. A large company with its own network of track will probably do its own switching.

Public Loading Facilities

The railroad must also provide places where shippers and consignees who don't have their own sidings can load and receive carload freight. The simplest of these are "team" tracks, sidings located and spaced so that trucks can back up to the cars. More elaborate railroad-owned facilities range from a small gantry crane up to the huge port terminals handling coal, ore, grain, and other bulk cargoes between car and barge or ship, with provisions for intermediate storage. For each service provided by these facilities a schedule of charges must be established by published tariff, subject to regulation to assure that the rates are not unduly discriminatory to those who do not opt for all services. Fig. 8-1 is an example of a team-track facility.

Short Line Railroading

Shippers who are some distance from a "line-haul" railroad may reach a line-haul road via a connecting line. If it is a plant-built and plant-owned facility only, the owner saves switching charges; if it is a common carrier, the short line receives a "division" of the freight rate (typically, considerably more than just the percentage of the mileage involved, since the costs of an originating or terminating carrier are recognized as being disproportionately high). In return, the short line must be prepared to accept freight from all comers, including competitors, and its divisions will be scrutinized closely to see that profits from them don't constitute, in effect, a rebate on the freight rate as compared to what's available to others.

The Commodities Clause

Since 1906, it has been illegal for a railroad company to transport any commodity (except timber and materials used in railroad operations themselves) that it owns. That

Fig. 8-1. Team-track loading facility

is, a railroad cannot own a coal mine or a steel mill and transport its output for general sale. This act was intended to equalize the situation between producers by requiring the carriers to divorce themselves from subsidiaries that could profit by manipulating freight rates. By raising rates exorbitantly, the railroad with captive mines could presumably put the squeeze on its competitors while using the freight income to offset the price paid on its product.

The converse is not prohibited; a nonrailroad company such as a big steel producer can build and own a railroad to serve its needs, but this line, as a common carrier, must provide equal service and charge equal rates to its parent's competitors. These are matters that, presumably, can be more readily controlled by the regulatory authorities.

Tariffs

What is the freight rate on a shipment? Unfortunately, that isn't an easy question for the friendly local freight agent. Tariffs are complicated, to say the least, when you multiply the thousands of stations by the dozens of routings by the hundreds of commodities, which results in millions of different combinations. Over the period of a hundred years, the tariff bureaus, acting for the "trunk lines" (the major carriers), have developed a system of published tariff documents that, by cross-referencing against each other, reduce the problem of presenting all needed combinations from being hopeless to merely challenging. The answer is contained in those documents, but is derived only by tracking down, adding, subtracting, multiplying, and dividing a number of different numbers that together reflect all the factors that go into a rate, factors far more numerous than simply how much the shipment weighs and how many miles it has to go. Examining a few of these and hinting at the rest may provide some insight into the philosophies underlying the system.

Class and Commodity Rates

One-of-a-kind or occasional shipments, such as a car of granite curbstones going to a small town in the Midwest to surround its new fountain in the park, are covered by class rates—those rates determined by finding the classification that includes "granite, rough finished" (with some other characterizations and qualifications) in a list of hundreds of other items of generally equivalent density, value, and nature with respect to the handling care required. Class rates have become so high that, in general, even for a single shipment, application will be made to quote a commodity rate, which is usually done. Class rates move less than one percent of traffic. Commodity rates move the rest.

More or less regular shipments (the bulk of the business) are likely to be covered by commodity rates—those rates for one particular commodity or item from one specific point or area to another. For example, raw copper ingots are shipped from a smelter town in Arizona to a processing plant in Illinois; or washing machines (boxed in accordance with another reference specification) are shipped from a plant in Kentucky to a distribution center in the state of Washington. These rates (lower than corresponding class rates) have been set up, for example, to let an area compete in various markets with sources elsewhere in the country or world, to make it economically possible for a particularly bulky commodity to travel that far, or to recognize economies possible from centralizing a particular manufacturing, processing, or distributing function at one point.

Ex Parte Changes

All of these class and commodity rates in turn may be changed (in inflationary times, raised) by the effects of across-the-board ex parte changes authorized from time to time

175

by the STB to recognize changes in costs affecting the whole level of rates. In turn, these are usually modified by "hold downs" on particular items for which raises are not requested for competitive or technical reasons.

Incentive Rates

To encourage shipments in amounts, forms, or under other conditions that will make more economical handling by the railroads possible, "incentive" tariffs (merely one form of commodity rate) may be established in return for the acceptance of such requirements as loading cars to more than the minimum carload weight. These are discussed in a little more depth in connection with unit-train operations.

Processing-in-Transit Rates

The general level of freight rates generates a great deal of discussion, controversy, and litigation, but the matter of freight rate comparisons between different sections of the country, different port cities, and even in different directions for the same commodity between the same areas is also ever more controversial. Over the years thousands of such matters have been determined by Congress, the ICC (now STB) and the courts, and are reflected in current tariffs.

In the case of our East-West System, for example, consider the matter of the farmers at A versus those on the branch leading west from U (both in the west-central area of Fig. 2-1). There is a flour mill at A, so grain processed there can go directly to the bakeries in the metropolitan area of J on the east coast. Wheat grown in the U area would be at a disadvantage as there is no mill in the area. It would have to be shipped as grain to the processor at F and reshipped to J, at greater freight cost since two shipments are involved. The answer, so far as the miller at F and the wheat growers at U are concerned, is the "milling-in-transit rate" established many years ago that treats the two "legs" of the trip from U to J, with a stopover at F where the grain becomes flour, as a single movement, accorded a rate equal to the through A - J flour rate. The flour mill at F can stay in business despite dwindling local supplies as shopping centers and apartment developments take over the wheat fields.

C H A P T E R   9

Car Types, Commodities, and Carloadings

To get any load from origin to destination, there has to be a suitable car. Standardized technology—air brake gear, couplers, trucks, track gage, and turnouts—makes it possible for almost any freight car to go anywhere, limited only by such constraints as clearances, weight restrictions on bridges, and curves that may be too sharp for extra-long cars. The variables involve what kinds of cars are needed and where they are located, who is going to acquire and maintain them, and how empties get back to their origin point.

Each freight car type is given a two- to four-letter designation by the Association of American Railroads (AAR). This designation is called a *mechanical designation*. It is stenciled on every car in the same place (immediately to the right of the capacity stenciling). This AAR mechanical designation indicates the general design of the car and what the general purpose of the car is (what commodity it was designed to carry). Examples of the alphabetic code are RB, which means bunkerless refrigerator car, and RBL, which means that the bunkerless refrigerator car has load-restraining devices. Ch. 9 shows a few of the mechanical designations as well as the commodities associated with that car type; there are many more.

The AAR, an industry association, assigns these designations as part of their responsibility to ensure safety standards (including design standards and approval), maintenance, operations, service and repair standards, and car service rules.

Freight Car Types

The freight car fleet in the United States in 2005 consisted of the following car types, with ownership as indicated in Table 9-1.

Except for rare instances where they may be used in unusual operating conditions (such as long backup movements), cabooses (also known as cabin cars) disappeared

Table 9-1. Car ownership

Car Type	Total All Owners	Class I Railroads	Other Railroads	Car Companies and Shippers
Boxcars:	132,094	74,346	41,197	16,551
Plain box	20,103	1,211	5,671	13,221
Equipped box	111,991	73,135	35,526	3,330
Covered hoppers	393,803	112,773	20,191	260,839
Flatcars	171,455	95,666	22,344	53,445
Gondolas	206,666	100,699	21,435	84,532
Hoppers	159,324	72,131	11,622	75,571
Refrigerator cars	23,492	17,577	2,895	3,020
Tank cars	254,778	1,053	38	253,687
Others	4,895	1,170	966	2,759
Total	1,346,507	475,415	120,688	750,404

Source: Railroad Facts, 2007 Edition, Association of American Railroads

from service many years ago. They have been replaced with EOT (end-of-train) monitoring and telemetry devices.

Traffic Distribution

For each principal class of commodity going from one producer to one receiver, one preferred freight car is designed to carry it. Many variables govern the type of car needed: (1) available loading and unloading gear; (2) the size, shape, and nature of the commodity; (3) its value and need for protection; and (4) the customary unit quantity of shipment. All these variables make a difference, large or small, in how satisfactory a particular car can be. Since there can't be an infinite number of different types of car, the one actually used will represent a compromise between what's ideal and what is practical for the car builders, railroads, and shippers.

Carloadings are reported in 15 major "commodity groups" that represent about 96 percent of the total loadings, exclusive of intermodal traffic (trailers or containers loaded on railcars, as discussed in Chapter 15). The number of trailers and containers loaded is now reported separately, without regard to the commodities involved, since the lading in most intermodal traffic is identified only as "Freight–All Kinds."

The following section presents the cars and their commodity groups in terms of the approximate carloads, tonnage, and revenues of each in traffic originated on railroads in the United States in 2005, the most recent year for which AAR statistics were available at the time of publication. Percentages (some of which may vary significantly from year to year) contributed by each commodity group are listed concerning total traffic, intermodal included.

Coal

Fig. 9-1. FreightCar America AutoFlood II aluminum hopper

Car Statistics:

Carloadings per year:	7.20 million (23.1%)
Tons originated:	804.14 million (42.4%)
Gross revenue:	$9.39 billion (20.1%)
AAR Mechanical Designation:	HT / GT
Examples of preferred cars:	Unit-train bottom-dump hopper and rotary-dump gondola

Most coal tonnage goes to generating stations, to export docks, and to steel mill coking plants, often in unit trains. Choice of bottom-dump hopper or high-side solid-bottom gondola depends upon unloading facilities at the receiving point. Cars unloaded by overturning them in rotary car dumpers may be equipped with a rotary coupler at one end that allows emptying without uncoupling; bottom-dump cars, which may also be unloaded in a rotary dumper, may be equipped with power-operated hopper doors for unloading in motion. Approximately 4,200 cu ft capacity is required for a 110-ton load (286,000 lbs gross rail load).

Fig. 9-2. FreightCar America BethGon Coalporter aluminum gondola

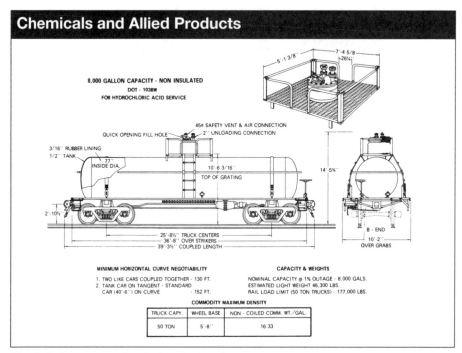

Chemicals and Allied Products

Fig. 9-3. Nonpressurized chemical tank car

Car Statistics:

Carloadings per year:	1.97 million (6.3%)
Tons originated:	167.20 million (8.8%)
Gross revenue:	$5.51 billion (11.8%)
AAR Mechanical Designation	T*
Example of preferred car:	Chemical tank car

*Tank construction and testing covered by numerous U.S. Department of Transportation (DOT) safety specifications for different commodity classes.

Tank car size increased rapidly following elimination of requirements for running boards. Use of the tank itself as the "center sill" strength member of car has allowed tank diameter to increase to the clearance limit. Since many chemicals require special tank linings or materials, and heater coils for unloading, most cars are leased, owned by, or assigned to individual shippers and carry only one class of product. Capacity ranges up to 150 tons (with six-wheel trucks) in some cars. Beginning in 2005, efforts were made to improve tank car safety. The AAR Tank Car Safety Project developed cars equipped with shelf couplers that prevent couplers from overriding one another and puncturing cars in a derailment. Some cars are equipped with head shields that provide additional protection against head punctures. Some also have thermal protection to assure that the lading vents safely in the event of a fire. Other safety improvements include bottom-fitting protection, improved steels, surge suppression devices, and more robust rupture discs.

Nonmetallic Minerals

Fig. 9-4. LO small-cube covered hopper car

Car Statistics:

Carloadings per year:	1.49 million (4.7%)
Tons originated:	169.70 million (7.7%)
Gross revenue:	$1.29 billion (2.8%)
AAR Mechanical Designation	LO
Example of preferred car:	Small-cube covered hopper

Many minerals such as salt or phosphate require protection from the weather and cannot be shipped in open-top cars. Special car linings may be needed to protect contents from contamination; most minerals are dense and load to 70- or 100-ton car capacity in twin-hopper cars of 2,500 to 3,000 cu ft capacity.

Farm Products (grain and other)

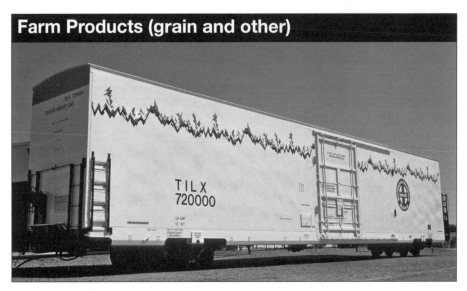

Fig. 9-5. RP Trinity TRINCool™ 86 ft refrigerated boxcar

Car Statistics:

Carloadings per year:	1.51 million (4.9%)
Tons originated:	140.44 million (7.4%)
Gross revenue:	$3.63 million (7.8%)
AAR Mechanical Designation	RP
Example of preferred car:	Mechanical refrigerator

The mechanical refrigerator car, with diesel-powered cooling unit and fuel capacity for as long as 2 weeks unattended operation, was developed to meet the subzero requirements of frozen food products. Virtually all refrigerator car cooling systems are mechanical and of general-purpose type; these systems are capable of maintaining temperatures required by various fresh or frozen products. Most are also equipped with cushioning and load-restraining devices. Many are now outfitted with remote temperature and tracking devices using GPS or satellite location systems.

Food and Kindred Products

Fig. 9-6. RB insulated refrigerator car

Car Statistics:

Carloadings per year:	1.49 million (4.8%)
Tons originated:	102.19 million (5.4%)
Gross revenue:	$3.25 million (7.0%)
AAR Mechanical Designation	RB
Example of preferred car:	Insulated refrigerator car

RB "bunkerless refrigerator" cars have the equivalent of at least 3-inch insulation on sides and 3½ inches on roof and floor but no cooling system. With plug doors and, usually, load-restraining devices (designation RBL), these cars can maintain the temperature of many food products within satisfactory limits throughout an extended trip without the expense of mechanical temperature control.

Metallic Ores

Fig. 9-7. HMA FreightCar America ore hopper

Car Statistics:

Carloadings per year:	662,000 (2.1%)
Tons originated:	59.94 million (3.2%)
Gross revenue:	$485 million (1.0%)
AAR Mechanical Designation	HMA
Example of preferred car:	Ore hopper

Ore is very dense, loading as heavily as 170 lbs per cu ft, so cars used exclusively in this service are of small cubic capacity. Cars in processed taconite pellet service have an added collar to increase cubic capacity and carry the same tonnage of this lower density product.

Metals and Products

Fig. 9-8. Alstom Transport coil steel gondola with removable cover

Car Statistics:

Carloadings per year:	716,000 (2.3%)
Tons originated:	57.85 million (3.0%)
Gross revenue:	$1.79 million (3.8%)
AAR Mechanical Designation	GBSR
Example of preferred car:	Coil steel car

Finished steel in sheet or coil form requiring protection from the weather is shipped in gondola cars with removable covers allowing it to be loaded and unloaded from

above by gantry cranes. The concentrated weight of coils requires heavy-duty load-securing devices, aided by end-of-car cushioning. Structural shapes, pipe, and other long products travel in open-top "mill gons" of 52 to 66 ft length, with drop ends to allow overhang above an "idler" flatcar for exceptionally long loads.

Fig. 9-9. Greenbrier Companies 66 ft open-top mill gondola

185

Petroleum and Coke

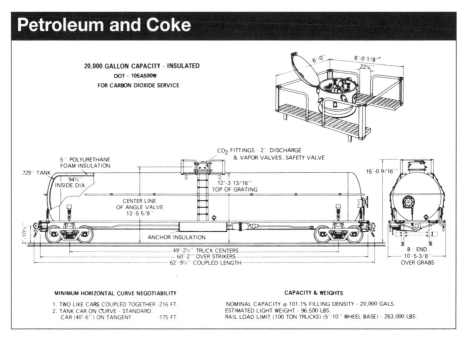

20,000 GALLON CAPACITY - INSULATED
DOT - 105A500W
FOR CARBON DIOXIDE SERVICE

CO_2 FITTINGS - 2" DISCHARGE
& VAPOR VALVES, SAFETY VALVE

5" POLYURETHANE
FOAM INSULATION

.729" TANK

94½"
INSIDE DIA

12'-3 13/16"
TOP OF GRATING

CENTER LINE
OF ANGLE VALVE
13'-5 5/8"

15'-0 9/16"

ANCHOR INSULATION

B - END
10'-5-3/8"
OVER GRABS

49'-2½" TRUCK CENTERS
60'-2" OVER STRIKERS
62'-9½" COUPLED LENGTH

MINIMUM HORIZONTAL CURVE NEGOTIABILITY

1. TWO LIKE CARS COUPLED TOGETHER -216 FT.
2. TANK CAR ON CURVE - STANDARD
   CAR (40'-6") ON TANGENT   -175 FT.

CAPACITY & WEIGHTS

NOMINAL CAPACITY @ 101.1% FILLING DENSITY - 20,000 GALS.
ESTIMATED LIGHT WEIGHT - 96,500 LBS.
RAIL LOAD LIMIT (100 TON TRUCKS) (5'-10" WHEEL BASE) - 263,000 LBS.

Fig. 9-10. Pressure tank car, 33,000-gallon capacity

Car Statistics:

Carloadings per year:	660,000 (2.1%)
Tons originated:	55.61 million (2.9%)
Gross revenue:	$1.42 billion (3.0%)
AAR Mechanical Designations	HTC (coke), DOT Class 112A (petroleum)
Examples of preferred cars:	Pressure tank car; coke hopper

Coke is used primarily in blast furnaces in the smelting of iron ore, and travels relatively short distances from coking plants to steel mills. Much lighter than coal, coke is

Fig. 9-11. CSX Transportation steel triple-hopper car

shipped in hopper cars built to larger cubic capacity or equipped with "coke" racks to accommodate its volume. Liquified petroleum gas (LPG) is one of the principal petroleum products carried by rail. LPG must be kept under pressure to remain liquid at ordinary temperatures. Special restrictions apply to the construction, handling, and equipment of cars in this "hazardous material" (hazmat) service.

Stone, Glass, and Clay Products

Fig. 9-12. Union Pacific DF boxcar

Car Statistics:

Carloadings per year:	603,000 (1.9%)
Tons originated:	55.23 million (2.9%)
Gross revenue:	$1.51 billion (3.2%)
AAR Mechanical Designations	GB, XL
Examples of preferred cars:	Gondola (stone), DF boxcar (glass and clay products)

Fig. 9-13. Typical load-restraining device used in a DF boxcar

DF cars are boxcars with special loading devices that prevent damage to the lading. Often, the cars are prominently marked with the letters "DF" to indicate their special purpose.

Lumber and Wood Products (except furniture)

Fig. 9-14. FreightCar America Flexibeam center-beam bulkhead flatcar

Car Statistics:

Carloadings per year:	611,000 (2.0%)
Tons originated:	47.60 million (2.5%)
Gross revenue:	$1.51 billion (3.2%)
AAR Mechanical Designation	FMS
Example of preferred car:	Center-beam bulkhead flatcar

The bulkhead car is ideal for transporting finished, packaged lumber because of the ease with which such lading can be handled by forklift trucks. The efficient car body structure, provided by the central girder or truss against which the bundles are secured, allows a car that is long enough to hold 100 tons of lading to remain within axle-load limits.

Waste and Scrap Materials

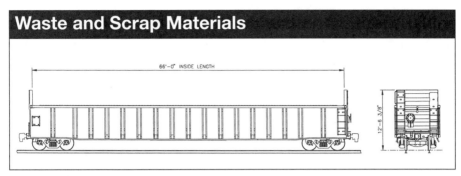

Fig. 9-15. Diagram of a Greenbrier 66 ft open-top gondola

Car Statistics:

Carloadings per year:	706,000 (2.3%)
Tons originated:	47.35 million (2.5%)
Gross revenue:	$1.07 billion (2.3%)
AAR Mechanical Designation	GB
Example of preferred car:	Gondola

The relationship of freight rates for "recycling" materials to those for shipping ores, minerals, and so on, used in the alternative process of meeting current needs by the use of new raw materials (and leaving the scrap to clutter up the environment) are major social and environmental issues. Scrap is not a time-sensitive commodity requiring expedited handling, but the volume fluctuates widely with changes in price, tending to cause alternating shortages and surpluses in car supply, both of which are costly to the railroads. Some gondolas, suitable for scrap and other heavy loads, are equipped with lading strap anchors for commodities requiring tie-downs.

Pulp, Paper, and Allied Products

Fig. 9-16. XL paper boxcar built by Greenbrier for CSX Transportation

Car Statistics:

Carloadings per year:	679,000 (2.2%)
Tons originated:	38.24 million (2.0%)
Gross revenue:	$1.95 billion (4.2%)
AAR Mechanical Designation	XL
Example of preferred car:	Equipped boxcar

Rolls of newsprint are subject to flattening from impacts of shifting within the car, with subsequent problems in the printing press and damage claims. The equipped box-car (equipped with load-restraining devices and end-of-car cushioning units adaptable to its particular load) is indispensable in handling such commodities. Paper products are also subject to damage if loaded in cars contaminated or roughed-up by previous loads.

Motor Vehicles and Equipment

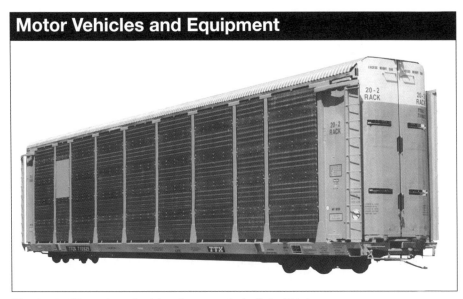

Fig. 9-17. FA enclosed tri-level autorack, built by Trinity

Car Statistics:

Carloadings per year:	1.79 million (5.8%)
Tons originated:	35.59 million (1.9%)
Gross revenue:	$3.80 billion (8.1%)
AAR Mechanical Designation	FA
Example of preferred car:	Enclosed tri-level autorack

The low rates made possible by carrying 12 to 18 automobiles per car not only regained the majority of this traffic for railroads (approximately 70 percent of all finished vehicles), but have also allowed the manufacturers to concentrate assembly of particular makes and models at single plants because of the greater distances over which shipping finished cars is economically attractive. The enclosed autorack car and other designs were developed to minimize damage in transit at the insistence of the manufacturers. These cars are typically equipped with premium trucks, couplers, and end-of-car cushioning to provide a smoother ride.

All Other Carloads (except intermodal)

Fig. 9-18. Combination-door boxcar

Car Statistics:

Carloadings per year:	2.71 million (8.7%)
Tons originated:	21.81 million (1.1%)
Gross revenue:	$2.37 billion (5.1%)
AAR Mechanical Designations	XM, FM
Examples of preferred cars:	Unequipped "free-running" boxcar, combination-door boxcar, general-service flatcar

Fig. 9-19. FreightCar America 89 ft all-purpose flatcar

This category (excluding intermodal loadings) includes merchandise and machinery of all types not falling within the other commodity categories. Since cars equipped for handling specific loads are usually assigned to such shippers, a typical car found in this service is the unequipped (XM) boxcar.

Versatility has remained a goal of the car designer for generations. The "combination-door" boxcar has been perhaps the most widely used example of a car with worthwhile if more modest claims to versatility. With "grain doors" across its regular sliding center doors, it can handle granular bulk commodities; packaged or palletized items are easily loaded or unloaded through the wider opening provided by the extra set of "plug" doors. The vulnerability of the latter to damage unfortunately results in restriction to "narrow-door" use whenever its operating mechanism becomes unserviceable. The general-service flatcar has a wood deck for nailed-down blocking of the load, standard-size stake pockets, and concentrated-load capacity to handle a wide variety of loads.

Intermodal Equipment

Evolving from standard but extra-long (75 ft) flatcars built for moving bulky but light circus wagons from town to town (since they were charged a flat rate by the car, the circus owners naturally wanted to do the job with as few vehicles as possible), piggyback car design has been driven by the height and length of highway trailers allowed by the most favorable laws the trucking interests have been able to push through Congress and state legislatures. The result has been a unique variety of railcar configurations, as illustrated here and in Chapter 15.

TOFC (trailer-on-flatcar) traffic generally requires accommodating the maximum cubic capacity, as represented by trailer lengths that have grown to as large as 53 ft. With the highway axle load at 18,000 lbs versus 55,000 lbs for a 70-ton railcar, emphasis has been on two-trailer/car or four-wheel single-trailer configurations. With COFC (container-on-flatcar) traffic by 2007 rising from a long-term minor role to far greater volume than TOFC, the economies of stacking have put the railcar emphasis back on load-carrying capacity.

Fig. 9-20. Greenbrier Husky Stack All-Purpose car, with trailers. This car can also handle containers.

The 125-ton truck has been generally accepted for unit-train service where every axle is pounding away at the track with a full load. In double-stack "three-pack" and "five-pack" COFC cars, where articulation tends to result in somewhat lower dynamic wheel-rail forces, heavy-axle loads are standard practice on many main lines.

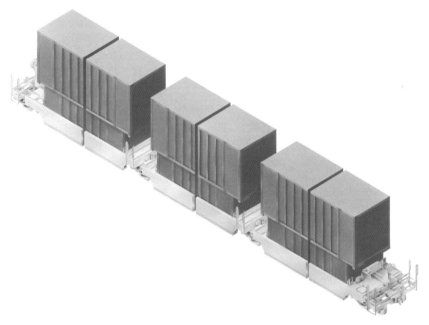

Fig. 9-21. "Three-pack" articulated well car that is set for double-stack service

Fig. 9-22. Heavy-haul double-stack container service accounts for a significant portion of railroad tonnage and revenues.

Car Ownership and Distribution

Each railroad wants to have just enough cars available for the shippers on its line, not too few (since sooner or later that means lost business), and not too many because the cost of providing freight cars is—after transportation labor—the railroad's largest single cost item. The cost of providing freight cars includes: (1) purchase, (2) depreciation, (3) maintenance, and (4) rental payments. Despite a continuing trend toward improved use, such car costs amount to about 15 percent of total expenses.

Some railroads are primarily *originating* carriers, located in areas where more products are mined, grown, or otherwise produced than are consumed. They will tend to be short of cars and under pressure to buy or lease more. Predominantly *terminating* carriers can depend on cars made empty on-line as their supply for loading if the cars are suitable for carrying the commodities that the terminating carriers originate with reasonable efficiency. But they may have large, unfavorable balances of car rental payments if they don't own their share of the fleet. Much traffic is seasonal; the "value" of a car to the shipper and the railroad fluctuates with demand at a particular time and region. For the best use of the entire fleet, cars must operate as a pool—available and able to be drawn in response to market forces.

Car Rental Systems and Rates

Car-hire systems. The conditions and rates for using and paying for cars belonging to another railroad or a private car owner are crucial factors in ensuring an efficient supply level of needed car types when comparing car-hire systems to the cost of owning cars. As of 2007, the number of privately owned cars (see table in Chapter 9) in the fleet exceeded the total of those owned by Class I and smaller railroads.

Bilateral agreements. Similar to the shift of rail traffic rate-making from rigid Interstate Commerce Commission-controlled tariffs to negotiated shipper-railroad contracts (as permitted by the Staggers Act of 1980), many car rental rates and conditions are now established by bilateral agreements between railroads covering their interchange (the transfer of cars from one road to another) of specified types of car. These are permitted by the Car Service and Car Hire Agreement with the Customer Operations Division of the Association of American Railroads, to which all railroads are signatories and under whose terms all car interchange takes place. Car-hire rules and rates directly under this agreement are discussed further.

In contract freight rates, the terms and rates of bilateral agreements are private. To keep the use of the car as a mutual advantage, the terms and rates are more "liberal" to the parties involved than the alternative—otherwise, they wouldn't be set up. Keeping track of all individual car movements and interchanges and the resulting car-hire charges, plus calculating interrailroad balances for monthly settlement, is handled on the AAR's Railinc subsidiary's computers (in strict confidence).

Car hire–per diem. Railroad-owned cars are identified by 2-, 3-, or 4-letter AAR-assigned "reporting marks" not ending in "X" (usually the initials of the railroad's name). Use of railroad-owned cars is paid for by what is still often referred to as a *per diem* rate (per day rate), although it is now on hourly instead of daily time intervals and also includes a charge for each mile run. (Regulated by the ICC for most of the 1920s and 1930s, the charge was a flat "dollar a day.")

The flat dollar-a-day charge was gradually raised after World War II; eventually, the prevalence of more specialized, productive, and sophisticated cars and the disproportionate increase in new-car prices (which increased sixfold between 1950 and 1980) caused the rental to be based on the initial car costs, minus depreciation for age.

Under daily rentals, the road on which a car was physically located at midnight each day owed the fee to its owner; hourly car-hire rates were substituted in 1979 to remove any incentive for a mad scramble (perhaps resulting in inefficient scheduling and operations) to shove cars onto connections just before the daily deadline.

What Should the Rate Be?

The objective is to set the rate high enough so that there will be a net return to the owner (to encourage an adequate total car inventory) and a strong incentive for railroads to keep "foreign" (rented) cars moving, yet low enough to encourage a receiving road to hang onto an empty long enough to find a return load and thus improve overall car use.

During the long period of railroad regulation, ICC authority for setting the rate rested on the principle that car rental is part of the cost base on which a level of "fair return" freight rates would be allowed. In matters of car distribution, the ICC also acted as guardian of the principle that a "commodity" (e.g., empty cars) in short supply should be doled out to claimants in even-handed, nondiscriminatory fashion, with shippers and communities of all sizes receiving equal consideration. This was, of course, in conflict with the idea of reducing the severity of a car shortage by allowing the assignment of cars to multi-car, quick-turnaround (unit-train) service.

The ICC also prescribed higher incentive per diem rates to encourage acquiring car types expected to be in shortage during certain times of the year. This it did for plain boxcars in the late 1970s—setting a rate that was high enough to make a new boxcar earning per diem an extremely profitable investment. The result was an unprecedented spurt in boxcar production, followed soon after by a huge car surplus and virtual cessation of all boxcar productions for a dozen years.

Who Prescribes Car-Hire Rates?

In line with the partial deregulation of railroad rates by 1980, the prescription of car-hire rates was shifted from the ICC to the railroad industry itself. The Equipment Assets Management Working Committee (within the AAR) has a membership broadly representing large and small carriers and establishes rates for recommendation to the Surface Transportation Board (STB). The STB (which replaced the ICC in 1995) retains oversight because of such matters as the antitrust implications of such an industrywide process. Mileage and per hour rates for each car type are prescribed by formula from the car's original cost and age. Typical prescribed car-hire charges, as of 2007, range from 18¢ per hour plus 5.4¢ per mile for an elderly 50 ft plain (unequipped) Class I-owned boxcar to $1.75 per hour plus 12¢ per mile for a relatively new, privately owned, expensive multilevel 89 ft flatcar.

A law was instituted in 1992 after a considerable period of discussion because it could affect different-sized railroads that own smaller or larger car fleets of differing age in radically different ways. The law was a 10-year process of deprescription for railroad-owned cars not moving under bilateral agreements or freight contracts. Cars with the reporting marks of Class III carriers (some of which had large fleets out of proportion to their own limited mileage) are exempt from deprescription and continue to earn car hire at a rate frozen at a 1990 level. New cars are deprescribed; owners can deprescribe one-tenth of their fleet each year, until at the end of the 10-year process all cars owned by the larger railroads will be earning car hire at market rates—rentals set by a bidding process reflecting their value at the time and place.

Private-Owner Cars

Private-owner cars (owned by shippers or leased from a car company) are identified by reporting marks ending in "X." If they are moving under the terms of a contract, the freight rate that is negotiated with the railroad reflects the value of the shipper-furnished car. In "tariff" service, they are paid for according to the loaded miles run. In effect, the railroad compensates the shipper for saving it the cost of supplying a car.

The shipper must make arrangements, similar to interchange rules regarding inspection, and so on, for the car to be accepted by the originating railroad. The railroad retains the option—a concern in car surplus situations—of supplying a suitable car of its own if available.

Car Service and Distribution Rules

As part of the partial railroad deregulation process, direct ICC control of car distribution was eliminated, leaving car service rules and their enforcement up to the industry itself. Car distribution not under bilateral agreement is regulated by the Customer Operations Division (COD) of the AAR under the previously mentioned car service agreement to which all railroads subscribe. They thus agree in a contract to follow its rules, directives, and orders for car handling and routing, under penalty of assessment (subject to arbitration) for violations.

Car service rules (established and amended by letter ballot of the subscribers, with votes in proportion to the number of cars owned) have two underlying objectives: *first,* ensuring the well-timed movement of empties to where they are needed for loading; *second,* reducing empty-car mileage. An example of a change aimed at the second objective is the revision of Car Service Rule 1 covering the loading of empty "foreign" cars (cars owned by another railroad).

Rather than requiring that such cars may be loaded only for a shipment routed in the direction of the home (owner) road, they may now be loaded "without regard to route or destination," recognizing that a short detour away from home toward a more likely source of long-haul traffic may result in a higher proportion of loaded mileage. Considering the unbalance between overall traffic flow in opposite directions, this system does fairly well in encouraging loaded backhaul. Nationwide, general-service, "plain" boxcars averaged 64 percent loaded mileage in a recent year.

How Does an Empty Get Back?

If no load is likely to be available soon, the empty will be sent back "via the service route" (Fig. 2-2), retracing the route it took on its last loaded trip. Thus, the railroad that got a piece of the revenue will bear the corresponding burden of the empty mileage.

If the demand for a type of car in an area is building up beyond that supplied by normal movements, however, a railroad may ask the COD to issue a Car Quota Directive requiring that its connecting roads route a daily quota of unassigned empties to it for loading. Grain cars may thus, for example, be diverted toward the Southwest in anticipation of the winter wheat harvest.

Assigned Service Cars

Cars specially equipped to handle specific commodities or products are in assigned service to cover the traffic between specified shippers and consignees. They are, in effect, in a pool making regular trips over a specific route. Car ownership is often shared by the railroads making up the route in proportion to the mileages involved. This may result in an empty owned by the terminating railroad being sent back empty to a "foreign" line for loading, but the car hire will balance out.

Cars in assigned service usually return empty; equipped boxcars, for example, that are usually in this service average only 54 percent loaded miles, but both railroad and shipper benefit from the more certain supply of suitable cars.

Free-runner is a term used by transportation people to describe cars that may be loaded in any direction (in accordance with the current version of Car Service Rule 1) rather than being returned empty on the reverse route.

Railbox-Railgon

To provide access to a fleet of cars of types not otherwise available in sufficient quantity at the time, TTX Corp. (owned by the major railroads) established its subsidiaries to acquire large fleets of "Railbox" (RBOX) and "Railgon" (GONX) standardized plain boxcars and gondolas to be available to railroads as free-runners on demand at rates generally lower than the ICC incentive rates in effect. Although many were later shifted to individual-railroad ownership, about 14,000 RBOX and GONX cars remain in service; despite the "X" in their reporting marks, they operate under railroad-owner rules. TTX (Trailer Train Corporation) itself owns and leases out a fleet of some 90,000 cars—all specialized, including five-platform piggyback spine and double-stack well cars along with 89 ft flatcars welded to railroad-owned multilevel autoracks.

How Do You Find an Empty?

In filling the order of a shipper for an empty to load, the traffic department of a railroad has its own computerized record of its own cars and the foreign cars on its line. For major traffic movements to be handled in nonassigned cars, however, it's not good enough to be seeking out suitable empties *after* the order has been place; suitable cars should already be moving toward the loading points. Several major communication, display, and data processing systems now aid the railroads, COD, and shippers in doing just that.

The operations department of the railroad directly controls car distribution; orders are received through centralized customer operations centers and are then matched by car distributors and filled by transportation officers and yardmasters.

UMLER

The *Universal Machine Language Equipment Register* (UMLER) is a data file updated daily by car owners to reflect car availability: added, retired, and bad order. The AAR subsidiary Railinc in Cary, North Carolina, maintains it. The data, which can be addressed to varying degrees of depth depending on need, include the following:

- Reporting marks
- Number
- Capacity
- Weight
- Mechanical designation
- Interior and exterior dimensions
- Special equipment
- Cost
- Periodic inspection
- Maintenance status

The data are for all freight cars, piggyback trailers, and containers in interchange service—a total of almost 4 million units. (UMLER also covers locomotives, maintenance-of-way equipment, and end-of-train reporting devices.)

It is a self-policing system, since only cars registered in UMLER may be accepted in interchange and be entitled to car-hire payments. In addition to its car fleet management functions, UMLER data is also used for such operating functions as determining the length of specific train consists in planning single-track meets.

TRAIN II

This second-phase version of the "Telerail Automated Information Network," continuously upgraded since going into operation at the AAR in 1975, receives information from all railroad car interchanges in the United States and Canada. Since 1992, all interchange data is received by EDI (Electronic Data Interchange) transmission from the interchange point. Its databank on the location and status of every freight car is updated hourly. Other data, most of which is received or updated no later than within one day of the event, includes such matters as the time of placement *for* loading, release time *after* unloading, *previous* loads (important for determining suitability for planned next load), and *current* routing. It serves as an automatic message routing system sending advance information from the originating road's computer to the computers of all bridge and connecting lines so they can plan car handling.

Car Tracing

Shippers are even more interested in the location, status, and arrival time of cars loaded with their goods, and railroad traffic departments have long maintained communication and office systems for providing such information as quickly as possible. Increasing computational capability has extended and automated the process. Starting in 1980, the AAR has provided a SAM (Shipper Assist Message) service whereby shippers with the capability of high-speed data communication can direct a query to the Railinc computer in Cary, North Carolina, and automatically receive data on any of the cars carrying their shipments from the computers of all participating railroads. "Third-party" agents will provide such service (for a fee) to shippers who do not have such message-transmission capability.

Car Routing Optimization

In a system with more than a million items moving throughout a network as complex as the North American rail network, the overall effect of a car service rule on the efficiency of fleet use is far from obvious. When it was responsible for car distribution, the ICC took steps toward understanding the way cars actually moved by basing studies on a more manageable database obtained by collecting a 1 percent sample (still over 200,000 a year) of all waybills. This database collection (for the Surface Transportation Board and for the FRA by the AAR) continues.

Based on inputs and mathematical network models of rail routes compatible with evolving computer capabilities, a variety of AAR studies (and other studies with extensive participation of various university researchers) have generated computer programs that have been, and continue to be, used to evaluate the net effect of car service orders and directly improve car-use strategies of railroads and car fleet managers.

Multilevel reload projects are a case in point. Implemented by the railroads and United States and Canadian automobile manufacturers in the mid-1980s, the reload projects direct the rack cars that were made empty at distribution terminals to the most productive reloading point rather than assigning cars to assembly plants. By 1985, empty-car mileage was reduced by an estimated 200 million miles per year by raising the loaded-mile percentage from 50 to about 63 percent.

Terminal Operations

The first step in the actual rail movement of a shipment occurs when the local freight crew, which also brings empties for loading and incoming loads, picks up the car. The actual operation of picking up a load is simple and quick, though the following important things need to be remembered:

- Closing the derail

- Checking the car to be sure the doors are closed and secured

- Checking that an open load is secured and no loose tie-downs or other material could drag or fall from the car

- Releasing the hand brake

Other cars complicate the process of picking up the load. As Fig. 11-1 shows, it makes quite a difference which way the siding is connected to the main track. Often the car to be picked up will be sandwiched between partially loaded or unloaded cars that will have to be respotted. The local freight crew may also have cars to deliver as well as pick up. Often, specific locations (spots) along the customer track are assigned to tasks (loading and unloading) or commodities. Cars may not be merely placed on the track in a convenient location or order. Fig. 11-1 shows that the simple operation of picking up a load may be as complicated as removing several cars from the track, setting over the load to be pulled, adding the cars to be placed to the string of cars that must be returned to the industry track, and respotting the track with all cars in the appropriate location.

In total, the switching involved in originating, terminating, and interchanging shipments is an expensive part of railroad operations. Road crews serve industries outside of terminal limits, and much yard switching is in connection with forwarding trains through intermediate yards. In a recent year, about one-quarter of all transportation expenses (mostly train-crew wages and benefits) on Class I railroads were chargeable to yard operations. Since only the roadhaul brings in revenue, the ability of yardmasters and trainmasters to provide reliable, timely service with a minimum number of switch and local crews and locomotives has a lot to do with whether or not the railroad makes money.

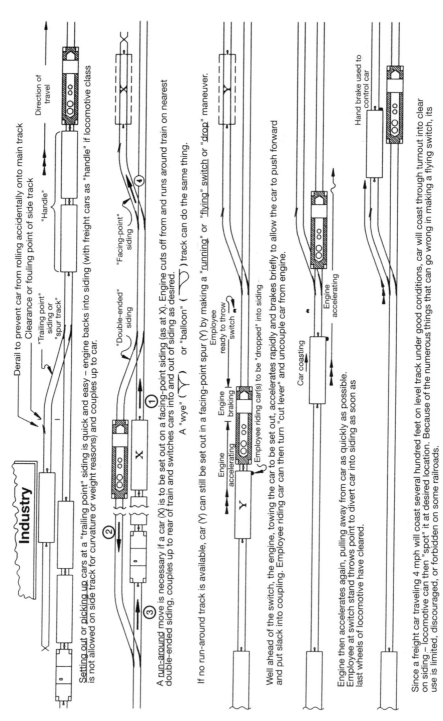

Fig. 11-1. Set-outs, pick-ups, run-arounds, and drops

The Switching District

For a simplified but representative bird's-eye view of some of the ways such operations may be arranged, consider our hypothetical East-West Railroad's situation in the metropolitan/port area of J. The principal trackage in the "J Switching District" (Fig. 11-2) is an area within which a shipper located on any one railroad is, in effect, served by all.

The tangle of trackage in Fig. 11-2 looks complicated, and it is, but it's not even in the same league as the actual situation in such areas as New York, New York; Chicago, Illinois; or Minneapolis-St. Paul, Minnesota. It will serve to illustrate some typical arrangements for getting freight into the line-haul system.

The Base of Operations

The East-West's principal operating base in J is its "77th St. Yard," (1) in Fig. 11-2. Trains to and from the west start and end their runs here, and most switching crews working within the J district work out of 77th St., where complete servicing facilities for locomotives are available.

Switching and Terminal Companies

Much of the trackage in the J area is owned and operated by the J Terminal Railroad, (marked in the system network map, Fig. 11-2, as a "joint facility" because it is owned by the line-haul railroads serving J). The E-W System "interchanges" cars for points on the J-T at a small yard (2) switched directly by 77th St. yard crews. To reach its huge export-import coal piers at (3), the E-W has trackage rights over the J-T and its key bridge across the harbor. Intercity passenger trains operated by Amtrak over the line-haul railroads continue without pause onto J-T trackage and into the Union Station downtown at (4).

Interchanges Large and Small

As our E-W map (Fig. 2-1) shows, the E-W and the NW & NE are mostly competitors in the J area, but there is some freight originating on one of them destined for points on the other that will be interchanged at J. This traffic, a few cars each way a day, is handled by the J-T crews, who pick it up at (2) and deliver it to the NW & NE's principal J Yard at "30th St." (5). This, unfortunately, is not likely to be a quick process since there isn't enough business to make it a principal factor in scheduling the various trips that make up the short crosstown connections.

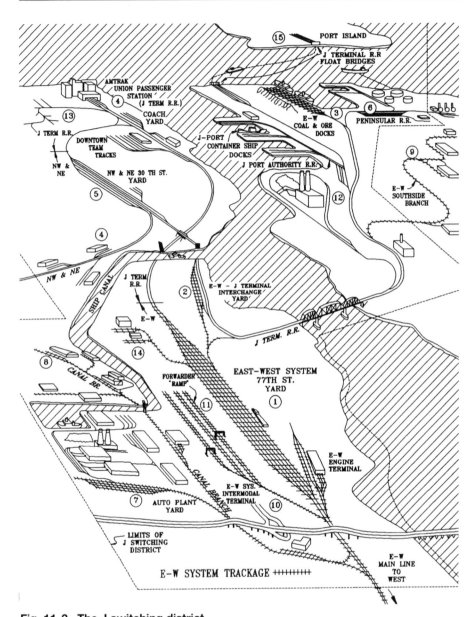

Fig. 11-2. The J switching district

The interchange between the E-W and the Peninsular Railway, on the other hand, is a big one, with many cars of feed for the farming country south of J coming in on the E-W. Interyard transfer runs from (1) to (6) handle this traffic on schedules closely tied to the arrival and departure of connections at both ends.

Reciprocal Switching

A shipper on the E-W "Canal Branch" at (8), a shipper on the J-T downtown in the congested old warehouse area at (13), and a shipper on the NW & NE at (5) with something to ship to the west can all choose either E-W or NW & NE for its initial segment of its line-hauling routing, and, under pre-1980 deregulation prevailing tariff rules, all three shippers will get the same rate. In one case, the E-W will:

- Order an empty from the NW & NE (to be delivered to them via the J-T).
- Place it for loading.
- Pick it up when released by the shipper.
- Deliver it to the J-T for transfer to the NW & NE for the roadhaul.

In another case, the situation is reversed. Within the switching district where these reciprocal arrangements apply, the origination line-haul road will "absorb" the switching and "per diem reclaim" charges payable to the other lines involved, giving up a chunk of its "division" of the through line-haul rate in exchange for being able to compete for the traffic from shippers not located on its tracks. Much of this balances out, of course, and the extra moves involved make it likely that service, speed, and reliability will cause the shipper to tend to route the freight via the line the freight is on. "Freedom of choice," uninfluenced by rate differences, is preserved. Under post-1980 Staggers Act conditions (with most regular shipments moving under contract terms more closely tied to the cost of handling individual classes of traffic) such absorption of switching charges is no longer a common practice.

Marine Railroading

Car floats serve Port Island's industries. The car floats are barges with tracks on their deck that receive strings of cars pushed aboard over "float bridges" (mating sections of track arranged to rise and fall with the tide). A tug then moves the float across the channel where its cars are offloaded and moved by switch engines to industry and dock trackage. Once a widely used method of serving harborside industries (and of bridging gaps in the main-line rail network), this flexible but expensive method of reaching across the water is now limited to a few operations in the ocean (notably between Alaska and the rest of the North American rail network) and in the Great Lakes' port areas. Here, as at J, services by individual line-haul railroads have been consolidated into joint operations.

Shifters, Locals, and Turns

The huge automobile plant at (7) is the principal source of traffic on the E-W "Canal Branch" that extends to (8), serving numerous industries within the J Switching District. Auto plant traffic requires several trips a day from 77th St. to the small Auto Plant Yard, where the plant's own locomotives and crews take over for the extensive intraplant rail operations.

Names for a particular crew assignment tend to have a strong local flavor, and what one line calls a shifter might well be dignified by an entirely different title on another railroad. All these crew assignments extending outside a yard but within a switching district have the common goal of picking up and delivering loads and empties as efficiently as possible, considering the constraints of long-standing work agreements, difficult physical track arrangements, congested grade crossings, and drawbridge interference.

Thus, what the E-W employees mean when they refer to the docks shifter is not a single 1,500 hp switch engine puttering around the waterfront but a set of up to five 6-axle road units that leave 77th St. with a massive train of coal that it hauls over the J-T to the docks and exchanges for equally heavy loads of ore; the five 6-axle road unit may also rearrange loads and empties at the pier that may be required to let the giant ship/car/stockpile/unloader do its work.

Local Freights

Outside of yard limits, local freight crews handle industry switching as they work their way along the line. Since the E-W's "Southside Branch" (9) extends beyond the J Switching District, the local freight crews do the daily switching. The branch is short but so busy that two crews are often used, one leaving 77th St. and working its way out to the far end, where a second crew takes over its locomotive, caboose, and papers for the trip back. Out on the main lines (Fig. 2-1), local freight crews are assigned segments of line long enough so that normal levels of traffic can be readily handled in a day's work, with an occasional overtime. One such run is from H to K, a fairly long distance but with relatively few plants to be switched. It is worked westbound on Monday, Wednesday, and Friday, and eastbound on the alternate days. Six-day service is often provided on this type of local by using two crews. Crew A runs west on Monday, Wednesday, and Friday, and returns on Tuesday, Thursday, and Saturday. Crew B runs west on Wednesday, Friday, and Sunday.

Combined Local and Through Service

If there is a concentration of industry with a day's local work of a terminal and no significant amount of industry for a great distance beyond, one-way-per-trip local service may be combined with through-freight service. The local works outward from the terminal (for example, B to E in Fig. 2-1) and consolidates the eastward cars it picked up for further movement by through-train at the end of the trip (at E). A westward through-train leaves the cars for delivery by the local (between E and B) at the local's turning point (at E).

Through-Freight Service

Some routes may not have enough industry to support dedicated local service. There may be no more than one or two industries in hundreds of miles. These industries will be served by through-trains, generally those handling the lowest priority traffic so that local work does not delay time-sensitive shipments.

Turns

Branches such as that from T to S may be handled by turns (runs that go out to the end of the line, turn, and come back). Through lines, such as between J and P, may be run as two shorter turns; one crew will work from H to M and back, meeting its counterpart (which is doing the same thing starting from P) at the midpoint and exchanging trains. This gets everybody back to the home terminal at the end of the shift, and the meeting point can be changed as necessary to equalize the time required on the two turns if the relative amount of business changes. Turns providing local service may also be used without a counterpart train starting from the opposite end of the line. This arrangement generally exists in urban areas where there is a concentration of industry for several miles either side of a yard, but no significant amount of industry beyond.

C H A P T E R   1 2

Classification and Blocking

O n our hypothetical East-West Railroad, the next step in the terminal operations is to assemble the cars from various sources into blocks headed for individual destinations (blocks, in this case, indicate groups of cars that are coupled and moving together, not to be confused with track "blocks" in the signal system); these blocks will then be combined into trains for the linehaul. Each block has a destination that represents the next processing point (yard or terminal) for the cars in that block. The destination yard of the block may be the destination of some of the cars, the yard at which some cars will be placed in local trains for delivery, or the yard at which some cars will be assigned to another block and train for further movement. The switching can be done in two principal ways—flat and gravity. The E-W, like most of the larger railroads, uses both.

Flat Switching

Fig. 12-1 is a condensed and shortened diagram of the E-W's 77th St. Yard at J. A real yard serving this large a metropolis would have many more tracks, but the operating scheme would be the same. Locomotive and car movements in any yard on a railroad are much the same, but the pattern and purpose of the operation is part of the railroad operating scheme as a whole, and each yard may be distinctly different in that respect.

Yards, Subyards, Tracks, and Leads

Yards of this size and complexity that exist today are also located in areas as sparsely populated and seemingly remote as J is densely populated and strategically situated. The logic for this is the FRA-mandated 1,000-mile inspection. All trains, regardless of commodity, terrain, or climate, must be thoroughly inspected every 1,000 miles or less

211

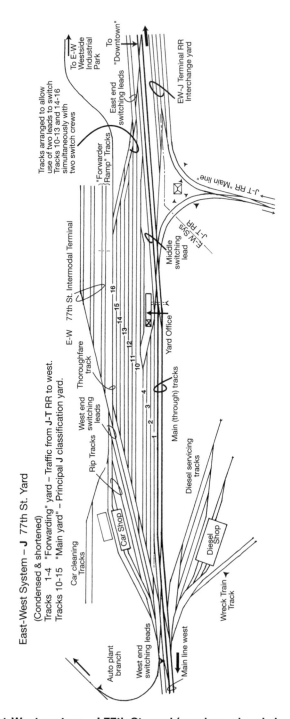

Fig. 12-1. East-West system—J 77th St. yard (condensed and shortened)

for safety-related defects by qualified railroad personnel. It is also quite convenient to perform major switching operations at these yards.

Within any major yard, the tracks will be arranged in several subyards, each with a somewhat more specific purpose. At our hypothetical 77th St., there is an engine terminal with tracks where the hostler's job is to:

- Fuel, sand, and water the diesels.

- Separate and rearrange units into new combinations, making up suitable locomotives for outgoing runs.

- Move engines into and out of the diesel shop for inspection, running repairs, and heavier maintenance work by the mechanical department's specialists.

Car repairs are performed on the "rip" (repair in place) track, in the car shop, and in the car shop yard on freight cars that need the repair. To the east is the E-W System (the J Terminal RR Interchange Yard), arranged so that cars placed by one road's switching crew can easily be picked up (after acceptance by the car inspector) by the other road's crew.

Two classification yards are in the 77th St. complex: Tracks 1 through 4, called the Forwarding Yard and Tracks 10 through 16, called the Main Yard. Each consists of a group of parallel body tracks connected by ladders (Fig. 3-14) at each end to switching leads extending from each end. Crossovers connect the switching leads to the main tracks (the main line to the west and the main line to downtown, and the line to the auto plant branch) that lead to the outside world. These are all hand-throw switches, operated by the switch crews themselves or, in the case of trains entering or leaving the yard in completing or starting their runs, by switch tenders. Some tracks, designated as through (or running) tracks, are normally kept free of standing cars so that yard and road engines can use them to get from one end of the yard to the other freely without fouling the main tracks.

Shuffling the Deck

To take one example of all the car-flows in which 77th St. is involved, consider the matter of getting empty cars to industries along the E-W's main line between J and I. Plenty of cars are available that have come into the J area from the west under load, and are consigned to team tracks, distribution terminals, and consuming industries all over the J Switching District. They come back into 77th St. from various switch runs, directly and via the J-T interchange, and will be found on tracks in the Main Yard assigned as "arrival tracks" by the yardmaster.

The Switch List

Yard and computer-generated data received on all empty cars entering the 77th St. yards are analyzed by the division's car distributor, who will identify suitable empties (in regard to ownership, type, or special equipment) to match against empty car orders received from the customers. Based on this information, the yard office will generate a switch list that tells a yard crew on which tracks and in what order cars currently sitting on other tracks are to be placed.

The objective in this particular case is to make up the "I Peddler" (the local freight that runs from J to I, serving the lineside industries en route). In the process, of course, the switch crew that assembles the train and the yard or local crew that delivers the cars will handle many cars as part of their day's work. The switch crew will generally consist of a foreman and perhaps one switchman (yard helper). There may be an engineer, but many yard engines are now operated by remote control, the yard foreman and helper wearing belt-mounted control boxes to operate the locomotive. A yard crew delivering the cars may be similar to the switch crew. A local crew operating on the main line outside of the terminal limit will generally consist of a conductor, an engineer, and perhaps one brakeman. When the I Peddler is complete, it will have both empties and loads for its industries, including cars that have come from the Peninsular, from the docks on Port Island, and even from eastbound trains. It may be quicker to bring a car destined for a point just west of J into 77th St. on a fast freight from the west and then take it back on the local rather than having it come all the way east from I in local service.

Station Order

To speed up the local's work, its train will be arranged in station order, (cars to be set out at the first station are placed at the head end, followed by those cars to be set out at the next station, and so on). Blocking cars by station order is particularly important in the case of through-freights that make set-outs and pick-ups at only a few specified points and whose schedules aren't compatible with any additional manipulating en route.

Batting 'em Out

To carry out the work put on paper by the switch list, the locomotive takes a cut of cars from one of the yard tracks, hauls it back onto the switch lead, and then proceeds to shove (kick) the cars into their assigned tracks. A capable, experienced crew will often have several cuts of cars moving at one time, coasting slowly toward the cars already on the body tracks after being cut from the string attached to the locomotive. The yard helper or brakeman will think ahead and be in the right position to line up a switch for the next cut. They may ride on a rolling car to be in position for the next move but are often prohibited by safety rules from getting on or off of a moving car or locomotive. The crew will kick cars taking into account their weight, the distance to be traveled, and any grades in the yard so that they do not impact at more than walking speed (4 mph or less). Yard leads are sometimes just a bit higher than the center of the body tracks so that a slight grade helps keep the cuts rolling. Cars with especially sensitive loads are moved all the way into coupling with the locomotive attached and other cars are not dropped onto them, as called for by the rules.

Nevertheless, flat switching is a relatively slow and consequently expensive process if a lot of rearranging is to be done. After the cars are in the proper tracks for their destination, they probably will not be in station order, so it will be necessary to pull them back out and shuffle them again. In flat switching a long train, the switch engine may take short cuts of cars and classify them, moving rather snappily in the process but having to go back several times to get more, or take longer cuts and have to accelerate sluggishly in making each move. Either way, it will move the equivalent of many train lengths in getting all cars into their assigned positions.

Gravity Switching

Because of the time and money consumed by flat switching, the E-W Railroad (like most fairly large railroads) does as much of its classification as possible by gravity. It has built what it likes to call "electronic classification yards," often simply known as "hump" or "retarder" yards, at D and H. The yard at H provides hump classification of westbound cars only, based on system traffic flow studies, while D Yard (located between the two main tracks) has separate gravity yards for handling eastbound and westbound traffic.

Systemwide Effects

Because of the capability for thorough classification of westbound trains at H, the J 77th St. Yard simply places into trains (in any order) all westbound cars arriving from every connection, branch, and station in the area (except for those going out in the I Local) and sends them off to H. Cars coming into H from the west are already blocked for the various connecting railroads, docks, yards, and major industries in the J area. As a result, about half the trackage in the main 77th St. classification yards was removed to make room for the new Intermodal Yards handling the E-W's steadily increasing piggyback traffic.

Very little eastbound traffic comes onto the E-W between D and H, so trains are blocked at D so thoroughly that they can go to their destinations without further classifications and bypass the H Yard; what little eastbound work must be done there can be done better by flat switching.

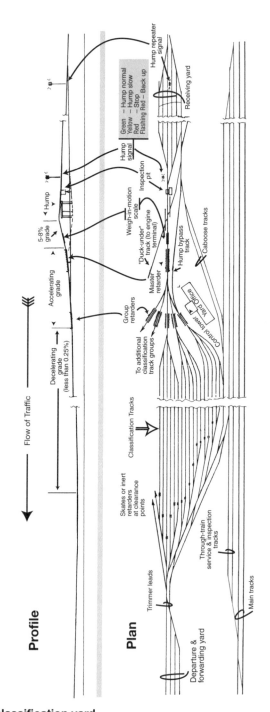

Fig. 12-2. Gravity classification yard

Systemwide Switching Strategy

When there is a sufficient volume of traffic for a single destination or a number of destinations beyond an en route terminal, cars may be accumulated to run in a train that bypasses other, intermediate, yards. It may be worthwhile to accumulate cars for a day or more and eliminate the time and trouble of intermediate handling one or more times. That strategy does not fit all traffic. The volumes on some routes and the origins and destinations of shipments may not allow this strategy. In the past, such shipments always moved from yard to yard to yard, being switched into a new block at each yard until it reached its destination. Sophisticated data processing systems have made it possible to reduce switching on such cars by developing a systemwide blocking strategy that sends all cars for a similar destination to a single point for switching and consolidation whether that yard is on the direct route of the shipment or not.

It may make sense to send a car out of route for a day or ultimately backhaul it for a day if that routing saves overall transit time or reduces en route switching of the cars or both. The routing may depend on the time and day that the car is released to begin its journey. The computer system may assign cars to a block after considering all of the available shipments throughout the system that are destined to a general area and the workload of several candidate yards at the time that the various trains handling the shipments will arrive.

The Hump Yard

Fig. 12-2 shows a gravity yard arrangement typical of that built by the E-W System at H. The basic idea, of course, is to push the cars being sorted over an artificial hill or "hump" and let gravity move them into the classification tracks. It is the most efficient classification method if the traffic pattern is such that most of the cars passing through are headed in different directions from their neighbors in the incoming trains. Running the whole train over the hump just to get one or two groups of cars headed in the right direction would not be worthwhile. But where the cars are really scrambled, the hump comes into its own; the hump locomotive need travel only one train length in classifying the entire consist, shoving the cut at a constant, slow speed.

The Receiving Yard

Incoming trains stop in the receiving or arrival yard, which must have enough tracks to accommodate trains coming in from all principal lines over a period of a few hours. Road locomotives and cabooses are removed, and the humping engine, often a six-axle unit with a slug attached, couples up to the rear of the cars on one track, generally after a mechanical inspection of the cars so that those in need of repair may be routed to a repair track or facility during the switching.

Other hump-yard facilities include an inspection pit, often provided on the single track approaching the hump itself so that each car's running gear can be thoroughly inspected for defects (sometimes as a replacement for inspection in the receiving track), which will get in-train or rip-track attention depending on the nature of the problem. Receiving yards may also be set up with track spacing and runaways so that inspectors can examine cars from small utility vehicles.

Before being pushed over the hump, air must be bled from brake cylinders so that the cars will roll freely. A switch list is provided to the "pin-puller" (who stands at the right side of the hump) so that person will know where the cars are to be separated. The upgrade leading to the hump ensures that the slack is in so the cut lever can be operated.

The Classification Bowl

The classification tracks themselves, often called the bowl because of their concave profile, fan out from the base of the hump in groups of five to nine tracks; the total number of tracks depends on the size and function of the yard and available land but may be as many as 60 to 70.

Coming over the hump, the cuts of one or more cars first encounter a steep grade, which quickly accelerates each cut so that there will be enough space between it and the next one for switches to be thrown. Usually, a "weigh-in-motion" scale automatically takes care of the requirement that each car loaded on-line must be weighed before it enters interchange (the point where the car crosses to another railroad) or reaches its destination.

Car Retarders

Electric or electropneumatic car retarders regulate the motion of the car during its descent; it is the computerized control of the switches and retarders that gives the modern hump yard its "electronic classification yard" title. The retarder is a set of powerful jaws on each side of and a few inches above the rail head that grasps the car wheels, slowing the car to the computed exit speed. This process produces loud squealing, and some yards located in populated areas now must meet environmental requirements by providing noise baffles alongside the retarders to reduce, to an acceptable level, noise radiated sidewise.

The retarders are arranged so that each car passes through only two retarders: a master retarder at the foot of the hump and one group retarder on the track leading into each group of classification tracks. Through the group retarders, the tracks are on enough of a grade to accelerate the cars and make sure that they will move through the turnouts into the classification tracks. Beyond that point, they flatten out to a grade that isn't quite enough to keep a free-rolling car moving at the speed at which it enters the track.

At the far end of the classification tracks is usually a slight upgrade that slows cars as they approach the turnouts and tracks leading to the departure tracks. Skates (wedge-shaped shoes placed atop the rail by a remote-controlled skate-placing machine) or inert retarders (spring-loaded versions of the master or group machines) are used to keep the cars from rolling too far and fouling the exit trackage.

Retarder Control

In the most modern electronic yards, the retarder and switch control system accepts "switch list" data telling it which track each cut is to take, along with waybill information on the weight of each car, and a count of the cars already in each track. Its memory includes such information as the length, grades, and curvatures of each track and its approaches. It gets individual data on the speed and "rollability" of each cut—on both curved and straight sections—from trackside radar devices, and keeps track of the wind velocity affecting car movement.

The retarders are controlled, using this computerized information, so that each car leaves the group retarder at a speed that will let it roll just far enough up the track to which it is being sent to couple with the cars already there. The hump tower operator monitors the whole operation from the tower vantage point where, day or night, each cut rolling down into the bowl can be watched and the automatic operation can be overridden or modified if any problem threatens to develop.

Distributive Retarders

Another type of coupling-speed control is provided by the distributive retarder system. A small forest of hydraulic cylinders located close alongside the rails in the classification tracks contain mushroom-shaped pistons that must be depressed by the wheels of a car as it rolls by. An orifice restricts the rate at which the piston may be pushed down so that a car traveling at more than 4 mph will be retarded to that speed. Spaced along tracks on a slightly descending grade, these cylinders act, without the complication of any centralized control, to maintain the desired constant speed up to coupling. As an option, units provided with an air supply can also nudge a car up to the set speed if it is traveling too slowly. This system, which trades system and installation costs for the upkeep of hundreds of spread-out mechanical units, has gone into service in North America in a few relatively small yards. In the interest of minimum wear on the retarders, these are double-ended yards in which locomotives need not enter the classification tracks and cars routinely pass the retarders only once.

Trimming

At the lower end of the yard, one or two trimmer locomotives take care of such chores as pushing cars together if they didn't quite come together, rearranging cars within a classification and rehumping any misclassified cuts.

Cars go over the hump at a rate of about 3 mph, which works out to one 50 ft car every 10 seconds or 300 cars per hour. With two hump locomotives on the job so that a second train can start over the hump as soon as the first has cleared, and with a reasonable allowance for trimming and other delays, a single hump can classify up to 1,500 cars per 8-hour shift. Traffic is rarely distributed evenly around the clock to fully utilize hump capacity on all three shifts, but processing of 3,000 to 3,500 cars per day is often achieved.

High-Capacity Yards

Since all the cars being classified into a single bowl must go over one track, yards that must handle more cars than this must either (1) have two hump tracks that (at least during some times of the day) can function as two separate subyards, each distributing cars into the tracks on its side of the bowl, or (2) the speed over the hump must be increased. This can be done by providing a third set of tangent-point retarders (located at the point where the cars enter the individual classification tracks) making the final speed reduction. Cars can then travel through the turnouts and group retarder area at higher speeds, increasing the rate at which the train can go over the hump without having the cuts too close together.

Departure

In some hump yards, trains leave directly from the classification tracks, but in most cases classified cuts are pulled forward into a departure and forwarding yard. Here they are combined into trains (perhaps by the road locomotive if agreements permit) with blocks in station order, fitted with the rear-coupler-mounted EOT (end-of-train) device that has generally superseded the caboose, and subjected to mandatory predeparture mechanical inspection and air brake tests.

Line-Haul Operations

To safely and efficiently conduct its line-haul operations, a railroad must coordinate many otherwise independent activities across a rail network. The coordination relies on communication, so its effectiveness is determined by its communication technology. In years past, communication was limited to hand and whistle signals, telegraph and telephone systems, and written instructions in timetables and train orders. In time, signal indications at block stations, at interlockings, and in CTC or ABS systems provided authority for train movements. This environment prevailed for many years, until advances in communication technology—especially direct dispatcher-to-train voice or digital radio communication—emerged. This breakthrough enabled the closing of many towers that existed largely to deliver a dispatcher's orders to a train crew by physical hand-off of written instructions. Direct dispatcher-to-train communication had a significant impact on both signaled and unsignaled operations:

- In ABS (Automated Block System) territory, it provided the means of authorizing movement into such territory.

- In CTC (Centralized Traffic Control) territory, it enabled the exceptional movements not handled by signal indication.

- In unsignaled territory, it had its largest impact, enabling the deployment of Track Warrant Control (TWC) and Direct Train Control (DTC) systems and their greater control of train operations.

With these technological advances came fundamental changes to the control of line-haul operations. Timetable and train order operation (T&TO) has largely disappeared. All trains are run as extras, and even Amtrak and commuter trains have been removed from employee timetables. "Hot" trains are no longer indicated by "Class of Train," but are given higher priority by the dispatcher's actions.

Control of Line-Haul Operations

Often, when line-haul operations are contemplated, one envisions high-speed operation on single- or double-track CTC. This may be typical of many high-density corridors, but nearly all trains must traverse territories—especially in or near terminals—where other control regimes dictate train movements. Let's examine the life of a typical road train from its origin to its destination.

Imagine the high-priority general-merchandise train H-CHINYC operating between Chicago and a freight yard outside New York City. A train schedule template (often called a base schedule) resides in a computer database, and the computer or dispatcher activates the schedule to initiate today's operation. As the time of the train's departure approaches, the following various activities start:

- The crew call system identifies the crew members to be called by the crew caller.
- The locomotive dispatcher and the service track foreman prepare locomotives
- The yardmaster and mechanical crews ready the cars for departure.

The locomotives must be moved from the ready tracks to the head end of the train, a function performed either by the road train crew or by dedicated engine hostlers. Their movement is entirely within the yard, so they operate under "other than main track" rules where they must look out for their own safety, being prepared to stop within one-half their line of sight and looking out for conflicting moves, turnouts improperly lined, and so on.

Once the power is attached to the train, the crew charges the air brake system and performs brake tests to ensure brake line continuity and proper brake application and release. (In some yards, "yard air" is available to charge the brake system, and mechanical forces certify that the system is functioning properly.) With dispatcher and yardmaster permission, the train departs the yard, often proceeding under "other than main track" rules until entering main track, so designated in the employee timetable. There, dispatcher authority, communicated either by signal indication or by a radio order transcribed by the crew, permits the train to enter the main track.

At various terminals en route, the train may enter "yard limits" (main track whose use is controlled by track warrant or other dispatcher authority). The train need not protect against other trains or engines, but it may proceed only at a low speed, typically restricted speed (20 mph, prepared to stop within one-half the line of sight of the crew) unless a signal indicates the route is clear.

Our high-priority Chicago–to–New York City general-merchandise train would very likely operate over territory equipped with CTC, where signal indications authorize train movement. The dispatcher would set up the meets and the overtakes consistent with the train's priority relative to other trains. The priority may change over time if the train is ahead of schedule or if a delay to other trains would cause them to miss service commitments or cause the crew to exceed its hours of service.

CTC systems will predominate on high-density corridors, but it is not uncommon that some segments of ABS control may be interspersed with the CTC. Entry into such territory requires dispatcher permission, but, once entered, authority to proceed with the "current of traffic" established for that track is conveyed by signal indication. If moving "against the current of traffic" (i.e., running "wrong main" in double-track ABS), a track warrant will establish the limits of its movement authority on that track. Since there are no approach signals to interlockings or junctions when running "wrong main," trains must approach the home signals of interlockings prepared to stop unless the home signal is seen to be clear.

Typically, a general-merchandise train would set out or pick up blocks of traffic or both en route. With cabooseless operations and all crew members at the head end, the order of the blocks on the train must be carefully managed so that cars may be picked up or set out without requiring a head-end crew member to walk a great distance to perform this work. Air brake rules can also limit the flexibility of work en route, since a full air brake test—often requiring an assist from the Mechanical Department—may be required if a train consist is dramatically altered with multiple block pick-ups and set-outs at any terminal.

It would be unlikely that our hot Chicago–New York City freight would encounter any unsignaled territory, but that might happen if the train had to be diverted off its normal route. Main-line unsignaled territory is controlled by radio-based block systems, where the block limits are either fixed (DTC) or are set according to dispatcher instructions (TWC). In either case, trains must get movement authority from the dispatcher via radio, and the crew must record the instructions onto forms and proceed accordingly. Crews will advise the dispatcher when they are approaching the limits of their current authority so that they receive new authority or when they are clear of the track specified so that they release track previously occupied for use by other train movements.

Railroads have installed numerous train defect detection devices across their networks, including sensors for hot bearings, dragging equipment, truck-curving performance, and wheel defects, especially flat wheels where WILD (wheel impact load detectors) are used. When a defect is detected, the train is typically stopped and the offending car must be set out, translating into a long delay if the head-end crew member must walk a great distance to the railcar.

Another important wayside device is the Automated Equipment Identification (AEI) reader, which communicates with electronic chips on railcars, locomotives, end-of-train devices, and many trailers and containers. This technology has automated many reporting functions and improved their accuracy. Most AEI tags simply provide stored information (i.e., car initial and number), but some are active tags that can communicate real-time data such as locomotive fuel levels and mechanical refrigerator temperatures. Although the AEI system is valuable for locating equipment, it does not inherently know the identity of the train that is passing. This function falls to the railroad computer system, which takes the AEI list, cross-references it by locomotive number to previously reported train consists, and appends a train ID to the AEI list.

Upon arrival at the train's terminus, the train must be put away in receiving tracks. Modern trains are often longer than tracks in yards built years ago, so the crew may have to "double" or even "triple" their train into two or three tracks. The inbound road crew may cut their engines off the train and operate the power to the locomotive servicing tracks, or they may be instructed to leave the power on the train and be transported by van to the yard office. There, they file trip reports, including statements of en route delays, and record their off-duty time. If this station is the "away from home terminal" for this crew district, the railroad will arrange to transport them to lodging for food and rest before they are again called for road service.

The Future

Rapid advances in computer and communication technology have produced remarkably swift changes in control of line-haul operations. For example, timetable and train order control, a mainstay for many years, virtually disappeared in one decade—the 1990s. Railroads are now testing and, in an increasing number of cases, deploying PTC (Positive Train Control) systems where movement authorities are communicated electronically and enforced by on-board computers should the engineer fail to apply brakes to bring the train into compliance with the authority. It might soon be possible to avoid the high cost of CTC installation while obtaining many of CTC's benefits if TWC can be combined with on-board control of power turnouts at sidings and junctions, eliminating the time wasted today when manually reversing and restoring turnouts for train meets.

Unit-Train Operations

The past several chapters have described the several components that make up a railroad trip:

- Switching at origin (industry, interchange, port, or intermodal ramp)
- Line-haul movement between railroad terminals
- Switching at terminals between origin and destination
- Switching at destination (industry, interchange, port or intermodal ramp)

In general terms, railroads have cost advantages over their highway competition in the line-haul component of the trip, especially for heavy commodities. However, switching at origin, destination, and intermediate points is an expensive and relatively fixed-cost operation. Therefore, to remain competitive, railroads must lessen this component of their operating cost. If they can pull multiple cars between an origin and a destination, they minimize the switching cost throughout the trip. The economics greatly favor railroads when a trainload can be handled at one time and the cars can be loaded and unloaded quickly. This is the principle behind multi-car and unit-train operations.

The efficiencies gained are not without some cost. Before the separation of large volume shipments into unit trains, traffic moved in the general-merchandise network, along with boxcars, tank cars, gondolas, and other shipments. With less traffic, the general-merchandise network is not as fluid, and fewer train arrivals and departures translate into longer dwell times in yards. Furthermore, efficient loading and unloading, plus efficiencies in line-haul operation, mandate the use of specialized equipment for unit-train service not suitable for reloading with other commodities.

Perspective

Large-scale movements of single commodities between large producers and large consumers has been a feature of railroads since the early days, but rate regulation under the Interstate Commerce Commission (ICC) prevented the railroads from lowering their prices when the economies of scale of unit-train operation lowered their costs. This policy reflected the ICC's concern that such rates would favor large shippers over small ones, which was considered bad public policy. Furthermore, railroad costs are very complex, and have a large fixed-cost element, making average costs high even if marginal costs are low. It took nearly a decade of submissions in the 1950s and 1960s to the ICC and numerous court appeals, including one to the U.S. Supreme Court, before railroads could reduce rates to reflect lower costs and regain traffic lost to competition. Legislative changes took longer, but regulatory relief arrived for U.S. railroads with the passage of the Staggers Act of 1980, giving railroads sweeping freedom to set rates, negotiate individual-shipper contracts, and provide new service offerings. This enabled railroads to better compete with the newly deregulated trucking industry. Railroad rates could only be reviewed by the government if their rates reflected that the railroad was exercising monopoly power in a market.

The Unit Train

In its simplest form, the unit train can be viewed as a conveyor belt on rails, moving large volumes of a commodity from one origin to one destination. Terminals at either end have been outfitted with efficient loading and unloading facilities, and the trainset's railcars are designed for rapid loading and unloading as well. Although the largest scale application of this principle has been in the movement of coal from mine to power plant, it is also used in handling such commodities as grain, ethanol, steel, orange juice, hot liquid sulfur, and intermodal equipment, especially double-stacked containers. A typical unit coal train is shown in Fig. 14-1.

At times, the volume of traffic available between a single shipper and an individual consignee is not adequate to justify a full unit train. Such shipments could move in the general-merchandise network, but they would be more efficiently handled in multi-car service. In many ways, this service mirrors unit-train efficiency in loading and unloading, but the individual shipments must be assembled from several sources into a train-load, then move to a common intermediate destination where they may be disassembled and disseminated to multiple destinations. They may appear as unit trains because their cars and commodity may appear identical, but they are not true unit trains.

Fig. 14-1. Unit coal train being "flood loaded"

Railcar and Locomotive Specialization

To extract the maximum efficiencies from the unit-train operations, the railroad equipment used is typically very specialized for the service to be performed. In many cases, top-loading open or covered hopper cars are used that can be rapidly unloaded from bottom hatches, with some cars equipped with air-actuated hopper doors. Coal is often transported in high-sided gondola cars that are unloaded by overturning the cars in a dumper (without uncoupling the cars if one end of each is equipped with a special rotary coupler). The specifics of the loading and unloading process depend, to a considerable extent, on the space available at the receiving end of the movement and the age of the unloading equipment, with newer installations generally equipped with rotary-dump facilities. Light weight yet strong aluminum cars have replaced steel-bodied equipment, especially for unit coal shipments. This permits as much lading weight as 116 tons per car without exceeding the prevailing 286,000 pound gross weight restriction. Moving in trains of 110 to 135 cars, over 15,500 tons of coal can be delivered in each train.

Like the railcars, the locomotives utilized in unit-train service may be very specialized. When transporting bulk commodities over long distances, the locomotives must produce sufficient tractive effort to overcome any grade they encounter, and adequate horsepower to propel the trains at track speed to avoid impeding other trains. Furthermore, the locomotives may be specially equipped to permit distributed power operation (DPU); the locomotives are typically deployed with multiple units in the lead and one at the rear, thereby reducing drawbar forces and improving train-handling and braking performance. Common practice in the United States is the assignment of a railroad's newest power to these trains because these locomotives are high-horsepower, high-tractive-effort units. This assignment also generates fuel savings, as these locomotives, the most fuel efficient in the fleet, are matched to the service that most rapidly produces ton-miles.

Depending on negotiations between the railroad and its customers, the railroad may provide the rail equipment, but carriers are moving increasingly to encouraging or requiring customers to provide their own cars, either through purchase or lease. Railroad-owned equipment may be used to supplement private car fleets when necessary.

Rates

Immediately after winning their right to enter into contracts with their customers in 1980, railroads placed much traffic, especially long-term, high-volume shipments, under contract. Contractual commitments enabled railroads to target their capital investments to areas of known growth, and provided them greater assurance that their investments would earn adequate returns. The contracts typically specified volume and service commitments, and many had clauses that automatically adjusted rates based on rail-cost inflation tied to the Rail Cost Adjustment Factor (RCAF) produced by the AAR.

Over time, various factors have led railroads and their customers to move away from long-term contracts. Customers want the flexibility to re-examine their pricing and sourcing options at shorter intervals, necessitating contracts of shorter duration. Similarly, railroads have found that long-term contracts are not consistent with market volatility, especially the highly unpredictable diesel fuel market. Contracts are still written for major market segments, but railroads often use published tariffs that permit the rates and conditions to be altered more rapidly.

Equipment Utilization

The utilization of dedicated cars can achieve mileage-per-day averages exceeding three times that of the general-service car. Although the length of haul varies widely, round-trip travel may reach 4,000 miles and consume 11 days. The repetitive, high-mileage moves have major consequences for maintenance of equipment, track, and structures. Entire trainsets may be taken out of service for preventive maintenance, because setting out an individual bad order car delays the entire train, reduces its lading capacity, and requires concerted efforts to return the repaired car to the trainset. The track and structures experience highly repetitive loading, which may produce accelerated wear that must be corrected by taking the line out of service, producing traffic bottlenecks.

Mini-Trains

For many railroads, economics dictate that a unit train be 50 or more cars. Short line railroads, with their lower costs and more flexible work rules, may profitably operate unit trains with fewer cars. This may enable penetration into markets long ago lost to trucks. Such point-to-point "mini-trains" may carry a commodity such as crushed rock, sand, or grain in 5- or 10-car units directly from a loading to a delivery point. They operate under tariffs requiring special "while-we-wait" loading and unloading and work rules allowing a one- or two-man train crew not restricted by normal divisional or yard/road limits.

The mini-train becomes, in effect, a 500- to 1,500-ton truck that can take grain from a country elevator to a terminal on demand without tying up expensive covered hoppers for days in the "normal" local freight set-out/load/pick-up/classify/roadhaul/yard switch/set-out/unload and return car cycle. As the unit train's low rates have made producers of low-value commodities competitive over distances previously impossible, the mini-train can make railhaul truck-competitive on short hauls.

Intermodal Traffic

In 2003, for the first time ever, intermodal surpassed coal as the leading source of revenue for the Class I railroads. This is a fascinating and dynamic story, resulting from the enormous demand for consumer goods, globalization and sweeping changes in logistics, and innovative railcar designs.

What Is Intermodal?

Intermodal is simply transportation involving more than one mode of transportation during a single journey. However, in the context of railroading, the definition is slightly more complex and further explained by Gerhardt Muller in his book *Intermodal Freight Transportation,* as "… transporting freight [in trailers or containers] on two or more different modes in such a way that all parts of the transportation process, including the exchange of information, are efficiently connected and coordinated."

History of Intermodal Transportation

Railroad intermodal operations date back to at least the 1880s, when the Long Island Rail Road shipped farm wagons on flatcars. The roots of current intermodal operations, however, began to sprout in the 1950s, with the near simultaneous occurrence of three key events. *First,* in 1956, Congress passed the Interstate Highway Act (officially called the Federal-Aid Highway Act of 1956), which created the nation's interstate highway system. The ever expanding and improving road network subjected the railroads to intense competition from trucks. Truckers offered shippers lower rates, faster transit times, and significant warehousing and inventory cost savings due to smaller shipment sizes.

Second, during World War II, railroads carried over 90 percent of intercity freight, but by the mid-1950s, railroad market share declined to less than 50 percent. To help counter this trend, railroads created trailer-on-flatcar service (TOFC), which permitted shippers to load their products into truck trailers and then ship by rail. Early trailers were 30-35 ft in length and secured to the flatcar using a combination of 40 jacks and chains. By 1955, railroads carried 284,000 trailers (168,000 carloads). That is barely 4 percent of what is carried today, but TOFC service marked the beginning of modern intermodal operations.

Also, the first container ship operations began in 1956. Launched in April by Malcom McLean (who later founded Sea-Land Steamship Lines), the *Ideal X* sailed from New York to Houston. While the maiden voyage only carried 58 containers, it is widely considered the beginning of "container revolution." Containerization reduced the time ships needed in port and diminished loss, damage, and pilferage. This resulted in enormous efficiency gains.

The *third* key event was the 1957 invention of the collapsible trailer hitch. When raised, the hitch grasped the trailer kingpin and no further tie-downs were necessary (eliminating the cumbersome 40 jacks and chains). Moreover, the hitch could be lowered, permitting trailers to drive over it. This was critical because during intermodal's early years, railroads loaded the trailers by driving them up ramps located at the end of the cars. Multiple cars were loaded by driving the trailers over each car, which were connected by bridge plates, until the desired loading location was reached (known as *circus loading*).

During the 1960s, domestic intermodal traffic grew by leaps and bounds, reaching 1.8 million annual trailers and containers by 1965 (a 640 percent increase over 1955). International traffic began to develop as well. In 1966, Sea-Land transported the first trans-Atlantic containers and trans-Pacific container services started in the late 1960s between Japan and the U.S. West Coast by American President Lines (APL), Nippon Yusen Kaisha (NYK Line), Kawasaki Kisen Kaisha (K-Line), and Mitsui O.S.K. Lines, among others. Interestingly, many of the containers from Japan routed via railroad to Northeastern U.S. ports for reloading onto container ships for Europe, and this service was known as "land-bridge" (Fig 15.1). The balance of the containers transported inland via rail for North American consumption was labeled "mini-land bridge" (also called IPI traffic for Inland Point Intermodal). Today, mini-land bridge is widespread, but land bridge has fallen out of use.

Railcar design developed, too. By 1960, flatcars increased in length to 89 ft, so they could handle two 40 ft trailers per car. Previously, railcars were either 50 ft or 75 ft in length, but as the trailers grew in size, longer railcars were required, and the 89 ft car became the backbone of the railroad intermodal fleet for the next 15 to 20 years.

The 1970s brought significant changes as well, and intermodal traffic continued to skyrocket, growing by 40 percent from just 5 years earlier. The railroads carried 2.4 million trailers and containers (1.4 million carloads) in 1970, and the vast majority was domestic freight carried in trailers. Truck trailers increased in size, too, quickly growing from 40 ft in length at the beginning of the 1970s to 45 ft, and then 48 ft long.

International traffic expanded rapidly as Asian economies produced consumer goods for the North American market and the railroads provided a lower cost alternative to trucking large volumes of containers from the ports to inland destinations.

One of the pricing trends that started in the 1960s and that gained momentum during the 1970s, was the railroads' shift from a retailer to a wholesaler of intermodal transportation (i.e., the railroads sold their transportation services to other transportation providers, such as trucking companies, steamship lines, freight forwarders and consolidators, who, in turn, provided rates and service to the producers or consumers

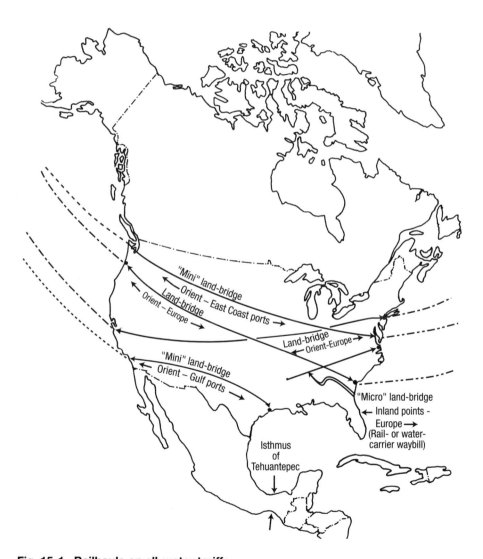

Fig. 15-1. Railhauls on all-water tariffs

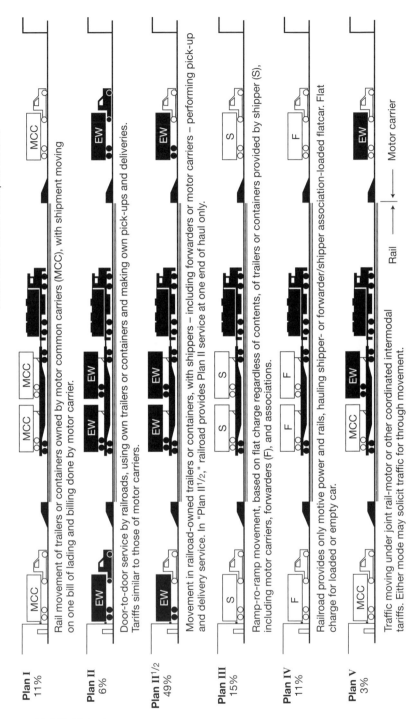

Fig. 15-2. TOFC/COFC plans

The following text appears within the figure:

Items shown in black provided (owned or leased) by railroad. Trailer/Motor carrier examples shown.

Plan I 11%
Rail movement of trailers or containers owned by motor common carriers (MCC), with shipment moving on one bill of lading and billing done by motor carrier.

Plan II 6%
Door-to-door service by railroads, using own trailers or containers and making own pick-ups and deliveries. Tariffs similar to those of motor carriers.

Plan II1/2 49%
Movement in railroad-owned trailers or containers, with shippers – including forwarders or motor carriers – performing pick-up and delivery service. In "Plan II1/2," railroad provides Plan II service at one end of haul only.

Plan III 15%
Ramp-ro-ramp movement, based on flat charge regardless of contents, of trailers or containers provided by shipper (S), including motor carriers, forwarders (F), and associations.

Plan IV 11%
Railroad provides only motive power and rails, hauling shipper- or forwarder/shipper association-loaded flatcar. Flat charge for loaded or empty car.

Plan V 3%
Traffic moving under joint rail-motor or other coordinated intermodal tariffs. Either mode may solicit traffic for through movement.

Rail ——— Motor carrier

234

of the goods). See Fig. 15.2. Today, railroads generally provide only wholesale transportation, but, like any rule, there are some exceptions.

Rail terminal operation changed rapidly in the 1970s, too. Instead of circus loading, the railroads mechanized the process, using overhead and side loading cranes to load and unload the railcars. This eliminated the need to drive the trailers over the cars. Not only was it more efficient to use cranes, it enabled railcar designers to eliminate substantial weight from the cars since solid steel decks running the entire length of the car were no longer needed.

This proved fortunate as oil prices dramatically increased in the early 1970s, and the railroads developed new lightweight, fuel-efficient "spine" cars. These cars are essentially just the center sill and trucks, along with a minimal platform to support either container pedestals or highway trailer wheels. Many of the cars were articulated to save further weight, and some designs included single-axle trucks (but those cars were not articulated). Figs. 15-3 through 15.7 show several intermodal equipment designs.

The most significant intermodal railcar design of the decade was the double-stack car, which made its initial appearance in 1977. The Southern Pacific, Sea-Land, and American Car & Foundry jointly developed the prototype, and the concepts for it date back to 1970. The first car was a "stand-alone well," meaning it was one car that carried two containers stacked on each other; the stand-alone well car is supported by two trucks, each with two axles. Subsequent designs created in 1979 used articulated trucks, which lowered the tare weight, improved fuel efficiency, and decreased the overall length of the car compared to a stand-alone well car. One interesting feature of the early well car design is that they did not have a center sill. The side sills supported the load. This weight-saving design continues in use today.

Compared to 89 ft flatcars and intermodal spine cars, double-stack cars literally carry twice the number of containers per foot of train length—a huge jump in efficiency. It is difficult to overstate the importance of the double-stack car. Without it, railroad intermodal growth and revenues would be a small fraction of what they are today.

Aside from the creation of the double-stack car, another far-reaching event that began in the 1970s was deregulation of intermodal pricing and service. Congress did not completely deregulate railroad pricing until 1980 (with the passage of the Staggers Act), but the 4-R Railroad act enacted by Congress in 1976 began the process that allowed railroads to change their prices without interference from regulators.

The Double-Stack Revolution

The combination of a fast growing market for consumer goods, newfound pricing freedom, and efficient railcar design, then, set the table for the double-stack revolution. In 1980, the railroads carried 3.1 million trailers or containers. By 1985, that number rose to 4.6 million, and by 1990, intermodal loads reached 6.2 million, an astounding 200 percent growth rate for the decade. Double-stack operations began in earnest in

Two-Axle Platform

Light weight, single-axle-truck platforms for 48 ft trailers in general service.

Clearance for nose-mounted refrigeration unit -----------

16 ft 1½ in. to rail with 13 ft 6 in. "high" trailers

28 in.-wheel low-deck, one-trailer units drawbar–connected in group of four. Minimum TOFC tare wgt. (24,000 lb/trailer), operable on low-clearance routes.

Articulated Skeleton

Light weight, center sill + single-end-platform units, articulated into groups of five or ten per "car."

Slack-free connectors, std. 70-ton trucks, 33-in. wheel trucks. Low tare weight, low-profile aerodynamics for major fuel savings on high-speed routes.

Articulated "Spine" COFC

Light weight center sill only "platforms" with crossbearers/attachments for containers only.

Provision for 20 ft containers on alternate platforms

48' max

Slack-free connectors, std. 70-ton trucks, minimal structure to accommodate containers of various lengths, heights. Tare 26,000 lb/platform

Articulated "Bulkhead" Double-Stack

Low-tare and reduced train-length, COFC-only configuration supporting, securing, upper-level containers directly on car bulkhead structure.

17'0" with 8'6" high boxes

40' well

Upper container support/restraint

Std. 100-ton intermediate trucks

70-ton end truck

Stacking reduces tare/container to 17,500 lb. Load limit/well 100,000 lb net.

High-Capacity "IBC" Double-Stack

Enlarged version of five-platform double-stack to accommodate longer, heavier containers in all combinations.

20'6" with two 9'6" boxes

40', 45', 48', 53'

24' ⟶ | ⟵ 20' ⟶ | ⟵ 20' ⟶

IBC's (interbox connectors) position secure upper containers

Std. 125-ton (78,750 lb axle load) intermediate trucks 70-ton end trucks
Higher capacity trucks raise net load limit/well to 122,000 lb.

Dual-Mode Trailer ("Carless" Intermodal)

Dedicated-service consists of trainable trailers equipped for rail and highway travel; trailers operated in slackless trains of up to 75 units. Minimum air drag with close-coupled, matched trailer bodies.

RoadRailer® MK IV

48'

13'6"

Forwardmost unit supported by adapter car

MK IV trailers equipped with dual (rail & highway) brake systems
Tare wt 19,000 lb

Two-axle highway/single-axle rail running gear, mutually retractable (train air)

RoadRailer® MK V (ex "Railmaster")

48' or 53'

MK IV & MK V trailers may be mixed in consist

Detachable rail bogie (with train brake system) – modified 70-ton car truck

MK V trailer has highway brake system + rail train-pipe only
Tare wt 16,000 lb (on highway)
Mark IV/Mark V consists may be hauled on rear of low-slack (e.g. double-stack) trains

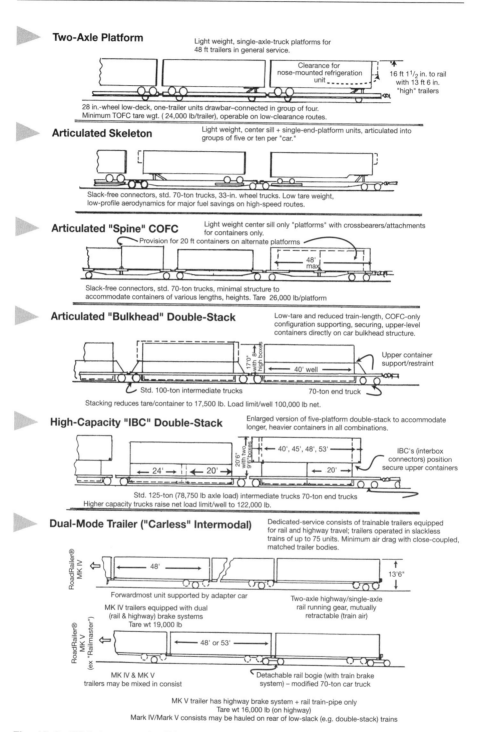

Fig. 15-3. "Third generation" intermodal equipment

1984 between Los Angeles and Chicago, after American President Lines contracted with the Union Pacific and Chicago & North Western railroads.

Intermodal Today

During 2006, North American railroads carried over 14 million intermodal loads. Imports now account for 60 percent of the shipments (compared to 1970, when domestic freight accounted for most of intermodal traffic). Containers now account for over 80 percent of the total intermodal volume, and 55 percent of domestic shipments now move in containers, rather than trailers (compared to the 1970s, when nearly all domestic freight moved in trailers).

International Freight Traffic and ISO Containers

The growth in international freight continues to be driven by North American demand for consumer products. Imported containerized freight includes clothing and shoes, electronics, furniture, hardware and lighting, toys, food, forest products, auto parts, machinery, and steel among the many thousands of products carried. Since 2000, the compound annual growth rate for international intermodal shipments is 8 percent, outperforming the U.S. economy by a considerable margin.

International containers vary in size, but are generally 20 ft (or 40 ft) long by 8 ft wide by 9 ft 6 in. high, and the industry refers to them as ISO containers since they conform to dimensions established by the International Standards Organization (ISO). A few 45 ft containers have crept into the fleet, but overall, the basic container size has not materially changed (infrastructure in Europe and Asia, such as narrow streets, simply cannot support larger containers). Frequently, container volume is reported in TEUs (Twenty-foot Equivalent Units). For instance, a 40 ft container is two TEUs. Last, the ISO containers are owned and controlled by the steamship lines, such as Maersk, APL, K-Line, OOCL (Orient Overseas Container Line), China Shipping, COSCO (China Ocean Shipping Company), and so on.

Major ports of entry for overseas containers include Los Angeles, Long Beach, and Oakland, California; Seattle, and Tacoma, Washington; Portland, Oregon; and Vancouver, B.C., on the West Coast. It includes New York, New York; Norfolk, Virginia; Savannah, Georgia; Charleston, South Carolina; and Houston, Texas, on the East and Gulf Coasts. Most of what is produced in Asia (that is shipped in containers) enters North America at western ports, and the portion of the freight that is not consumed locally travels to inland destinations via rail. The railroads possess a large market share of the long-haul container traffic moving inland (to cities such as Chicago, Memphis, and New York). However, a growing percentage of Asian container traffic is routed to the U.S. East Coast via the Panama Canal (known as *all-water traffic*). Unfortunately, the railroads enjoy a much lower market share of this traffic as it fre-

Fig. 15-4. Five-unit articulated 48 ft well car with 125-ton intermediate trucks, adaptable for double-stacked ISO marine (8 ft wide) or domestic (8 ft 6 in. wide) containers

quently is consumed within the local port area, and does not require lengthy transportation to inland locations.

Domestic Freight Traffic, Containers, and Trailers

Compared to international traffic, the growth rate for domestic intermodal shipments is lower, averaging 2 percent growth per year since 2000. The slower growth results from increasing domestic container sizes (larger containers mean fewer shipments), and more intense truck competition. Regarding container sizes, in 2000, about 75 percent of the domestic containers were 48 ft in length; today that number is less than 20 percent, as 53 ft containers continue to replace older 48 ft units (a cubic capacity increase of about 10 percent). The overall dimensions of a domestic container are 53 ft long by 8 ft 6 in. wide by 9 ft 6 in. high.

Further, contrasted to the steady growth of the international container volumes, domestic intermodal traffic is more cyclical, caused by competitive dynamics between

Fig. 15-5. Mobile side loader (piggy-packer) capable of loading trailers and containers on single- or double-stack railcars, stacking containers three high on ground.

truckers and the railroads. Domestic intermodal shipments tend to be a shorter haul than international freight, which makes it more susceptible to truck diversion. Interestingly, this dynamic occurs even though trucking companies (such as Hunt, Schneider, Swift, UPS, and Yellow) are some of the largest intermodal shippers. In the longer haul domestic markets, truckers, and railroads cooperate more, especially as trucking companies try to cope with driver shortages and high fuel costs but compete fiercely in shorter haul traffic lanes.

Regarding trailer ownership, in intermodal's early days, the railroads also usually owned or controlled the trailers. Today, the major Class I railroads own virtually no trailers at all, with the truck lines, freight consolidators and forwarders, and some shippers providing them (although a few short line railroads still furnish them). One exception is the Norfolk Southern's ownership of "RoadRailer" trailers. RoadRailers are specially equipped highway trailers that will connect directly to railroad trucks. Once connected, the trailers can be pulled by locomotives in trains up to 150 trailers long, without the need to load them onto flatcars.

Concerning ownership of containers, these are again supplied by trucking companies, consolidators, and shippers, but a good number are still provided by certain railroads through national pools. For instance, the UP, NS, KCS, CN, and CP jointly own or participate in the North American-wide EMP (Equipment Management Pool) container pool.

Fig. 15-6. Well cars

Fig. 15-7. Spine cars

Transloading

Precise data are hard to find, but perhaps as much as 10 percent of the arriving ISO containers are transloaded (i.e., transferring the cargo from an ISO container to a domestic container, usually within the metropolitan area of the port where the cargo arrived). It occurs for several reasons, such as to gain lower freight rates, or to improve logistics. For example, it may be cheaper to transload the contents of three ISO containers that arrive on the west coast into two 53 ft containers for shipment inland than to ship the same three ISO containers intact. Factors to consider are the freight rates for the shipments and the cost of transloading the goods, which includes the costs of shipping the ISO container to the transloading facility.

Most likely, though, transloading occurs because it adds value to the product shipped, rather than just a cost savings. For instance, suppose a major home improvement chain imports snow shovels but does not yet know where severe winter weather will hit. By warehousing goods near their arrival port, the retailer can wait to determine where to ship the snow shovels.

The Railcar Fleet

The greatest portion of railcars in service today is double-stack wells along with a fair amount of spine cars used to carry "conventional" traffic (trailers or containers in single stack). The most common double-stack car types are five-unit articulated cars with either 40 ft or 48 ft wells, and three-unit articulated cars with 53 ft wells. The spine car fleet consists of mostly three-unit articulated cars with short platforms that will support both two 28 ft "pup" trailers and 48 ft and 53 ft trailers (or containers). A few spine cars will handle 57 ft trailers. Most of the older 89 ft flatcars have fallen out of service, but occasionally the railroads operate them during periods of strong demand.

About two-thirds of the railcars are supplied by TTX, (owned by the Class I railroads). TTX operates similar to a cooperative, where the railroads share or "pool" the cars. Also, in some cases, railroads own or lease their equipment.

Railroad and Terminal Operations

Upon a ship's arrival in port, the containers are unloaded and usually stacked on the dock. Many of the ships carry between 6,000-8,000 TEUs (Twenty-foot Equivalent Units) and a few even carry a whopping 12,000 TEUs. The containers are then loaded onto waiting railcars ("on-dock" loading), drayed (trucked) to a nearby railyard for loading ("near-dock" loading), drayed to a transloading warehouse, or trucked directly to a local customer. When draying the containers, they are placed on chassis (a platform with wheels to support the container, and when combined with a container, the entire unit looks similar to a trailer) and like the containers, the chassis are owned by the steamship lines, although at some terminals, steamship lines engage in limited chassis pooling.

From the port, the containers travel in unit trains (with minimal switching en route) to inland railroad terminals. In some cases, the inland terminals handle international containers exclusively (and, as a practical outcome, operate separate terminals for domestic container traffic). When that is the case, after the containers are unloaded, the railcars are reloaded with ISO containers for the trip back to the port. Usually the containers are empty, but the steamship lines will try to find loads (and revenue). If loaded, the container could contain domestic freight, but more likely it would contain exports, such as scrap paper, scrap metal, food products, hay, and grain.

Also, although the recent trend by the railroads has been to create separate terminals for international and domestic freight, many terminals handle both ISO and domestic containers. When that is the case, a train might arrive carrying ISO boxes and then reload with domestic containers for routing to another inland terminal. Whether railroads operate exclusive or mixed terminals is a function of traffic mix, overall volume, and individual railroad network (there is no right or wrong answer). Similar to the ports, the inland terminals need a constant supply of chassis because the containers need to be drayed to the receivers of the goods. Typically, the railroads own the chassis that handle the 53 ft containers (although some discussion of pooling occurs), and the steamship lines own the chassis that carry the 20 ft and 40 ft ISO containers.

The Intermodal Future

Forecasters expect intermodal traffic to double again in the next 10 years. Continued strong growth in consumer spending (i.e., strong demand for the goods carried by intermodal), plus increasing highway congestion and fuel costs, and continuing truck driver shortages are all expected to spur the increasing intermodal volume. Moreover, railroads have recently spent billions in capacity improvements to handle burgeoning demand, a marked contrast from the disinvestment of the 1970s.

No doubt the anticipated growth will also foster major changes. Many ports will be challenged with congestion. Also, questions remain, such as will expansion of the Panama Canal negatively impact the demand for mini-land bridge service? Intermodal has always been a dynamic story, and the coming years will be as exciting as the past.

Special Freight and Package Services

T he primary business of the railroads in North America is now, as it has always been, the transportation of freight in standard carload lots. Nevertheless, the transportation of LCL (less-than-carload) and express package shipments has always had a relatively higher degree of public visibility because of the sheer number of customers directly concerned and the perceived dependence of big versus small-business competitiveness on the relative shipping costs in large versus small lots. The handling of loads too large or too heavy for other overland transport modes also focuses attention on the rail network.

Large and Heavy Loads

Standard clearances and load limits are included by reference as a part of railroad freight tariffs, indicating the size and weight of shipments that can be handled in regular service. Most routes provide at least AAR "Plate B" clearance and 220,000 lbs weight on rail for eight-wheel cars. Many main lines have been modified to be able to handle piggyback and autorack traffic without restriction, to the extent that typical limits, beyond which special arrangements are required, are 20 ft above rail, 11 ft 6 in. wide, and 125 tons net weight.

High-Wide Load Coordination

Nevertheless, thousands of oversize shipments per year on U.S. railroads require special coordination. Railroads maintain special offices for this purpose to work with shippers in finding routes (sometimes unbelievably roundabout) that will bypass close clearances, bridge load limitations, and other bottlenecks. Railroad limits may actually determine the largest size to which bridge girders, pressure vessels, or generators may be designed and what provisions must be made for piecemeal shipment and on-site assem-

Fig. 16-1. 12-axle FD depressed-center flatcar with 325-ton capacity [Photo by Dennis More, courtesy of KASGRO Rail Corp.]

bly. Finally, the operating department of the railroad is involved in determining and observing any special restrictions necessary en route, such as the following:

- Low-speed travel by local freight or special train
- Scheduling to avoid trains on adjacent tracks
- Uncoupling levers inactivated on multi-car shipments

Generally, all railcars of 16 axle or more configuration, when loaded, require Special Train Service that consists of a dedicated power unit and crew.

Special Equipment

A few of the Class I's still own heavy-duty equipment but the majority of that equipment is provided by companies that specifically own and manage heavy-duty railcars. A small number of private car owners also provide heavy-duty equipment. The various types of railcars are special depressed-center, well, or high-capacity flatcars for oversize or overweight loads. These types of railcars have a range of 4-, 8-, 12-, 16-, 18-, and 20-axle configurations (AAR Mechanical Designations FD, FW, and FM. See Figs. 16-1 and 16-2). Car Use and applicable Detention Fees are based on published tariff rates and are charged each time a car is loaded. When loads are too long or too heavy for one railcar, they are shipped as bolstered loads. This typically means the load weight is spread across two different railcars, allowing more weight to be carried (Fig. 16-3).

For the very largest power-generating machinery, "Schnabel" cars (AAR Mechanical Designation LS) have been built so that the load forms the central part of the car structure (Fig. 16-4) and extends to the very limits of the clearance diagram if needed. Schnabel-type cars also move only in Special Train Service when loaded.

Fig. 16-2. 16-axle FD depressed-center flatcar with 450-ton capacity [Photo by Wade Beard, courtesy of Specialized Rail Transport]

Some include special hydraulic jacking devices to shift the load a few inches in any direction to clear specific obstacles. Maximum capacity is about 500 tons for a 20-axle car. A 36-axle Schnabel car may have a maximum capacity over 800 tons. Since most main-line tracks are spaced on 14 ft centers, the disruption involved in moving an object 20 ft in diameter can only be overcome with the best in advanced planning.

LCL Traffic

With the general availability of over-the-road truck service handling less-than-carload shipments on a regulated common-carrier basis, most railroads have been permitted to discontinue handling LCL traffic, which has traditionally been unprofitable. However, several million tons per year in small freight shipments ride the rails in forwarder- and shipper-association traffic.

Forwarders

A *forwarder* accepts LCL and LTL (less-than-truckload) shipments for transportation at a package rate and puts them together in carload lots for the long haul. This allows three things to happen: (1) The railroad has a carload to haul, (2) the forwarder makes a profit from the difference between the two rates, and (3) the quantities involved allow the dispatch of cars on regular schedules that individual shippers could not support.

Most forwarder traffic is now handled in piggyback service, giving the forwarders reduced terminal and handling costs and making them more competitive with the common-carrier or contract trucker. On the East-West system, the forwarder traffic on his

Fig. 16-3. Two FM-type 8-axle flatcars carrying a bolstered load weighing approximately 500 tons [Photo by Wade Beard, courtesy of Specialized Rail Transport]

own leased and loaded Trailer Train flatcars (Plan IV) is enough to warrant running Train 151, a first-class schedule, as the first leg of a run-through train to the West Coast. Accepting only TOFC/COFC traffic, 151 is allowed 70 mph and provided enough horsepower to vigorously climb the mountain. Since the completion of a 1988 tunnel enlargement program to eliminate height/width restriction on the Allegheny Division main line, traffic on the E-W hotshot is primarily COFC (domestic and import/export) riding on double-stack equipment.

Shipper Associations organized on a cooperative, nonprofit basis to perform similar functions to forwarders in obtaining carload rates and larger scale and more regular traffic flows for their members were specifically exempted from regulation in 1940 when forwarders were brought under the purview (range of function and power) of the ICC. With the advent of piggybacking, these organizations, although forbidden from advertising their services commercially as a condition of nonregulation, grew rapidly and handled a major portion of LTL shipments. Deregulation essentially negated the advantages of such arrangements (particularly, with decisions allowing a company to handle its traffic in either owned or contract trucks that acted essentially as common carriers in accepting backhaul traffic).

Shipper agents or *consolidators* may be grouped (with forwarders) in a "third party" category as intermediaries between transportation companies and shippers in the management and handling of freight traffic. They handle shipments on land, sea, and air common-carriers at their rates, charging a fee for the services they provide shippers in maintaining regular service patterns and handling the details of the transportation

Fig. 16-4. Twenty-axle "Schnabel" car or 500-ton load capacity

process. The complex transportation alternatives characteristic of expanding international and intermodal traffic—including trade-offs involved in the "just-in-time" inventory-control philosophy of manufacturing—have resulted in expansion and proliferation in both the number and diversity of these organizations.

To provide a more even flow of traffic, railroads may find it to their advantage to establish reduced multi-trailer rates. A piggyback broker can therefore undertake to eke out a profit by consolidating individual trailer loads solicited from shippers whose traffic flow would not otherwise qualify for the bargain rates.

Rail-Passenger Services

R ail-passenger services involve direct contact with millions of customers and often share the same right-of-way and other facilities with freight railroad operations. Public awareness of this rail-passenger service is often limited and its importance is little appreciated. Table 18-1 indicates that less than 5 percent of U.S. railroad revenue is from passenger services, and in North America throughout railroading history, passenger traffic has been a relatively minor segment of the business.

Passenger Service

When does a system with two rails and guiding wheels stop fitting the classification of "railroad"? Fig. 17-1 does not answer this question directly but lists a spectrum of rail-passenger-carrying systems ranging from light rail (yesterday's streetcar or interurban) to main-line intercity and commuter passenger-train service.

The terminology used is generally that of the U.S. Department of Transportation, with a separation of railroad commuter service into two categories: *primary,* where the line exists because of the passenger service; and *ancillary,* where other traffic predominates, at least when rated by revenue. Typical characteristics of the different passenger systems are listed as a means of showing similarities and differences. Several existing systems don't fit any mold in all respects, and technical developments further complicate the picture (such as diesel-propelled light rail sharing right-of-way with freight services). Taken as a whole, the train consist, accommodations, fare, schedule, right-of-way, and performance characteristics lay out the differences between rapid transit, railroad commuter, and intercity systems.

	Mass Transit			Commuter		Railroad		
	Light Rail	Heavy Rail/Transit		Primary	Ancillary	Intercity		Auto Ferry
		Urban	Commuter			Corridor	Long-Haul	
Typical Train Consist	Single or two-car articulated "light-rail vehicles"	Self-propelled multiple-unit passenger cars	Self-propelled multiple-unit passenger cars	Self-propelled multiple-unit cars	Locomotive-hauled (push-pull) or self-propelled cars	Locomotive-hauled or self-propelled (multiple-unit or fixed consist) passenger & snack cars	Locomotive-hauled baggage passenger & nonrevenue cars	Locomotive-hauled automobile-transporter, passenger & nonrevenue cars
Typical Passenger Accommodations (Typical) — Low density = 40 psgr/car; Lim seating & standees - 125-200 psgr/car; Single-deck commuter - 100/car; Medium density = 70 psgr/car; Double-deck = 160/car	Single-deck limited seating & standees	Single-deck limited seating & standees	Single-deck, full seating & limited standees	Single or double-deck & limited standees	Single or double-deck & limited standees	Medium-density coach snack & limited 1st class (low density)	Single or double-deck coach, lounge sleeping, dining	Single-deck low-density coach, lounge, sleeping, dining
Fare Structure, Sale & Collection (Typical)	Flat fare, single-trip farebox or machine ticket random insp.	Flat or zone single-trip fare machine-issued turnstile collection	Graduated single-trip fare machine-issued, faregate collection	Multi-ride zone-fare agent-sold flash ticket	Multi-ride zone fare, agent-sold, on-train ticket collection	Single-trip, agent-sold, reserved accommodations on-train coll.	Single-trip, agent-sold, reserved accommodations on-train coll.	Single-trip reserved accommodations check-in
Schedules: Trips/day (each way, per line)	50-150	100-200	25-150	25-75	1-25	4-40	1/2-4	1
Min. headway (rush hr. per track) (Typical)	5 min.	1 1/2 min.	3 min.	3 min.	10 min.	15 min.	N.A.	N.A.
Hours of service	Day-evening limited weekend	Day, evening, weekend	Weekday, evening, weekend, limited owl	Rush-hour, limited off-peak evening	Rush-hour weekday	Daily, day & evening	Daily (or tri-weekly) overnight(s)	Daily (overnight)
Miles between passenger stops (average, typical)	0.2	0.5 (local) 1.5 (express)	1.5	2.5 (local) up to 20 (express)	3.0	35 200 (express)	80	900
Length of route-miles (typical)	10	15	25	35	50	85-300	300-2500	900
Speed/mph Average incl. stops	15	25	35	30 (local) 45 (express)	35	75	50	50
Speed/mph Maximum	50	55	75	70 (ABS) 100 (cab sigs)	79	79 (ABS) 110-125 (cab sig ATC)	79 (ABS) 90 (ATS cab sig.)	79
Right-of-Way Principal Locations, Exclusivity	Surface - street or private right-of-way (with grade crossing)	Tunnel, elevated surface (no grade crossing)	Elevated tunnel, surface (no grade crossing)	Surface, tunnel (no grade crossing)	Surface (some grade crossings)	Surface (few grade crossings)	Surface (many grade crossings)	Surface (many grade crossings)
Other Non-Pasgr Rail	None or lim freight	None	None	Limited freight	Freight	Freight	Freight	Freight
Number of Tracks	2	2 to 4	2	2 to 6	2	2 to 4	1 to 2	1 to 2
Signaling/Control	ABS (on private rwy)	ABS/ATC	ABS/ATC	ABS/ATC	ABS	ABS/ATC	CTC/ABS	CTC/ABS
Station Platforms	Low	High	High	High	Low	High & low	Low	Low
Train Characteristics (Typical) Propulsion/Power Distribution/Voltage (Low Voltage = 600-750v, High = 11-25 KV)	Electric-overhead trolley wire/low voltage DC /Diesel-electric	Electric-third rail/low voltage DC	Electric-third rail/low voltage DC	Electric-overhead catenary/high V, AC, third-rail/low V. DC	Diesel-electric and diesel-hydraulic	Electric overhead catenary, high V, AC, gas turbine diesel-electric	Diesel-electric	Diesel-electric
Cars/Train	1-4	2-12	4-12	2-12	3-18	4-12	4-18	25-45
Train Wgt/Passenger (lb)	300 (w/standees)	450 (w/standees)	700	800	1000	2000	5500	8000
Acceleration~ mph/sec. @ Medium Speed	4.5	3.5	3.0	3.0	1.0	1.5	0.3	0.2
Acceleration Control	Operator	Automatic	Computer	Automatic	Operator	Operator	Operator	Operator
Braking	Dynamic/air magnetic	Electro-pneumatic	Dynamic/ elec-pneu	Electro-pneumatic	Automatic air	Dynamic/ elec-pneu	Automatic air	Automatic air

ABS = Automatic Block Signals
ATC = Automatic Train Control
CC = Centralized Traffic Control

Fig. 17-1. Rail-passenger systems

Heavy Rail Transit

"Heavy rail" rapid transit systems are characterized by an exclusive right-of-way. Although most trackage is usually surface (in cut or on fill), enough must usually be in tunnels (subways) to make third rail electric propulsion the choice in the interest of affordable tunnel size. Right-of-way and structure costs typically dominate track and vehicle costs. Newer North American steel rail systems (such as San Francisco's BART) have typically been designed for 70-75 mph speeds with computerized train control in which the operator serves primarily a monitoring and emergency manual-control function. Their traffic pattern approaches that of a commuter railroad.

In common with older (but typically more extensive) 50-55 mph systems upgraded with higher performance, air-conditioned equipment, and signaling that is capable of 90-second rush-hour headways (see New York City Transit in Fig. 17-3), ultimate line capacity is primarily a matter of the number of doors for each train (governing factor is the rate at which passengers can get off and on). With trains of eight to twelve 75 ft cars, comfortable rush-hour line capacity of 40,000 per hour exceeds that of a hypothetical 20-lane expressway dominated by the typical single-occupant commuter automobile.

About half of the heavy rail systems in business in 2007 represent new (since World War II) starts. As a result, nationwide impact of this rapid transit concept increased (even in such automobile-based areas as Southern California), although declines in inner-city population and commercial activity in the larger cities already served by the older systems have held overall ridership at a relatively constant level of 7 million trips per day over the last three decades. Typical heavy rail farebox recovery of operating costs averages somewhat above 50 percent, although some systems do considerably better.

Light Rail Systems

With nearly 2 dozen new (post-1978) light rail systems in business or under construction by 2007 joining a half-dozen others in cities that never completely lost their "streetcars," light rail has become an increasingly attractive and significant alternative to bus (including busway) transit. (Light rail as an alternative is judged by ridership, environmental, and farebox cost coverage ratio considerations.) The newest systems (Fig. 17-4) are characterized by limited central business district street-running coupled with time-saving overall transit times made possible (financially and environmentally) by using the existing rail freight corridors that reach growing suburbs. The recent introduction of diesel-electric-propelled LRVs (light rail vehicles) has expanded the scope and capabilities of light rail, chiefly in that the high cost of electrification is eliminated. Such vehicles, defined as "noncompliant" by the Federal Railroad Administration (because they do not meet the crashworthiness standards of freight and commuter/intercity passenger rolling stock) must be operated under temporal (time) separation arrangements with freight services. Recent developments in signaling and traffic control, however, have provided opportunities for limited "extended temporal

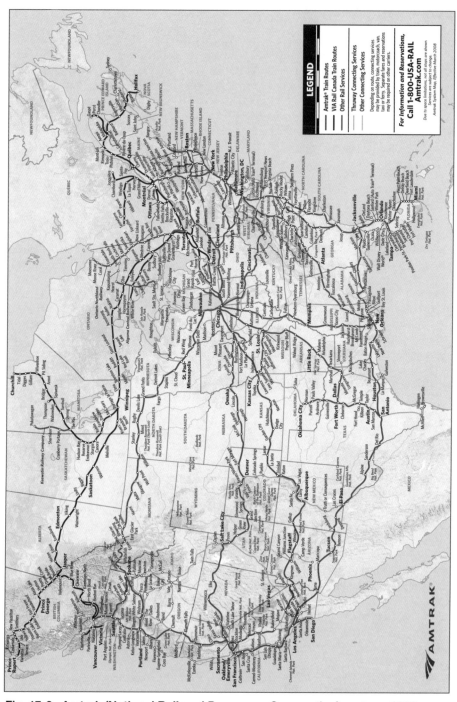

Fig. 17-2. Amtrak (National Railroad Passenger Corporation) routes – 2008
[Courtesy Amtrak]

Fig. 17-3. The R142 is one of New York City Transit's newest subway cars, numbering over 1,000 units in a fleet of nearly 7,000 vehicles.

separation" operations under which freight and light rail can operate within the same time frame on shared track.

Light rail is the fastest growing segment of rail transit. Farebox cost recovery percentages (on average, in the low 30s, but with some much higher) are typically a few points above transit bus levels. To date, the key to a winning combination of amenities attracting ridership and acceptable operating costs has been the availability of high-capacity articulated cars, capable of running in trains to carry 1,500 to 6,000 passengers every hour at peak periods, of service-proven reliability. Incremental rather than radical performance and technological advances have carried the day.

Railroad Commuter Service

By 1984, the operation (including employment of train, maintenance, and management personnel) of all railroad commuter services had been taken over by public authorities. These railroad commuter services had not been self-supporting for many years and had generally been operated by freight railroad companies under some form of cost-

Fig. 17-4. California's San Diego Trolley is typical of the numerous modern light rail systems that have been built since the late 1970s.

of-service contracting by municipal, regional, or state authorities (Fig. 17-5). Right-of-way ownership of all primary and some ancillary routes has now also generally been acquired. After bottoming out in the early 1970s, ridership has increased significantly. Although fewer than 2 dozen urban areas in the United States and Canada currently have some commuter rail service, traffic amounts to well over 700,000 round trips per workday. On average, commuter rail fares cover about 50 percent of operating costs.

Most of the nearly 5,000 cars in commuter service have been built or rebuilt within the past 25 years with push-pull locomotive-propelled equipment, requiring no turning at terminals (the choice for diesel ancillary services). Wherever clearances permit, car designs have settled on "gallery" (single-row upper-deck seating with fare-checking capability from the open lower deck) or full double-deck configurations providing 160 to 170 seats for each car. All cars in service are air-conditioned.

Intercity Passenger Service

Amtrak, formally the National Railroad Passenger Corp., was created by Congress effective May 1, 1971, to take over money-losing rail-passenger operations from the privately owned freight railroads. At the time of Amtrak's creation, many freight railroads were either bankrupt or on the verge of bankruptcy and the quality of their pas-

Fig. 17-5. The Northeast Illinois Regional Commuter Railroad Corporation in Chicago operates Metra, one of the most extensive systems of its type in the United States. Metra employs bi-level gallery-style cars on all of its trains.

senger operations was deteriorating rapidly. The intent of Congress was to create a national interconnected rail-passenger network to preserve, improve, and expand the rail alternative to commercial airlines, motor coach, and private-automobile travel.

It was neither practical nor feasible to create a new track network, so the intent was for Amtrak to operate passenger trains over the privately owned track of the freight railroads, with Amtrak paying a user charge. The freight railroads, in exchange for a tax write-off or other considerations, donated their passenger-fleet equipment to Amtrak, which also inherited the freight railroad employees who had operated the passenger-rail service—an intended seamless transfer to ensure, to the largest extent, continuity of operations with minimal disruption to those depending on passenger-train availability. Freight railroads also agreed to give Amtrak trains priority access and handling to help ensure on-time arrivals, although this agreement frequently is breached and is a source of continuing disharmony with the freight railroads.

Amtrak, in 2007, operated a 21,000-route-mile system serving 500 locations in 46 states, employing some 19,000 and carrying more than 25 million passengers annually. Virtually all Amtrak routes are over freight railroad tracks, the primary exception being the Northeast Corridor linking Washington, D.C., with Philadelphia, New York, and Boston, which the federal government acquired following the 1970 bankruptcy of freight railroad Penn Central Railroad. Small segments of the Northeast Corridor between New York and Boston are owned by state governments.

Since its creation, Amtrak has struggled financially, owing to a congressional failure to provide Amtrak with a consistent source of federal funding. Annually, since Amtrak's first year of operation, it has had to fight for a congressional appropriation that its officials and supporters consider insufficient. This inconsistent and inadequate funding has preoccupied Amtrak officials, adversely affected operational improvements, and slowed acquisition of a modern fleet.

Since the 1980s, there has been increasing political pressure to eliminate Amtrak and invite either private or state-regional entities to take over various routes and create separate, high-speed passenger corridors. Amtrak's lone high-speed corridor is the Northeast Corridor where its Acela Express trains operate at speeds in excess of 100 mph over some segments and up to 150 mph in others (Fig. 17-6). Amtrak trains over freight railroad tracks generally are limited—for safety reasons—to speeds below 79 mph.

In some instances, states have provided additional funding to operate intercity passenger routes, some contracting with Amtrak to operate the trains, and others hiring other operators. Amtrak also provides commuter services under contract in a number of locations.

Setting Amtrak apart from freight railroads goes beyond the difference in their customer base. Amtrak survives only by convincing Congress to appropriate sufficient money to make up the difference between Amtrak's costs of operation and the revenue it generates from operating passenger trains. This requires two specialties: (1) knowledge of train operations and (2) an understanding of the congressional appropriations process.

The one Amtrak president said to be most expert at both was Graham Claytor (1982-1993), who had been CEO of freight carrier Southern Railway, secretary of the Navy, and acting-secretary of transportation before becoming president of Amtrak. Prior to Amtrak's creation, the Southern Railway, under Claytor, prided itself on operation of passenger trains, and even chose to continue operating (at a financial loss) some of those passenger trains for a period after Amtrak's creation. Also highly regarded was Alan Boyd (1978-1982), who had been the nation's first transportation secretary, chairman of the Civil Aeronautics Board, a state transportation official, and president of Illinois Central Railroad from 1969-1972. Boyd succeeded Paul Reistrup (1975-1978), a Naval Academy graduate and railroad operating executive with substantial experience in operating passenger trains for CSX predecessor Baltimore & Ohio. Reistrup is remembered the best for fighting for sufficient funds to replace much of the antiquated passenger-car fleet that Amtrak had inherited from freight railroads.

Two Amtrak presidents—Tom Downs (1993-1998) and George Warrington (1998-2002)—had considerable commuter-railroad experience at New Jersey Transit, which also required significant state and federal appropriations. David Gunn (2002-2005) was highly respected as a freight railroad operating officer (Santa Fe) and rail transit chief (Washington Metropolitan Transit Authority). Gunn was succeeded in 2006 by Alexander Kummant, a former Union Pacific Railroad marketing officer, who had held executive positions in different industries before arriving at Amtrak.

Fig. 17-6. Amtrak's Acela Express operates high-speed service between Boston and Washington, D.C., on the electrified Northeast Corridor at speeds up to 150 mph. (William C. Vantuono photo)

Federal Amtrak appropriations have declined steadily as the proportion of total passenger-operation expenses paid by passengers have risen from less than half to 80 percent in the early 1990s (fares more than cover all "above the rail" train-operating costs). Operations remain dependent on establishing a program that supports continuing capital expenditures (primarily for rolling stock, especially sleeping cars) to expand service in additional profitable markets, reducing unit overhead costs.

Amtrak Equipment

All passenger-train cars and locomotives used in regular service are owned by Amtrak, as are all major maintenance and overhaul shops and most passenger-station facilities. Diesel, electric, and dual-mode diesel (also equipped to operate on third rail) in passenger service is well into its second generation; all of which has been acquired since the start of Amtrak service. In the "High-Speed Rail" paragraphs, note that 18 of the 150 mph Acela Express trainsets and 15 HHP-8 (8,000 hp) electric locomotives supplemented the 55 AEM-7 (7,000 hp) electric locomotives in Northeast Corridor service by 2000.

With the exception of those trains operating through the tunnels restricting access to New York City, all long-haul (overnight) Amtrak trains were re-equipped with 550 double-deck Superliner I and II coaches, sleepers, dining, and sightseer-lounge cars by 1996, essentially retiring the Heritage fleet of 1948-1969 stainless-steel cars inherited from the pre-Amtrak railroads. Viewliner single-deck sleeping cars entered service on the low-clearance Eastern routes in 1996.

Other corridor and day-train services are covered by 635 Amfleet I (medium-density) and Amfleet II (low-density) coaches, food-service, and club (first-class) cars, supplemented by 100 conventional 1989 Horizon cars and additional double-deck medium-density short-haul cars and Talgo-articulated trainsets in expanding state-sponsored corridor service in California and the Northwest.

In the interest of service reliability and all-weather maintainability, all locomotives and cars are equipped for HEP (head-end power) electric heating and air conditioning; steam-heated Amtrak equipment made its last runs in 1983.

Amtrak Operations

Since the mid-1980s, train crew members (previously employed by the contracting railroads) have become Amtrak employees (retaining some freight-service re-employment rights), as are on-train service, station, and maintenance personnel in full-time passenger-train operations.

Amtrak contracts with the railroads over which its trains operate to cover direct costs for any services provided (Amtrak normally buys and puts aboard fuel and supplies), for trackage rights, and for a contribution toward overhead. Contracts are subject to renegotiation since 25-year stipulations regarding such matters as track quality in the original Amtrak act expired in 1996; the contracts may include incentives for on-time performance above a certain standard. Competitively, Amtrak is, in turn, a contract train operator for some governmental commuter rail agencies.

Other Passenger Services

VIA Rail Canada was established by the Canadian government as a Crown Corporation to take over the intercity passenger operations of the Canadian National and Canadian Pacific railroads in an arrangement somewhat similar to Amtrak. Although VIA's network does include some "corridor" short-haul routes in Ontario and Quebec, and total ridership is higher than Amtrak's per capita (per person), cost recovery over the entire sparsely populated country, including some lines on which service has been decreed as necessary for otherwise completely isolated communities, has remained far lower.

Automobile ferry service between the Washington, D.C., area and central Florida was operated, starting in 1971, by the Auto Train Corporation under a specific exemption in the Amtrak authorization act. Equipment deterioration and losses from a similar service on a Kentucky-Florida route resulted in termination of a highly successful service; Amtrak acquired rights to the name and resumed daily Auto Train service (mandated to be fully profitable) in 1986.

Tourist railroads provide train rides for the public, ranging from regional common carriers (operating long passenger consists as an adjunct to their freight traffic) to volunteer-staffed museums with an abundance of rolling stock and a few hundred feet of track. The principal attraction varies: reaching world-famous or merely pleasant scenic areas, recreating (with wildly varying degrees of "authenticity") rail travel of the recent or more historical past, or perhaps providing a trip-to-nowhere dining experience.

Longevity of the operations also varies—from less than a single season to more than 160 years; ownership covers the spectrum from struggling, definitely nonprofit local museums to the U.S. National Park Service. (Class I or other railroads with an Amtrak-member heritage may run passenger excursions but are prohibited by the Amtrak act from running scheduled service.)

Train length and patronage typically varies directly with the size and rarity of the motive power in use as it ascends from industrial switcher through vintage diesel to main-line steam, with trolley operations a popular alternative. More than 100 lines in the United States and Canada provide at least some scheduled (usually seasonal) trips; some lines attract as many as 400,000 riders in a season; and safety of operations are just as critical a matter as in main-line railroading—tourist railroading can no longer be dismissed as a trivial part of the industry!

High-Speed Rail

Although one service in North America (the high-speed rail in the Washington–New York–Boston Northeast Corridor) does fit the definition, high-speed rail is not shown separately in Fig. 17-1. This term is generally accepted to include passenger service operating at a speed of 125 mph or higher between station-pairs where resulting downtown-to-downtown journey times are competitive with air for business travelers. Some examples are the Japanese "Bullet Train," the British Rail HST-125 ("High-Speed Train – 125 mph," the only diesel-powered example) or the French TGV (Train á Grande Vitesse), of which there is an extensive network in France. In recent years, high-speed systems have been built in Korea and Taiwan. Typically, aerodynamically refined, steel-wheel, nontilting fixed-consist trainsets operate over sufficiently curve-free alignments on new and exclusive or highly improved conventional routes to achieve 90 to 110 mph or better start-to-stop times. Unique in the continued presence of significant heavy freight traffic on the same trackage is Amtrak's 135-150 mph Washington–New York–Boston Acela Express. Under present conditions it appears that, whatever their overall ecological, congestion-relief, or other social benefits, proposals for high-speed systems in corridors in North America must first demonstrate financial feasibility founded primarily (if not wholly) on credible private-sector support.

Technologically, high-speed rail developments worldwide follow two identifiable thrusts:

- *Steel-wheel* technology, based primarily on the practicalities of light axle loads (no freight), sound track, and suspension design, and intensive maintenance in smoothing the track. With French TGV trains in service at speeds above 200 mph, the TGV's 2007 cracking of the 350 mph figure in a test cannot be entirely dismissed as a stunt—such flat-out runs in the past have in a matter of a decade or two proven to be precursors of similar service speeds. Given a population pattern allowing a "straight" route to be followed, the hill-climbing ability of such hot trains has kept economical line construction (with relatively few tunnels and major bridges) in the picture. Early on considered incapable of much more than 100 mph, locomotive-propelled (e.g., power-car at each end) rather than fully MU-powered consists are now operating at the high end of the speed spectrum.

- *Tilting trains,* tested early on (1937) by three railroads in the United States. They maintain physical (and mental) passenger comfort while rounding curves at velocities far higher than the balancing speed for the track superelevation. Tilting the car body keeps the passenger comfortable but does not alter the direction or magnitude of the wheel rail forces down below, which must (and can, up to "cant-deficiencies" in the 15 in. range for passenger-train axle loads) remain within the limits of track and car-suspension stability. Despite earlier (1960s-1970s) experiences on both sides of the Atlantic leading to abandonment of the concept after years of development, tilting trains are now routinely allowing usefully faster schedules—at top speeds below as well as above the 125 mph threshold—over existing or less expensively improved curvy routes in several European countries. Cars on 18 Acela Express trainsets, designed for 150 mph Amtrak Northeast Corridor service that began in 2000, tilt to attain 3-hour New York–Boston schedules despite numerous curves remaining on an upgraded and electrified line north of New Haven, Connecticut.

Magnetic levitation, with or without benefit of high-temperature superconductivity discoveries, undoubtedly rates highest on the glamour scale. Maglev can push trains to speeds beyond 300 mph, where aerodynamic drag—anywhere except in an evacuated tunnel—limits the practicality of any further acceleration.

The Railroad Organization

Railroads come in all shapes and sizes, from less than 1 mile to more than 30,000 miles of line (route-miles exclusive of yards and multiple-track routes) and with annual revenues from less than 1 million dollars to billions of dollars. The Surface Transportation Board (STB), the agency responsible for economic regulation of the railroad industry, has split the railroads into the following three Classes according to annual revenues (adjusted annually for inflation):

- Class I roads, of which there were seven in North America as of 2007 (Each has annual revenues in excess of $319.2 million, and totaling each railroad's mileage, operated some 96,000 route-miles of railroad.)

- Class II roads, with annual revenues of more than $25.5 million but with less than $319.2 million

- Class III roads, the true "short lines" of the industry, with annual revenues of less than $25.5 million

In compiling data for the industry, the Association of American Railroads (AAR) uses the STB revenue threshold for Class I railroads and further divides the Class II and Class III roads into "regional" (more than 350 route-miles and annual revenues exceeding $40 million) and "local" roads with route-miles and revenues under the regional threshold.

There are also "switching and terminal" railroads or "S&Ts" that may be all or partly owned by a combination of Class I roads. They do not necessarily count revenue dollars and may have expense reimbursement arrangements that are unique to this group. Examples include the Belt Railway of Chicago, the Conrail Shared Asset Areas, the Terminal Railroad Association of St. Louis, and the Indiana Harbor Belt.

The AAR for 2005 listed 30 regionals operating just over 15,000 route-miles with revenues of $1.48 billion and 523 local railroads (generally referred to as *short lines,* though this term may apply to some regionals as well) with over 29,000 total route-miles and $1.94 billion total revenues. Putting this in perspective, the seven Class I roads in 2005 generated revenues of more than $44 billion or 93 percent of the industry total.

On the smallest of lines, the general manager and a clerk may constitute the entire office force, whereas the Class I and larger Class II roads will have employee counts in the thousands and staffs of commensurate size. But regardless of route-miles or annual revenues, every railroad's tracks and trains are part of a North American rail system. The same things have to be done and the essentials of the organization are much the same, whatever the size.

Names and titles may vary, as well as the ways some of them may be linked together on the organization chart. But a look at the corporate structure of one of the larger systems, one with 40,000 employees and 2006 revenues of about $15 billion, will show one way in which a railroad corporation can be organized to successfully carry on its business. We will use this railroad as our example in the discussion that follows.

Corporate Structure

All Class I roads, plus a few of the Class II's and a handful of companies that operate multiple short lines, are corporations, with a board of directors headed by its chairman, who is sometimes also designated as the chief executive officer (CEO), responsible for long-term plans and practices. The railroad president, who more often than not is the CEO, may also be designated as the chief operating officer (COO), and is directly responsible to the board for running the railroad by making decisions on a shorter term basis. Reporting to the President and COO are the Chief Financial Officer (CFO), the Chief Commercial Officer, and several other Executive Vice Presidents (VPs) or Senior VPs who manage key support disciplines such as government affairs, investor and press relations, law, human resources, and taxation (Fig. 18-1). We will go into greater detail below on the activities and responsibilities of the CFO, COO (whether or not also President), and the Chief Commercial Officer who sometimes has the title of EVP (Executive Vice President) for Marketing and Sales.

The Chief Commercial Officer oversees the revenue-generating activities of the enterprise. The railroad is a service industry and as such the whole organization exists to create revenue by selling customers a transportation service that is, in the customer's mind at least, better than that offered by any competitor. (See also Chapter 21 on railroad marketing and sales.) The marketing and sales function on any railroad from the smallest short line to the mighty Union Pacific is a circular function.

The sales representative calls on the customer to sell the service now offered and if that will not get the order, the representative asks the customer what it will take to win the company's business. Armed with that information, the representative goes back to the marketing department and (with the counterparts in operations and finance) tries to design a service that will meet the customer's requirements. With that service package now in hand, the sales representative goes back to the customer and asks for the order.

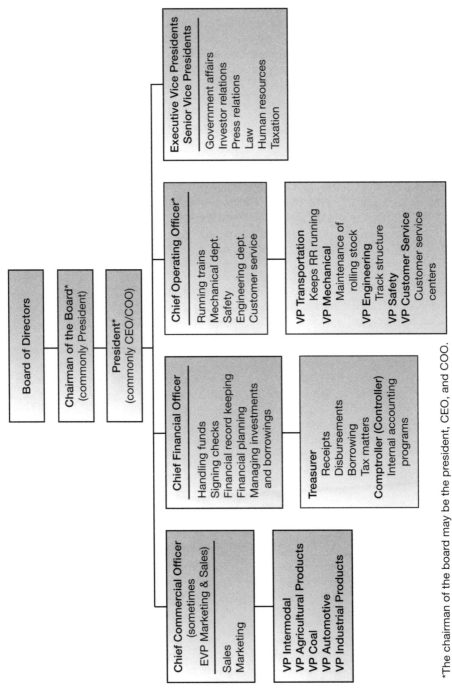

Fig. 18-1. Example of railroad corporate structure

The marketing and sales department is generally aligned along commodity lines with vice presidents and group heads for intermodal, agricultural products, coal, automotive, and "industrial products," including everything else the railroad moves, typically in carload lots. Every commodity is assigned a Standard Transportation Commodity Code (referred to as a STCC or *"stick" code*), a seven-digit number that goes from the general to the specific. Raw corn is listed in STCC 01 (zero-one), canned corn is in STCC 20, lumber is in STCC 24, Chemicals is in STCC 28, and the steel coils for the metal for the cans for the corn is in STCC 33 (specifically STCC 33 123 32, "steel, sheet, in coils, plain or galvanized"). That's an example of how specific STCCs are.

The COO is in charge of every activity on the railroad that supports the generation of revenue, from safety to running trains to track work to equipment maintenance to customer service centers and—in cooperation with the marketing department—service design. Under the COO we have the VP Transportation who keeps the railroad running, the VP Mechanical (rolling stock maintenance, sometimes Chief Mechanical Officer), the VP Engineering (track and structures and in many cases signaling and communications), VP Safety, VP Customer Service, and various other support group leaders.

Out on the railroad there are regional and divisional VPs, Terminal Superintendents, Road Masters (who oversee track conditions) and Road Foremen of Engines (who keep the locomotives running and the crews qualified to run them). Readers who would like to see how a typical operating department is set up are encouraged to turn to Fig. 22-1.

The Chief Financial Officer is the executive officer responsible for handling funds, signing checks, keeping financial records, and financial planning for the railroad. Reporting to the CFO are the treasurer (receipts, disbursements, borrowing and tax matters) and a comptroller or controller (internal accounting programs). The financial planning office is there both to keep the company from running out of cash and to manage its investments and borrowings, so the overall cost of meeting its obligations is as low as possible. This includes maintaining as good a financial rating for the railroad's financial paper and as low an interest rate as its operating results can support.

Financial Results

One of the theories behind railroad regulation is the determination of a level of rates that will not result in profits beyond a rate of return considered "reasonable." Since the way in which a company's books are kept can have a big effect on its reported profits, the law requires that railroad accounting and financial reports to the STB follow very specific rules.

The financial community, which rates and handles railroad securities, wants its reports in accordance with "generally accepted accounting principles" (GAAP), which change from time to time in accordance with Financial Accounting Standards Bureau. The FASB is a private, not-for-profit organization whose primary purpose is to develop GAAP within the United States in the public's interest. The Securities and Exchange

Commission (SEC) designated the FASB as the organization responsible for setting accounting standards for public companies in the United States.

As companies doing business in the United States and selling shares in the open market ("publicly held"), railroads are required by the SEC to disclose pertinent financial and other data to permit informed analysis by potential investors. The SEC Act of 1934 requires annual and quarterly reports of financial condition (Forms 10-K and 10-Q, respectively). These reports may be found on any publicly held railroad website under the Investors or Investor Relations tab.

The three most important parts of the quarterly and annual reports are the Income Statement, the Balance Sheet, the Statement of Cash Flows and the notes relating to each. Any serious student of the railroad industry must have a basic understanding of each and how they relate to each other.

The *Income Statement* shows total revenues from railroad operations, the expenses incurred in providing those revenues, and the operating income (equivalent to gross income for nonrailroads). These three are sometimes called "above-the-line" results be-

Table 18-1. Condensed income statement

Condensed Income Statement		
(Amounts shown in millions)		
	2006	2005
Total operating revenue	$52,152	$46,118
Freight	50,315	44,457
Passenger	70	65
All other revenues	1,767	1,597
Total operating expenses	40,980	37,843
Net operating revenue	11,172	8,275
Other income	1,049	811
Miscellaneous deductions	945	725
Interest charges and amortization of discount	1,151	1,220
Income taxes on ordinary income	2,857	1,946
Provision for deferred taxes	786	278
Unusual or infrequent items (Dr) Cr	0	0
Ordinary income	6,482	4,917
Net railway operating income	7,560	6,075
Rate of return on net investment	10.2%	8.5%

Source: Railroad Facts 2006

cause they relate solely to the core business of providing a transportation service. See Table 18-1 for details.

A key measure of railroad operating efficiency is the operating ratio or the percentage of total operating revenue represented by total operating expense. (The *operating ratio* is the complement of what nonrailroads call gross margin, or gross income as a percentage of revenue.) A well-run railroad will have an OR (operating ratio) in the low to mid-70s though some particularly well-run railroads (for example, Canadian National and before that the Illinois Central) have reported operating ratios in the low 60s.

Improved asset utilization, better operating practices, and fewer accidents produce greater profitability and therefore will tend to bring the operating ratio down. The extent to which the ratio fluctuates with changes in traffic level may well be more a matter of the railroad's traffic mix than of management efficiency. If most of the line's business is in mineral traffic, which can be handled satisfactorily by running proportionally fewer trains of the same length, the ratio may go down with reduced traffic because the latest, most efficient equipment can do the whole job. On the other hand, if most of the traffic is premium-priced or time-sensitive freight handled in trains that must run on schedule, any revenue fall-offs will push up the operating ratio exponentially.

Continuing down the income statement are (1) "other income" from land sales and cash receipts not related to the core railroad operations, (2) interest paid on debt less the interest received, and (3) income taxes paid or due and other noncore items coming down to Net Income and Earnings per Share (net income divided by the number of common stock shares). The Income Statement section between Operating Income and Net Income is sometimes referred to as "below the line" and can vary widely among railroads. Net income is a number of more importance to investors than to those who merely want to know how good the company is at generating income from the core business.

The *Balance Sheet* not only shows assets, liabilities, and equity but also shows the capital structure of the organization, or capitalization. The Balance Sheet also sheds a great deal of light on three other items: the amount of net debt relative to equity and capitalization, how cash is managed, and, in conjunction with the Income Statement, return on capitalization (on assets and on equity).

In railroad parlance (specific to this industry), the total capitalization is defined as net debt (long-term debt minus cash) plus equity. Most railroads try to keep the debt-to-capitalization ratio between 30 percent and 50 percent. At debt-to-capitalization ratios of more than 50 percent, investors may be less willing to lend money at "investment-grade" rates, demanding the higher interest levels of subinvestment grade debt.

The *Cash Flow Statement* starts with the net income figure from the Income Statement and puts back noncash items like depreciation and changes in current assets and liabilities to arrive at "cash generated by operating activities." As a general rule, the higher the ratio of operating cash flow to net income, the better.

Railroads are capital-intensive industries because so much of the asset base is either consumed (fuel) or wears out (track, locomotives, and cars) and must be continually replaced. Short-lived assets like diesel fuel and locomotive filters are expensed as they are used and show up under operating expenses on the Income Statement. Money for longer lived assets—track, bridges, buildings, locomotives, cars—is shown under capitalized expenses *(capex)* on the Cash Flow Statement.

Next are dividends paid to shareholders as a distribution of earnings deducted from operating cash flow along with capex to arrive at Free Cash Flow, a measure that affects the investment community's comfort with the firm's ability to continue to function as a going concern. Another consideration on the Cash Flow statement is the money spent repurchasing shares on the open market. Share counts go up as new shares are issued or as employees cash in shares received as options as part of their compensation.

These options are shown on the Income Statement as part of the diluted share count used in calculating earnings per share (EPS). They are called *diluted shares* because the exercise of options results in the issuance of new shares that dilute the EPS from what it would have been absent these shares. Thus, railroads buy back shares to reduce the dilution and to increase earnings per share. Ideally, share repurchases are paid from free cash flow, though sometimes additional debt may be incurred to buy back shares.

Another financial measure frequently used by short lines or nonpublicly traded railroads is Earnings Before Interest, Taxes, Depreciation and Amortization (EBITDA). It is a measure of operating cash flow and is useful in determining a smaller company's ability to stay in business. The EBITDA-to-revenue ratio is useful in evaluating companies that do not capitalize major expenditures but do take depreciation on them. Moreover, EBITDA is used in evaluating what a short line is worth in a sale. In the mid-2000s, for example, investors saw sales-to-EBITDA multiples in the eight-to-ten times range and even above in some cases.

The Financial Effects of Railroad Regulation

Federal regulation of railroad rates was partially eliminated with the passage of the Staggers Act in 1980. Various other long-standing aspects of regulation were eliminated on December 31, 1995, by the Interstate Commerce Commission Termination Act. The effects of these eliminations will continue to show up in railroad organization and operations for some time to come. Under the jurisdiction of the Surface Transportation Board (STB), which inherited remaining ICC functions, railroads remain subject to some constraints beyond those applying to all businesses of similar size, and various aspects of previous restrictions are covered in Chapter 21 under "Railroad Marketing."

There is, however, one valuable historic precedent pertinent to this discussion, and that has to do with railroad ownership of nonrailroad enterprises. Until 1996, for example, under the "Commodities Clause" of the 1906 Elkins Act, it was illegal for a railroad to own mines or factories whose products (other than timber or materials needed for the railroad's own use in producing transportation) would be shipped over its tracks. This law was passed to break up such combinations as coal mining and railroad companies, which were judged to represent unequal competitors for independent producers. A mining or metals company could still own a railroad, but as a common carrier, its rates and operations were regulated by the ICC to ensure that it would serve all shippers, particularly its owner's competitors, on an impartial basis.

As a result of this restriction, some railroads were set up as subsidiaries of railroad holding companies ("East-West Industries," for our fictional East-West Railroad Co.). The holding company could then own and operate other nonrailroad businesses without being subject to such restrictions. In recent years, however, corporations like Norfolk Southern (North American Van Lines) and Union Pacific (Overnight Transportation) gradually shed these noncore businesses. Moreover, many nonrailroad companies that owned railroads (Georgia-Pacific, ALCOA, and so on) sold off their rail operations to short line businesses to focus on their own core competencies and leave the business of running a railroad to railroad operating companies like RailAmerica and Genesee & Wyoming.

In connection with the Staggers Act's partial deregulation of rail rates, the ICC was to make an annual determination as to the revenue adequacy of each railroad—the relationship of its "return on net investment" (ROI) to the cost of capital. The cost is the premium realized by the company to gain access to the financial resources and the return is the reward that the company realizes from making those investments. These investments are, of course, made possible from the financial resources ("retained earnings") obtained in the first place. Logically, to make these investments successful and sustainable, their returns must be greater than the cost of obtaining the funds to make the investments. How much of those returns are meted out to stockholders (through dividends, or share buybacks) and how much is directed to retained earnings for the purpose of further capital investment (both renewals as well as expansion) will depend upon many factors.

The STB also uses the rail cost recovery index or Rail Cost Adjustment Factor (RCAF) as the measure of inflation experienced by railroads in the course of their operations. The application is designed to allow railroads to adjust rates commensurate with inflation without the potential for challenge by rail customers. While still in use in 2007, the application of this mechanism appears to be applied to a somewhat lesser volume of rail traffic than previously was the case.

The implications of a carrier becoming "revenue adequate" (over a relevant length of time) in the eyes of the STB are not definitively known, but there is general agreement that the regulator would be likely to assess the needs of revenue-adequate railroads differently from those carriers that are not revenue adequate. Neither the statute nor regulations set out exactly how such a possible change in approach would unfold, but it is probable that the impact on rate reasonableness decisions will be decidedly more important that any impact on the RCAF.

Post-Staggers railroad earnings have been far above those in most of the previous years. However, industry-average ROI on this ICC basis (8.46 percent in 2005) has not approached "revenue-adequate" cost-of-capital (12.2 percent in 2005) levels. Since boxcar and intermodal (piggyback) traffic has been completely deregulated, most other traffic moves under contracts rather than tariffs, and competitive pressures have continued to restrain rail rates (revenue-per-ton-mile averages have declined relative to the cost index for every year since deregulation), the effect on the few roads that have attained revenue adequacy has been essentially nil.

During the pre-Staggers years of the 1970s, the freight railroads as a whole were able to acquire sufficient equipment to handle the traffic only by borrowing money (selling more equipment trust certificates than were paid off). They paid high rental rates for privately owned cars; capital expenditures were more than double for the retained funds, and maintenance was deferred to the point that roadway capital expenditures were only about one-third of those for equipment. Tie conditions got so bad that on some railroads there were "sanding derailments" where rail simply rolled over under the weight of a stationary car.

However, in most of the years since the early 1980s, retained funds have been sufficient to exceed a greatly increased level of capital expenditures. At the cost to car and locomotive builders of a disastrous decline in orders, improved car and locomotive utilization permitted applying the bulk of these funds to restoring the condition of a slimmed-down track network to a state generally conceded to be free from deferred maintenance.

In recent years, retained funding (augmented by massive private investment in leased rolling stock) has generally supported a level of capital spending better balanced between equipment and roadway needs but sometimes strained in meeting the needs of increased traffic.

In 2007, there was such a ground-swell of interest in railroad regulation and control that it put the whole future of a healthy, post-Staggers railroad industry in question.

There were three very real governmental initiatives. In Ex Parte (EP) 646, the STB sought to make its rail rate dispute resolution procedures "more affordable and accessible to shippers of small and medium-size shipments." Since small shippers dominate the industrial commodity base of the railroads at large, the threat of more rate cases to defend could very well make these small shippers less attractive to the Class I's. The STB still allows the Class I's to base rates on cost-of-service and as those costs escalate, rates go up (or yields go down), and the whole matter spirals out of control.

In EP 664, the STB stated its intention to change the way railroads determine their cost of capital and thus "revenue adequacy." The Board conceded that "rail carriers should have an opportunity to earn adequate revenues defined as those that are sufficient to cover operating expenses, support prudent capital outlays, repay a reasonable debt level, raise needed equity capital, and otherwise attract and retain capital in amounts adequate to provide a sound rail transportation system." The then-current cost of capital methodology put that number at 12.2 percent for 2005 and the calculation proposed in 2007 dropped it to 7.5 percent, a 40 percent reduction. So even as the STB allowed rates at the 180 percent of variable cost model (variable means if you don't run the train you don't incur the cost, never mind that payrolls and maintenance budgets remain), if total ROI exceeded the 7.5 percent cost of capital, the offending railroad could become too revenue adequate and thus invite STB scrutiny.

The result was that if revenues were to be constrained, Class I resources would be directed to the commodity origin-destination pairs that produce acceptable revenue-cost ratios. That could conceivably lead to a lot fewer single-car movements. The impact on short lines could be devastating because the very low-margin moves thus threatened were the short lines' bread-and-butter traffic.

Finally, in September 2007, Congress had before it a pair of bills called the "Railroad Competition and Service Improvement Act," HR 2125 and S 953. This was clearly an attempt to roll back the clock to the pre-Staggers era (before the age of contract pricing, before the railroads could shut down money-losing services, before the days of short lines that were created out of money-losing Class I branch lines).

Looking back, there was a common thread among the three proposed actions. Some members of the rail-shipper community felt they were paying too much for rail service and called in their chits from their representatives in Congress. The members of the Congress, in turn, asked the STB to look into the situation, and the first thing the Board did was to go after revenue-adequacy and cost-of-capital calculations. Then, the Board made it easier for shippers to ask for redress when they feel they have been overcharged. Both cost-of-capital and small-rate cases were embodied in HR 2125 and S 953.

The Class I railroad community was not pleased. Union Pacific Chairman Jim Young summed up the Class I feeling when he wrote in a September 2007 letter to the STB, "The Board's recent proposal on the calculation of the industry's cost of capital, its new regime for rate regulation, and the re-regulation legislation introduced in Congress, if adopted, will compel us to reconsider our future investment policies ... This legislation would undo much of the progress our industry and company have made during the last twenty years."

Infrastructure Maintenance

The nature of railroad track is such that it can go for quite some period of time without major repairs or much apparent deterioration. Thus, should management want to present a favorable-looking operating ratio, it can make major cuts in the maintenance-of-way account. In periods of reduced traffic, of course, the track is receiving less wear, and some reduction in maintenance expense would not result in a net decline in track condition. Beyond this point, the track is accumulating "deferred maintenance." To look for this, rail and crosstie replacement figures may be studied and compared to those of previous years.

To some extent, the same is true for maintenance of equipment, though this will usually show up in the "bad order ratio" (the percentage of cars and locomotives in unserviceable condition). A conscientious management, of course, wants to have a good estimate of any deferred maintenance it may be incurring. In the past, making accurate estimates was difficult at best. However, with changes in technology, a good estimate of the life of improved rail or of a new type of crosstie may be made in short order, often before installation has begun.

In the pre-Staggers days of rate regulation, the ICC sometimes required that all proceeds from general rate increases that it permitted be used to reduce deferred maintenance; whether and to what extent it existed was often a topic of great importance to the railroad's financial planners.

Since the Staggers Act, the railroads have had much more freedom in how they allocate maintenance, repair, replacement, and capacity improvement funds. Deferred maintenance of main-line track, the general infrastructure, and rolling stock is largely a thing of the past.

Equipment Depreciation

When parts of the track or some cars are repaired, the cost is a business expense that reduces net income for the year, and therefore, no income taxes are involved. In theory, a car wears out at the rate for which "depreciation" is allowed by the STB and could be replaced at the end of its life for the original cost. The money that had been set aside (tax-free) in the depreciation account during the car's lifetime would purchase another. The railroad would be right back where it started, with a new car and no money in the depreciation account.

But what's a repaired car and what's a new car? A car that is in need of major repairs may be rebuilt into something bigger, better, and suitable for some entirely different lading that has become important in the railroad's traffic mix during the car's lifetime. If it is determined to be a repair and replacement-in-kind job, it is done with tax-free money. If it is a retirement of one car and purchase of a new one, the increase in value is made with "retained income" money (on which income tax has been paid) or by borrowing money to be paid back over a period of years, with interest. Since the income tax rate for large corporations can be as much as 35 percent or more, a good part of the net income of the railroad can rest on these rules and decisions. The car body may be virtually replaced at one time and the trucks and couplers at another, resulting in a car that is nominally 50 or more years old but which actually contains no parts that are anywhere near that ancient.

Equipment Trusts

The relatively unattractive rate of return in past years and the resulting difficulty in borrowing money at advantageous rates has meant that major improvements in the railroad physical plant, such as the new multi-million dollar computer-controlled classification yards, had to be paid for out of retained earnings from current operations. Since general-purpose rolling stock can be "repossessed" and resold if necessary, financing has been more readily available to help pay for cars and locomotives. In one common, long-used arrangement called the "Philadelphia Plan," equipment trust notes covering about 80 percent of the cost of specific equipment are issued by a financial institution, with the railroad making a down payment of 20 percent. The notes are paid off in installments by the railroad, with the bank retaining title to the rolling stock until the last notes are retired, usually in 15 years.

Equipment Leases

Investment tax credits and provisions for accelerating depreciation (in effect deferring income taxes) intended to encourage industrial investment in productive facilities have at various times had a major effect on investment decisions. As a result of the legalization of contract freight rates, railroads and shippers may share the benefits (which will exist only if equipment and the traffic for which it is suited last long enough) of more expensive but cheaper-to-haul equipment. Since railroads at some times may not have had enough earnings to take full advantage of the tax savings resulting from ownership and so many other circumstances affect the relative risks and benefits of ownership, a variety of leasing schemes exist within the following two principal categories:

- *Capital leases* are those in which the terms are such that the lessee (renter) is so committed to the use of the equipment over an extended period that the lease is required to appear on its balance sheet; the lessee is entitled to any associated tax benefits under these conditions.

- *Operating leases* are those in which the lessor (owner) retains sufficient responsibility for the continued use of the equipment to be entitled to associated tax and depreciation benefits.

Track: Depreciation Versus Addition/Betterment Accounting

Until 1982, railroad accounting for track and structures was required to be on a basis in which only "additions and betterments" could be capitalized. If 90 lb rail was replaced with 132 lb rail, for example, $^{42}/_{132}$ of the cost of the rail could be capitalized and its cost charged off as depreciation over a period supposed to be related to its useful life. The rest of the rail and the entire cost of installing it was an expense and so would reduce net income immediately, even though the benefits of the resulting improved track conditions would endure for a number of years.

As a result, there was a great incentive to hold down income taxes by plowing money into the track during periods of good traffic and correspondingly maintaining bottom-line profit figures during low-traffic periods by sharply cutting track programs, even though it has long been known that such peak-and-valley track maintenance represents a much less efficient use of manpower and materials. In 1983, such roadway maintenance was essentially capitalized by shifting it to a "ratable depreciation" basis tending to iron out the humps. Capital expenditures and net earnings reported earlier in the year are therefore not comparable with current figures.

Tunnels and Embankments

The cost of boring a tunnel or building an embankment to run trains efficiently through the mountains has been a tough question for the tax accountants and lawyers— do such things depreciate? Since it's literally nothing, the hole through the hill will never "wear out." But it must be expected that with the passage of time, it may become less useful as traffic patterns and the relative power, weight, and cost of trains change. The hole will be as good as ever, but in the wrong place or, perhaps, not quite big enough. Rulings in the late 1970s allowing such depreciation under certain circumstances were of considerable one-shot benefit to some railroads.

Deferred Taxes

Several tax decisions in recent years (on such subjects as tunnel and grading cost depreciation and temporary or regular changes in the tax laws intended to encourage industrial investment in production facilities and produce jobs) have had the effect of allowing companies to set aside money for depreciation at a faster-than-normal rate and thus pay less income tax during the early years of the life of the facilities. Since you can only depreciate anything once, depreciation in later years will be less, and the taxes then will be higher.

CHAPTER 19

Administration, Law, Accounting

The many corporate functions not directly involved in attracting and handling traffic or operating and maintaining the railroad can be arranged in as many different ways as there are railroads. Many of the matters under the various titles within these areas are reasonably self-explanatory and are what would be expected in any organization of this size, with appropriate adjustments for a railroad's singular characteristics. Some offices that are found only on a railroad are worth some discussion.

Information Technology (IT)

Networked computer systems are as important to the railroads as to any other industry. So many different parts of the railroad organization (operations, sales, accounting, purchasing and materials management, and human resources) use computers. It is now standard practice to have a special group develop, maintain, and operate an integrated central system and the computer programs used to receive, process, and display the data for the entire company. Even if the railroad does not have its own computer facility (leased or owned), it will still need people who can handle the company's input/output data exchange with the UMLER and TRAIN II systems of the AAR Car Service Division. Like most modern industries, the railroads are increasingly using the Internet to facilitate communications and information sharing, including interfaces with customers.

Labor Relations

While the railroad industry is not a closed shop, its operations in almost all aspects are governed by contracts with a relatively large number of separate unions, often referred to as "The Brotherhoods," representing both railroad-only occupations (such as train and engine service or car maintenance) and general trades. While the railroad managements are usually represented in industrywide bargaining by the National Carriers Conference Committee, local agreements govern actual operations on each railroad. Chapter 20 covers labor relations in detail.

Human Resources

The human resources (personnel) department of a railroad, similar to that found in general industry, makes sure that the company has complied with all applicable laws, regulations, and interpretations of the EEOC, IRS, NLRB, and other agencies, plus their counterparts in the various states where the railroad has employees. In addition, railroad operations are subject to the Federal Hours of Service Law, which provides severe penalties for allowing any employee concerned with train operation from being on duty more than 12 hours at a stretch.

Training programs are of increasing importance with the continual rise in the complexity of technology, both railroad and nonrailroad, that employees must be able to handle. Most railroaders will continue to learn the critical aspects of their work on the job, but many skills are being developed through more formal training programs and facilities.

Purchasing and Materials Management

"Purchasing and Stores," as it is known on many railroads, is often set up as a separate department, though on the smaller railroads it may be located within the operating department. It is responsible for spending almost one-quarter of all the railroad's revenue.

Inventory-carrying costs are now so high and the volume and variety of materials and supplies used so great that a railroad's net income can practically be consumed if the purchasing organization consistently buys items too far in advance of need or in quantity not closely related to need.

Running out of critical items can be even more serious, and buying competitively and in quantity can also lead to major savings, so the purchasing organization has the clear-cut job of handling its affairs so that its "customers" throughout the railroad have confidence in its responsiveness and reliability. Otherwise, every operating group could squirrel away material, and the railroad may be buying items it already has in surplus. Most purchasing and materials management departments are computerized, but the manager out in the field is still very much a key person.

Public Relations/Corporate Communications/Investor Relations

Beyond its specific assignments of handling the railroad's advertising, generating press releases, and publishing whatever newsletter or employee magazine the management authorizes, Public Relations (PR), more commonly called Corporate Communications, has the job of keeping the company's image as positive as possible throughout its territory. PR is truly everybody's business, and an undamaged shipment delivered *on* time *every* time counts more than a catchy slogan. The public relations staff cannot in any way offset the effects of a sloppy railroad with disgruntled employees. What it *can* do is help keep the record straight with timely, correct, well-phrased information about the capabilities and accomplishments of a good railroad and help the president or the chairman of the board make each employee a plus rather than a minus in establishing the railroad's identity in all the many communities through which it passes. Most Class I railroads also have a separate Investor Relations department that prepares annual reports, quarterly financial statements, and other materials distributed to stockholders and analysts. Investor Relations also organizes quarterly analyst presentations as well as annual investor conferences.

Law and Public Affairs

As public utilities regulated by federal, state, and local authorities, railroads are in need of legal counsel to a degree beyond that typical of most businesses of the same size. The impact of changes in laws and court rulings on the railroad is such that many lines, including our example, find it worthwhile to have officers of high rank located at key points in the various areas served whose main duties are concerned with such "public affairs" matters.

Accounting

The various financial matters handled by the office of the comptroller or accountant on a railroad include those such as billing customers and paying the company's bills, plus the extra complexities of auditing inputs from dozens or hundreds of agents, conductors, or collectors and keeping track of freight car per diem and car hire charges and revenues resulting from interchange service. Certain STB (Surface Transportation Board) rules must also be observed.

Traffic

The direct interface with the railroad's customers is the Traffic Department, the agents who quote rates, receive and receipt shipments, prepare bills of lading, notify consignees their goods are in, and (on occasion) try to find out why the goods haven't arrived.

Corporate Development

On a small railroad, the chairman of the board or the president may be the only person specifically planning ahead in terms of the direction the company should follow in enhancing its future. It helps to have everyone in the organization working today to make tomorrow better, but studying the company's choices is a top management function. In this structure, since the main opportunities are in developing new transportation needs that the railroad can profitably meet, a corporate planning staff is located in the marketing/planning area.

Real Estate and Insurance

All railroads own at least one long, narrow piece of real estate, the right-of-way. Additionally, most companies have adjacent land they own that is zoned for industrial or commercial use and can be used to help induce important shippers and receivers of freight to locate where the railroad can readily serve them. Thus, real estate management, contracts, insurance, and related functions find a logical home in the department charged with developing the market for freight service.

The *insurance* organization of the railroad is concerned with providing appropriate protection against major loss. In general, a railroad's property is so spread out or relatively indestructible that all but the most major catastrophes are more economically handled by relying upon self-insurance rather than by taking out insurance. The insurance manager's job is to study these trade-offs. On a smaller railroad, particularly with respect to public liability, the practice may be considerably different.

Marketing and Business Development

The development of particular types of business, including some that may not exist at present, is promoted by offices attached directly to the chief of marketing and business development.

For example, many railroads continue to foster the development of agriculture and forestry practices suitable for their territory through agribusiness agents. Many important products that are quite literally "growth industries" can be traced back to improved species, fertilizers, and crop-management schemes pioneered by such experts.

The *services industries* office works on a long-term basis to develop auxiliary services, such as warehousing, which the railroad can provide as add-ons to its basic transportation to do the following:

- Increase its overall profitability
- Attract more business
- Create a function that makes money itself

The *industrial development* organization's success in convincing companies who are planning new or expanded plants that the best location is at some available site along the railroad (or accessible to its intermodal service) will have a lot to do with what the company's income looks like years from now. A good *plant hunter's* business is to know more about plant sites, zoning laws, water supply, labor availability, tax rates, and possible new-business concessions than anyone else in the area, as well as respecting the confidential nature of such inquiries.

Chapter 21 covers business development and marketing in more detail.

Economic Forecasting

To handle the business, the railroad still has to have the cars, locomotives, and track capacity. If new or different traffic is forecast, lead time may be anywhere from 6 months to 2 years or more for ordering new equipment and constructing new track (sidings or double track). As much as anything, the general level of business activity at this future date will determine whether or not the railroad should commit its capital funds to be in a position to make money later. The railroad thus finds it advisable to have an economist on its staff to provide as informed a basis as possible for making the necessary investments.

Sales

The direct contact with the customer occurs mostly through the sales organization. Headed up by a regional sales manager, agency sales offices are located in all the major shipping and receiving localities on the railroad. The outposts of the system are the *off-line* agencies that solicit or make arrangements for interline traffic. Since over 75 percent of all railroad freight shipments travel over more than one line, such agencies are maintained by most roads, and several have agencies in foreign countries.

Much of the push for marketing actions originates from the sales organization, which also has the job of making sure that customers are made aware of what a new rate, schedule, or service can mean for their traffic.

Since familiarity with the customer's particular product, processes, and needs is often the key to effective sales and marketing, individual sales agents will specialize in one or more commodity groups. On some railroads, the entire traffic organization is set up on this basis, with its major groupings by coal, merchandise, forest products, grain, or other traffic elements. Railroad expenses charged to "traffic" as a whole amount to less than 2 percent of revenues, but it's a vital function if there is to be enough for the operating department to haul to keep the railroad profitable.

Labor Relations and The Railway Labor Act

L abor relations in the railroad and airline industries is governed by the Railway Labor Act, which is notably different than the National Labor Relations Act (which governs almost all other workers, including those in the trucking industry). The Railway Labor Act, or RLA, was enacted into law in 1926. It was the first law in America guaranteeing workers the right to organize and choose their own bargaining representatives. Passage by Congress of the RLA followed decades of labor unrest that included widespread and often violent work stoppages, frequently pitting federal soldiers against striking workers. The RLA was the entry point for labor legislation at the federal and state levels affecting employees in other private-sector industries and the public sector. It applied initially only to railroads and their employees. Airlines and their employees were brought under RLA coverage in 1936. Employers and workers in most other industries gained similar rights under the National Labor Relations Act of 1935.

Although labor unions trace their roots to the mid-1800s, these early unions were little more than fraternal organizations, created for mutual insurance protection in the event of injury, death, or family emergencies at a time when employers provided no benefits to employees. Organized protests of any sort were promptly halted by courts, and workers typically were fined or jailed. Unions were judged by courts to be unlawful combinations in restraint of trade. Notwithstanding the law, workers frequently engaged in work stoppages in an effort to gain improvements in wages, benefits, and working conditions.

At the urging of President Calvin Coolidge in 1924, railroads and their unions jointly drafted legislation to ease more agreeable labor-management relations aimed at reducing the threat of widespread railroad shutdowns. The product of that unprecedented collaboration was called the Railway Labor Act, which President Coolidge signed into law on May 20, 1926. Its premise was that arms-length negotiations would promote more stable labor relations in the railroad industry. The law's constitutionality was upheld by the Supreme Court in 1930.

The RLA was the first federal law guaranteeing the right of workers to organize and join unions and elect representatives without employer coercion or interference.

"Otherwise," said the Supreme Court, "collective action would be a mockery." Upon its passage, Pennsylvania Railroad President W. W. Atterbury called the RLA "machinery for peace" rather than "a manual for war." Labor leader Bert Jewell said in 1926 that the RLA lays the foundation "for the most far-reaching development yet achieved in any industry through genuine cooperation between employees and managements."

Rather than regulating wages, rules, and working conditions, the RLA recognizes that railroads and their employees can settle their own disputes the best, and that government ought to intervene only when they fail. The Supreme Court observed that wages, rules, and working conditions "may be as bad as the employees will tolerate or be made as good as they can bargain for." To encourage voluntary settlements, the RLA makes it the duty of all carriers and their employees to exert every reasonable effort to voluntarily settle disputes—a provision the Supreme Court called "the heart" of the RLA.

The RLA covers all employees and subordinate officials of any express company, sleeping car company, or railroad carrier subject to the jurisdiction of the federal Surface Transportation Board. The RLA also applies to railroad affiliates (such as warehouse companies that provide services in connection with railroad transportation). The RLA's underlying philosophy is almost total reliance on collective bargaining for settlement of disputes over wages, rules, and working conditions. The RLA also contains a stick—a presidential emergency board by which neutrals make nonbinding recommendations for procedures or terms on which a dispute might be settled.

The RLA contains five basic purposes:

1. To avoid any interruption to commerce

2. To ensure an unhindered right of employees to join a labor union (added in 1934)

3. To provide complete independence of organization by both parties to carry out the purposes of the RLA

4. To assist in the prompt and orderly settlement of disputes covering rates of pay, work rules, or working conditions

5. To assist in the prompt and orderly settlement of disputes growing out of grievances or out of the interpretation or application of existing contracts covering the rates of pay, work rules, or working conditions

The term of collective bargaining agreements under the RLA is not of a fixed duration, meaning RLA contracts do not expire. Contracts remain in force until changed. There is no time limit by which contracts must be negotiated to avoid a work stoppage. Under Section 6 of the act, either side may propose changes to an existing collective bargaining agreement, but agreements—for purposes of stability and labor peace—generally contain agreed-upon moratorium clauses that provide that no change may be demanded on specified subjects for a prescribed period of time. Either side seeking to change existing agreements must provide 30 days' written notice—Section 6 notices—about the desired changes, and within 10 days of receipt of such notice the sides must agree upon a time and place for the negotiation. Each side is to select its negotiators without interference from the other. Once Section 6 notices that propose the changes to an existing agreement have been served, the parties must maintain the *status quo* (no strikes or lockouts or promulgation of changes) until all procedures of the RLA have been fully exhausted.

The National Carriers Conference Committee

Until 1963, negotiations generally took place on a regional basis in Eastern, Western, and Southeastern rail territories. In 1963, the railroads established a permanent National Railway Conference, whose National Carriers Conference Committee (NCCC) negotiates nationally with the various railroad unions in what is commonly called "national handling." Members of the NCCC today include BNSF Railway, CSX, Kansas City Southern, Norfolk Southern, and Union Pacific. Other major railroads, including Amtrak, bargain individually with their unions. Some unionized regional and short line railroads also negotiate under the NCCC umbrella.

Although unions have no similar permanent organization such as the NCCC that engages in national handling, it is not uncommon for multiple unions, on an *ad hoc* basis (for a specific purpose and for no other purpose), to negotiate jointly with the NCCC. So-called national handling generally covers wages, rules, and working conditions. Matters such as job assignments and bidding, division of work assignments, and reporting times and places generally are negotiated between an individual railroad and the various unions' local or regional (general committee) officers.

Under the RLA, there are three categories of disputes: Representation disputes, major disputes and minor disputes. *Representation disputes* concern controversies arising among employees over the choice of a collective bargaining representative and are settled through elections monitored by the federal National Mediation Board. *Major disputes* involve formation or modification of a collective bargaining agreement covering wages, rules, and working conditions. *Minor disputes* involve grievances over interpretation or application of existing collective bargaining agreements.

Major Disputes

For major disputes, the RLA provides for a three-member National Mediation Board (NMB), appointed by the President of the United States and confirmed by the Senate, with the power to mediate any dispute between carriers and their employees at the request of either party or upon the board's own motion. No time limit is on the mediation procedure. The NMB controls the schedule of talks and only the NMB may release the parties from mediation.

If the NMB is unable to bring about an amicable settlement of the controversy through mediation, the board is required to use its influence to induce the parties voluntarily to submit to binding arbitration. The law is specific in that arbitration is voluntary and not compulsory. If both sides voluntarily agree to binding arbitration, an Arbitration Board of up to six members is established. Carriers and labor each select an equal number of arbitrators, who then select the additional member or members. If the arbitrators named by the two parties fail to agree upon the neutral arbitrator or arbitrators, the NMB makes the appointment.

If either labor or management decline voluntary arbitration, and if in the opinion of the NMB, the continuance of the controversy threatens substantially to interrupt interstate commerce in any section of the nation, the NMB is required to notify the President, who may, at his discretion, create a fact-finding Presidential Emergency Board (PEB). At this point, the parties must maintain the *status quo* (no strikes or lockouts) for 30 days. If the president chooses not to appoint an emergency board, strikes or lockouts may occur after the 30-day cooling-off period. Emergency boards are comprised of neutral members whose job is to make an investigation and submit to the President, within 30 days of its creation, a fact-finding report with nonbinding recommendations for procedures or terms on which a dispute might be settled. During this period, the parties must maintain the *status quo* (a second 30-day cooling-off period). Upon submission of the PEB report, the parties are required to maintain the *status quo* for an additional, or third, 30-day cooling-off period (they may mutually agree to extend the period of *status quo*). The nonbinding recommendations of the PEB are expected to carry the weight of public opinion and induce a voluntary agreement among the parties.

At this point, the RLA has run its course. If no agreement has been reached, either side becomes free to act in its own economic interests—a work stoppage (or strike) by labor, a lockout by management, or unilateral implementation of management proposals (that generally would force a work stoppage). The Supreme Court has held that the RLA's machinery for resolution of major disputes would become "meaningless" if courts could prohibit the parties from engaging in self-help. However, Congress may—and frequently does—impose, through legislation, additional machinery in an effort to gain a voluntary settlement. Congress also may—and frequently does—impose its own settlement. Such congressional action is not part of the RLA. The constitutional authority for Congress to impose its own settlements is found in the Constitution's commerce clause—Article I, Section 8, Paragraph 3—which is the basis of all transportation economic and safety regulation.

Minor Disputes

For minor disputes (interpretation and application of existing collective bargaining agreements), the RLA provides for binding arbitration. The purpose of binding arbitration for minor disputes is to limit the number of potential strikes. Federal courts may issue strike injunctions to "compel compliance"—halt strikes or management promulgation—when it rules a dispute is minor.

Labor Protection

Labor protection, which guarantees a wage floor for railroad employees adversely affected by mergers, consolidations, and acquisitions (as well as by track-abandonments, lines sales, and leases of uneconomic or surplus track), is provided through separate legislation, regulation, and contracts, and is not part of the Railway Labor Act. So-called labor protection is, in fact, income protection.

When two or more Class I railroads merge, the merged carrier must, under a provision of the Interstate Commerce Act, provide adversely affected employees (terminated or displaced) of the unifying railroads with income protection for at least 6 years. This means that no employee, as a result of the merger, will lose their pre-merger income through furlough, displacement, or demotion for up to 6 years. Lesser protection is provided when smaller regional railroads merge.

In February 2000, the United Transportation Union reached a negotiated settlement with major railroads that when two Class I railroads merge and there is more than one collective bargaining agreement at merger, the affected unions will determine the surviving contract. The agreement ended the so-called practice of "cramdown," whereby the STB would override or modify collective bargaining agreements in the implementation of mergers, consolidations, and acquisitions.

So-called labor protection has been called the "key that unlocks the door" to merger implementation and intended operating efficiencies. Otherwise, railroad mergers might be delayed or otherwise frustrated by labor strife. Labor protection ensures that the unifying railroads are able to cease to operate as a collection of separate railroads and fully enjoy the operating economics of being a unified system while providing income protection to affected employees. Similarly, when railroads abandon uneconomic track, or sell or lease that track to other operators, adversely affected employees of the selling railroad are entitled to up to 6 years of income protection (based upon length of employment). This protection was imposed by the Interstate Commerce Commission (now the Surface Transportation Board) and is known as New York Dock conditions, after a case involving a small railroad by that name.

Business Development and Marketing

The American Marketing Association defines "marketing" as "an organizational function and a set of processes for creating, communicating, and delivering value to customers and for managing customer relationships in ways that benefit the organization and its stakeholders." A critical part of this is determining what products the organization can provide to create more customers while still maintaining the desired margins.

For more than 100 years, the railroads were not permitted to do any of this. The Interstate Commerce Act of 1897 created the Interstate Commerce Commission (ICC), charged with regulating both pricing and service design of not only the railroads but also the few other means available for the transport of goods and people. The railroads consumed most of the ICC's attention. The ICC was formed largely because there was a growing sentiment that railroads were effectively monopolies and could charge whatever they wanted and deliver whatever level of service they felt was appropriate. At issue were rate discrimination between large and small markets, and between short-haul and long-haul pricing, plus preferential treatment of large customers over small, and the practice of giving free passes to politicians.

To its credit, however, the ICC invented the "what the traffic will bear" concept, made clear by one Judge Cooley, the first ICC Chairman: "Rates have been made on the principle of 'what the traffic will bear' theory to prevent unjust discrimination between competing places and commodities. 'Cost of service' fixes the minimum below which rates must not sink, just as 'what the traffic will bear' fixes the maximum above which they must not rise." So, the market value of the commodity was one of the earliest factors that the ICC considered in determining "just and reasonable" rates. If the railroads were to charge more for their transportation services than they are worth to the shipper, little or no volume would be available to pay for the costs and capital that goes into owning and operating a railroad. The question thus becomes one of attracting freight volume for the sake of volume at low cost versus charging what the traffic will bear—"market pricing."

Freight rates don't really change the quantity of goods that anybody ships. A reduction in Norfolk Southern (NS) freight rates between Harrisburg, Pennsylvania, and Atlanta, Georgia, won't cause a manufacturer to increase volumes in that lane. Lower railroad rates may cause a shipper to pick NS over trucker Arkansas Best, but the railroad's "customers' customers" (consumers) are the real determinants about what volumes move in what lanes.

The ICC's power grew increasingly oppressive for the railroads over the next 70 years, by which time the superior service offered by trucks and the interstates had siphoned off much of the railroads' high-rated traffic while the private auto and jet planes siphoned off most of the long-haul passenger train business. As a result, the railroads were more concerned with shrinking their asset base to save money than they were with finding new business that competed with trucks while still making a profit and fitting within the ICC's highly regulated pricing structure.

Finally, Congress began to take notice. The Staggers Act of 1980 eliminated most of the ICC's activities and positions that were the root causes for the systematic economic dismemberment of the industry. Gone were the extensive and expensive litigations surrounding perceived rate and service discrimination, prohibitions against any real marketing and new business development initiatives, the inability to come even close to earning the cost of capital, and the requirement to keep branch lines open well beyond their useful life. Named for Congressman Harley Staggers (D-W.Va.), who chaired the House Interstate and Foreign Commerce Committee during these proceedings, the legislation freed the railroads from the restrictive regulatory arm of the ICC, promoting free market competition for the first time. It deregulated the railroad industry significantly, diluting the regulatory structure that had existed since the Interstate Commerce Act.

From this point forward, U.S. railroads were permitted to determine where they ran trains and what rate they charged their customers. Moreover, Staggers prompted industrywide restructuring and was the catalyst for hundreds of new short line and regional railroads. Railroads could price competing routes and services differently to reflect the demand for each, and enter into confidential shipper contracts covering rate and service provisions. Moreover, Staggers recognized the need for railroads to earn adequate revenues and streamlined line sales, leases, and abandonments.

Congress ratified the Interstate Commerce Commission Termination Act of 1995, abolishing the ICC completely and creating the Surface Transportation Board (STB), an economic regulatory agency charged with resolving railroad rate and service disputes and reviewing proposed railroad mergers. The abolishment of the ICC and the ability of railroads to market, price, and design their services to meet customer needs has paid off handsomely for the railroads, the government, and the freight-shipping public at large. Railroads are now a growth industry as measured by Wall Street. They are beginning to earn their cost of capital, and by 2007, were spending more than $9 billion a year in capital improvements. Clearly, the ability to market railroad transportation services and get paid "what the traffic will bear" is working.

Business Development Functions

A railroad's business development and marketing people are concerned with the longer range aspects of getting freight onto trains. The job of making up a package of rates and service, often including innovations in loading, unloading, or railroading technology that will capture, increase, or retain traffic has several essential parts:

1. *Cost and price analysis* considers the rate the railroad must charge to make handling traffic profitable. It must cover the out-of-pocket costs and make some contribution toward the overhead costs of the railroad. It also calculates how much the transportation is worth to the customer, taking into account the costs and alternatives, such as decentralizing the customer's plants so that less transportation is required, or shipping via the competition.

2. *Market research* generates information on the amount of prospective traffic. In general, goods aren't produced just because a wonderfully low freight rate may become available but rather because somebody has a use for the item, though a favorable transportation situation may make a new producing area become competitive.

3. *Customer service* engineering develops concepts for hardware that will cut costs, reduce damage, or otherwise significantly improve the total process of getting the goods from where they are to where they're needed.

4. *Service design* (rates, routes, and divisions) considers the various routes over which the traffic can be moved, the rates that can be established legally (considering their relationships to others in effect), and the division of the revenue between the carriers involved.

All of this must be done in collaboration with the operating department before a business development program can be devised. A major change in the rate structure may keep the law and public affairs people busy for a long time overcoming tariff suspensions, rate appeals, and other roadblocks. Aggressive, imaginative, and precise work in marketing is the key to railroad prosperity.

Tariffs and Contracts

Freight doesn't move unless somebody needs the goods to be someplace else. The value of that move to the receiver is a function of what the goods are worth in the new place versus their value where they began their journey. For example, a 1,000 board-feet of two-by-fours may be worth $300 in Spokane, Washington, and $400 in Chicago, Illinois. That $100 spread is mostly transportation and it doesn't matter to the buyer whether it comes by rail or truck. But then there's the time value. BNSF says it can deliver on the fourth day; an independent trucker may offer second-day delivery. But that 2-day savings in transit time carries a price, say, $50 a thousand. The freight payer then has to decide whether 2 days' additional inventory in-hand is worth the extra cost. It's up to the railroad to determine what the customer really needs to keep his supply chain filled in the most economical manner and then offer the product that meets those needs.

In cases like these, prices are typically found in tariffs published by the railroads and generally posted on their websites. Then there are customers like Archer Daniels Midland and Pennsylvania Power & Light that buy their transportation by the trainload, or customers like Perdue Farms and General Motors, where annual railroad shipments number in the tens of thousands. Here's where Staggers really paid off: The railroads can negotiate package prices (contracts) that spell out how much is to be shipped over what routes, in whose equipment, and at what cost. This is contract pricing—confidential documents between the carriers and their customers. (See Chapter 8, "Contract Rates.") But either way, contract or tariff, the rate charged to the customer has to cover the avoidable costs, plus a portion of fixed costs and a profit margin. As a rule, crew, fuel, and equipment (car ownership or car hire plus locomotive opportunity cost) eat up about 75 to 80 percent of variable cost.

As an example, consider that lumber shipment from Spokane to Chicago. Let's use a railroad-owned center-beam flatcar loading to 100 tons. The railroad's avoidable costs are estimated to be $3,300 (80 percent of which is for fuel, road power, freight car usage and crew dispatching, and clerical costs). The revenue-to-cost ratio is 1:3 (1 to 3), which is the median where 1:0 is break-even and 1:6 is for highly rated commodities like toxic chemicals. That yields a freight rate of $4,280.

At this point it's up to the sales representative to go out and sell this package to the freight-payer. This is no longer a handshake business like it was pre-Staggers. This actual want ad excerpt shows how serious and demanding a position a railroad sales representative can be: "Union Pacific Railroad Marketing & Sales Account Representative headquartered in Omaha, Nebraska. Account Representatives are responsible for the full account management of Union Pacific's medium and lower volume accounts. Responsibilities: identifying customer requirements, developing creative solutions, establishing and negotiating prices, coordinating company resources, implementing strategies, satisfying customers, and driving revenue growth. Candidates in this area should have an undergraduate or graduate degree in marketing, management, finance or business. The candidate must possess excellent communication skills, strong analytical skills and display initiative and creativity in developing customer requirements."

The Customer Viewpoint

Transportation is part of supply chain management and adds to the cost of goods sold. A good transportation buyer seeks to lower the costs, and the railroad sales representative has to be attuned to whether the customer is trying to cut freight bills or lower inventory cost. It all starts with inventory management; the higher the unit cost of raw material and finished goods, the higher the inventory costs. Moreover, the railroad representative needs to know whether the customer takes title at origin or destination because of the impact on inventory-carrying costs.

The term "working capital" refers to the difference between current assets and current liabilities and is a function of the time it takes to convert raw materials into finished goods, finished goods into sales, and accounts receivables into cash. The supply chain manager must therefore balance inventory requirements against transportation costs, production schedules, customer requirements, and cash flow.

One of the chores every railroad marketing or sales manager has to face is repeated requests for tracing cars. Shippers don't ask trucker J. B. Hunt where their trailers are, but they do want to know if their carload has left UP's Bailey Yard in North Platte, Nebraska, for Portland, Oregon. The real question, never asked in so many words, is, "when will I see my car at the destination?" So, the customer's focus is more on the goods movement information than it is on the goods. They want to be able to tell carriers how many loads are available on what dates and where to have the appropriate vehicles in place at the appointed time. And they want to know when the goods will arrive at destination. So tracing is less important than reliable arrival times.

Information technology is invaluable. Over the past 20 years, most shippers have undergone massive process transformations to stay competitive. They pass on to the carriers the performance expectations that mirror their own drive for quality and consistency. Yet the basic transaction processing tools that the railroads use to meet these expectations are in some instances out of sync with customer IT (information technology) systems. Granted, the railroads were among the first industries to computerize the building systems to support complex order fulfillment, traffic classification, and train control processes. The systems were adequate to enable transactions, but using them to drive the business was not a consideration. Now, the need for IT systems able to aggregate customer requirements to shape operating activity has become evident.

The concept of the scheduled railroad is finally getting some respect. Historically, railroads have been limited in this effort by the complexity and size of their operations and the massive amount of data used to describe those operations.

Most core railroad business processes are still supported by manual input activities (customer service centers or dispatching offices). By collecting data as close to the business activity itself (ideally as a byproduct of the work activity—e.g., AEI), railroads are improving data accuracy and objectivity, and reducing data gathering cost.

With improved, timely, flexible information, tactical management (resource planning, plan adjustment, and local crew deployment) is getting more effective and efficient. Feedback as events take place is providing process measurement and control in terms of train performance, connection performance, shipment cycle time, performance reliability or variability, and asset utilization. All of it pulled together provides the information stream that customers require.

The New Realities

Value drivers are those things a company does to increase the value of its product or service to its customers. For railroads, they are: (1) customer knowledge (how much is known about how the customer's business works), (2) a service delivery system designed around the customer's logistical process, (3) the ability to renew and replace equipment and personnel to stay ahead of the other two, and (4) a customer service system that makes the service offered hassle-free. Let's take a look at each and an example of how a railroad used it to improve profitability.

1. *Customer knowledge.* Railroad A won the bid for a new distribution center for low-margin consumer goods. Revenues were modest, and car hire was high due to slow turns. After a year of experience working together, both railroad and customer began to see ways to take additional costs out of the rail delivery system. Working together, they revamped the place-and-pull process, coordinated schedules with the vendors and connecting Class I's, and even fine-tuned the warehouse floor to minimize car dwell time. As a result, demurrage was eliminated, car cycle time went down to 30 hours interchange to interchange, car hire went down, and business and profits came up.

2. *Service delivery system.* Railroad B was losing share at a barge transload on a major waterway adjacent to its tracks. The railroad sales representative asked the facility manager what was causing this downturn in rail loading. The answer was direct and to the point: "The freight service you're providing isn't what we're buying." With the help of the plant operating personnel who had to use the service and the railroad operating personnel who had to deliver the service, they came up with a coordinated scheduling system that cut demurrage, cut train-crew dwell time waiting to place and pull, cut car hire, and increased rail profits from that user.

3. *Renew and replace.* Locomotive failures and bad track add to costs for everything from fuel to car hire to labor. Reliability drops and shippers defect. In other words, at the same time the operating ratio is increasing, cash revenue is dropping. On one line, locomotive failures and derailments had gotten to the point that the customers were talking about picking up stakes and moving. Fortunately, about this time a re-railing program was under way as was a locomotive rehabilitation program. The net result was that a major customer came visiting and saw several miles of "new" CWR, more modern power, a freshly painted depot, and happy people. The talk of leaving stopped cold.

4. *Customer service.* An eastern short line teamed up with an under utilized seaport and a steamship operator to put steel coil in ships at a lower net cost than to truck to a bigger port. Rail rates were actually a bit higher than it would cost to truck, but the customer, being able to get only two of the 18,000 lb rolls on a 40,000 lb capacity truck, saw he was "paying for 4,000 lb of air per truckload." It wasn't an easy move to assemble, either. The manufacturer really didn't want either the rail or the local seaport. Three

railroads and five yards were in the route. They needed a connecting Class I's high-performance specially equipped boxcars. A tremendous amount of hand-holding was required to put all the pieces together.

An added value was the efficient use of space and equipment. Space constraints at the port left little room for 56 truckloads for each vessel to queue up waiting to unload. Offloading the trucks into a storage area pending loading on shipboard was out of the question. Now, the handful of railcars are tucked quietly away at the small port and taken quietly away by railroad personnel when made empty. The process worked so well that the port and steamship company had a new service they could sell, proving once again that customer service produces revenue, and the increased revenue contributes to the capital expenditure (capex) required to produce new revenue.

The four *customer* value drivers feed *owner* value drivers in quite a direct manner. Railroad A's customer knowledge added to revenues by increasing car use, doubling the number of cars that could be unloaded at once. Railroad B cut the costs of service to the customer and lopped some points off its operating ratio. The Bad Track Road (renewed and replaced) spent capex wisely. And the Short Line used exceptional customer service to take the hassle out of the plant-to-ship move.

The Short Line Railroad Advantage

Short line railroads have been with us since the *Best Friend of Charleston,* which saw service on the 136-mile South Carolina Canal and Railroad Company starting in 1830. Short line operators today are typically entrepreneurs who saw the need to *preserve* (as opposed to building new) rail service in an era when the Class I's were shedding lines. Many are independent businesses whose aim is to carve out a niche in the rail business by offering a superior rail service that is run by, with, and for the communities they serve.

Short lines are about as close as one can get to custom service in a batch-process industry. They can provide a level of customer knowledge and competitive advantage the Class Is are simply too big to match. The short lines can switch cars when the customer needs them switched, block for the distant destination at interchange if the connecting Class I wants them to, and generally design the service to meet the needs of the customer and the network.

And because they are local businesses, short lines can keep close tabs on their own customers' customers. Short line constituencies fall into what one might call "The Four Cs"—Customers, Class I connections, Coworkers, and Communities. And it's this last, *community,* that gives the short line operator a competitive edge over the competition.

Short lines also give a shipper options. The most successful short lines connect with more than one Class I, meaning their customers can offer the short line–Class I combination that offers the best value in terms of convenience, reliability, and price.

Moreover, the short line sales representative usually knows the internal cultures of the connecting Class I's and can be of invaluable assistance in guiding the selection of a Class I for the long haul.

But at the end of the day, it is the sales and business development teams of all rail-roads, large and small, that get the freight on the rails and give the operating people something to do.

CHAPTER 22

Operations

About 85 percent of railroaders work in the Operations Department. This is the lowest level in the organizational structure where Transportation (the operation of trains and yards) and Engineering (the maintenance of rolling stock and fixed plant) are viewed together. These activities are highly interrelated: they compete for track time, meaning large maintenance projects periodically shut down railroad operations while high train volumes interfere with the engineering improvements needed to maintain or increase train speeds. Fig. 22-1 is a typical organization chart for this department of a large railroad, condensed by leaving out many important staff and support positions attached to officials at various levels and by listing only examples of the many employee classifications at the working level throughout the department. Small railroads, including the many short lines in North America, will greatly simplify this structure by consolidating positions and removing intermediate levels of management.

On a large railroad, the Operating Department is headed by an executive who may serve as Chief Operating Officer (COO) and whose title may be Senior Vice President or Executive Vice President reporting to the railroad's President and Chief Executive Officer (CEO). Organizational structures vary among railroads, but the office positions reporting to this executive are typically:

- Vice President, Transportation: Manages train and yard operations (see Chapter 23)

- Vice President, Engineering: In charge of the maintenance-of-way functions

- Vice President, Mechanical: In charge of motive power and car organizations. (Some roads may combine the Engineering and Mechanical functions into a single Vice President, Engineering.) Depending on the railroad, other organizations may be supervised directly by the head of the Operations Department, since their functions are concerned with both train operations and maintenance of facilities.

- Vice President, Safety: Seeks to reduce injuries to employees and the public and accident damage to railroad track and equipment. The department may include Freight Claims as well, because technology, training, and discipline to minimize personal injury and equipment damage also contribute toward reducing damaged shipments.

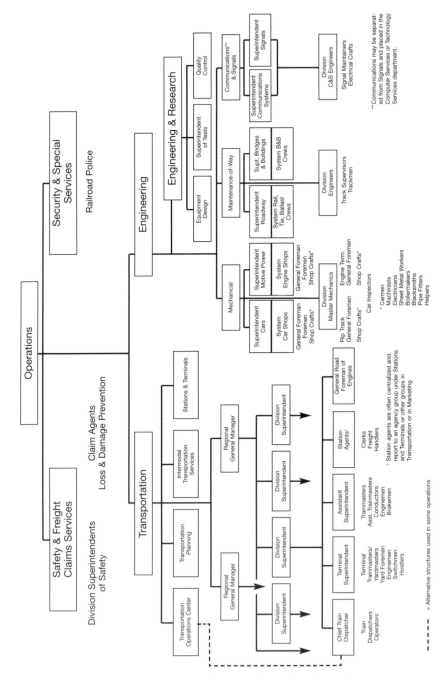

Fig. 22-1. Condensed organization chart — Operation Department

- Vice President, Security: Supervises the railroad's police forces. Growing concern about terrorism and public safety has magnified the importance of this function.

- Vice President, Purchasing: Manages acquisition and disposition of railroad assets, the vast majority of which are employed in or consumed by Operations.

- Vice President, Labor Relations: Negotiates and interprets agreements with the railroad's unions; at some roads, this function might be placed within the Human Resources Department.

Military Parallels to the Operations Department Structure

Railroads, especially their Operations Department, function much like a military organization. Some of this derives from historical precedents: Former soldiers and officers played major roles in the construction, management, and operations of railroads following the Civil War. The similarity is not simply coincidental. Both organizations have (1) a headquarters function that develops and articulates plans that move the organization in the desired direction, and (2) many widely scattered individuals and groups of individuals who must work toward this common goal while executing their responsibilities away from their supervisors. To encourage the desired behavior of the latter individuals, railroads adopted a carrot-and-stick approach: Road and yard crews who could not be directly supervised were often given incentives to finish a day's work quickly to get an early quit, while strict rules were issued and enforced to redirect undesired behavior. In time, railroads may be able to move away from the military model, since communication improvements enable employees to be supervised regardless of their location and fewer truly independent decisions need be made.

Field Staff Structure for Operations Department Functions

Although the following chapters describe in detail how the major Operations Department responsibilities are organized in the field, it is useful to give a general overview here. Many functions lend themselves naturally to a divisional (geographic) structure, since the level of their activities—like equipment and track maintenance—correlate to road and yard operations. Some railroads, recognizing how closely Transportation and other Operations activities must be coordinated, have officers for the various functions reporting to Division Superintendents in what is called a "Divisional" form of organization. Other roads follow a "Departmental" form of organization, where each department is organized into divisions that largely mirror the Transportation divisions, but have the officers in these functions report to senior departmental officers at the regional or headquarters level. Given the need for these responsibilities to respond to both local (division) and corporate (headquarters) needs, it is often said that these officers have "dotted-line" reporting relationships in that they may have more than one supervisor. Whether "departmental" or "divisional," the managers of these functions are:

- Division Engineer, responsible for maintenance and construction of track and structures (including buildings). Reporting to him will be Track Supervisors and Bridge and Building officers responsible for specific territories within the division.

- Division Master Mechanic, responsible for maintenance of railcars in his territory and repair and servicing of locomotives assigned to the division or routed through on road trains. He will have assistants at repair facilities.

- Division Communication and/or Signal Engineer, responsible for maintenance and construction of signal and communication equipment. Some roads combine communication and signal functions into one department; others separate the functions, often placing signals within Engineering but placing Communications in Technology or in its own department.

Railroad Safety and Accident/Incident Reporting

A major responsibility of the Operating Department is promoting safety and lowering employee and public injuries. These long-standing functions are increasing in importance as corporations and society as a whole strive for zero injuries.

Prior to January 1, 1975, railroads made monthly reports of "collisions, derailments, and other accidents" under the Accident Reports Act of 1910. Passage of the Occupational Safety and Health Act of 1970 (OSHA) required all employers, including railroads, to "maintain accurate records of ... work-related deaths, injuries, and illnesses," and redefined the record keeping rules. Railroads continue to make their monthly reports to the Federal Railroad Administration (FRA), a branch of the U.S. Department of Transportation. The reclassification seeks to separate incidents unique to railroads (e.g., derailments) from those that could happen in any industry (e.g., falling while walking in an employee parking lot), so that railroads' safety performance could be more readily compared with that of other industries. The 1975 reporting rules remained unchanged until May 1, 2003, when revisions were made to align with revised OSHA rules. Consequently, comparisons among FRA statistics before 1975, before May 1, 2003, and after May 1, 2003, must be done cautiously; in general, the changes give the impression that safety has declined, when actual trends are extremely favorable.

Train Accidents/Incidents

The term Accident/Incident is used to describe the entire list of reportable events. The term refers to any event that falls within the following subcategories:

- Train Accident: "Any collision, derailment, fire, explosion, act of God, or other event involving ... on-track equipment" resulting in total damages greater than the current reporting threshold. Note that this definition excludes costs derived from loss and damage to lading, liability claims, disruption of operations, and cost of clearing wrecks.

- Train Incident: "An event involving the movement of on-track equipment that results in a reportable casualty but does not cause reportable damage above the threshold established for train accidents." (Note that casualty is defined as "a reportable death, injury, or illness arising from the operation of a railroad.")

- Nontrain Incident: "An event that results in a reportable casualty, but does not involve the movement of on-track equipment nor cause reportable damage above the threshold established for train accidents." Nontrain incidents, which account for more than 85 percent of all employee injuries, are essentially similar to those resulting from the hazards to which workers in any heavy industry are exposed.

The "Reporting Threshold" referred to in these definitions is "The amount of total reportable damage resulting from a train accident, which, if exceeded, requires" the event to be reported. This number is adjusted annually to reflect inflation and thus maintain some degree of comparability over longer periods of time. For 2007, it is $8,701.

When reporting statistics, the FRA often groups data according to the following categories:

- Train Accidents: A safety-related event involving on-track rail equipment (both standing and moving), causing monetary damage to the rail equipment and track above a prescribed amount.

- Highway-Rail Grade Crossing Incidents: Any impact between a rail and highway user (both motor vehicles and other users of the crossing) at a designated crossing site, including walkways and sidewalks associated with the crossing.

- Other Incidents: Any death, injury, or occupational illness of a railroad employee that is not the result of a "Train Accident" or "Highway-Rail Incident."

Railroad Safety Performance

Traditionally, a railroad has been a hazardous workplace, given the hardness, mass, and inertia of rolling wheels, track equipment, and machine tools that make any careless move potentially life threatening. Fortunately, concerted attention by railroad management and work by groups such as the joint railroad/public authority educational program "Operation Lifesaver" have resulted in significant declines in railroad-related deaths and injuries. Nowhere is this more evident than in reports compiled by the Bureau of Labor Statistics where reportable injuries and illnesses per 100 employees— once about the same for railroads as for all private-sector employment—is now nearly half that of the rest of the private sector and roughly one-quarter of what it once was (see Table 22-1). Other proof of the railroads' remarkable safety achievement is evi-

Table 22-1. Employee injury – illness rates in various industries

Industry Category	Reportable injuries/illnesses per 100 employees			
	1976	1984	1994	2004
Railroad	10.1	8.7	5.1	2.7
Trucking, warehousing	15.1	14.5	14.8	7.0
Water transportation	15.2	13.2	9.5	4.4
Transportation by air	14.2	13.1	13.3	10.1
Construction	15.3	15.5	11.8	6.4
All manufacturing	13.2	10.6	12.2	6.6
All private-sector employment	9.2	8.0	8.4	4.8

Source: Bureau of Labor Statistics
Note: Trucking, warehousing statistic for 2004 is a combination of trucking and warehousing.

denced in Table 22-2, where the activity that led to a railroad employee's lost time injuries are tallied. Note that the two most common activities—Walking and Standing—preceded nearly one-quarter of all lost time injuries and that the first uniquely railroad-related activity—Riding—is, at 6.9 percent, the third most common activity leading to lost time. In recent years, U.S. railroads have brought the railroad employee annual death toll from train accidents to single digits, dropping to as few as four in 1998 and 2003 (see Table 22-3). This decline comes at a time of increasing railroad traffic, and the accident/incident rate per 1 million train-miles plus train-hours has declined by 40 percent in slightly more than a decade, dropping from 19.1 in 1994 to 11.5 in 2004 (see Table 22-4). Railroads celebrated their safest year to date in 2006, with the lowest employee casualty count and rate, the lowest grade crossing collision count and rate, and nearly the lowest train accident rate.

Another measure of the railroad's success in lowering casualties is its progress in reducing Federal Employees Liability Act (FELA) payments. This act, passed in 1908, preceded state workmen's compensation laws that now cover workers in all other industries. Unlike the no-fault workmen's compensation laws, tort-based FELA—now applying only to railroads (including Amtrak and commuter rail agencies)—requires that compensation for death or injury be obtained via individual litigation establishing the employer's fault and allowing, if the employee's suit is successful, an eventual lump-sum award for compensatory and punitive damages (including contingency legal fees) of unlimited amount. In spite of the potential for large awards, the railroad industry was able to reduce FELA payments by 20 percent between 1994 and 2004, largely due to reductions in employee casualties.

Table 22-2. Major sources of employee lost time[1]

Activity	Count	Percentage
Walking	882	14.9
Standing	422	7.1
Riding	407	6.9
Operating	240	4.1
Sitting	217	3.7
Getting off	187	3.2
Stepping down	172	2.9
Using hand tool	167	2.8
Lifting equipment (tools, parts, etc.)	144	2.4
Lining switches	139	2.3
Opening	134	2.3
Lifting other material	130	2.2
Pulling	130	2.2
Driving (motor vehicle, forklift, etc.)	101	1.7
Repairing	100	1.7
Descending	95	1.6
Climbing over/on	93	1.6
Hand brakes, applying	92	1.6
Handling, other	83	1.4
Cleaning	82	1.4
Loading/unloading	80	1.4
Closing	79	1.3
Bending, stooping	78	1.3
Getting on	72	1.2
Adjusting, other	69	1.2
Spiking (installation/removal)	68	1.1
Hand brakes, releasing	68	1.1
Other (Narrative must be provided)	67	1.1
Inspecting	62	1
Total - All Causes	**5,923**	**100**

[1] The number of cases that resulted in employees being absent for work at least one day
Source: Railroad Safety Statistics Annual Report 2004 – FRA

Table 22-3. Fatality rates from train accidents and other causes

Train Accidents Excluding Highway-Rail Crossing (HRC) Incidents

Type	Person	Fatalities by year											
		1993	1994	1995	1996	1997	1998	1999	2000	2001	2002	2003	2004
A -	Worker on duty (rr empl)	13	8	10	14	11	3	7	4	4	3	2	7
B -	Employee not on duty	2	-	1	-	-	-	-	-	-	-	-	-
C -	Passenger on train	49	2	-	9	1	-	-	-	1	7	-	1
D -	Nontrespasser	-	2	-	-	-	-	1	3	-	-	-	1
E -	Trespasser	3	-	3	2	4	1	1	2	1	4	2	1
F -	Worker on duty (contractor)	-	-	-	-	-	-	-	-	-	-	-	1
G -	Contractor (other)	-	-	-	-	-	-	-	-	-	-	-	-
J -	Nontrespasser, off rr prop	-	-	-	-	1	-	0	1	-	1	-	3
Total		67	12	14	25	17	4	9	10	6	15	4	13

Grand Total — All Causes

Type	Person	Fatalities by year											
		1993	1994	1995	1996	1997	1998	1999	2000	2001	2002	2003	2004
A -	Worker on duty (rr empl)	47	31	34	33	37	27	31	24	22	20	19	25
B -	Employee not on duty	4	5	2	-	-	2	1	1	1	1	1	-
C -	Passenger on train	58	-	-	12	6	4	14	4	3	7	3	3
D -	Nontrespasser	489	505	443	365	362	324	304	332	269	266	204	232
E -	Trespasser	675	682	660	620	646	644	570	570	673	646	634	628
F -	Worker on duty (contractor)	6	3	7	9	6	2	2	-	2	3	3	2
G -	Contractor (other)	-	-	-	-	5	3	10	3	2	7	2	2
H -	Worker on duty (volunteer)	-	-	-	-	-	-	-	-	-	-	-	-
I -	Volunteer (other)	-	-	-	-	-	-	-	-	-	-	-	-
J -	Nontrespasser, off rr prop	-	-	-	-	1	2	1	3	-	1	1	6
Total		1,279	1,226	1,146	1,039	1,063	1,008	932	937	971	951	867	898

Source: Railroad Safety Statistics 2004 Annual Report and Railroad Safety Statistics 2000 Annual Report – FRA

Table 22-4. Accident/Incident Rate

Year	Rate*	Year	Rate
1994	19.14	2000	13.94
1995	16.60	2001	13.56
1996	15.05	2002	12.18
1997	14.14	2003	11.95
1998	13.78	2004	11.59
1999	13.72		

*Using this equation: (Total accidents and incidents reported) x 1,000,000 / (train miles + train hours)
Compiled from Federal Railroad Administration website, Rail Equipment Accidents, 2004

Improved safety performance has reduced casualties, but it has not translated into reductions in the number and cost of train accidents. Comparing 1994 and 2004, the number of train accidents increased from 2,788 to 4,479, while the expenditure for repair to track and equipment damaged in accidents increased from $181 million to $339 million. On a dollar basis, track defects were the largest single cause, followed by human factors, equipment failure, and other causes (see Tables 22-5 and 22-6). Clearly, accident costs remain a burden warranting continual efforts to root out or cut down accident causes and consequences.

Freight Claims

After a long period in the 1.2 to 1.6 percent range, the ratio of loss-and-damage (L & D) claims to freight revenue now hovers around 0.3 percent. The percentage is small, but the annual payments still exceed $100 million, warranting continued efforts to further reduce the costs.

Table 22-5. Causes of FRA Accidents-Incidents (1994)

	Human Factors	Equipment Failure	Track Defects	Other	Total Number Train Accidents	Total Damage to RR Property
Collisions	218	10	7	32	267	$31M
Derailments	451	270	897	267	1,185	$125M
Other	263	29	47	103	442	$13M
Highway Grade Crossing				194	194	$12M
Total Number Train Accidents	932	309	951	596	2,788	
Total Damage to RR Property	$44M	$32M	$55M	$49M	-	$181M

Source: Compiled from Railroad Accident-Incident report, FRA - 1994

Table 22-6. Causes of FRA Accidents-Incidents (2004)

	Human Factors	Equipment Failure	Track Defects	Other	Total Number Train Accidents	Total Damage to RR Property
Collisions	399	16	6	32	453	$35M
Derailments	888	338	1126	404	2,756	$260M
Other	590	127	52	228	997	$31M
Highway Grade Crossing	1			272	273	$13M
Total Number Train Accidents	1,878	481	1,184	936	4,479	
Total Damage to RR Property	$90M	$58M	$127M	$64M	-	$339M

Source: Compiled from Railroad Accident-Incident report, FRA - 2004

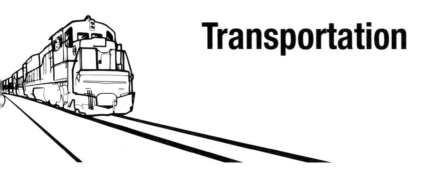

Transportation

A little more than half of a railroad's employees are in the transportation segment of the operation organization (which, put simply, runs the trains and the yards). Railroads carefully scrutinize the structure of their transportation organization to maximize effectiveness, and it is not uncommon to find that the organization chart may differ between companies. The organization at its base, however, faces the same issues as its predecessors over a hundred years ago—how to efficiently control train and yard operations.

At the heart of every railroad transportation organization is the crew district. The length of a district is primarily derived from the distance over which a crew and locomotive can operate without needing to be relieved, but the following factors play a role as well:

- An established city or a marked change in the terrain, as in going from prairie to mountain territory

- Number of hours that a crew is permitted to operate a train before requiring rest (known as "Hours of Service" and regulated by government authorities)

- Amount of track that can be managed by an individual (dispatcher or trainmaster), which is tied to communication capabilities and operational intensity (congestion, terrain, and major traffic origins and destinations)

Their actual lengths vary due to the factors noted above, but the length of a district upon which crew pay was based was once set at 100 miles for freight trains (150, for passenger trains), which was the distance that a train could be expected to travel in a "basic day" of 10 hours (although crews could work as long as 16 hours, later changed to 12 hours under Hours of Service rules in the United States). Over time, the distance to be traveled in a "basic day" (now, 8 hours) increased, currently standing at 130 miles. (Note that some railroads have eliminated all mileage-based pay, instead compensating their road train crews strictly by the hour.)

Even though 130 miles remains the basis for pay, the actual length of crew districts has often been increased, eliminating the intermediate crew change. Several factors have made this possible:

- Road diesel locomotives, unlike their steam predecessors, can run many hundreds of miles between servicings.

- Communication and control technologies have greatly improved. An extensive network of radio towers, linked to dispatcher offices by microwave or fiber-optic cable, permit direct communication between dispatchers and trains. Centralized Traffic Control, where dispatchers manage train movement authority by signal indications and set train routes by power switches, speed the movement of trains. Numerous systems are now available that permit train crews themselves to line their own routes in advance, subject to dispatcher permission.

- The ability to run ever longer trains means that fewer trains can handle the same amount of traffic, so the number of train meets, and their attendant delay, has been reduced.

- Network rationalization and decline in on-line business have reduced the need for road trains to do work en route. Locals and road switchers can now handle much of the traffic originating or terminating between the crew change points, requiring fewer stops by road trains.

- With its higher train speed and dispatching priority, Amtrak can operate hundreds of miles in a "basic day," and has extended its crew districts commensurately.

In addition to its road train responsibilities, the Transportation Department must operate the railroad's yards, where trains are assembled, disassembled, and switched and where many of the railroad's customers are served. Often, yards are in the middle of a crew district and are supervised as part of the road operation's line. On the other hand, if a railroad has several main lines coming together in one city, it may set up all its tracks and yards in the area as a terminal, with only a few miles of line but hundreds of miles of track to manage.

District Organization

Railroads refer to officers assigned to districts and terminals as "Front Line Supervisors," since they have the most direct contact with train and yard employees. Each district or small group of districts will have a trainmaster, who is responsible for the safe and efficient management of road and yard operations, and who will possibly be aided by one or more assistants. (A major terminal may have Terminal Trainmasters distinct from those responsible for road operations.) The trainmasters must be experts in national and local labor contracts to ensure that contractual constraints do not unduly limit their ability to manage operations efficiently. They must also be experts on operating rules and safety policies, as they test crews for rule compliance and conduct investigations of infractions, meting out punitive discipline when appropriate.

Because of the specialized skills required of a locomotive engineer, each district or small group of districts will be supervised by a Road Foreman of Engines (also known as a Traveling Engineer or Transportation Engineer). A Road Foreman of Engines' focus is the safe and efficient operation of the train from the train engineer's perspective, advising and monitoring throttle, brake, train makeup, and other practices. These supervisors often lead the analysis of train accidents, scrutinizing output from the train event recorders (often called *black boxes*) and establishing whether any action by the engineer (e.g., rapid throttle changes, excessive speed, or heavy or improper braking) contributed to the incident. They will also be heavily involved in any change in train operating policy such as longer trains, distributed power, and speed limit changes.

Although some individuals and activities are confined to a single crew district, many supervisory and "overhead" functions can be shared among several crew districts, giving rise to railroad *divisions*. Crew districts then became known as *districts* or *subdivisions*. Divisions could represent many thousands of miles of railroad. In time, *regions* were created to further centralize common work and to recognize that some divisions had common characteristics based on traffic, geography, or topography. These organizations are described below.

Division Organization

Railroad divisions were formed to handle the many functions common among crew districts. For example, the train dispatcher associated with one crew district may also be able to handle another, and the dispatchers associated with all the districts in a division can be assembled in a common place and report, in turn, to the division's Chief Dispatcher.

The size of the railroad often dictates the division's organization. For a small railroad, there may be only one division, and its supervision is assigned to a General Manager. Similarly, large railroads, each of whose divisions is the size of a small railroad company, may assign a General Manager to each of its divisions. On other properties, divisions are managed by Superintendents. Typically, the General Manager or Superintendent has a staff of one or more Assistant Superintendents and possibly one or more Terminal Superintendents. The assistant positions may be organized along geographic or functional lines. Reporting to these individuals are:

- *Trainmasters,* who usually report to an assistant superintendent and who are responsible for specific districts within the division. They supervise train and yard movements, ensuring that the operation is consistent with the railroad's operating plan established at headquarters.

- *Terminal Trainmasters,* who report to a Terminal Superintendent or Terminal Manager in the case of major terminals. They supervise yardmasters, yard crews, switch tenders, and hostlers in making up trains, getting locomotives to them, switching cars to local industries, and moving road trains into and out of the terminal, again according to the railroad's operating plan.

- Division *Road Foreman of Engines,* who supervises the operation of locomotives and locomotive engineers in moving the traffic of the division.

- *Chief Dispatcher,* who directs the safe and efficient operation of road trains. The Chief Dispatcher serves as a coordinator between road, yard, and terminal operations and manages the interaction between maintenance-of-way crews and trains. Many North American railroads have moved the dispatching function from the division to central dispatching offices, but the chief dispatcher's function remains unchanged.

Regional Organization

The reasons that some railroads combine divisions into regions are:

- Railroads have become so large that headquarters management has difficulty having the large number of railroad divisions reporting to them directly.

- Some regions enable a certain line of business (say, production of coal or other bulk material) to be almost completely encompassed within its limits, allowing its officers to focus on the needs of that commodity.

Transportation Headquarters Organization

The Transportation headquarters organization will be staffed to take care of those systemwide functions that cannot logically be handled by region or by division. Among these functions are:

- **Locomotive distribution.** This function assigns locomotives to road trains and to division pools to support local operations, flows locomotives to match supply and demand, manages locomotives in run-through service with other railroads, routes locomotives to shops for their periodic inspections, and coordinates locomotive purchase, rebuild, and retirement programs with the Mechanical Department.

- **Car distribution.** This function forecasts railcar supply and demand for each "car distribution territory" (some division of the railroad's network) and issues movement instructions to flow cars accordingly; working with Marketing and Sales, it sets policies on customer use of railroad-owned equipment, and it coordinates railcar purchase, rebuild, and retirement programs with Mechanical and Marketing and Sales Departments.

- **Crew calling.** Once a local function, technology now permits train and yard crews to be called from a central office. Computer systems assist in managing the complex work rules and contractual constraints associated with crew assignment.

- **Train dispatching.** Like *crew calling,* this was once a local function, but many railroads now exploit modern communication and control technology to perform this task from centralized or regionalized dispatching offices. In such cases, the Chief Dispatchers of adjacent divisions or all the Chief Dispatchers of a Region may report to a Corridor Superintendent who coordinates their activities across extended territories.

- **Station agency.** Like *crew calling* and *train dispatching*, "station agency" functions were once performed locally. Before modern communication, a physical presence near major customers was critical to the paperwork flow required by railcar movements. Station agents received bills of lading, produced waybills, arranged for cars to be spotted and pulled, and coordinated weighing and other ancillary services. Today, the paperwork largely moves through Electronic Data Interchange (EDI) and Internet-based systems, although some is communicated by fax and entered into the railroad's computer system. Railroads now centralize these functions.

- **Customer service.** Closely related to *station agency,* this function answers customer inquiries like, "Where is my shipment?" Often, Customer Service is co-located with station agency. Because this function now represents the "face" of the railroad as the shipper sees it, the function may be operated by the Marketing and Sales department.

- **Central yard office.** Many of the clerical functions at railroad yards—keeping track inventories and reporting train arrivals and departures—can now be performed remotely, and some roads have relocated these responsibilities from the terminals to a central facility.

- **Transportation planning/Service design.** The efficient operation of a railroad requires coordination of the activities of literally thousands of individuals working across the railroad network. To achieve this coordination, railroads develop "Operating Plans" that detail how cars will be switched into "blocks," how blocks will be assembled into trains, and how those trains will be scheduled and routed across the railroad network. *Transportation planning* tasks encompass the following subfunctions:

  - *Maintenance of blocking and classification tables:* Defines what grouping of cars (blocks) will be produced at each switching location, and assigns cars to the blocks based on each shipment's characteristics, including destination, commodity, weight, height, and several dozen other factors.

  - *Maintenance of train schedules:* Defines what blocks a train will carry (including block set-outs and pick-ups en route), train arrival and departure times, routes, priority relative to other trains, locomotive requirements and physical constraints such as weight and length.

  - *Monitoring of transit time performance and transportation efficiency:* To determine if the Operating Plan is effective and to identify improvements, analysts examine the voluminous data generated by railroad operations. A critical tool for this work is a computer system, known as Trip Planning or Car Scheduling, which predicts the movement of cars across the railroad according to the Operating Plan. In effect, the computer creates a plan for each shipment that mirrors the plan that the trainmaster, yardmaster, and dispatcher are instructed to follow when handling that shipment. The computer then monitors the shipment's movements relative to the plan that it has devised, and issues alerts when the car deviates from the plan. If the railroad cannot recover from the deviation, the computer creates a new schedule from that point, and monitors future events relative to the new schedule. Some railroads use the output from such systems to predict train size and yard workloads into the near future, tuning the operating plan consistent with the system's predictions.

– *Support for differentiated service:* Not all shipments are equal, and the railroad must recognize the unique characteristics of each shipment. Much of a railroad's traffic can be adequately handled within a single Operating Plan, but groups of shipments with special handling requirements (related to time-sensitivity, large volumes, or commodity characteristics) warrant their own Operating Plan. It is common for railroads to have staffs that develop plans specifically for intermodal and automotive shipments; unit-train operations; dimensional shipments (excessive size or weight); and hazardous shipments, especially those characterized as explosive, poisonous, or posing an inhalation hazard. Complementing these planning groups may be departments within Transportation responsible for day-to-day operation of these specialized subnetworks (e.g., intermodal operations).

– *Numerous small but critical functions* including designing and deploying systems to control train, yard, and dispatching functions; creating and monitoring transportation contracts (especially those related to interaction with other railroads); developing and implementing operating rules and monitoring adherence; and monitoring and correcting data quality issues.

A Railroad's Transportation Philosophy

A railroad can only be successful if it efficiently coordinates the activities of the hundreds of railroaders involved in the movement of each shipment. In time, technology may permit railroad operations to be optimized in real time, using communications for instantaneous transmission of the railroad's operational status and computers for creation of the optimal plan given that status. However, such technology has only recently begun to be developed, so railroads follow a simpler operating principle that divides transportation into strategic and tactical realms. This specialization of labor mirrors the military, where headquarters devises the broad strategic plan and soldiers are locally responsible for the tactical implementation of the plan. For a railroad, the strategic view is expressed in the railroad's Operating Plan, which reflects the railroad's goals and priorities.

The railroad's tactical perspective reflects how that plan is implemented in the field given a reality fraught with real time constraints (e.g., budget limits, locomotive and crew imbalances, derailments, traffic surges and dips, and track outages). At many railroads, a constant tension exists between strategic and tactical planning. A fundamental question revolves around how "scheduled" the railroad should be—*highly* scheduled (closely adhering to the plan under any circumstances), or *less* scheduled (using the plan as a guide but adjusting train operations to maximize train size by annulling or consolidating trains). Companies favoring the former believe that a highly scheduled railroad provides a more predictable and disciplined operation, improving service to the customer while driving down costs overall; some see greater benefit to a less scheduled railroad, where operations are adjusted to drive down directly measurable costs such as train crews.

The Engineering and Mechanical Departments

A railroad's Vice President-Engineering, which on many roads is now called Vice President-Engineering and Mechanical, typically has charge of departments responsible for the railroad's cars and locomotive and building and maintaining its track, roadway, and structures (including wayside signals and highway-rail grade crossing warning devices, which fall under Communications & Signals). The reason for assigning both responsibilities to one vice president is that there is so much cross-functionality between the two disciplines (as defined by the "wheel-rail interface"). On many railroads, these departments (usually known as Mechanical and Engineering, respectively) report directly to the official in charge of Operations. In either case, their task is to provide the rolling stock and right-of-way that Transportation uses to haul the traffic.

In the sample organization chart shown in Fig. 22-1, the Vice President-Engineering has three staff groups responsible, systemwide, for engineering design of equipment to meet the railroad's requirements; planning and conducting tests of track and rolling stock in the field and in the railroad's research laboratory (or with the Transportation Technology Center, operated by the AAR for the Federal Railroad Administration); and methods for quality control of materials and supplies used by the railroad.

Maintenance-of-Way (Engineering)

When railroad construction began in the 19th century, there were only two types of engineering, military and civil, so the title *chief engineer* on the railroad continues to refer to the person in charge of its roadway and structures, while his counterpart in charge of the mechanical department is usually known as the *chief mechanical officer.* The maintenance-of-way (M/W) department responsibility is actually broader than indicated by its title, since it is in charge of both maintaining and building tracks, bridges, buildings, and other structures.

Fig. 24-1. High-speed production tampers, such as this Plasser Unimat 4S, which tamps ballast under switches as well as tangent and curved track, does the work of what many years ago required dozens of workers using hand tools. [Photo courtesy Plasser American Corporation]

The modern M/W department has evolved with the high degree of mechanization of almost all track work in recent years. Most rail laying, tie replacement, and track-surfacing operations are done by large crews equipped with highly specialized equipment enabling one or, at the most, a few of them to take care of the entire system. Such equipment can include production tampers (Fig. 24-1), ballast distributors (Fig. 24-2), and ballast undercutter/cleaners. These crews, and the system M/W engineering and planning office can come under the Superintendent of Roadway, who also has a single shop maintaining all the track maintenance equipment for the system. A similar organization takes care of system bridge and building work.

Division Engineers

The M/W organization located at each division point is headed by the division engineer, with a staff to handle design and minor construction projects on the division. Track supervisors (or foremen) and their crews, assigned segments of track, handle all maintenance not accomplished by the system crews, and have the field responsibility for the quality and safety of the railroad's most basic item—its track.

Fig. 24-2. Ballast distribution equipment, such as this massive Plasser BDS-100 used by Amtrak on the Northeast Corridor, delivers and distributes thousands of tons of ballast to a track work site. [Photo courtesy Plasser American Corporation]

Communications and Signals

Communication and signaling system responsibilities are usually combined organizationally, since both are primarily electronic and electrical. This area has a superintendent at the system level, sharing a common organization out in the field at the division level where wayside signals, microwave terminals and relay stations, hump-yard car retarders, highway-rail grade crossing warning devices, and fault detection devices—hot wheel bearing (hotbox) detectors, wheel impact load detectors, dragging equipment detectors, and so on—are installed, maintained, and modified. Signal maintainers are responsible for the entire job of installation of these items, including a variety of both light and heavy work.

Mechanical Department (Motive Power and Cars)

Like M/W, the Mechanical Department is responsible not only for the maintenance and servicing of the items under its care but also for selecting or designing and obtaining them. Even though diesel locomotives are basically designed by their manufacturers rather than by the railroad, there is still a strong "do-it-yourself" tradition and capability. The superintendent of cars and the superintendent of motive power typically have strong design and industrial engineering staffs to develop specifications for equipment and procedures for its servicing and maintenance.

In recent years, the cost-saving from certain mechanized maintenance operations has tended to result in more centralized repair facilities, such as automated wheel shops capable of turning out all the freight car wheelsets needed on an entire railroad system or locomotive heavy repair shops rebuilding all the engines of one manufacturer for the system in a production line. These system shops come directly under the system superintendent's organization, though they may not all be located at the same terminal.

The heavy cranes and other equipment necessary to lift and position cars and locomotives for heavy repair work can do the same thing in a manufacturing operation. So, some railroads, of all sizes, make use of their shops for car building programs (often using "kits" supplied by car builders) and major locomotive rebuilding and upgrading (modernizing) work. The organization for these shops, with general foremen and foremen of the various trades required, along with planning and quality control elements, is not unlike that in a production-line manufacturing business.

Division Master Mechanics

Heading up mechanical department organizations at the divisional level are the master mechanics. Each division has the following points at which the mechanical department will operate:

- Maintenance, service, and inspection facilities

- RIP (repair in place) tracks for running repairs to cars (called rip track for repair, inspect, and paint)

- Heavy repair car shops

- Engine terminals, varying in capability from simple fueling and sanding to major repairs

- Interchange points where cars received from connections are inspected

The employees performing the maintenance and inspections tasks in these facilities include the following:

- *Carmen* (specialists in a variety of inspection and maintenance operations particular to railroad cars—Fig. 24-3)

- *Machinists* and *electricians* concerned primarily with locomotive maintenance and inspection

- *Members of the metal-working trades* (sheet metal workers, boilermakers, blacksmiths, and pipefitters) who can repair, rework, or rebuild car, locomotive, and shop structural and accessory parts

- *Storekeepers, equipment operators,* and *helpers* to make up a team matching the job (which must be expected, particularly in isolated areas, to include the unexpected)

Fig. 24-3. A carman undergoing training in freight car air brake system inspection and repair procedures [Photo courtesy BNSF Railway]

Strategic Planning

A good measure of the strength of a railroad's management is its ability to "get it all together" (temporarily or continually) and produce the results that can only come from the coordinated efforts of people with experience and responsibility working as a team. The interrelated nature of the responsibilities of the organizational units discussed in this chapter as well as Chapters 22 and 23 are such that the railroad's degree of success in selling and producing transportation depends not only on how well organized, staffed, equipped, and trained the individual departments are but even more on how effectively they work together. This shows up particularly if a railroad (whose operations are by nature day by day, repetitive, and likely to get into a comfortable rut) enters a transportation market in which it has been inactive. This is where Strategic Planning comes in. Strategic Planning involves all of a railroad's primary functions—Engineering, Mechanical, Operations, Transportation, Marketing and Sales, Legal, and so on.

Suppose that a railroad has found that, under existing conditions, traffic bringing fairly large quantities of grain from various small elevators on its lines to a huge processing mill is highly unprofitable. Utilization of expensive covered hopper cars used for this service is poor because of erratic loading at the elevators uncoordinated with less than daily train service on the branch lines and slow unloading at the mill. Since raising rates on this traffic under the existing operating conditions will make them un-competitive with trucking, while the covered hoppers, of which there are frequent shortages, can earn impressive profits in long-haul service, the railroad has been plan-ning to simply leave this market, jeopardizing some branch lines, elevators, and the economic health of affected communities.

However, if rapid-turnaround train movements (operating within the area without in-termediate crew changes) coordinated with multi-car elevator loading and speeded-up unloading (achieved with minor improvements to dedicated cars by matching modified facilities and switching at the mill), car use may improve to the extent that the traffic becomes profitable to the railroad at rates sharing the benefits among all parties in-volved. It is clear that almost every part of the organization will be involved in devel-oping this new service and the operating plan that accompanies it. All of this is coordi-nated by Strategic Planning.

Glossary

A

AAR or **A.A.R.** (Association of American Railroads) An industry association whose responsibilities include safety standards (including design standards and approval), maintenance, operations, service and repair standards, and car service rules research.

AAR Manual of Standards and Recommended Practices (MSRP) Publication containing the technical specifications and quality assurance requirements for interchange freight cars and components. Considered mandatory when specifically referenced in *AAR Interchange Rules.*

AB brake The standard freight car brake system that consists of the AB or ABD control valve, brake cylinder, auxiliary and emergency reservoirs, trainline, and other associated parts. The system allows rapid serial brake applications on each car in a train, controlled from the locomotive cab. The AB brake has an emergency and a service part that controls the charging, application, and release of the brakes.

AB brake valve The operating control valve of the AB freight car brake, consisting of three portions: the service portion, the emergency portion, and the pipe bracket. The AB valve controls the charging, application, and the release of the air brakes on each car.

ABD brake valve A modification of the AB valve that is an integral part of the AB brake system for freight cars. The ABD valve substitutes certain internal parts, and features a quick-release mechanism that helps the rapid evacuation of air from the air brake cylinder when the brakes are released. It was the first complete redesign of the AB control valve; D stood for diaphragm. The orientation of the control valve piston was changed from horizontal to vertical so the pistons would not be affected by slack action from the train.

ABDW brake valve A further modification of the ABD valve involving a substitution of the emergency portion only. The ABDW valve provides accelerated buildup of brake cylinder pressure during service brake applications, and decreases the time required to achieve effective braking. The need for a B-1 quick-service valve is eliminated when a car is equipped with the ABDW control valve. It was developed by Westinghouse engineer Richard Wilson; the W stood for Wilson. This valve was called the *accelerated application* valve and operated during a service brake pipe reduction to reduce brake pipe pressure at the individual car.

ABS (Automatic Block Signals) On a specific section or length of track, an arrangement of automatic signals governing each block.

ACI (Automatic Car Identification) System used to provide for automated identification of cars in a train by owner, number, and equipment classification when read by a wayside scanner. See **AEI**.

adhesion A measure of the ability of locomotive driving wheels to generate tractive force, usually expressed as a percent of the total weight on the drivers.

ad hoc (from *Latin,* meaning "to this") **1.** Formed for, or concerned with, one specific purpose. **2.** Improvised and often impromptu.

AEI (Automatic Equipment Identification) An automatic car scanning system to assist railroads in tracking and tracing cars. The system requires a transponder mounted on diagonally opposite corners of each railcar or other equipment to respond to radio-frequency interrogation.

air brake The general term used to describe the braking system used on most railways operating in North America.

AL (A-end left) Referring to the corners of a railcar.

alternating current (AC) An electric current that reverses its direction at regular intervals, usually abbreviated AC. See **direct current** (DC).

alternator A device that generates alternating current electricity, or, an electrical machine on a locomotive unit, driven by the diesel engine. When rotated, the alternator generates alternating electrical current subsequently adapted for use by the traction motors.

ambient temperature Refers to the temperature of the surrounding atmosphere. This term is not definite unless accompanied by an actual temperature figure or range.

ammeter An instrument for measuring electric current in a circuit.

amperage A unit of measure of electrical current.

Amtrak The name "Amtrak" is the blending of the words "America" and "track." It is properly used in documents with only the first letter capitalized. It is also known as the National Railroad Passenger Corporation.

ancillary Helping; auxiliary; held to use as a reserve, as in an *auxiliary power generator.*

angle cock Manually operated valve at ends of car or locomotive opening or closing air brake trainline.

anti-creeper See **rail anchor**.

APB (Absolute Permissive Block) On a specific section or length of track, an arrangement of signals and circuits automatically providing absolute protection from control point to control point against opposing train movements while permitting following movements under block signal protection. The name APB combines *absolute,* meaning "stop," and *permissive,* meaning "stop-and-proceed."

APL (American President Lines)

approach locking A time-sensitive electrical locking system that prevents the movement of track switches in a given route after a train is committed to that route, while at the same time protecting that route from opposing or conflicting movements.

AR (A-end right) Referring to the corners of a railcar.

AREA (American Railway Engineering Association) Professional organization whose membership is comprised of railroad maintenance-of-way officials. The AREA develops and establishes material specifications and track construction standards. AREA is now part of AREMA. See **AREMA**.

AREMA (American Railway Engineering and Maintenance-of-Way Association) Organization formed in 1998 encompassing the AREA, Roadmasters and Bridge and Building Associations and the AAR Communications & Signals Division in establishing and maintaining standards and recommended practices across the board.

armature The rotating part of a direct current motor or generator. It consists of a laminated iron cylinder or core keyed to a shaft. Armature coils of insulated copper wire or bars are wound in the slots of the cylinder. In alternating current machinery, the armature is frequently the stationary element.

articulated cars Two or more car bodies permanently coupled by slackless connections over shared trucks.

aspect The appearance of a roadway (fixed) signal conveying an indication that is viewed from the direction of an approaching train; the appearance of a cab signal conveying an indication that is viewed by an observer in the cab.

ATCS (advanced train control systems) See **automatic train control system**.

ATSI (advanced technology safety initiative)

automatic brake The air brake system used on a train. The automatic brake is controlled by a pressurized air pipe or brake pipe that runs the length of the train. A reduction or drop in the pressure in this trainline, called a brake pipe reduction (BPR), causes air brakes to apply on each car.

automatic coupler See **coupler**.

automatic interlocking An arrangement of signals, with or without other signal appliances, that functions automatically, as distinguished from those functions that are controlled manually. These signals are so interconnected by electric circuits that their movements must succeed each other in proper sequence.

automatic train control system (ATC or ATCS) **1.** A trackside system working in conjunction with equipment installed on the locomotive, so arranged that its operation will automatically result in the application of the air brakes to stop or control a train's speed at designated restrictions if the engineman does not respond. **2.** When operating under a speed restriction, an application of the brakes when the speed of the train exceeds the predetermined rate and which will continue until the speed is reduced to that rate. ATC usually works in conjunction with cab signals.

automatic train operation (ATO) A system by which speed and other control signals from the wayside are automatically received and translated into train response, with appropriate ATC supervision to assure operating safety.

automatic train stop system (ATS) A trackside system working in conjunction with equipment installed on the locomotive, so arranged that its operation will result in the automatic application of the air brakes should the engineman not acknowledge a restrictive signal within 20 seconds of passing the signal. If the restrictive signal is acknowledged, ATS will be suppressed.

axle The steel shaft on which the car wheels are mounted. The axle holds the wheels to gage and transmits the load from the journal bearing to the wheels.

B

balance speed A speed at which the tractive effort of the locomotive exactly balances or equals the sum of all the train, grade, and curve drag forces. At balance speed, there is neither acceleration nor deceleration.

ballast Material selected for placement on the roadbed for the purpose of holding the track in line and surface.

ballast car A car for carrying and distributing ballast for repair and construction work, usually of either the flat, gondola, or hopper type.

ballast regulator A track-mounted machine for moving ballast to provide the desired cross section, usually including brooms to clear ballast from the ties.

ballast undercutter cleaner A production machine that removes the ballast from the track, cleans it, and returns it back to the track in one continuous operation.

BART (Bay Area Rapid Transit) San Francisco's steel rail passenger service.

B-end of car The end on which the hand brake is located. If the car has two hand brakes, the B-end is the end toward which the body-mounted brake cylinder piston moves in the application of brakes or the end on which the retaining valve is located (if such a valve is used). If none of the above definitions are applicable, the car owner shall arbitrarily designate the B-end.

Bessemer process A steelmaking process whereby liquid pig iron is converted to steel by forcing air at atmospheric temperature through the metallic bath in a converter in which no extraneous fuel is burned, resulting in the oxidation or reduction of the carbon, manganese, and silicon to the extent desired and their removal in the form of slag.

bill of lading A carrier's contract and receipt for goods specifying that the carrier has received certain goods that it agrees to transport from one place to another, and to deliver to a designated person or assignee for such compensation and upon such conditions that are specified therein.

BL (B-end left) Referring to the corners of a railcar.

block **1.** In cars, a block or group of cars that are coupled and moving together. They are assembled in the process of classification for movement to a specified common destination. **2.** In railroad tracks, a length of track of defined limits, used by trains and governed by block signals, cab signals, or both.

block signal A fixed signal at the entrance of a block to govern trains and engines entering and using that block. (Standard Code)

body center plate A circular cast or forged steel plate on body bolster at the car centerline. Its function is to mate with the truck center plate and transmit the body bolster load to the truck.

body side bearing Flat steel bearing pads fastened to the body bolster, a standard distance outboard from the center pin hole. Its function is to support the car or the mating truck side bearing when variations in track cross level or other train dynamics cause the car to rock transversely on the center plates.

bolster See **container bolster**, and **truck bolster**.

bolster anchor rods The rods that are positioned one at each end of the bolster of passenger car trucks, the ends of which are mounted in rubber. One rod is on an arm integral with the truck frame and the other on the end of the bolster to guide the lateral and vertical movement of the bolster. They position the bolster so that it is always free from contact with the truck transoms.

bolstered load A load with the weight spread across two different railcars.

bolster gibs Small projections at each end of a truck bolster that engage the side frame column guides and provide vertical guidance for the bolster and lateral restraint to the side frames when assembled as a truck.

bolster pad In a tank car, a plate welded directly to the exterior of the tank at each body bolster location to which the remaining body bolster structure is attached.

bolster spring The secondary suspension element in a car truck, supporting the truck bolster, on which the weight of the car rests. The bolster spring rests on the truck frame or on swing hangers.

boxcar A closed car having a floor, sides, ends, and a roof with doors in the sides (or sides and ends). Used for general service and especially for lading that must be protected from the weather, and from subsequent damage.

BR (B-end right) Referring to the corners of a railcar.

brake beam The immediate supporting structure for the two brake heads and two brake shoes acting upon any given pair of wheels. In freight service, the virtually universal type is of truss construction consisting primarily of tension and compression members fastened at the ends and separated at the middle by a strut or fulcrum to which the truck brake lever is attached. Brake beams are said to be inside hung or outside hung, according to whether they are in the space between the axles or outside the axles.

brake pipe A term properly used, applied to describe the continuous line of brake pipe extending from the locomotive to the last car in a train, with all cars and air hoses coupled. It acts as a supply pipe for the reservoirs and also is usually the means by which the car brakes are controlled by the engineman. When a train is made up and all brake pipes on the cars are joined, the entire pipe line comprises what is commonly called the *trainline*. The term is often used to refer to the brake pipe on a single car.

brake pipe reduction (BPR) A reduction in air pressure in the train brake pipe. This pressure reduction causes air to flow from the air reservoir on each car to the brake cylinder, thus causing the brake to apply and produce a retarding force on the train.

branch line A secondary line of a railway, as distinguished from the main line, sometimes defined as a line carrying from 1.0 to 5.0 million gross tons per year.

bridge plate A hinged device affixed to a TOFC flatcar at the BR and AL corners used to span the gap between coupled cars to enable circus loading of trailers. Flatcars with 15 inches of end-of-car cushioning require auxiliary bridge plates at the BL and AR corners to provide the additional spanning length necessary when coupled to standard draft gear cars.

buff A term used to describe compressive coupler forces. The opposite of draft.

B-unit A diesel unit without a cab and without complete operating controls. B-units are usually equipped with hostler controls for independent operation at terminals and enginehouses.

C

cab car A passenger-train car equipped with trainline-connected controls so that it can serve as the lead unit in a train being pushed by a locomotive at the rear of the consist.

caboose A car that used to be placed at the rear of a train to provide an office and quarters for the conductor or trainmen or both while in transit, and to carry the various supplies and tools that were used in freight train operations. From the caboose, the crew was also able to observe the condition of the train and initiate measures to stop the train if unfavorable conditions arose. Sometimes called *cabin car, way car,* or *van.* Most railroads no longer use cabooses.

cab signal A signal located in engineman's compartment or cab, indicating a condition affecting the movement of a train or engine and used in conjunction with interlocking signals and in conjunction with, or in lieu of, block signals.

C&S (Communications and Signals)

cant (of a rail) A rail's inward inclination effected by using inclined surface tie plates, expressed as a height-to-width ratio (e.g., 1:20).

cant deficiency See **underbalance**.

capacity As applied to a freight car, the nominal load in pounds or gallons that the car is designed to carry. These figures, formerly stenciled on the car, are identified as CAPY. Car capacity figures are recorded in UMLER. Capacity is not to be confused with load limit, which is the maximum weight that can be loaded in a given car. See **UMLER.**

car body The main or principal part in or on which the load is placed.

car days An expression referring to the number of days a car owned by one railroad is on the line of another railroad.

car float A flat-bottomed craft without power and equipped with tracks upon which cars are run from the land by means of a float bridge, to be transported across water. See **float bridge**.

car-mile An operating term defined as one car that is moved over 1 mile of track.

car retarder A braking device built into a railway track to reduce the speed of cars being switched over a hump. Power-activated shoes press against the lower portions of the wheels and slow the car to a safe coupling speed.

car service A term applicable to the general services of railroads with respect to car supply, distribution and handling, involving such matters as demurrage, interchange, per diem charges and settlements, private car line mileage statements, and allowances.

car service rules Rules established by agreement between railroads governing interchange of cars. See **interchange rules**.

catenary On electric railroads, the term describing the overhead conductor that is contacted by the pantograph or trolley, and its support structure that supplies electricity to propel railroad trains.

center pin The large steel pin that passes through the center of both body and truck center plates and assists in keeping the two plates in proper alignment as the car is being placed on its trucks. In passenger-train cars; it also locks truck to car.

center plate See **body center plate** and **truck center plate**.

center sill The center longitudinal structural member of a car underframe, which forms the backbone of the underframe and transmits most of the buffing shocks from one end of the car to the other.

centrifugal force The force that seems to push a rotating object or its parts outward from a pivotal point.

CEO (chief executive officer)

CFO (chief financial officer)

chassis A platform with wheels to support the container. When combined with a container, the entire unit looks similar to a trailer.

Chessie System The Chesapeake & Ohio (C&O) acquired the Baltimore & Ohio (B&O) in 1962, and the Western Maryland merged with the C&O and the B&O to become the Chessie System. The Chessie System later merged with the Seaboard System and became the CSX. See **Seaboard System**.

circus loading A term used to describe an older method of loading highway trailers on TOFC (piggyback) flatcars, whereby a tractor backs the trailer up a ramp placed at one end of a cut of cars, and along the decks of the cars to the point of securement. Circus loading requires bridge plates at each end of all cars to enable the trailer and tractor to pass from car to car. See **side loading**, and **overhead loading**.

Class I railroad A railroad whose operating revenues are more than an annually designated amount—in 1998, it was $255 million.

Class II railroad A railroad whose operating revenues are between $20.4 million and the Class I threshold.

classification track **1.** One of the tracks in a classification yard, or a track used for classification purposes. **2.** Tracks with a concave (bowl-shaped) profile that fan out from the base of the hump in groups of five to nine tracks. The total number of tracks depends on the size and function of the yard and available land but may be as many as 60 to 70.

classification yard A railyard consisting of a number of usually parallel tracks, used for making up trains.

clearance diagram An outline or cross section drawing representing the maximum limiting dimensions to which rail equipment can be built. Specific limiting dimensions have been established and are shown on standard clearance diagrams known as "plates."

closure rails The rails located between the parts of any special track work layout, such as the rails between the switch and the frog in a turnout; sometimes called the *lead rails* or *connecting rails;* also the rails connecting the frogs of a crossing or of adjacent crossings but not forming parts of it.

CN (Canadian National)

CO (carbon monoxide) A colorless, odorless, highly poisonous gas formed by the incomplete combustion of carbon or a carbonaceous material, such as gasoline.

CO² (carbon dioxide) A colorless, odorless, incombustible gas, formed during respiration, combustion, and organic decomposition and used in food refrigeration, carbonated beverages, inert atmospheres, fire extinguishers, and aerosols. Also called carbonic acid gas.

COD (Customer Operations Division)

COFC An acronym for container-on-flatcar. A type of rail-freight service involving the movement of closed containers on special flatcars equipped for rapid and positive securement of the containers using special pedestals or bolsters.

cog railroad A tourist railroad that climbs steep grades (e.g., 25+ percent) with the aid of a locomotive cog wheel engaging a rack rail.

coil spring A spring made by winding round wire or rods in a helical pattern around a circular core, used extensively in railcar suspension systems.

coke rack A slatted frame or box, applied above the sides and ends of gondola or hopper cars, to increase the cubic capacity for the purpose of carrying coke or other freight, the bulk of which is large relative to its weight.

commodity A general term used to describe the contents of a car. Other terms such as *lading,* or *product,* mean the same thing and are often used interchangeably.

common carrier One who holds himself out to the general public to transport property and passengers in intrastate, in interstate, or in foreign commerce, for compensation. Common carriers must operate from one point to another over routes or in territory prescribed by the Surface Transportation Board (U.S. interstate) and by a Public Service or Public Utilities Commission (intrastate).

consignee The one to whom something, such as goods or merchandise, is delivered for custody or sale.

consist (noun) The coupled vehicles making up a railroad train.

consist report A report that now lists only time, date, location, and car numbers for the makeup of a train since on any sophisticated system the waybill date is previously entered, and train symbol itinerary is already established in the computer.

container bolster A container securement device generally used on raised center sill COFC cars. Container bolsters are arranged to mount transversely on a flatcar, and support the container at each end.

continuous action tamper (CAT) A production machine equipped with a small internal tamper unit that starts and stops while the rest of the machine moves constantly.

continuous-welded rail (CWR) Rail links welded end to end into strings without bolted joints. The rail links that make up continuous-welded rail come in lengths up to 1,600 feet long before being welded together to form even longer strings of rail. Due to the length of the rail links, special rail trains are required to transport them into position where they are eventually welded together.

conventional traffic Trailers or containers in a single stack.

conversely Meaning reversed, as in position, order, or action; something that has been reversed; an opposite.

COO (chief operating officer)

coupler A device located at both ends of all cars and locomotives in a standard location to provide a means for connecting locomotive units together, for coupling to cars, and for coupling cars together to make up a train. The standard AAR coupler uses a pivoting knuckle and an internal mechanism that automatically locks when the knuckle is pushed closed, either manually or by a mating coupler. A manual operation is necessary to uncouple two cars whose couplers are locked together. See **E coupler,** and **shelf coupler,** and **interchange rules**.

coupler shank That part of a coupler behind the head and containing either a slot or a pin hole at the rear portion for connection to the yoke and draft system.

coupler yoke A cast steel component of the draft system that functions as the connecting link between the coupler and the draft gear.

covered gondola A gondola car that has been equipped with some form of removable cover that can be placed over the lading to protect it from weather exposure in transit.

covered hopper car A hopper car with a permanent roof, roof hatches, and bottom openings for unloading. Used for carrying cement, grain, or other bulk commodities requiring protection from weather.

CP (Canadian Pacific)

creep See **rail creep**.

crossbar A bar with locking devices at each end that fit and lock to belt rails in DF (damage free) boxcars to provide longitudinal restraint for lading.

crossing In track work, an arrangement of four frogs allowing one line to cross another.

cross level The distance one rail is above or below the intended level of the other— not to be confused with superelevation on curves.

crossover Two turnouts in which the track between the frogs is arranged to form a continuous passage between two nearby and generally parallel tracks.

crossover platform A drop step located on the engine front and rear, permitting movement of personnel between units.

crosstie Intermediate transverse structural members of a freight car underframe extending from the center sill to the side sill.

crossing In track work, an arrangement of four frogs allowing one line to cross another.

CSX (Chessie and Seaboard Railroad, which are made up of many consolidated railroads that merged to become CSX Transportation.) See **Chessie System** and **Seaboard System**.

CTC (Centralized Traffic Control) A term applied to a system of railroad operation by means of which the movement of trains over routes and through blocks on a designated section of track or tracks is directed by signals controlled from a designated central point. Also called TCS *(Traffic Control System)*.

curve (of a railroad line) In the United States, it is customary to express track curvature as the number of degrees of central angle subtended by a chord of 100 feet. The degree of curvature is equal to 5,750 divided by the radius in feet.

curved track A bend in the track where the track changes direction.

cushion underframe A term generally used to describe a freight car designed so that a hydraulically cushioned inner sill, free to slide with respect to a rigid outer sill, isolates the car body from a major portion of the end impact loads experienced in switching. Not to be confused with end-of-car cushioning devices, which are independent long-travel units installed in the draft gear pockets behind each coupler.

cushioning A term referring to the energy-absorbing capabilities of a car underframe or draft system. Although standard draft gears do have energy-absorbing capabilities, the term *cushioning* or *hydraulic cushioning* is generally understood to mean systems with a minimum travel of 10 inches.

D

dampener Any material or device used to reduce vibration by absorbing energy.

dark territory A section or block of railroad track that has no signals.

deadhead An operating term used to describe off-duty travel of a train crew member from some point back to his or her home terminal. Sometimes the term is used to identify any railroad employee traveling on a pass.

decentralization Corporations that make and distribute products have the choice, over a period of time, of arranging their plants and distribution centers to reduce the amount of transportation involved in the whole process. They often build smaller plants closer to their customers instead of having one central plant.

deferred maintenance The accrued expenses chargeable to current operations for the estimated cost of repairs that cannot be made during the year due to priorities for materials and supplies or shortage of labor.

demurrage A tariff established and assessed by individual railroads to encourage shippers to load and unload quickly to get the cars back in revenue service.

depreciated value The reproduction value of a freight car adjusted for depreciation up to the date of damage.

depressed center flatcar A flatcar having that portion of the deck between the trucks lower or closer to the rail to accommodate loads with excessive vertical dimensions.

deration Equipment performance reduction caused by operating or environmental conditions

DF A term used to describe an interior lading restraint system for boxcars, using transverse bars (crossbars) engaging special belt rails mounted to the car sides. The initials DF stand for "damage free." See *crossbar*.

diesel-electric locomotive A locomotive in which power developed by one or more diesel engines is converted to electrical energy and delivered to the traction motors for propulsion. See **prime mover**.

diesel engine An internal-combustion engine invented by Rudolf Diesel, differing from other internal-combustion engines because its compression is high enough to cause combustion without the necessity of introducing a spark for ignition. It uses the heat of highly compressed air to ignite a spray of fuel introduced after the start of the compression stroke.

direct current (DC) An electric current that flows in one direction only. See **alternating current** (AC).

ditch The part of the right-of-way that is lower than the ballast section, which drains the water from the track into a stream or drainage facility.

division On some railroads, the part of a railroad generally under the control of a Division Superintendent.

division of revenue The share of revenue enjoyed by one carrier in an interline movement.

dog Any of various hooked or U-shaped metallic devices used for gripping or holding heavy objects.

domestic cars Cars owned by the railroad on which it is running.

double-slip switch A combination of a shallow-angle crossing and two other tracks, located within the limits of the crossing, each connecting a right-hand switch from one crossing track and a left-hand switch from the other, to provide routes between the crossing tracks without additional frogs.

double-stack cars Five-unit articulated cars with either 40-foot or 48-foot wells.

DP (distributed power) Powered locomotives that can be distributed throughout a train allowing more locomotives to pull longer trains without separation from overpowering.

draft A term used to describe forces resulting in tension in the coupler shank. The term *draft* means the opposite of the term *buff*.

draft gear A term used to describe the energy-absorbing component of the draft system. The draft gear is installed in a yoke that is connected to the coupler shank and is fitted with follower blocks that contact the draft lugs on the car center sill. So-called "standard" draft gear uses rubber or friction components or both to provide energy absorption, while "hydraulic" draft gear uses a closed hydraulic system consisting of small ports and a piston to achieve a greater energy-absorbing capability. Hydraulic draft gear assemblies are generally called *cushioning units*. See **cushioning**.

draft system The arrangement on a car for transmitting coupler forces to the center sill. On standard draft gear cars, the draft system includes the coupler, yoke, draft gear, follower, draft key, draft lugs, and draft sill. On cushioned cars, either hydraulic end-of-car cushion units and their attachments replace the draft gear and yoke at each end; or a hydraulically controlled sliding center sill is installed as an integral part of the car underframe supplementing the draft gears.

dragging equipment detector (DED) A sensor between and alongside the rails to detect dragging equipment.

draw head The head of an automatic coupler.

drawbar pull A tensile coupler force. Locomotive pulling power is sometimes expressed in terms of "pounds of drawbar pull."

drawbridge Another term to describe a movable bridge.

DTC (direct train control)

dump car A car from which the load is discharged either through doors or by tipping the car body.

dynamic hunting See **hunting** and **truck hunting**.

dynamic track stabilizer A track machine that consolidates ballast by subjecting the track to high vibratory forces. A compactor applies forces through the rails themselves, simulating the stabilizing effects of accumulated train traffic and thus reducing or eliminating post-track work slow orders.

dynamometer A device for determining the power of an engine.

dynamometer car A car equipped with apparatus for measuring and recording drawbar pull, horsepower, brake pipe pressure, and other data connected with locomotive performance and train-haul conditions.

E

EBITDA (earnings before interest, taxes, depreciation, or amortization)

E coupler A standard AAR automatic coupler. Type E couplers are cast in several grades of steel, and have several shank configurations to meet varying service requirements.

ECP (electronically controlled pneumatic)

EDI (electronic data interchange)

EEOC (equal employment opportunity commission)

electrification A term used to describe the installation of overhead wire or third rail power distribution facilities to enable operation of trains hauled by electric locomotive or electric MU cars.

electronically controlled freight brake Braking system using the communication capability of digital electronics over a two-wire trainline to provide instantaneous control and monitoring of all air braking functions throughout trains of any length, initially applied in special service pending standardization in the late 1990s.

Electronic Track Warrant See **PTS**.

electropneumatic Combination of electrical and compressed air devices and equipment used in controlling and operating such devices as power track switches and car retarders.

electropneumatic brake A braking system used in multiple-unit (MU) electric passenger trains. Brakes are applied and released on each car through the action of electropneumatic valves energized by current taken from contacts on the engineman's brake valve and continuous train wires. Brakes can be applied instantaneously and simultaneously, eliminating undesirable slack action and providing more positive control of train speed.

elliptic spring A spring whose shape resembles an ellipse (an oval shape). Made of two sets of parallel steel plates called *leaves,* of constantly decreasing length. Because of the damping provided by friction between the leaves, such springs have been widely used for bolster springs for passenger cars.

EMD Formerly Electro-Motive Division of General Motors. Since General Motors (GM) sold it in 2005, it is now known as Electro-Motive Diesel.

EMP (equipment management pool) In the EMP, railroads jointly own or participate in the North American-wide EMP container pool.

empty-and-load brake A freight car air brake incorporating gear to increase braking power automatically when the car is loaded.

empty weight See **light weight**.

EMU (electronic multiple unit) See **multiple-unit cars**.

end-of-car cushioning device A unit installed at the ends of a car that develops energy-absorbing capacity through a hydraulic piston arrangement supplemented by springs to assure positive repositioning of the unit. These devices replace the standard draft gear and provide up to 15 inches of travel.

end-of-train device A device that monitors air brake system and train integrity on trains being operated without a caboose. Includes flashing marker light (night) and rear-of-train emergency brake application capability.

energy The ability to do work. See **work**.

entrepreneur A person who organizes, operates, and assumes the risk for a business venture.

EOT (end of train) An end-of-train device that monitors the air brake system and train integrity on trains being operated without a caboose.

EP (ex parte) *Latin* term used in legal and congressional writing. Example: EP 646.

EPA (Environmental Protection Agency) Established in 1970 by Presidential Executive Order, it brings together parts of various government agencies involved with the control of pollution.

EPS (earnings per share)

equalizer In six-wheel and some four-wheel truck arrangements, a system of bars, rods, levers, and springs that serves to equalize the loads on the axles and provide improved riding qualities for the truck.

ergonomics Applied science of equipment design for the workplace, intended to increase productivity by reducing operator fatigue and discomfort. Also called *biotechnology, human engineering,* or *human factors engineering.*

EVP (executive vice president)

extra train A train not represented on, and authorized to move by, the timetable.

F

fail-safe A term used to designate a design principle of any system that tries to eliminate the hazardous effects of a failure of the system by having the failure result in nonhazardous consequences.

fall-offs A reduction or decrease, as in revenue *fall-offs* that push up the operating ratio.

false-clear An unsafe train signal.

false-proceed (Railway Signal Indication) A clear or green signal displayed because of a system failure when a more restrictive indication should be displayed. Sometimes called *false-clear.*

fare box recovery ratio Measure of the proportion of operating expenses covered by passenger fares; found by dividing fare box revenue by total operating expenses for each mode or for expenses systemwide or both.

FASB (Financial Accounting Standards Bureau)

FAST An acronym for The Facility for Accelerated Service Testing located at the Transportation Technical Center near Pueblo, Colorado.

FCC (Federal Communications Commission)

FELA (Federal Employees Liabilities Act)

Field Manual of the AAR Interchange Rules One of two manuals that together form the *AAR Code of Interchange Rules* governing the condition and repair of railway equipment used in interchange service. Also called *Field Manual.* The Field Manual is published annually, along with occasional updates, and contains technical information concerning mechanical condition, wear limits, and repair criteria for interchange cars. See also ***Office Manual of the AAR Interchange Rules.***

field weld A weld joining two rails together after rails are installed in a track.

flange Any projecting surface or area, generally small with respect to the main component of which it is a part, included to serve some special purpose.

flange of a wheel The vertical projection along the inner rim of a wheel that serves (in conjunction with the flange of the mating wheel) to keep the wheelset on the track, and provides the lateral guidance system for the mounted pair.

flatcar A freight car having a flat floor or deck laid on the underframe (with no sides, ends, or roof), designed for handling commodities not requiring protection from weather.

flat switching The switching movements in a yard where cars are moved by a locomotive on relatively level tracks as opposed to being moved over a hump.

float bridge A structure with an adjustable apron to connect tracks on land with those on a car float, thus permitting cars to be transferred between the land and the car float at varying water levels.

force-fit A force-fit is used to keep the wheels in place, but it causes stress in the axle at the inner face of the wheel. The raised wheel seat axle lowers this concentrated stress.

foreign car Any car not belonging to the particular railway on which it is running.

4R Railroad Act (The Railroad Revitalization and Regulatory Reform Act of 1976)

FRA (Federal Railroad Administration) An agency of the U.S. Department of Transportation with jurisdiction over matters of railroad safety and research.

frog A track structure used at the intersection of two running rails to provide support for wheels and passageways for their flanges, thus permitting wheels on either rail to cross the other.

frog number The length in units along the frog point at which it is one unit wide—a measure of the sharpness of its angle.

fusee A red flare used for flagging purposes.

G

GAAP (generally accepted accounting principles)

gage **1.** The distance between the rails of a railroad track, and the distance between the wheels of a wheelset. **2.** Some measuring containers for air, water, or oil. **3.** A thickness of metal.

gage line **1.** The spot on the side of the rail head ⅝ of an inch below the rail tread where track gage is established. Gage lines other than ⅝ of an inch are found on light rail transit. **2.** The side of the rail head of a third rail where the third rail gage is measured.

gallery car A passenger car normally employed in commuter service that contains a main seating level and an upper deck level with an open aisle or passageway through the center that gives a "gallery" appearance to the car interior.

gantlets Sections of double track on bridges or in tunnels where the two lines overlap or are so close together that only one train can pass at a time.

gate Sometimes used to describe the bottom door assembly that serves as a discharge opening on covered hopper cars, usually called the *discharge gate.*

gauge A measuring tool, or a container to measure something.

g/bhp-hr (gram/brake horsepower-hr)

GE (General Electric)

genset (generator set) A separate diesel engine provided on the locomotive, typically in the rear of the unit below the cooling system. This generator set generates head-end power (HEP) with minimal involvement from the locomotive systems. The new locomotives must meet applicable EPA emissions requirements.

gibs The vertical ridges on each end of a truck bolster that engage the column guide surfaces of the side frame when the truck is assembled.

gigabytes **1.** A unit of computer memory or data storage capacity equal to 1,024 megabytes. **2.** One billion bytes.

girder rail A special rail cross section for use on light rail trackage in paved streets incorporating an integral flangeway on the gage side of the rail head.

gondola car A freight car with low sides and ends, a solid floor, and no roof. It is used mainly for transportation of coal, iron, and steel products, and other lading not requiring protection from the weather. Special types of gondola cars are built with high sides (for coal), removable covers, load-scouring devices, and drop-ends (for long loads) for specialized service.

GPS (Global Positioning System)

grade The rise or fall in elevation of a railroad track. A rise of 1 foot in elevation in 100 feet of track is a 1 percent ascending grade. Similarly, a decrease of 0.75 of a foot or 9 inches in elevation in 100 feet of track is a 0.75 percent descending grade.

grade crossing An intersection of a highway with a railroad at the same level. Also, an intersection of two or more railroad tracks at the same elevation.

grade resistance The resistance to motion of a train on a gradient due to the pull of gravity. Grade resistance is always 20 pounds for each ton of train weight for each percent of grade. Thus, a train on a 0.75 percent grade (0.75 of a foot or 9 inches change in elevation per 100 feet of length of track) would have 15 pounds grade resistance for each ton of train weight. If the track rises, the grade drag is positive; if the track decreases in elevation, the grade drag is negative.

grain door A temporary arrangement for sealing the openings around boxcar sliding doors so that the car may be used for bulk handling of grain. One common type consists of heavy reinforced paper nailed to strips of wood that are fastened to the door posts one either side of the car door opening.

gravity switch move A switching maneuver whereby gravity causes a stationary car to roll when the hand brake is released rather than being propelled by an engine.

GRL (gross rail load)

GTO (gate turn-off)

guardrail 1. A short, heavily braced rail placed opposite a frog to prevent wheels from striking the frog point or taking the wrong route. **2.** Auxiliary rails between the running rails on bridges, in tunnels, or near other obstacles or hazards to keep derailed cars from leaving the roadbed before exiting the danger area.

H

hand brake 1. A device mounted on railway cars and locomotives to provide a means for applying brakes manually without air pressure. Common types include vertical wheel, horizontal wheel, and lever type, so named because of the configuration or orientation of their operating handles. **2.** The brake apparatus used to manually apply or release the brakes on a car or locomotive.

hazardous material 1. When used with respect to lading in transportation vehicles, a term identifying the lading as subject to specific safety requirements set forth by the Department of Transportation or the Surface Transportation Board (which replaced the Interstate Commerce Commission) or both. Examples of hazardous materials are explosives, poisons, flammable liquids, corrosive substances, and oxidizing or radioactive materials. **2.** A substance or material that is capable of posing an unreasonable risk to health, safety, and the environment.

HC (hydrocarbons) Any of numerous organic compounds, such as benzene and methane, that contain only carbon and hydrogen.

heavy rail transit An electric railway constructed on an exclusive right-of-way to transport passengers in an urban environment. Operations generally consist of trains with several passenger cars coupled together, operating on a subway, elevated, or grade-separated surface right-of-way, usually with power via third rail.

heavy repairs As reported to the Association of American Railroads, repairs to revenue freight cars requiring over 20 man-hours.

held for orders Cars in repair facilities waiting on authorization to proceed with repairs.

helper locomotive A locomotive usually placed toward the rear of a train, to assist in the movement of the train over heavy grades. Helper locomotives can be either manned, or remotely controlled from the lead unit in the train.

HEP (head-end power)

high and wide A term referring to outside dimensions of a car or open-top load that exceed the normal clearances on the route to be traveled.

high-side gondola car A gondola car, with sides and ends over 36 inches high, for carrying coal or minerals.

high-speed rail Passenger-rail transportation system in densely traveled corridor over exclusive right-of-way at speeds of 125 mph (200 kmph or kilometers per hour) or greater.

horsepower (hp) A unit of power equivalent to 33,000 foot-pounds per minute or 746 watts.

horsepower-limited speed The maximum speed obtainable from the horsepower developed by the locomotive.

hostler One who services a large vehicle or engine, such as a locomotive.

hotbox Railroad slang for a dangerously overheated journal bearing.

hotbox detector A heat-sensitive device installed along railroad main-line track at strategic locations for measuring the relative temperatures of passing journal bearings. Bearing temperatures may be transmitted to wayside stations and monitored by personnel who can act to stop a train if an overheated journal is discovered. Most detectors report any bearing temperatures above a threshold value by radio directly to the train crew for appropriate action.

hp-hr (horsepower-hour)

hump yard A railroad classification yard in which the classification of cars is accomplished by pushing them over a summit, known as a "hump," beyond which they run by gravity into their assigned track.

hunting Side-to-side movement of railcars at high speed. See **truck hunting**.

Hz (hertz) This derived unit measures frequency. It is a unit of frequency equal to 1 cycle per second and is written cycles/s (cycles per second). It is named after Heinrich Rudolf Hertz.

I

ICC (Interstate Commerce Commission) This commission was superseded by the Surface Transportation Board in 1996.

ID (identification) The train ID tells what particular train it is.

idler car Usually a flatcar used in the transportation of a long article or shipment, which extends beyond the limits of the car carrying the shipment; the idler being a car on which the shipment or article does not rest, but overhangs. Also, a car used to move cars into or out of trackage (e.g., car float) where a locomotive may not go.

IDT Initials that stand for In-Date-Test, periodic test of the air brake equipment on every car to assure its continued proper operation. The month, day, and year of the most recent IDT must be stenciled on every car.

IGBT (integrated gate bipolar transistor)

independent brake The air brake control valve on a locomotive unit that controls the brakes on that locomotive (or multiple-unit consist) independently from the train brakes.

indication (of a signal) This tells the train engineer whether to stop, or stop-and-proceed. It tells the engineer what is safe.

inert retarders A spring-loaded device or system for holding a classified cut of cars and preventing it from rolling out the bottom of a railyard.

insulated rail joint A joint in which electrical insulation is provided between adjoining rails.

interchange or **interchange service** **1**. The transfer of cars from one road to another at a common junction point or the operation of cars owned by parties other than the railroad on which it is operating. **2**. A railroad intersection designed to permit traffic to move freely from one railroad to another without crossing another line of traffic.

interchange delivery report Confirms that the car or cars have been turned over to the railroad of its destination. This report includes the initial and number of the car, its contents, destination, and the time and date that it was delivered to the railroad of destination.

interchange rules The rules that are established and maintained by committees made up of representatives of railroad and car owners. If offered in interchange, a car complying with all interchange requirements must be accepted by an operating railroad and passed on to another operating railroad at a common junction point.

interface (noun) **1.** The surface where two objects or areas touch. On the rail, it is where the wheel and the rail are touching (the wheel-to-rail interface); it also refers to the surface (e.g., handles or levers) touched by an operator when operating a machine or engine. **2.** The point of interaction between a computer or any other entity, such as a printer or a human operator.

interlocking At a point where one or more routes meet or cross, an arrangement of signals and signal appliances (e.g., power switch machines) so interconnected that their movements must succeed each other in proper sequence, train movements over all routes being controlled by signal indication.

interlocking, automatic See automatic interlocking.

intermodal traffic Transportation of goods in containers or trailers involving more than one mode—rail, water, and highway.

interterminal switching The movements from a track of one road to a track of another road with the same district. It involves complex agreements between the railroads in every city.

intraplant switching The movement from one track to another or between two points on the same track within the same plant or industry.

intraterminal switching The movement from a track, industry, or firm to another track, industry, or firm on the same road within the same district.

inverse 1. Reversed in order, nature, or effect. **2.** Something that is opposite, as in sequence or character; the reverse.

invert The inverted arch in the lower portion of the cross section of a tunnel supporting the track, walls, and roof.

IPI (Inland Point Intermodal)

IRS (Internal Revenue Service)

ISO (International Standards Organization) The organization that sets standards in many businesses and technologies, including computing and communications.

ISS (Interchange Settlement System)

IT (Information Technology)

J

joint The junction of members or the edges of members that are to be joined or have been joined.

journal bearing The general term used to describe the load-bearing arrangement at the ends of each axle of a railcar truck. So-called plain journal bearings are blocks of metal, usually brass or bronze, shaped to fit the curved surface of the axle journal, and resting directly upon it with lubrication provided by oil supplied by spring-loaded wick-fed lubricator pads beneath the axle in the journal box. Journal roller bearings are sealed assemblies of rollers, races, cups, and cones pressed onto axle journals and generally lubricated with grease. Vertical loads are transferred from the journal bearing to the truck side frame through the journal bearing wedge (in plain bearing designs), or through the roller bearing adapter in roller bearing trucks.

journal box The metal housing on a plain bearing truck that encloses the journal of a car axle, and the journal bearing and wedge, and that holds the oil and lubricating device.

K

KCS (Kansas City Southern)

KCSM (Kansas City Southern de Mexico)

kg/m (kilogram per meter)

kilowatt-hour (kW-hr) A unit of energy measured equal to the continuous flow of 1 kilowatt (1,000 watts) for 1 hour.

K-Line (Kawasaki Kisen Kaisha)

knuckle 1. The pivoting casting that fits into the head of a coupler to engage a mating coupler. **2.** The pivoting hook-like casting that fits into the head of a coupler and rotates about a vertical pin to either the open position (to engage a mating coupler) or to the closed position (when fully engaged). Coupler knuckles must conform to a standard dimensional contour specified by the Association of American Railroads.

kV (kilovolt)

kW (kilowatt)

L

ladder (of a track) A track connecting successively the tracks of a yard.

ladder (on a railcar) Bars of iron or steel attached by bolts or rivets to the side or end of a freight car or caboose to form steps by which persons may climb to and from the car. The typical freight car ladder assembly consists of vertical stiles with a number of horizontal treads.

L&D (loss and damage)

LCL (less-than-carload) A term that applies to a quantity of freight that is less than the amount necessary to make up a carload.

light engine A locomotive or locomotive consist running as a train without cars.

light rail An urban/suburban passenger system employing manned vehicles (LRV's—usually articulated) operating singly or in short trains over routes, including some in-street running on overhead catenary or trolley wire power.

light weight Empty or tare weight of a railroad car, new or as determined by reweighing after any repairs, stenciled on car in conjunction with the load limit abbreviated LT. WT.

linehaul The movement over the tracks of a carrier from one city to another, not including switching service.

link and pin coupler An old type of connection between cars employing a single link attached to each draw head by a vertical pin manually inserted when coupling.

local service The service rendered by a train that stops to deliver and receive freight by setting out and picking up cars at intermediate points along its route.

locomotive unit A single car body with power and transmission equipment, but not necessarily with controls. Also called a *power unit,* or in the case of diesel-electric locomotives, a *diesel unit.* The least number of self-propelled machines running on rails that convert energy into motion for the purpose of pulling or pushing on a train. A locomotive is made up of one or more locomotive units.

LPG (liquid petroleum gas)

LRV (light rail vehicle)

LTL (less than truckload)

L/V ratio The L/V ratio is defined as the ratio of the lateral force to the vertical force of a car or locomotive wheel on a rail. An important factor affecting the tendency of the wheel to overturn or climb the rail; it is often a point of discussion in evaluating the cause of a train derailment.

M

magnetic field A term applied to the space occupied by electric or magnetic lines of force.

main lines The primary tracks of a railroad, those carrying more than 5 million gross ton per year.

main track A track extending through yards and between stations over which trains are operated by time table, track warrant, train order, or signal indication.

manifest A document giving the description of a single shipment or the contents of a car.

manual block signal system A block signal system where the use of each block is governed by block signals controlled manually or by block-limit signals (or both) on information by radio, telephone, or other means of communication.

MCS (minimum continuous speed) The speed of a train where the motor heat generation is balanced against the ventilation system capability.

Mechanical Designation An alphabetic code, usually two- to four-letters, assigned by the Association of American Railroads to every freight car to designate its general design characteristics and its intended purpose (e.g., XF = food-service boxcar).

mechanical refrigerator A term applied to refrigerator cars equipped with a self-contained power plant and mechanical refrigeration equipment including a compressor, condenser, evaporator, and fans for distribution of cold air around the lading.

Metra Chicago's transit system.

Mitsui O.S.K. Lines Mitsui Osaka Gyosen Kaisha (Osaka Mercantile Steamship company) Lines

motive power A term relating to the self-propelling equipment of a railroad, usually taken to mean locomotives.

mph (miles per hour)

mph/s (miles per hour per second)

MU (multiple unit)

multiple-unit operation Practice of coupling two or more locomotives or electric passenger cars together with provision made to control the traction motors on all units from a single controller. Sometimes referred to as *MU-ing.*

multiple-unit cars A term referring to the coupling together of two or more electrically operated passenger cars with provision made to control the operation of the cars from a single controller. Sometimes referred to as *EMU.*

M/W (maintenance-of-way)

N

NCCC (National Carriers Conference Committee)

NLRB (National Labor Relations Board)

NMB (National Mediation Board)

normally aspirated (internal-combustion engine) An engine that uses air at atmospheric pressure for combustion.

NOx (nitrous oxide) Nitrogen oxide is the generic term for a group of highly reactive gases, all of which contain nitrogen and oxygen in varying amounts. These oxides form when fuel is burned at high temperatures, as in a combustion process. One of the oxides is nitrous oxide, N_2O, a greenhouse gas that is colorless, sweet-tasting, and used as a mild anesthetic in dentistry and surgery. Another oxide is nitrogen dioxide, a poisonous brown gas, NO_2, often found in smog and automobile exhaust fumes and synthesized for use as a nitrating agent, a catalyst, and an oxidizing agent. NO_2 is often seen as a reddish-brown layer over many urban areas.

NS (Norfolk Southern)

NYK Line (Nipon Yusen Kaisha)

O

Office Manual of the AAR Interchange Rules One of two manuals that together form the *AAR Code of Interchange Rules* governing the condition and repair of railway equipment used in interchange service. Also called the *Office Manual*. The Office Manual is published annually, along with occasional updates, and contains the pricing and billing information used for preparing bills for repair work done on foreign cars. See also ***Field Manual of the AAR Interchange Rules***.

OOCL (Orient Overseas Container Line)

open-top car Any of a group of cars with or without sides and ends, and with no roof, all being intended for transportation of commodities not requiring protection from the weather, such as steel products, coal, or rough forest products. Flat, gondola, and hopper cars are all classed as open-top cars.

operating ratio The ratio of operating costs to gross revenue.

ore car An open-top gondola or hopper car designed specifically to carry iron or some other metallic ore. Because of the high density of most ores, cars for this service are built with relatively low cubic capacities, and some are equipped with empty-and-load brake equipment.

OS (on sheet) A train passing is recorded on sheet.

OSHA (Occupational Safety and Health Administration)

O.S.K. Lines See **Mitsui O.S.K. Lines**.

overhead loading A method of loading highway trailers or containers on intermodal cars by the use of an overhead (usually a gantry type) crane.

P

pantograph A device for collecting current from an overhead conductor (catenary) and consisting of a jointed frame operated by springs or compressed air, and having a suitable collector at the top.

PEB (Presidential Emergency Board) A board by which neutrals make nonbinding resolutions for procedures or terms on which a dispute might be settled.

per diem The amount or rate paid by one carrier to another or to a private car owner for each calendar day (or each hour) that it uses a car belonging to the other.

permissive A railroad signal that means stop-and-proceed.

pick-up A car or cars added to a train en route between dispatching and receiving yards, or cars added at a dispatching yard to a train operating over two or more divisions on a continuous wheel report.

piggyback A term referring to of transporting highway trailers on railroad flatcars. See **TOFC.**

piggyback cars Flatcars designed and equipped for the transportation of highway trailers.

pilot A qualified employee assigned to a train or other on-track equipment when the engineer, conductor, or driver is not qualified on the physical characteristics or rules of the portion of the railroad over which movement is to be made.

pin-puller A person who operates the cut lever to separate cars in the receiving yard—before the hump.

plain journal bearings See **journal bearing**.

Plates B, C, E, F, and **H** An AAR-clearance diagram for unlimited interchange. See **clearance diagram**.

platform An intermodal freight car unit capable of carrying a 40-foot container or trailer. The term used to clarify a situation since platforms permanently connected (by articulation or drawbars) are given a single car number. Also called a *slot*.

plug door 1. A type of side door used on insulated box and refrigerator cars that fits flush with the interior car side when closed. Plug doors provide a better seal and are therefore more desirable than the common sliding door for insulated car applications. **2.** A freight car door designed to fit into the door opening rather than sliding across it.

PM (particulate matter) Material suspended in the air in the form of minute solid particles or liquid droplets, especially when considered as an atmospheric pollutant.

power Work done by a force divided by the time required to do the work. A high power locomotive can do a relatively large amount of work in a short amount of time.

PR (public relations)

pre-empt Having the right to purchase something before others, especially the right to purchase public land that is granted to one who has settled on that land.

pre-emptive 1. To undertake or initiate to deter or prevent an anticipated, usually unpleasant situation or occurrence. **2.** Having or marked by the power to pre-empt or take precedence.

preventive maintenance Inspection to discover if something needs repairing before it fails and performing the necessary work in order to stop or slow that failure.

prime mover 1. A machine or mechanism that converts natural energy into work. **2.** The initial force, such as electricity, wind, or gravity, that engages or moves a machine.

propagation 1. The process of spreading to a larger area or a greater number. **2.** *Physics* The act or process of propagating, or to cause to move in some direction (as a wave) or through a medium.

PTC (positive train control) A generic term used to describe any microprocessor-based system of train control the will (1) prevent train-to-train collisions (positive train separation), (2) enforce speed restrictions, including civil engineering restrictions and temporary slow orders, and (3) provide protection for roadway workers and their equipment operating under specific authorities.

PTS (positive train separation) 1. One of three core features of a PTC system. 2. A nonvital (non-safety-critical) form of communications-based train control, employed as an "overlay" on a freight or main-line passenger railroad. Overlay systems supplement rather than replace existing, traditional track-circuit-based signaling and train control.

pull-aparts The separation of both rail ends in a bolted rail joint to the extent that the gap is very large and track bolts in one rail end are usually sheared as one rail end pulls away from the other.

push-pull train operation Passenger service, typically over commuter or medium-haul routes, with locomotive-powered consists that are trainline connected for control from either end that can shuttle between terminal stations without being turned.

puzzle switch See **double-slip switch**.

R

rack rail A notched rail mounted between the running rails that engages the gears of a locomotive so equipped, for traction when ascending and braking when descending on a cog railroad.

rail As used in car construction, any horizontal member of a car superstructure. The term is usually used in combination with some additional identifying word such as *belt rail* or *hand rail*. As used in track, a rolled steel shape, commonly a T-section, designed to be laid end to end in two parallel lines on crossties or other suitable support to form the supporting guideway constituting a railroad.

rail anchor A device attached to the base of a rail bearing against a crosstie to prevent the rail from moving longitudinally under traffic.

rail creep The occasional lengthwise movement of rails in track. Rail creep is caused by the movement of trains or temperature changes. It is common practice to stop the effect of creeping by the use of rail anchors or resilient fasteners.

rail head The physical rail.

railhead The farthest point on a railroad to which rails have been laid.

rail, head-hardened A rail with only the rail head heat treated to a higher hardness for reduced wear, and longer life on curves.

rail section The shape of the end of a rail cut at right angles to its length. The rail mills identify the different shapes and types of rails by code numbers (e.g., 131-28 for the 131 RE rail section).

rail tread The top portion of the rail head where rail/wheel-tread contact occurs. Also called *running surface*.

rail web The vertical member of a rail connecting head and base to form a beam.

raised wheel seat axle Current design of axle in which wheels are pressed onto the enlarged, parallel section of an axle, eliminating failures caused by stress concentration at the wheel-axle interface.

RALES (Research and Locomotive Evaluator – Simulator)

R&D (research and development)

rapid transit Heavy-rail systems for urban/suburban passenger service not directly connected to the lines of commuter or freight railroads.

rate bureau The tariff-setting and publication agency for all carriers within a certain freight classification territory in the era prior to deregulation.

rate of return The ratio of net operating income (also called *net railway operating income* in railway accounting) to the value of the property in common carrier use, including allowance for working capital.

RCAF (Rail Cost Adjustment Factor)

real estate Land, including all the natural resources and permanent buildings on it.

receiving yard A railyard used for receiving trains from over-the-road movements in preparation for classification.

regenerative braking The retardation system on electric cars or locomotives that can return power developed by traction motors acting as generators to the third rail or catenary for use by other units.

remote control A term denoting the control of any apparatus from a location apart from the location of the apparatus.

REN (Rate EDI Network)

repair 1. Reconstruction of a car, or a part or parts of a car to its original design. **2.** Physical work performed on a railcar in order to restore original structure because of damage, decay, injury, deterioration, or partial destruction. See also **preventive maintenance**.

resilient fastener Any of a variety of proprietary designs of rail fastener other than cut spikes that provide a more positive connection between the rail and tie or a track support slab.

reverser The handle on a locomotive control stand that selects the direction in which the locomotive will move by reversing the traction motor field connections.

right-of-way 1. The strip of land on which a railroad track is built. **2.** Sometimes, the real property of a railroad other than its rolling stock.

rip track A small car repair facility, often simply a single track in a classification yard or terminal. In larger yards, the rip track may be quite extensive with several tracks and shop buildings. Larger car repair facilities are generally known as "car shops." The name *rip track* is derived from the initials RIP, which stands for "repair, inspect, and paint."

RLA (Railway Labor Act) An act of Congress, May 20, 1926. This act was amended June 21, 1934, providing for the disposition of disputes between carrier and employees. The 1934 Amendment created the National Railroad Adjustment Board and National Mediation Board.

roadbed The material below the subgrade that supports the track and loads placed on the track.

rock-and-roll A slang term for the excessive lateral rocking of cars, usually at low speeds and associated with jointed rail. The speed range through which this cyclic phenomenon occurs is determined by such factors as the wheel base, height of the center of gravity of each individual car, and the spring dampening associated with each vehicle's suspension system.

ROI (return on net investment)

roller bearing The general term applied to journal bearings that employ hardened steel rollers to reduce rotational friction. Roller bearings are sealed assemblies that are mechanically pressed onto an axle. The bearings transfer the wheel loads to the truck side frames through a device known as a roller bearing adapter that fits between the bearing outer ring and the side frame pedestal.

rolling resistance A part of train resistance that includes the resistance to wheels rolling on the rail, friction in the journal bearings on the cars, and wind resistance.

rolling stock General term for all locomotives and cars.

rotary-dump car Open-top car equipped with rotary coupler at one end allowing load to be dumped by overturning without need for uncoupling.

rotating end-cap roller bearing Modern type of journal roller bearing in which the outer grease seal is between the car/ridge-type bearing assembly and a cap attached to the axle.

route-miles The total number of miles (length of roadway) included in a fixed-route transit system network, excluding yard tracks and sidings.

rpm (revolutions per minute) The abbreviation refers to the rotational speed of a wheel or shaft.

RPO (railway post office)

running rail The parallel rails that rolling stock and on-track equipment run directly on as opposed to guardrail, rack rail, or third rail. The rail or surface on which the tread of the wheel bears.

running surface See **rail tread**.

S

SAM (Shipper Assist Message)

S&Ts (switching and terminal) Referring to railroads that provide switching and terminal service.

Schnabel car A specially designed car used for transportation of extremely large and heavy machinery. The car is constructed with two separate units, capable of empty movement as a single car when bolted together. The load is placed between the two carrying units, and rigidly fastened to them, thus becoming literally part of the car body.

Seaboard System The Seaboard Coast Line, Atlantic Coast Line, Louisville, Nashville, Clinchfield, and others became the Seaboard System. Later the Seaboard System and the Chessie System merged to become CSX.

SEC (Securities and Exchange Commision)

sectional route locking Unlocks portions of the route as soon as the train has cleared so that other routes can be set up promptly.

shatter cracks A rail defect in the form of minute cracks in the interior of rail heads, seldom closer than one-half inch from the surface, and visible only after deep etching or at high magnification. They are caused by rapid (air) cooling, and may be prevented from forming by control cooling the rail.

shelf coupler A special coupler, required on some cars designed for transporting hazardous commodities, having top and bottom "shelves" cast integral with the head to prevent vertical disengagement of mating couplers in the event of an excessive impact, as in a derailment. Shelf couplers are fully compatible with other standard AAR couplers.

shopping The removal of a car from service for repair, maintenance, or inspection.

short line railroad A railroad company that originates or terminates freight traffic on its track, participates in division of revenue, and is usually less than 100 miles in length.

side bearing A load-bearing component arranged to absorb vertical loads arising from the rocking motion of the car. Various types of side bearings range from simple flat pads to complex devices that maintain constant contact between the truck bolster and car body. See **body side bearing**.

side frame In the conventional three-piece truck, the heavy cast steel side member that is designed to transmit vertical loads from the wheels through either journal boxes or pedestals to the truck bolster springs.

side loading A method of loading or unloading containers or highway trailers on or off flatcars by physically lifting the unit over the side of the car with heavy-duty mobile loading equipment.

siding A short section of railroad track connected by switches with a main track.

signal indication The information conveyed by the aspect of a signal relative to speed and conditions on the track ahead.

skate A metal skid or chock (wedge) placed on a rail to stop the movement of rolling stock.

slack Unrestrained free movement between the cars in a train.

sliding sill A term used to describe a type of hydraulic cushioning for freight car underframes. In sliding sill designs, a single hydraulic unit is installed at the center of the car and acts to control longitudinal forces received at either end of an auxiliary center sill, which is free to travel longitudinally within a fixed center sill. See **cushion underframes**.

slug A cabless locomotive that has traction motors but no means of supplying power to them by itself. Power is provided by power cables from an adjacent unit. Slugs are used where low speeds and high tractive effort are needed, such as in hump yards.

snubbers Hydraulic or friction damping devices used in suspension systems of cars to improve lateral stability. Some snubbers are designed to replace one spring in the truck spring group, some are incorporated as part of the truck side frame or bolster design, and others require special installation. Supplemental hydraulic snubbing is used most often on cars with high centers of gravity such as 100-ton coal hoppers or gondolas and tri-level automobile rack cars.

solid-state inverter A sophisticated, computer-driven device used to generate, modify, or alter electrical waveforms and frequencies, an essential component used to generate and regulate alternating current for the AC induction traction motors of modern locomotives.

spike A long, steel, square nail with a cutting edge used to secure a rail to a crosstie.

spike killing The damage and reduction of the holding power of a tie resulting from repetitive removal and installation of spikes in changing or transposing rail.

spiral When used with respect to track: a form of easement curve in which the change of degree of curve is uniform throughout its length in going from tangent to curve.

spring A general term referring to a large group of mechanical devices making use of the elastic properties of materials to cushion loads or control motion. See **coil spring**, **elliptic spring**, and **truck springs**.

spring group Any combination of standardized coil springs used in each truck side frame, and selected to match car capacities and obtain desired vertical suspension characteristics. Cars are often stenciled to show the number of specific springs of various designations (e.g., 5 D5 outer, 3 D5 inner) that make up the spring group standard to the car.

SS (steady state) The EPA is referring to smoke emissions. Steady state means the locomotive is under load for an extended period.

Staggers Rail Act of 1980 An act of Congress that fundamentally altered the regulatory environment of the railroad industry by reducing regulations, including the elimination of antitrust immunity in certain areas of activity.

stake pocket A U-shaped collar attached to the side or end sill of a flatcar to receive the lower end of a stake used for securing open-top loads.

standard gage The standard distance between the rails of North American railroads of 4 feet 8½ inches measured between the inside faces of the rail heads and ⅝ of an inch below the rail head.

static load The load or weight on the roadbed applied by track material or standing rolling stock.

station order In the trainyard, cars to be set out at the first station are placed at the head end, followed by those cars to be set out at the next station, and so on.

STB (Standard Transportation Board)

STCC (Standard Transportation Commodity Code)

subballast Any material that is spread on the finished subgrade of the roadbed below the top ballast to provide better drainage, prevent upheaval by frost, and better distribute the load over the roadbed.

subgrade The finished surface of the roadbed below the ballast and track.

sun kink A small irregularity in track alignment caused by excessive compression in the rails.

superelevation The vertical distance the outer rail is raised above the inner rail on curves to resist the centrifugal force of moving trains.

swing hanger Bars or links, attached at their upper ends to the frame of a Swing Motion truck, and carrying the spring plank at their lower ends. Also called *bolster hanger.*

swing-nose frogs A frog in a turnout with a movable frog point connected to a switch machine to match the switch position.

switch A track structure with movable rails to divert rolling stock from one track to another in a turnout. By eliminating the gap across which wheels must pass, the swing nose eliminates impact and also allows the use of frogs longer than No. 24 (e.g., No. 32, allowing 80 mph operation through the diverging route of a turnout).

switch and lock movement A device that performs the three functions of unlocking, operating, and locking a switch, movable point frog, or derail.

system car A car owned by the subscriber railroad.

system repair A repair performed by owner of the car.

T

T&TO (timetable and train order)

tangent track A track segment without any curves.

tappet A lever or projecting arm that moves or is moved by contact with another part, usually to transmit motion, as between a driving mechanism and a valve.

tariff (freight) A schedule containing matter relative to transportation movements, rates, rules and regulations.

Tariff Circulars (STB) Circulars issued by the Surface Transportation Board (formerly ICC) containing rules and regulations to be observed by the carriers in the publication, construction and filing of tariffs and other schedules.

TCS (traffic control systems) A block signal system under which train movements are authorized by block signals whose indications supersede the superiority of trains for both opposing and following movements on the same track. See also **CTC**.

team tracks Sidings located and spaced so that trucks can back up to the railroad cars.

tee rail (or T-rail) The typical rail shape used in track construction. The tee rail consists of a head, web, and base, and is so called because of the inverted "T" shape it assumes.

TEM (Train Energy Model)

TEUs (Twenty-foot Equivalent Units)

third rail A current distribution system for electric railroads consisting of an insulated rail laid parallel to one of the running rails and arranged to provide a continuous supply of power to electric locomotives.

tie The portion of track structure generally placed perpendicular to the rail to hold track gage, distribute the weight of the rails and rolling stock, and hold the track in surface and alignment. The majority of ties are made from wood. Other materials used in the manufacture of ties include concrete and steel. Also called *crosstie*.

tie-down Any device for securing a load to the deck of a car. Chain tie-downs with ratchets are probably the most common type and are used to secure wheeled vehicles and lumber products on flatcars.

tie plate A steel plate interposed between a rail or other track structure and a tie.

TLV (track loading vehicle)

toe (of a frog) End of a frog nearest the switch.

TOES (Train Operation and Energy Simulator)

TOFC An acronym for *trailer-on-flatcar* intermodal service or equipment.

TPD (truck performance detectors)

track An assembly of fixed location extending over distances to guide rolling stock and accept the imposed dynamic and static loads. See **track structure** and **rails**.

trackage rights The privilege of using the tracks of another railroad, for which the owed railroad is compensated.

track circuit An electrical circuit of which the rails of the track form a part.

track gage (measurement) Measured at right angles, the distance between running rails of a track at the gage lines.

track geometry car A passenger or self-propelled car equipped with necessary instrumentation to provide quantitative track evaluations.

track maintenance The process of repairing a track defect or track condition.

track modulus A quantitative measure of the vertical deflection of track under wheel loads (pounds per inch per inch of length) used to assess the suitability of track structure and subgrade for heavy axle-loading traffic.

track structure A term relating to the various components that comprise a track, such as tie plates, fasteners, ties, rail anchors, and guardrails. See **track**.

traffic control systems A block signal system under which train movements are authorized by block signals whose indications supersede the superiority of trains for both opposing and following movements on the same track. See **CTC**.

train For dispatching purposes, an engine or more than one engine coupled, with or without cars, displaying markers (e.g., headlight and rear-end device).

TRAIN II (Telerail Automated Information Network)

train consist The composition of the complete train excluding the locomotive. The cars in a train.

trainline A term properly applied to describe the continuous line of brake pipe extending from the locomotives to the last car in a train, with all cars and air hoses coupled. The term is often used to refer to the brake pipe on a single car.

train resistance A force that resists or opposes movement of a train. Resistance to motion along the track, attributed to bearings, wind and air resistance, flange contact with rail, and grade.

transcontinental Spanning or crossing a continent.

transloaded Transferring the cargo from an ISO container to a domestic container.

transpose rail To swap the rails of a track to extend their service life.

trimmer A signal located near the summit in a hump yard that gives indication concerning movement from the classification tracks toward the summit.

truck bolster The main transverse member of a truck assembly that transmits car body loads to the side frames through the suspension system. The ends of the bolster fit loosely into the wide openings in the side frames and are retained by the gibs, which contact the side frame column guides. Truck bolster contact with the car body is through the truck center plate, which mates with the body center plate and through the side bearings.

truck center plate The circular area at the center of a truck bolster, designed to accept the protruding body center plate and provide the principal bearing surface, often fitted with a horizontal wear plate and a vertical wear ring to improve wearing characteristic and extend bolster life.

truck center spacing On a single car, the distance between the truck center pins as measured along the center sill from the centerline of one body bolster to the centerline of the other.

truck hunting A lateral instability of a truck, generally occurring at high speed, and characterized by one or both wheelsets shifting from side to side with the flanges striking the rail. The resulting motion of the car causes excessive wear in car and truck components, and creates potentially unsafe operating conditions. For freight vehicles, the phenomenon occurs primarily with empty or lightly loaded cars with worn wheelsets.

truck side bearing A plate, block, roller, or elastic unit fastened to the top surface of a truck bolster on both sides of the center plate, and functioning in conjunction with the body side bearing to support the load of a moving car when variations in track cross level cause the car body to rock transversely on the center plates.

truck springs A general term used to describe any of the several types of springs used in the suspension of trucks to provide a degree of vertical cushioning to the car and its load.

TTCI (Transportation Technology Center, Inc.)

TTX (Trailer Train Corporation)

turbocharger A centrifugal blower driven by an exhaust gas turbine used to supercharge an engine.

turn-around time The time required to complete the cycle of loading, movement, unloading and placement for reloading of a freight car.

turnout An arrangement of a switch and a frog with closure rails by means of which rolling stock may be diverted from one track to another. Engineering term for *track switch*.

TWC (Track Warrant Control)

U

UMLER Acronym for *Universal Machine Language Equipment Register.* A continuously updated computerized file maintained by the Association of American Railroads. UMLER contains specific details on internal and external dimensions of equipment, carrying capacities, and equipment weight for freight cars, as well as special equipment and the general information (e.g., data on intermodal trailers, and locomotives) shown in *The Official Railway Equipment Register.*

underbalance The practice of operating a train through a curve at a higher speed but without the additional superelevation required to achieve balance speed.

unit 1. A car, multi-unit car, articulated car, or multi-level superstructure that is identified by a unique reporting mark and number. **2.** A locomotive unit. See **locomotive unit.**

unit train A train transporting a single commodity from one source (shipper) to one destination (consignee) in accordance with an applicable tariff.

UP (Union Pacific)

V

variable cost A cost that varies in relation to the level of operational activity.

VHF FM (very high frequency/frequency modulation)

vital circuit A circuit that must operate properly to prevent an unsafe indication even if some of its components malfunction.

voltage A unit of electromotive force that causes electrical current to flow in a conductor. One volt will cause an electrical current of 1 ampere to flow through a resistance of 1 ohm.

VVVF (variable-voltage variable-frequency)

W

waybill The primary written documentation of every freight shipment that forms the basis for railroad freight revenue accounts; a contract between the railroads that are moving the shipment.

well car A flatcar with a depression or opening in the center to allow the load to extend below the normal floor level when it could not otherwise come within the overhead clearance limits.

wheel The specially designed cast or forged steel cylindrical element that rolls on the rail, carries the weight, and provides guidance for rail vehicles. Railway wheels are semipermanently mounted in pairs on steel axles, and are designed with flanges and a tapered tread to provide for operations on track of a specific gage. The wheel also serves as a brake drum on cars with on-tread brakes.

wheel flange The tapered projection extending completely around the inner rim of a railway wheel, the function of which, in conjunction with the flange of a mate wheel, is to keep the wheelset on the track by limiting lateral movement of the assembly against the inside surface of either rail.

wheel plate The part of a railway wheel between the hub and the rim.

wheel report A listing of the cars in a train as it leaves a yard, made from waybills, on which the conductor posts set-offs and pick-ups.

wheelset The term used to describe a pair of wheels mounted on an axle.

wheel slip Rapid slipping of the wheels on the rail. An operating condition where there is driving wheel rotation on its axis with motion of the wheel at the point of contact with the rail. Wheel rotation speed during wheel slip is greater than it is during rolling, to the extent that tractive force is significantly reduced.

wheel tread The slightly tapered or sometimes cylindrical circumferential surface of a railway wheel that bears on the rail and serves as a brake drum on cars with conventional truck brake rigging.

wide gage Track defect caused by failure of tie-rail fastening system to withstand lateral wheel forces, leading to derailment when wheel drops off the rail head.

WILD (wheel impact load detectors)

woodchip hopper Open-top hopper or gondola car of high cubic capacity used to transport woodchips.

work The force exerted on an object multiplied by the distance the object moved. The work a locomotive does is the tractive effort of the locomotive multiplied by the distance the train moves as a result of the tractive effort.

Y

yard A system of tracks defined by limits within which movements may be made without schedule, train order, or other authority for the purpose of classification, and so on.

yard engine An engine assigned to yard service and working wholly within yard limits.

yard plant Compressed air supply facility allowing charging of train air line and conduct of terminal air brake tests before arrival of road locomotive.

yoke The component in a railroad car draft system that transmits longitudinal coupler forces to the draft gear. See **coupler yoke**.

Z

zeroed To adjust an instrument or a device to zero value.

Suggested Readings

Accounting and Finance

Railway Accounting Rules. Mandatory and Recommendatory Interline Accounting Rules and Forms and Rules of Order. Accounting Division, Association of American Railroads Annual.

Economics and History

American Railroads, by John F. Stover. 2nd ed. University of Chicago Press, 1998. 302 pages. (Hard/paper editions) LC No. 97-449. ISBN: 0-226-77658-1.

Domestic Transportation, by Roy J. Sampson et al. 6 Vols., 6th ed. Houghton Mifflin, 1990.

The Economics of Transportation, by D. Philip Locklin. 7th ed. Richard D. Irwin, 1972. 925 pages. LC No. 76-187057.

Enterprise Denied: Origins of the Decline of American Railroads, 1897-1917, by Albro Martin. Columbia University Press, 1971. 402 pages. LC No. 71-159673.

Modern Transportation Economics, by Hugh S. Norton. 2nd ed. Charles E. Merrill, 1970. 463 pages.

Railroad Land Grants, by Frank N. Wilner. Association of American Railroads, 1984.

Railroad Mergers: History Analysis Insight, by Frank N. Wilner. Simmons-Boardman Books, Inc., 1809 Capitol Avenue, Omaha, NE 68102, 1997. 474 pages.

Rails Across America. Edited by William L. Withuhn. Smithmark Publishing Co., 1994. 192 pages.

Railway Pricing and Commercial Freedom: The Canadian Experience, by T. D. Heaver and James C. Nelson. The Centre for Transportation Studies, The University of British Columbia. 1977.

Transportation: Economics and Public Policy, by Dudley F. Pegrum. 3rd ed. Richard D. Irwin, 1973. 612 pages. LC No. 72-90533.

Transportation Law, by John Guandolo. 4th ed. Wm. C. Brown, 1983. 1,054 pages.

Transportation Subsidies – Nature and Extent. Edited by Karl M. Ruppenthal. University of British Columbia, 1974. 125 pages. LC No. 73-93911.

Engineering and Maintenance

Car and Locomotive Cyclopedia – 1997. Simmons-Boardman Books, Inc., 1809 Capitol Avenue, Omaha, NE 68102. 1,136 pages.

Fuel-Saving Techniques for Railroads, by Paul Rhine. Omaha, NE: Simmons-Boardman Books, Inc., 2007. 174 pages. ISBN: 978-0-911382-55-6. LC No. 20-07940433.

Fundamentals of Railway Track Engineering, by Arnold D. Kerr. Omaha, NE: Simmons-Boardman Books, Inc., 2003. 393 pages. LC No. 2003114205.

Fundamentals of Transportation Engineering, by Robert G. Hennes and Martin I. Ekse. McGraw-Hill, 1955. 520 pages.

Introduction to North American Railway Signaling, Institution of Railway Signal Engineers, Omaha, NE, Simmons-Boardman Books, Inc., 2008. 210 pages. ISBN: 978-0-911382-57-0, LC No. 2008928725.

Railroad Engineering, by William W. Hay. 2nd ed. Wiley, 1982. 758 pages. ISBN: 0-471-36400-2.

Track Cyclopedia – 1985. 10th ed. Simmons-Boardman Books, Inc., 1809 Capitol Avenue, Omaha, NE 68102. 459 pages.

Transportation Engineering – Planning and Design, by Radnor J. Paquette, Norman Ashford, and Paul Wright. Ronald Press, 1972. 760 pages. LC No. 79-190209.

Geography

Geography of Transportation, by Edward J. Taaffe and Howard L. Gauthier, Jr. Prentice-Hall, 1973. 226 pages. LC No. 72-8995.

A Geography of Transportation and Business Logistics, by J. Edwin Becht. Wm. C. Brown, 1970. 118 pages. LC No. 70-11884.

Guide to Industrial Site Selection, by M. J. Newbourne and Colin Barrett. The Traffic Service Corp., 1971. 37 pages.

Labor Relations

Collective Bargaining and Technological Change in American Transportation, by Harold M. Levinson, Charles M. Rehmus, Joseph P. Goldberg, and Mark L. Cahn. The Transportation Center at Northwestern University, 1971. 723 pages. LC No. 71-154981.

The Hoghead – Industrial Ethnology of the Locomotive Engineer, by Frederick C. Gamst. Holt, Rinehart and Winston, 1980. 142 pages. LC No. 80-12232.

Labor in the Transportation Industries, by Robert Lieb. Praeger, 1974. 125 pages.

Railroad Retirement – Past, Present and Future, by Frank N. Wilner, Association of American Railroads, 1989.

The Railway Labor Act & the Dilemma of Labor Relations, by Frank N. Wilner. Simmons-Boardman Books, Inc., 1809 Capitol Avenue, Omaha, NE 68102, 1990. ISBN: 0-911382-12-7.

Technological Change and Labor in the Railroad Industry, by Fred Cottrell. D. C. Heath, 1970. 160 pages. LC No. 71-114364.

Logistics, Traffic, or Distribution Management

Business Logistics – Physical Distribution and Materials Management, by J. L. Heskett, Robert M. Ivie, and Nicholas A. Glaskowsky. 2nd ed. Ronald Press, 1973. 789 pages. LC No. 73-78570.

Cargo Containers: Their Stowage, Handling and Movement, by Herman D. Tabak. Cornell Maritime Press, 1970. 386 pages. LC No. 78-100658.

Container Services of the Atlantic, by John R. Immer. 2nd ed. Work Saving International, 1970. 396 pages. LC No. 69-20211.

Distribution and Transportation Handbook, by Harry J. Bruce. Cahners Books, 1971. 393 pages. LC No. 76-132669.

The Essentials of Distribution Management. Edited by Herschel Cutler. Distribution Economics Educators, 1971. 311 pages. Accompanying workbook, Freight Classification, Rates and Tariffs.

Intermodal Freight Transportation, by Gerhardt Muller. Eno Transportation Foundation and IANA, 1999.

Logistics Management, by Grant M. Davis and Stephen W. Brown. D. C. Heath, 1974. 441 pages.

Management of Physical Distribution and Transportation, by Charles A. Taff. 7th ed. R. D. Irwin, 1984. 545 pages.

Management of Transportation Carriers, by Grant M. Davis, Martin T. Farris, and Jack J. Holder. Praeger, 1975. 289 pages.

Model Legal Forms for Shippers, by Stanley Hoffman. Transport Law Research, Inc., 1970. 508 pages. Available from Traffic Service Corp. LC No. 73-114997.

Modern Transportation: Selected Readings, by Martin T. Farris and Paul T. McElhiney. 2nd ed. Houghton Mifflin, 1973. 466 pages. LC No. 72-6891.

Physical Distribution Case Studies, by Jack W. Farrell. Cahners Books, 1973. 489 pages. LC No. 72-91987.

Piggyback and Containers: A History of Rail Intermodal on America's Steel Highways, by David J. DeBoer. Golden West Books, 1992.

Practical Handbook of Industrial Traffic Management, by Richard C. Colton and
Edmund S. Ward. 5th ed. Revised by Charles H. Wager. The Traffic Service Corp.,
1973. 640 pages. LC No. 72-95464.

Railroad Management, by D. Daryl Wyckoff. D. C. Heath, 1976.

Readings in Physical Distribution. 3rd ed. Edited by Hale C. Bartlett. The Interstate
Printers and Publishers, 1972. 576 pages. LC No. 72-075080.

Traffic Management, by Kenneth U. Flood. 3rd ed. Wm. C. Brown, 1974. 505 pages.

Transportation and Traffic Management, by E. Albert Owens. College of Advanced
Traffic, 1972-1973. 4 volumes.
Volume 1 – 13th edition (1972)   Volume 3 – 9th edition (1977)
Volume 2 – 11th edition (1976)   Volume 4 – 11th edition (1976)

Rates and Regulation

Cases and Materials on Regulated Industries, by William K. Jones. 2nd ed.
Foundation Press, 1976. 1,278 pages.

Criteria for Transport Pricing. Edited by James R. Nelson. The American University,
1973. 320 pages. Available from Cornell Maritime Press. LC No. 73-4373.

Economic Considerations in the Administration of The Interstate Commerce Act, by
Marvin L. Fair. The American University, 1972. 182 pages. Available from Cornell
Maritime Press.

Freight Transportation: A Study of Federal Intermodal Ownership Policy, by Robert
C. Lieb. Praeger Publishers, 1972. 225 pages. LC No. 79-168341.

A Glossary of Traffic Terms and Abbreviations. 8th ed. The Traffic Service Corp.,
1972. 37 pages.

Miller's Law of Freight Loss and Damage Claims, by Richard R. Sigmon. 4th ed.
Wm. C. Brown, 1974. 425 pages.

Railroad Revitalization and Regulatory Reform. Edited by Paul W. MacAvoy and
John W. Snow. American Enterprise Institute for Public Policy Research, 1977.
246 pages.

Railroads and The Marketplace, by Frank N. Wilner. Association of American
Railroads, 1987.

Tariff Guide No. 9, by E. Albert Owens. The Traffic Service Corp., 1973. 20 pages.

Transport Competition and Public Policy in Canada, by H. L. Purdy, University of
British Columbia, 1972. 327 pages, LC No. 72-81827.

Transportation Regulation, by Marvin L. Fair and John Guandolo. 7th ed. Wm. C.
Brown, 1972. 608 pages.

Statistics

Moody's Transportation Manual. Published annually by Moody's Investors Service.

Transport Statistics in the United States. Published annually by the Bureau of Accounts, U.S. Interstate Commerce Commission. U.S. Government Printing Office.

Urban Transit

Beyond the Automobile: Reshaping the Transportation Environment, by Tabor R. Stone. Prentice-Hall, Inc., 1971. 148 pages. LC No. 72-140266.

Additional References

All About Railroading, by William C. Vantuono. 2nd ed. Simmons-Boardman Books, Inc., 1809 Capitol Avenue, Omaha, NE 68102. 112 pages.

The Future of American Transportation. Edited by Ernest W. Williams, Jr. Prentice-Hall, Inc., 1971. 211 pages. LC No. 72-160529.

The Practice of (Transport) Law, by Colin Barrett. The Traffic Service Corp., 1971. 51 pages.

The Railroad Dictionary of Car and Locomotive Terms. 3rd ed. Simmons-Boardman Books, Inc., 2006. 158 pages. ISBN: 0-911382-51-8.

Research in Transportation: Legal/Legislative and Economic Sources and Procedures, by Kenneth U. Flood. Gale Research, 1970. 126 pages. LC No. 72-118792.

Transportation: Management, Economics, Policy, by John L. Hazard. Cornell Maritime Press, 1977. 608 pages.

Transportation: Principles and Perspectives, by Stanley J. Hille and Richard F. Poist. Interstate Printers and Publishers, 1974. 561 pages. LC No. 73-93578.

Transportation Research Forum Proceedings. Published annually by The Transportation Research Forum.

Periodicals

International Railway Journal. Published monthly by Simmons-Boardman Publishing Corporation. Subscription rates on request (Circulation Dept., 1809 Capitol Avenue, Omaha, NE 68102. Phone: 1-800-895-4389. www.railjournal.com). Reports the latest developments and practices the world over. Articles are in English with resumés in French, German, and Spanish.

The Official Intermodal Equipment Register. Published quarterly by Commonwealth Business Media, East Windsor, NJ 08520-1415. www.railresource.com. Contains information on dimensions and capacities tariff for containers, trailers, and chassis in intermodal use by U.S. and foreign companies. Lists ramp locations and port facilities and names of officials concerned with reports and payments.

The Official Railway Equipment Register. Published quarterly by Commonwealth Business Media, East Windsor, NJ 08520-1415. www.railresource.com. Contains information on dimensions and capacities tariff for freight cars operated by railroads and private car companies of North America. Includes interchange points for railroads and home points for private car owners, with instructions regarding payments, movements, and repairs. LC A19-162.

The Official Railway Guide, Freight Service Edition. Published bi-monthly by Commonwealth Business Media, East Windsor, NJ 08520-1415. www.railresource.com. Contains names and addresses of railroads operating freight service in North America. Includes rail freight schedules, mileages, connections, and other facilities of North American railroads, as well as systems maps and personnel listings. Station index for 50,000 points, with line and schedule cross-references.

The Official Railway Guide, Passenger Travel Edition. Published monthly, except February and August, by Commonwealth Business Media, East Windsor, NJ 08520-1415. www.railresource.com. Complete Amtrak and other timetables for the United States, Canada, and Mexico, with fares, equipment, ticket offices, and station index cross-references. Also, connecting bus and ferry, short-haul and commuter service tables.

The Pocket List of Railroad Officials. Published quarterly by Commonwealth Business Media, East Windsor, NJ 08520-1415. www.railresource.com. Contains the names, titles, addresses, and phone numbers of 20,000 officials of railroads, truck affiliates, transit systems, and associated industry and governmental bodies. Covers railroads in North America, Central America, and South America, Australia, the Philippines, and Japan. Carries advertising of 400 supply companies, whose products and sales representatives are listed. LC 7-41-41367.

Railway Age. Published monthly by Simmons-Boardman Publishing Corporation. Subscription rates on request (Circulation Dept., 1809 Capitol Avenue, Omaha, NE 68102. Phone: 1-800-895-4389. www.railwayage.com). Circulates extensively among railway officers and others interested in railway affairs. Discusses current railway problems, progress and developments, and carries general news and statistics of the railway industry. LC CA8-3111; CA19-395.

Railway Line Clearances. Published annually, with interim change circulars, by National Railway Publication Company. www.railwaygazette.com. Presents weight limitations and vertical and horizontal clearances for more than 250 railroads of North America.

Railway Track and Structures. Published monthly by Simmons-Boardman Publishing Corporation. Subscription rates on request (Circulation Dept., 1809 Capitol Avenue, Omaha, NE 68102. Phone: 1-800-895-4389). Published for railway employees who build and maintain tracks, bridges, buildings and other parts of the railway plant. LC 14-435; 54-31791. www.rtands.com.

The Short Line. Published bi-monthly by Pioneer Railroad Services, Inc. Meghan Peterson, editor. A journal of short line and industrial railroading. Covers news, operations, and motive power rosters and acquisitions. Every other issue features a location survey for a particular state or metropolitan area. www.the-short-line.com.

Traffic World. Published weekly by the Traffic Service Corporation. Publishes news concerning U. S. Interstate Commerce Commission decisions and hearings, legislation affecting rates and railway service, rate revisions, and other transportation developments of special interest to shippers and industrial, commercial, and railway traffic officers. LC 42-22198. www.trafficworld.com.

Trains. Published monthly by Kalmbach Publishing Co., P.O. Box 1612, Waukesha, WI 53187. Railroad industry news and history. www.trains.com.

Our thanks to the Association of American Railroads for the assistance provided in compiling this list.

Contributors

Several railroad industry practitioners provided their expertise and time producing this Fifth Edition of *The Railroad: What It Is, What It Does.* Simmons-Boardman Books, Inc. gratefully acknowledges their contributions.

Roger W. Baugher, Director-Service Design, BNSF Railway, has over thirty years experience in railroading, having worked for four North American railroads and several consulting firms, including his own. He received an M.S. in Civil Engineering from the Railroad Engineering program at the University of Illinois, and an M.B.A. in Transportation and Finance from Northwestern University. His career has focused on railroad operations, including service design, equipment management, network analysis, transportation systems development, and operations planning.

Kendrick Bisset is Senior Systems Engineer at Safetran Systems Corporation, a Fellow of the Institution of Railway Signal Engineers, and Chairman of the IRSE North American Section. He received his B.S. in Electrical Engineering from the Illinois Institute of Technology. While in school, he was a cooperative education student, and worked for the Milwaukee Road and the Chicago Transit Authority. Bisset was with the CTA full time for sixteen years, moving up in the signal and communications engineering department to Director of Power & Way Engineering. After the CTA, he worked for various consulting firms in the Chicago area in signaling, among them Gibbs & Hill and LTK Engineering Services. Prior to Safetran, he was a staff engineer at General Railway Signal (now Alstom Signaling).

Roy H. Blanchard founded The Blanchard Company in 1989 to provide general management, marketing, and strategic planning support for short line railroads. He also provides assistance to rail transportation users on commercial and technical matters from rate negotiation to demurrage management and supply chain support. Blanchard publishes The Railroad Week in Review, an electronic compendium of railroad industry news analysis and comment. He is also a *Railway Age* Contributing Editor and for fifteen years wrote a column on industry best practices.

Rick Ford is Assistant Vice President, Mechanical & Utilization-Railcar Fleet Management/Repairs at Kasgro Rail Corp. He has over twenty years' experience in various aspects of railroading, having worked for a boiler manufacturing company, handling tie-downs and inspections for over-dimensional rail shipments. Ford currently is working for Kasgro Rail handling heavy-duty dimensional railcar fleet management issues of railcar supply and repair. He has been an active member of the Railway Industrial Clearance Association for seven years and is Director of RICA's Equipment Committee.

Stephen T. Gerbracht is currently Manager, Global Locomotive Development & Proposal Engineering, for GE Transportation in Erie, Pennsylvania. After graduating from Cornell University with a B.S. in Mechanical Engineering, he was hired by GE Transportation and has held positions in Remote Diagnostics/Services, Commercial Proposals, Systems Engineering and Finance. He holds an M.B.A. from Penn State University.

Thomas R. Gerbracht retired from GE Transportation in 2001 after thirty-seven years of service. He held Engineering assignments in Diesel Engine, Traction Motor, and Alternator, and worked in Locomotive Engineering, Product Planning, Application Engineering, Product Service, and Locomotive Marketing and Sales. He worked regularly with CSX, Amtrak, and Metro-North, and managed requisitions for locomotives for CN, Norfolk Southern, BC Rail, Union Pacific and others, including overseas customers.

William C. Vantuono is editor-in-chief of railway industry trade journal *Railway Age*. He joined the magazine in 1992. Vantuono has authored or co-authored two books, *All About Railroading* and *Off the Beaten Track: A Railroader's Life in Pictures* (with Robert G. Lewis and Robert H. Leilich), both published by Simmons-Boardman Books. He has been a contributor to or editor of several Simmons-Boardman Books publications, among them the *1997 Car & Locomotive Cyclopedia* and *Railway Age's Comprehensive Railroad Dictionary*. He also contributed to the *Encyclopedia of North American Railroads* (Indiana University Press). Vantuono holds a B.A. in Communications from Rutgers University and an M.A. in Public Media from Montclair State University.

Thomas White has over twenty years of experience as a train dispatcher, including trick dispatcher and assistant chief dispatcher assignments and special assignments in dispatcher training, service planning, scheduling, capacity management, infrastructure design, and new passenger service implementation. His prior experience includes train order operator, towerman, freight agency, yard clerk, and crew caller positions. He has been a railroad operations consultant since 1997 and has written three textbooks on railroad operations: "Elements of Train Dispatching" (Volumes I and II), and *Managing Railroad Transportation,* all available through Simmons-Boardman Books, Inc.

Frank N. Wilner was assistant vice president at the Association of American Railroads, where he drafted industry public policy positions. He later held a Clinton White House appointment as chief of staff to the vice chairman of the Surface Transportation Board, and currently is Director of Public Relations at the United Transportation Union. He also worked in management posts for the former New York Central, Penn Central and Norfolk & Western railroads, was a congressional correspondent writing on transportation for the Economist Magazine group, and has long been a contributing editor to *Railway Age* magazine. He is the author of four books on railroad economics and public policy, among them *Railroad Mergers: History, Analysis, Insight* and *The Railway Labor Act & The Dilemma of Labor Relations,* both published by Simmons-Boardman Books, Inc. Wilner also was editor-in-chief of the Journal of *Transportation Law, Logistics & Policy.* He earned undergraduate and graduate degrees in economics and labor relations from Virginia Tech.

Dr. Allan M. Zarembski is an internationally recognized authority in the fields of track and vehicle/track system analysis, railway component failure analysis, track strength, and maintenance planning. He is president of ZETA-TECH Associates, Inc., a technical consulting and applied technology company, which he established in 1984. Prior to that he served as Director of R&D for Pandrol Inc., Director of R&D for Speno Rail Services Co. and Manager, Track Research for the Association of American Railroads. Zarembski has authored or co-authored over 140 technical papers, over 120 technical articles, and two books, *The Art and Science of Rail Grinding* and *Tracking R&D,* both published by Simmons-Boardman Books, Inc. He has a Ph.D. and M.A. in Civil Engineering from Princeton University, and an M.S. in Engineering Mechanics and a B.S. in Aeronautics and Astronautics from New York University. He is a registered Professional Engineer in five states.

Additional input for Chapter 4 was provided by Peter J. Lawson, Product Manager-North American Locomotive, GE Transportation, Mark L. Nicolussi, Principal Engineer-Proposals & Systems Integration, GE Transportation, and Brian E. Kelly, Emissions Compliance Manager, GE Transportation.

Several individuals from TTX Company contributed to Chapter 15, Intermodal Traffic: Peter Wolff, Director Market Development; Jim Panza, Senior Manager, AAR Planning & Maintenance Assessment; John Flagello, Assistant Vice President, Market Development; Maia Pykina, Manager, Forecasting & Planning; and Bob Hewett, Consultant.

Index

In this index, colons separate main headings from subheadings, and subheadings from sub-subheadings; semicolons separate main headings when there is more than one; commas are used to indicate an inverted heading or to separate items in a list. Italicized page numbers indicate an illustration or table.

E